or

The

PASSCHENDAELE

—— 1917 ——

*For the grandfather I never knew,
Lance Bombardier Ernest Cyril Hicks,
Royal Field Artillery, and all the other men
who fought in that terrible battle*

The Welsh at
PASSCHENDAELE
—— 1917 ——

DR JONATHAN HICKS

First impression: 2017

The publishers wish to acknowledge the support of
Cyngor Llyfrau Cymru

Cover photograph: Daphné Vangheluwe
Cover design: Y Lolfa

ISBN: 978 1 78461 374 7

Published and printed in Wales
on paper from well-maintained forests by
Y Lolfa Cyf., Talybont, Ceredigion SY24 5HE
website www.ylolfa.com
e-mail ylolfa@ylolfa.com
tel 01970 832 304
fax 832 782

Contents

Preface

THE WORD 'PASSCHENDAELE' has become a byword for the death and suffering of the Great War. A remorseless slog by Allied soldiers up towards the village itself, through mud, rain, cold, and dead bodies, it was the most horrific of battles. By the time the fighting in this sector paused on 10 November 1917, hundreds of thousands of men on both sides had been killed or wounded. The landscape was scarred and desolate, and the men who fought there and survived would never forget the experience.

My paternal grandfather, Ernest Hicks, fought at the Third Battle of Ypres, as it is officially known, serving with the Guards Divisional Artillery. He did not recover from the experience and it led to his early death post-war. Thousands of other families across Great Britain suffered the consequences of their men fighting in this battle and the war memorials across Wales bear testimony to the fact.

This detailed work brings together the personal experiences, poignant stories and vivid accounts of the soldiers who fought at the Third Battle of Ypres in the battalions of the Welsh regiments and their support arms, as well as those men of Welsh origin who served in other regiments.

Today the countryside between Ypres and Passchendaele is a mixture of green arable land and industrialisation, but the memorials and headstones are never too far away, reminding one of its bloody past, and of the fact that many of the men who fought there still lie in Flanders Field, including those whose final resting places are in graves marked 'Known Unto God' and those who have no marked graves at all.

Jonathan Hicks

The Structure Of The British Army In The Great War

ARMIES: comprised of 200,000 to 300,000 men commanded by a General

CORPS: 50,000 men commanded by a Lieutenant-General

DIVISIONS: 16,000 to 18,000 men commanded by a Major-General

BRIGADES: 3,000 to 4,000 men commanded by a Brigadier-General

BATTALIONS: 800 to 1,000 men commanded by a Lieutenant-Colonel

COMPANIES: 160 to 200 men commanded by a Captain

PLATOONS: 40 to 50 men commanded by a Lieutenant

SECTIONS: 10 to14 men commanded by a Lance Corporal

(Regiments usually had two or more battalions)

CHAPTER 1

The Third Battle of Ypres

THE YPRES SALIENT had been a battlefield since 1914. The British summer offensive of 1917, officially known as the Third Battle of Ypres but today more commonly known as the Battle of Passchendaele, was fought in Belgium from 31 July to 10 November 1917, and lasted a total of one hundred and three days.

Fighting had first occurred around Ypres on 19 October 1914 and the First Battle of Ypres lasted until 22 November that year. The German advance into Belgium was halted but with over 300,000 casualties on both sides.

The Second Battle of Ypres had seen the first mass use of poison gas by the Germans on the Western Front. The battle had begun on 22 April 1915 and by the time it ended on 25 May the Allies and Germans had suffered over 122,000 casualties.

By 1917, the third year of the Great War, the Belgium town of Ypres had been surrounded on three sides by the German Army since the end of the First Battle of Ypres in the autumn of 1914. The Allies had held conferences in November 1916 and May 1917, and part of their strategy for 1917 was to seize from the Germans their control of the ridges to the south and east of Ypres, ground from which they were able to observe and fire upon Allied positions. Passchendaele village sits on a ridge east of Ypres and, when this was taken, the plan was to continue the advance to close the German supply railway which ran through the important junction of Roulers, some five miles from Passchendaele.

The 1917 campaign in Flanders was controversial from the outset. It was opposed by the British Prime Minister David Lloyd George and by the French Chief of the General Staff, Ferdinand Foch. The previous French campaign, the Nivelle Offensive, had failed to such an extent that it had led to mutinies in the French Army. Field Marshal Sir Douglas Haig, commander of the British Expeditionary Force, insisted it go ahead and was eventually granted approval by the War Cabinet on 25 July, just six days before the offensive began.

The Battle of Messines, from 7 to 14 June 1917, had proved to be an unqualified success. The objective of this plan was to attack the German positions south of Ypres and to drive them from the Messines Ridge. If this failed, the German artillery would continue to be able to pour enfilade fire into the right flank of any future British attack.

Prior to the advance at 3.10 a.m. on 7 June, 21 mines, dug since 1915 under the German lines and containing nearly a million tons of ammonal explosive, were detonated. Two failed to go off but 19 did explode and caused chaos in the German front lines. The ridge was taken with far fewer casualties than anticipated and the Allies now held the high ground in this area; the attack planned for 31 July could now proceed.

For the next six weeks, men and matériel were gathered in huge numbers in preparation for the onslaught. The weather was clear and sunny, and the success of the Messines operation gave the attackers confidence. Holding the high ground east of Ypres, however, meant that the Germans could observe the preparations. They responded on 12 July by firing 50,000 artillery rounds into the British lines and releasing their new weapon – mustard gas, which caused temporary blindness, severe burning and itching of the skin, abdominal pain, fever and vomiting, plus respiratory problems.

Nearly 2,500 soldiers were gassed as a result, 87 of them dying. The British bombardment began on 17 July and lasted for the next two weeks. Over 4,280,000 shells were fired, including 100,000 chloropicrin gas shells.

The main thrust of the attack was to be made by Fifth Army, under the command of Lieutenant-General Sir Hubert Gough. It was to attack between Zillebeke and Boesinghe, ground that rose up the ridge that ran along the Menin Road to the Gheluvelt plateau in the south and north to the village of Passchendaele. Criss-crossing this ground was a network of streams or *beeks*, which were to have consequences for the progress of the Allied forces. General Antoine's French First Army was to secure the left flank and Lieutenant-General Sir Herbert Plumer's Second Army would protect the right flank.

The British had amassed 3,091 artillery guns, 406 aircraft, nine divisions and 136 tanks in readiness for the attack. Opposing them on the high ground were the thirteen divisions of the German Fourth Army and six divisions of the Sixth Army to the south. They had around 600 aircraft and numerous artillery pieces.

After a number of delays, the battle was scheduled to start on 31 July 1917. It was ultimately to be composed of several phases. The Battle of Pilkem lasted from 31 July to 2 August; this was followed by the capture of Westhoek on 10 August. The Battle of Langemark opened on 16 August and finished on 18 August. A lull then occurred before the Battle of the Menin Road which ran from 20 to 25 September. The following day, the Battle of Polygon Wood commenced and this ended on 3 October. The Battle of Broodseinde lasted just one day, 4 October, as did the Battle of Poelcappelle on 9 October. The First Battle of Passchendaele also began and ended on one day, 12 October, but the Second Battle of Passchendaele commenced on 26 October and did not finally end until 10 November.

When the fighting ceased, only to then resume on 20 November at the Battle of Cambrai in France, the British casualties had exceeded 244,000 and the total of German dead, wounded and missing had reached nearly 400,000.

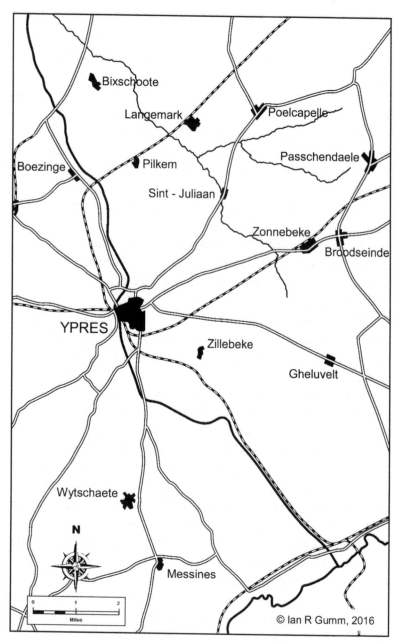

Map of the battlefield of Third Ypres

CHAPTER 2

From Mametz Wood
to Pilkem Ridge

THE 38TH (WELSH) Division had successfully captured Mametz Wood on the Somme in France during the second week of July 1916, although it had received some undeserved criticism in some quarters within the senior ranks of the Army for the time it took to do so, much of it propounded by one of their own brigadiers – Brigadier-General Llewelyn Price-Davies V.C. Nevertheless, the wood had been taken, despite some 4,000 casualties, and when the battalions who had been involved in the battle were relieved and taken out of the line, they left behind hundreds of their former comrades who had been killed in the fighting for the largest wood on the Somme.

Many of the dead were afforded burials in temporary cemeteries, their graves remaining undisturbed until the war ended; others had their final resting places destroyed by shellfire and subsequent fighting so that their graves were lost. An enormous number simply disappeared and were never seen again – victims of the terrible power of artillery shells. Some still lie within Mametz Wood.

Among the casualties suffered by the division were the Tregaskis brothers. Leonard and Arthur served as lieutenants with the 16th Welsh (Cardiff City) Regiment and they now lie side by side in Flatiron Copse Cemetery after being killed during the attack on the first day – 7 July 1916.

The Tregaskis Brothers:
Leonard (seated left) and Arthur
(seated right)

On 27 January 1919 their father wrote of his sons' deaths:

2nd Lieut. Leonard Tregaskis was born at Cardiff on the 14th March 1883 and was educated at Wycliffe College, Stonehouse, Glos.

2nd Lieut. Arthur Tregaskis was born at Cardiff on the 2nd May 1884.

When the war broke out they were farming in Canada. They at once decided that it was their duty to offer their services. By the time they had found someone to look after their farm, the Canadian first contingent was filled up. They would not wait for the next but came home and enlisted in the Cardiff City Battalion towards the end of 1914. After going through their training they were offered commissions which they accepted. They went to France with their battalion in 1915 and saw a good deal of active service. They were both killed in the attack on Mametz Wood on July 7th 1916.

Major Smith O.C. 16th Battalion Welsh Regt. Wrote, 'They fell leading their men in the attack on a big wood in which attack we suffered considerable losses. Leonard was undoubtedly the most popular man in the Battalion, beloved by everyone. Arthur was quiet but very sincere and possessed of great courage.'

The army chaplain wrote, 'They were both among the noblest and bravest of our valiant officers. I always found them true hearted men. The whole Battalion regarded them with deep affection and real pride. I shall always cherish their memories with devout thankfulness on accord of what they were and what they accomplished for God, King and Country.'[1]

Private George Harry Tomlin also served with the 16th Welsh Regiment. He was killed on 7 July and was buried in Flatiron Copse Cemetery. Born in Snodland, Kent, he was living in New Tredegar and working in the local lead wool works when he enlisted in 1915.

Corporal David George Lewis from Priory Street, Carmarthen, was laid to rest in Flatiron Copse Cemetery. Known as David 'Benjamin' Lewis, he was killed on 10 July during the second day of the fighting for Mametz Wood. Born in Carmarthen in April 1887, he was 29 when he fell while serving with the 13th Battalion of the Welsh Regiment (2nd Rhonddas).

Lance Corporal Frederick Ludlow of the 10th South Wales Borderers was also killed on 10 July, aged 31. He lived with his wife Minnie at 9 Oak Street in Cwm, Monmouthshire.

George Tomlin   David Lewis   Frederick Ludlow

Flatiron Copse in 1917

C.S.M. Albert Willshire of the 16th Welsh (sitting apart) with his men in training.
He was killed on 7 July and has no known grave.

His body was identified, and he too lies in Flatiron Copse Cemetery.

Besides the men who were afforded burials in the cemeteries in the area around Mametz Wood, the remains of over 700 soldiers of the Welsh Division who have no known grave were left behind when the survivors were moved north to the Ypres sector – the Immortal Salient. These men have no known graves and are officially listed as 'missing'.

Among these was Private David John Williams who was killed on 7 July while serving with the Cardiff City Battalion, aged 19. He had lived with his parents at Melin Cottage, Melingriffith, Whitchurch, in Cardiff. His remains could not be identified later and he is named on the Thiepval Memorial to the Missing.

Private Titus Philip Meyrick of the 16th Welsh fought at Mametz Wood but survived the war, being commissioned

David Williams (standing) with his brother

into Princess Charlotte of Wales' (Royal Berkshire) Regiment in 1917. In 1918 he was awarded the Military Cross, the citation reading:

For conspicuous gallantry and devotion to duty. When the enemy developed a strong attack and drove in the left of the line, he held a forward position with his platoon, in the face of heavy fire from front and flank. He inflicted heavy loss on the enemy, and held up the attack long enough to allow a strong line to be formed in the rear. Later, he again repelled a strong attack, and by his choice of position and tenacity succeeded in holding it up and eventually breaking the enemy's advance at this point.[2]

A newspaper article gave details of his career:

Official news is to hand that Second-Lieutenant T.P. Meyrick (youngest son of Mr. Philip Meyrick) of Manselton-road, Swansea, has been awarded the Military Cross for gallantry in the field. He joined the Welsh Regiment in the early days of the war, and saw much active service in the ranks at Ypres and Mametz Wood. Recommended for a commission by his commanding officer, he received a commission in the Berkshire Regiment early last year, since when he has been continuously at the front taking part in the Cambrai push and in all the recent heavy fighting. Second-Lieutenant Meyrick is 22 years of age, and before joining the Army was with Mr. Gunning at the local offices of the Sailors' and Firemen's Union.[3]

After the war Meyrick married and became a minister of religion. He died at Abergavenny Hospital on 21 March 1945.

Killed on 7 July was Sergeant Thomas G. Llewellyn of the 11th South Wales Borderers. He was from Fleur-de-Lis in Monmouthshire and was aged 19. His name is also among those on the Thiepval Memorial.

Another of the missing was Private Bethuel Harcombe, whose uncle, Councillor Mark Harcombe, was known as the 'Czar of the Rhondda' for his time on the Rhondda Council and as executive member of the South Wales Miners' Federation. Mark Harcombe had received a letter in December 1914 from Francis Wrentmore of the Somerset Light Infantry which gave him some idea of the conditions his nephew was later to endure:

> I suppose you want to know how the boys are getting on here. It is very cold and freezing hard. We have had a lot of rain, so it has been very rough in the trenches. We have been up to our knees in water. We had a good skirmish on December 19, when we were successful in taking the trenches of the Germans opposed to us.

Titus Meyrick   Thomas Llewellyn

We, however, had to retire from them because they were full of water so I suppose they were glad to leave them. We lost a lot of men in the skirmish – roughly speaking about six officers and 127 men killed. The Germans acted very well on Christmas Day. They helped us to bring in our dead, and we did the same for them. Some of theirs had been there two months. But under the circumstances we did well. The Germans and ourselves climbed out of the trenches and we shook hands with each other. We stopped firing from five o'clock until midnight, and we visited each other's trenches.[4]

Bethuel Harcombe of the 15th Welsh had landed in France a year later, in December 1915, and took part in the attack on Mametz Wood on 10 July, where he was reported missing. His body was never identified and he is commemorated on the Thiepval Memorial to the Missing. Born in Trealaw, he was just 18 years of age, having enlisted at the age of 16.

Another man whose body could not later be identified was Private Daniel Davies of the 13th Welsh Regiment who was killed on the same day, aged 30. He and his wife Mary had lived at 2 Wern Ddu Cottages, Pontrhydyfen, Port Talbot. He is named on the Thiepval Memorial.

Jabez Thomas from Briton Ferry was also killed on 10 July and his body was lost. He was 25 and serving as a Lance Sergeant with the 13th Royal Welsh Fusiliers. His name too is on the Thiepval Memorial.

Private John Henry Absalom was listed as missing after the fighting on 10 July. Born in Rudbaxton in Pembrokeshire, he served with the 14th Welsh – The Swansea Pals. Captain Melbourne Williams wrote to John's mother in August:

I was very sorry to read in the paper last night of the death of your son and I wish to offer you my sincerest sympathy in your terrible loss. Your son was in my platoon when I first joined the Battalion and was afterwards transferred to my company when I changed and I saw a lot of him. He was with the machine gun section on July 10th. I saw nothing of him after the advance started as I was

Jabez Thomas

Daniel Davies

John Absalom

wounded early in the day. From what I hear I believe he was killed instantaneous. Your son was most popular with everybody and was an excellent soldier. The work with the machine gun section for which he volunteered was most important.[5]

John Absalom was just 17 years of age.

Two brothers – John (known as 'Jack') and James Jones – who served with 'B' Company of the 15th Welsh (Carmarthen Pals), were killed on 10 July, aged 24 and 21 respectively. Their remains could not be identified and they are commemorated on the Thiepval Memorial to the Missing. They had lived with their parents at 4 Towy Avenue, Llandovery, in Carmarthenshire.

In August 1916 their father wrote to their officer enquiring as to the fate of his sons and received this reply:

I am glad you have written to me for information concerning your two sons Pte. James Jones and Corpl. Jack Jones and I will try and tell you what little I know but I am afraid I cannot give any hopes that either is alive. What hopes we cherished that they might have been wounded and gone to hospital without our knowledge have been dispelled by your letter.

The battalion went into action on the morning of the 10th July, the objective being a certain wood. From the evening of that day until we came out on the morning of the 12th, B Company was under my charge. On the afternoon of the 11th the battalion received orders to clear the left side of the wood of any of the enemy who might still be lurking there and it was after we had accomplished this and the men were digging themselves in that I last saw your two sons alive. At that time they were both trying to make what little cover they could for themselves before it got dark. From this time onward until we were relieved the next morning the enemy shelled us continuously, several shells falling right among the company, and it was during this period that we lost all trace of the two boys. As soon as it was light the next morning I searched the position we held for any wounded and to see who had been killed but I did not come across either of your two sons. Once, I came across a body lying face downwards which looked like your son James and I asked a man who was in a hole close by but he gave me the name of someone else. I turned the body

John Jones

half over but could not recognise the features. After I had been all round I came back intending to look at the identity disc but before I could reach the body a shell came and cut down a tree alongside which fell, covering the whole body.

When I found that the two were missing, for James was my orderly, I enquired of their platoon Sergeant (their officer had been killed), but the only thing he could tell me was that when last seen, which was sometime during the night, the two were together, what had become of them afterwards he did not know.

I am exceedingly sorry but that is all I can tell you. I should have written to you before and I am very sorry now I have not done so, only there was a possibility that perhaps they might have been wounded and in the dark gone out without our knowledge, but after this lapse of time even that hope is shattered.

James was my orderly and a more fearless and truehearted boy it will be very hard to find. To me he was more of a companion than an orderly and I will miss him very much. In Corporal Jones we have lost a very capable and willing soldier for even though he was not in my platoon, I am only saying what his officer would have said had he been alive to do so and that is, that he was a real good man.

I wish to tender my sincerest sympathy to you and to Mrs. Jones in your heavy sorrow and trust that you will not take the cruel blow too much to heart, for you have reason to be very proud of the two brave boys who so cheerfully gave their lives for their country.

I hope your wounded son will have a speedy recovery and that he, at any rate, will be spared you.

2nd Lt. W.S. Williams[6]

Private Griffith Jones of the 13th Royal Welsh Fusiliers still lies in Mametz Wood. He was killed on 10 July, aged 23, and is remembered on the Thiepval Memorial. He had lived with his parents at The Factory, Rhydygwystl, Chwilog, Caernarvonshire and had enlisted after hearing a sermon in Ebenezer Chapel, Four Crosses, near Pwllheli.

Private Richard Rowland Humphreys from Talybont, Cardiganshire, served with the 15th Welsh. He was killed on the following day, 11 July, aged 20, and is commemorated on the Thiepval Memorial.

Private Alfred Priestley of the 16th Royal Welsh Fusiliers was killed on the same day, 11 July. He was 20 and was from Shepley, Huddersfield. He too is named on the Thiepval Memorial to the Missing.

Corporal Thomas Davies was born at Brynonen, near Bwlchnewydd Chapel, Laugharne, in 1886. He enlisted in the 10th Welsh and landed in France in December 1915. Wounded on 10 July, he was taken to the Casualty Clearing Station at Heilly Station before being evacuated to a hospital, and was then put aboard a hospital ship to return to Britain for further treatment. He died in the 1st Western General Hospital in

Griffith Jones   Richard Humphreys   Alfred Priestley

William Owen

Liverpool on 23 July, aged 29. It may be that he was buried in Bargoed, where his mother was living. However, he is remembered on the Brookwood Memorial in Surrey.

Private William George Owen from Ynysyboeth served with the 2nd Battalion of the Welsh Regiment. His battalion had entered Mametz Wood on 15 July after the fighting for it was over. Whilst they were at the northern edge of the wood, enemy rifle fire came from Bazentin-le-Petit Wood to the north. His battalion was ordered forward and William Owen was killed during the advance. He has no known grave.

***

Leaving their fallen comrades and the wounded behind, the division moved to the Ypres area at the end of August. Here it was employed in routine front line duties: trench repairs, laying duckboards, wiring parties, but it also took part in raids on German positions – most notably on the High Command Redoubt from which the Germans could direct artillery fire and snipe at the British front lines. This was carried out on 17 November 1916 by elements of the 14th Battalion of the Welsh Regiment and a party of Royal Engineers. A three-minute artillery barrage fell on the German trenches and the infantry, who were already stationed in no man's land fifty yards behind the falling shells, rushed the German trenches once the barrage advanced to fall on the German second line.

The war diary of the 14th Welsh for the day recorded that at 11 p.m:

Second Lieutenants Gundrey (officer commanding raid), Vaughan, Kelk, I. Williams, England, Lewis, T.O. Williams and 145 other ranks raided High Command Redoubt. The operation had been carefully prepared and was well carried out. The co-operation between the artillery and infantry was excellent. The enemy's front and support lines were entered. Five Germans were killed, one German was found dead in our lines, one was found mortally wounded by our artillery. Two wounded and 18 unwounded prisoners were brought in. Our losses were two killed (behind our lines), eight slightly wounded. A machine gun and a quantity of documents and other articles were brought in. The R.E. party demolished machine gun emplacements and concrete dug outs.[7]

Victor Gareth Gundrey was born in Taunton, Somerset in 1892. For his part in the raid he was awarded the Military Cross. His citation read: 'For conspicuous gallantry in action. He led a successful raid with great courage and determination, capturing twenty prisoners and accounting for many of the enemy.'[8]

Gundrey later penned an account of the raid. Of the artillery bombardment he wrote:

It will take a long time for anyone who was within five miles of the scene of operations to forget that zero. The raiders or the raided will never forget it. Our own divisional artillery had been supplemented by guns both from the Corps reserves and from flank Divisions. The combined effort can only be described as terrific – it was as if the Redoubt had become involved in a miniature earthquake. All known gun positions in the enemy's rear were included in the torrential downpour of shells; all suspected machine gun emplacements were hurtled out of existence within the first few minutes of a trench mortar bombardment and all the enemy's roads or other communications were harassed with bullets from our Vickers and Lewis Guns.[9]

He wrote of the Redoubt:

High Command was built mainly of concrete. It was a veritable fort. The trenches were concrete faced, the dugouts built into solid masses of stone, and each fitted with a steel door. The furnishing even included braziers, framed pictures and beds, a state of affairs which presented anything but a favourable contrast to the miserable accommodation available on the Welsh side of no man's land. One dugout appeared to have been elaborately equipped as a signal office – it was possible that it was a 'listening set' station. This, together with a concrete observation post and a number of dugouts, was totally destroyed with gun-cotton at the termination of the raid.[10]

Gundrey also described the fighting that took place:

Like fish from shells the Germans were hauled forth on steel points from their hiding-places. They were presented with an alternative of either surrendering or being blown to pieces by hand grenades. Most of them chose the former, some of them suffered the latter. On the right flank of the attack there was a little hand-to-hand fighting, the result being that the German list of dead was that night increased by a score of names.[11]

The party then began the task of gathering booty:

Sandbag after sandbag was crammed with documents, maps and letters. It transpired that papers of considerable value to our Intelligence Staff were included in the jumble of papers, the most important being an artillery officer's log-book taken from the Observation Post. Practically every man secured some article of German equipment. One keen hunter possessed himself of an Iron Cross.[12]

Twice awarded the Military Cross, his second citation, which occurred the following year, read:

T./Lt/ Victor Gareth Gundrey, M.C. 14th Bn. Welsh R. – For marked gallantry and devotion to duty in the attack across the River Selle on October 20th, 1918. He went forward under heavy fire to ascertain the position, and finding two companies not quite on the final objective he led them forward and filled a gap in the

Victor Gundrey in later life

line. He then went round the whole line and sited the fire trenches, his runner getting shot by his side. His coolness and capacity were of the utmost value and materially assisted in the success of the day.[13]

Two weeks after this deed, at Morval Wood, Second Lieutenant Gundrey received a wound to his left leg which resulted in amputation at a field hospital. He worked in the film industry after the war, directing several feature films in the late 1920s. He also co-wrote the screenplay for *Journey's End*, about life in the trenches, under the director James Whale in 1929. He died in Chertsey, Surrey, in July 1965.

The two members of the battalion killed during the raid on High Command Redoubt were Corporal Godfrey Arthur Browning and Private Oliver Richard Jackson. Gundrey described what happened: 'The two lads who had made the greatest sacrifice were killed in our own trenches by a round from an enemy trench mortar. They were carrying the captured machine gun and were immediately in front of me when the round exploded.'[14]

Browning was born in Newport, Monmouthshire, and had enlisted in Swansea, landing in France on 2 December 1915. Jackson was 19 and was born in Waunarlwydd in Swansea. He had served with the Glamorgan Yeomanry before transferring to the Welsh Regiment. The two men were buried alongside each other in Essex Farm Cemetery.

Second Lieutenant Arthur Frederick Hastings Kelk received the Military Cross for his work that night. His citation stated: 'He hastily reorganised the men, led them to their objective, and

Arthur Kelk

was instrumental in finding and capturing the majority of prisoners taken.'[15]

Kelk was the son of the Reverend Arthur Kelk of Goldsborough Rectory, Knaresborough in Yorkshire and a graduate of Magdalene College, Cambridge. He had studied Theology in preparation for a career in the church. Arthur Kelk was killed in action a few months later on 9 March 1917, aged 25.

Second Lieutenant John David Vaughan, from Mansell Street, Burry Port, near Llanelli, was also awarded the Military Cross. His citation read: 'For conspicuous gallantry in action. He carried out a daring reconnaissance with great courage and determination, obtaining most valuable information.'[16]

Vaughan was killed on 18 March 1917, aged 30.

John Humphrey England and another lieutenant were hospitalised when the train on which they were travelling after returning from the raid, in order to rejoin the rest of the battalion, was involved in a collision with a light engine. England was later killed in action on 31 July 1917.

Four other ranks were each awarded the Military Medal for their part in the raid.

On 15 February 1917 the trenches of the 15th Welsh were raided in return by the Germans. The war diary described what happened:

At 1.30 a.m. the enemy opened a heavy artillery and trench mortar bombardment on the whole of our front line... Barrage on the left company commenced behind the front line and then shortened onto the front line itself. At the same time pocket barrage was placed round No.9 Post which was raided by a party estimated at about 25 strong. One of the garrison was killed, four wounded and Lewis Gun captured. One German was killed by the garrison. At same time No.7 Post was also raided and the garrison of 1 N.C.O. and three men apparently taken prisoners as no trace can be found of them, although no gap could be found in our wire near this post, and nothing was seen or heard as far as can be at present ascertained by the posts on either side.[17]

The casualties were: two other ranks killed, four missing and sixteen wounded. One of the wounded was Second Lieutenant F.W. Evans.

On 22 March 1917 the trenches held by the 10th and 13th Welsh were raided after an intense artillery bombardment lasting fifteen minutes. The enemy inflicted 39 casualties on the 10th Welsh, with four killed and four wounded of the 13th Welsh. The Germans captured three members of a working party in no man's land and killed Second Lieutenant E. Hadfield. Lance Corporals H. Colwell and A.W. Cullerton of the 10th Battalion were awarded Military Medals for their work in using their Lewis Guns to drive off the attacking Germans, while Private J. Class won the Military Medal for his work as a runner.

Edgar Hadfield was the husband of Miriam H. Hadfield of 13 King Street, Waterloo, London. A report of his death appeared in a newspaper:

Sec. Lieut. Edgar Hadfield, youngest son of Mr. S. Hadfield, of 'Avondale', Aughton, near Ormskirk, who was killed in France on the 22nd inst. whilst returning from patrol duty, and when only fifteen yards from his dugout. He was attached to the Welsh Regiment, and had been out in France since September last, returning for a brief leave in January last to be married to a Waterloo lady. He was 25 years of age, and before enlisting in the ranks in September, 1914, he was engaged in the Liverpool cotton trade.[18]

Edgar Hadfield

Retaliation was ordered and on the night of 29 March the 15th Welsh raided Morteldje Estaminet. A Bangalore torpedo, a tubular explosive device, was placed in the enemy wire but failed to detonate. Lieutenant T. Landman tried to light the fuse by hand but failed, so Lance Corporal Bamber volunteered to cut it out, which he did by 4.30 a.m., earning the Military Medal for his courageous work.

Another raid on the German front line at midnight on 31 March was successful. Three Germans were captured and nine were killed. Lieutenant T. Landman and Second Lieutenant H.E. Simmons won the Military Cross, and Sergeant J. Schofield won a bar to his Military Medal. Three further Military Medals were awarded and two officers were wounded in the raid.

Thomas Landman won the Military Cross twice. His first citation read: 'For conspicuous gallantry and devotion to duty when in command of a raiding party. Although severely wounded he continued to lead his men, and succeeded in carrying out the task allotted to him. He has previously done fine work.'[19]

His second award came in 1919 and read:

For conspicuous gallantry and ability to command. On taking his company to the support of another battalion he found the latter withdrawing in some confusion. The night was very dark and the conditions most trying, as the men had been exposed to heavy shelling for some hours. Thanks to his cool courage and determination, however, the battalion, which had lost its commanding officer, was rallied and led back to its evacuated position, which he succeeded in holding against repeated enemy counterattacks.[20]

Thomas Landman, a graduate of University College, Aberystwyth, was commissioned into the Welsh Regiment in April 1915. He survived the war, rising to the rank of captain, and relinquished his commission in January 1919. When the Second World War broke out he was commissioned into the Royal Artillery, but resigned in September 1940 owing to ill-health.

Horace Enfield Simmons' citation read: 'For conspicuous gallantry and devotion to duty during a raid on the enemy's trenches. He displayed great courage and skill in fixing a torpedo in position in the enemy's wire. He has at all times set a fine example.'[21]

He later joined the R.A.F. and won a bar to his Military Cross in Russia in 1920:

> At Cherni War, on 27th August, 1919, Lieutenant Simmons, flying a D.H.9, carried out work usually assigned to Scout machines. Descending to water level, he attacked a large fleet of enemy vessels, being hotly received by enemy fire from every description of guns. This daring attack created the utmost confusion amongst the Bolshevik troops, who suffered heavy casualties. Lieutenant Simmons has always displayed courage and ability of a high order during the operations in South Russia.[22]

A further raid on the same German position was conducted on 30 April which resulted in the capture of ten Germans and a machine gun, with the loss of two dead, three missing and twenty wounded. Captain Daniel, Lieutenant I.S. Morgan and Second Lieutenant J. Williams received Military Crosses, Sergeant D.A. Jones a bar to his Military Medal, and eight other Military Medals were awarded.

James Alfred Daniel's citation read: 'For conspicuous gallantry and devotion to duty. He commanded a raiding party with great success. To his careful training beforehand and gallant leading during the raid, much of the success is due.'[23]

He was also awarded the Distinguished Service Order in 1919:

> For conspicuous gallantry during an attack. He organised a patrol and advanced covering party, who established a bridgehead and covered the crossing over the river of the remainder of the battalion, enabling them to start the attack punctually. He subsequently dealt with some enemy machine guns, and brought on the rear companies to the final objective. It was largely due to his personal influence and power of command that the advance was so successful.[24]

Daniel was born in Ireland in 1893 and was a pre-war regular soldier who played for the 15th Welsh rugby team. He was wounded on the Somme in August 1918, but continued his Army career post-war, serving with the Army of Occupation in Germany. He died in 1959.

Isaac Stanley Morgan had fought at Mametz Wood the year previously and survived the war. His citation read: 'For conspicuous gallantry and devotion to duty. He commanded a platoon in a successful raid on the enemy lines. He was wounded during the operation, but continued to control his men until they withdrew from the enemy trenches. He set a splendid example throughout.'[25]

John Williams won the Military Cross twice. His first citation read: 'For conspicuous gallantry and devotion to duty. He led his platoon with great courage and ability. His able training beforehand was of the greatest value to the success of the enterprise.'[26]

In 1919 he was awarded a bar:

> For conspicuous gallantry in an assault on a village. When his commanding officer was wounded, he led the battalion with such effect that the enemy were enveloped before they could concentrate their machine gun fire on the attacking waves. After the objective was taken he headed the party which mopped up the machine gun posts in the rear who were hindering

consolidation with their fire. He displayed fine courage and leadership.[27]

Williams was promoted to major and fought the Bolsheviks in north Russia in 1919. He was awarded the M.B.E. and the Russian Order of Saint Stanislaus, 2nd Class, with Swords.

On the night of 30 April/1 May 1917 a large-scale raid by the 13th Welsh took place, with over 300 men taking part. All the enemy dugouts in the area known as 'von Kluck's Cottages' were destroyed by the supporting Royal Engineers and a dozen prisoners were captured. Lieutenant W.G. Forster, Second Lieutenants H.R. Perkins and H. Wilcoxon won Military Crosses, and nine Military Medals were awarded, with a bar to Company Sergeant Major D.E. Williams.

The battalion suffered one man missing and seventeen wounded, two of whom subsequently died of their wounds. The missing man was Corporal Gwilym Morris who had joined the Welsh Regiment at the outbreak of war. Before enlisting he was a certificated teacher at the Hendrefadog School, Tylorstown. A past student at the University College of South Wales and Monmouthshire, he had passed the inter-B.Sc. examination. In a letter to his father, the

commanding officer stated that Gwilym Morris had done excellent work and had been recommended for a commission. His name is among those on the Menin Gate.

Besides the constituent battalions of the 38th (Welsh)

Gwilym Morris

Division, other battalions of the four Welsh regiments – The Royal Welsh Fusiliers, The South Wales Borderers, The Welsh Regiment and The Welsh Guards – were stationed in the Ypres Salient in preparation for the coming offensive.

On 4 June the award of the Military Cross was made to Second Lieutenant John Rowland Morris of the 11th South Wales Borderers. Morris was to survive the war and rose to the rank of captain.

The Battle of Messines was planned to begin on 7 June but, prior to this, it was decided that information was needed to be obtained on the German forces that were opposing the 9th Royal Welsh Fusiliers. So, a trench raid was ordered to capture, not kill, the enemy. 'C' Company, led by Second Lieutenants E.O. Roberts and D.W. Thomas, consequently discharged these orders. They broke through the German front line and reached the support line.

The official report on the raid by the commanding officer Lieutenant-Colonel L.F. Smeathman stated:

The raid on the whole was a great success. The objective was easily reached. 37 prisoners passed by Battalion Headquarters but it is known that a considerable number of the prisoners captured by this Battalion were cleared down Chicory Trench and thus went through the 56th Brigade. It is impossible to say at present really how many casualties have occurred. The following are known:

1 Officer seriously wounded. (2/Lt. D.W. Thomas)

2 Men killed. One of these was brought in.

9 Men wounded.

1 Man missing but a party of 1 NCO and 2 men have, it is thought, found him in no man's land and are waiting to bring him in tonight.

The Front Line German Trench is almost demolished. Three dugouts were found in it, two of which were concrete and contained Germans. 15 Germans are known to have been killed with the bayonet.[28]

Officers of the 16th Welsh Regiment at Boesinghe in March 1917

John Morris

As a consequence of their actions that night seven men received decorations. Second Lieutenant Douglas Walter Thomas was awarded the Military Cross. His citation read:

> During a raid on the enemy lines in the Wytschaete area on the 5th June 1917, he set a magnificent example to all NCOs and men. It is known that he shot two Germans and stunned another with the butt of his revolver. He was seriously wounded. This officer has on numerous previous occasions done most excellent patrol work in the enemy line.[29]

Thomas had only arrived in France in January. He survived the war, being promoted to lieutenant, and returned to his home in Fulham.

Sergeant C. Bannister was awarded the Distinguished Conduct Medal:

> This Sergeant was in command of a platoon, the duty of which was to guard the right flank of the Battalion. Owing to his able leadership, this platoon thoroughly performed its allotted task. This Sergeant, with Sergeant Evans, then, with a complete disregard of his own safety, attacked and destroyed a German machine gun in a concrete emplacement, which was firing on the flank of the raiding party. His plucky action undoubtedly saved many lives.[30]

Charles Bannister survived the war and was demobilised in March 1919.

Sergeant T. Evans was one of five men who won the Military Medal. His citation read: 'He, in company with Sergeant Bannister, and with a complete

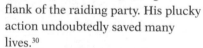

Charles Bannister

disregard of his personal safety, attacked and destroyed a German machine gun which was causing much trouble to the right flank of the raiding party.'[31]

Thomas Evans was a regular soldier who had landed in France on 11 August 1914. He survived the war.

Corporal H. Bonsall's citation read: 'He displayed the greatest ability in leading his section. It is established beyond doubt that he killed two Germans with the bayonet and captured five more personally.'[32]

Herbert Bonsall was born in the village of Chelmorton in Derbyshire and was a cotton operator in Ashton-under-Lyne. After joining the Army he was subsequently promoted to Lance-Sergeant and was killed in action on 4 January 1918, aged 22, while the battalion was holding front line trenches near Ribécourt in France. He is commemorated on the Thiepval Memorial to the Missing. Among the items returned to his mother was a damaged metal watch, possibly the result of the shellfire which took his life.

Private E. Siviter won his Military Medal because:

> He performed numerous acts of great gallantry. He continuously
> left our own line to help and dress wounded in spite of heavy
> machine gun fire from the enemy. He ultimately crawled out,
> in full daylight up to the enemy front line to a lance corporal
> who was wounded and gave him water. He has previously been
> recommended four times but so far has not had any recognition of
> his most valuable services.[33]

Edwin Siviter survived the war and was demobilised in March 1919.

The citation for Private F. Weeks read:

> This man was the last to leave the enemy lines. He found a
> wounded lance corporal who he could not carry, came in and
> reported and returned to the lance corporal across no man's land
> in broad daylight and in spite of heavy enemy machine gun fire.
> He also assisted in the saving of a badly wounded officer on the
> same occasion.[34]

Frederick Weeks was promoted to corporal but died of wounds on 20 October 1918 and was buried in Delsaux Farm Cemetery, Beugny in France. Born in the Rhondda, he had enlisted in Pentre and had landed in France in September 1915.

This was the second occasion that Private T. Jones had won the Military Medal. His second citation read:

> When 2/Lieut. D.W. Thomas was badly wounded... this man, in spite of heavy enemy fire from machine guns, and with complete disregard of his own personal safety, dashed out from our own lines and brought 2/Lieut. Thomas in. On four other occasions during the same raid he brought in wounded men at great personal risk.[35]

Trevor Jones was to be killed just a short time later, on 31 July 1917. He had served on the Western Front since 19 July 1915. Born in Llanelli, he worked at The Old Castle Tinplate Works before enlisting. He was 22 and is remembered on the Menin Gate Memorial to the Missing in Ypres.

The three Royal Welsh Fusiliers who were killed during the raid were Lance Corporal C. Crawford and Privates S.M. Jones and A.L. Hawkins.

Charles Crawford, the badly wounded man that Siviter and Weeks tried so hard to save, was born in Liverpool and was buried in Croonaert Chapel Cemetery. He had been a carter who claimed to be living with his sister, Mary Roberts, at 23 Dorset Road, Liverpool before enlisting, aged 28, in October 1915. However, his personal effects and his medals were unclaimed and subsequent enquires found that neither he nor anyone by the name of Roberts had ever lived at that address.

Buried three graves away from him is Sydney Meredith Jones who had served first with the Northamptonshire Regiment before being transferred to the Royal Welsh Fusiliers. Born in Manchester, he was the husband of Mrs F.M. Jones of 65 Regent Street in Kettering.

Arthur Lewis Hawkins was buried in Klein-Vierstraat British Cemetery. Born in Great Doddington in Northamptonshire, he had also previously served in the Northamptonshire Regiment. He was 23 and had lived with parents.

The officer who wrote the report of the raid, Lovel Francis Smeathman, lost two brothers during the Great War. A newspaper reported how his father came to receive the news:

Widespread regret has been occasioned by the news of the deaths of Lieutenant Julian M. Smeathman and Lieutenant Cecil Smeathman, two sons of Mr. and Mrs. Lovel Smeathman, of South Hill, Hemel Hempstead, and the deepest possible sympathy is felt for the parents in the great loss they have sustained. The news came as a great shock. It was known that Lt. Cecil Smeathman had been wounded, a telegram from the War Office having been received announcing the fact that he was in hospital. On Tuesday evening both Mr. and Mrs. Smeathman, whose interest in anything for the welfare of the community is so well-known, were present at the committee for the relief of Belgian refugees, at the Town Hall, little suspecting that soon they were to hear sad news, which later was followed by even worse intelligence. At the conclusion of the meeting Mr. Smeathman received a telephone message to say that a telegram had been received, which he ought to have as soon as possible. It was handed to him, and when he opened it he found it contained the news that his son, Lt. Cecil Smeathman, who was wounded on October 21st, had died on Sunday. Unhappily, more terrible news was to come. Barely half an hour had elapsed when a further telegram was

received, which stated the sad fact that another son, Lt. Julian M. Smeathman had been killed outright whilst serving his King and Country in the firing line on Saturday.[36]

Lt.-Col. Smeathman unveiling the War Memorial at Moor End, Hemel Hempstead, 26 June 1921, on which his two brothers were named

Two parties of fifteen men of the 16th Welsh were ordered to conduct two simultaneous raids on the German trenches across the canal which ran near to Boesinghe. The raids took place on the same night of 5/6 June under a Stokes Mortar barrage. The southern party, under the command of Second Lieutenant A.O. Jones, brought back three prisoners. The northern party missed their point of entry and ran into strong German resistance. Their commanding officer, Second Lieutenant J.O. Jones, was killed and over half of the men were wounded.

John Owen Jones was 22. Attempts were made to recover his body but it was eventually lost and he is commemorated on the Menin Gate. Born at Cemaes on Anglesey in June 1895, he had graduated from University College, Bangor, and worked as a builder and contractor. He was commissioned into the 15th Welsh but then posted to the 16th Welsh, surviving the fighting at Mametz Wood.

Second Lieutenant A.O. Jones was awarded the Military Cross, and five other ranks received the Military Medal. Sergeant Walter Ernest Richards survived the war, as did Corporal Trygve Bernard Tobiason of Grange Gardens, Cardiff. Tobiason, an apprentice engineer, had enlisted in November 1914, aged 19, and was promoted to Sergeant in September 1917 while he was recovering in hospital after sustaining a leg wound. After over three months in hospital, he trained as a bombing instructor and survived the war, being demobilised in January 1919 to take up a post with Palmers Shipbuilders at Jarrow-on-Tyne.

Private Robert Henry Pugh was one of the two privates awarded the Military Medal. He was commissioned in May 1918 and later awarded the Military Cross. The other was Private William Johnson of Caroline Street in Cardiff who had enlisted in December 1914, aged 28. He was wounded in the right thigh on 1 August 1917 and spent the next two months in hospital. On 1 January 1919 he deserted and went to his parents' home in Macclesfield. He was eventually arrested and fined.

Less than thirty-six hours after these three raids, the Battle of Messines began. The attack commenced with the detonation of nineteen enormous underground mines which blew huge holes in the German line. This was accompanied by a ferocious and effective artillery bombardment which allowed the infantry to move forward and capture the strategically important Wytschaete-Messines Ridge south of Ypres.

The 9th Royal Welsh Fusiliers and the 9th Welsh Regiment were both attached to 58th Brigade, part of 19th Division and were in the line to the left of Wytschaete, near the Hollandscheschurr Farm mines. 'D' Company of the 5th South Wales Borderers was also attached to 58th Brigade, and 'A' Company to the 57th Brigade, which was part of the second phase of the attack. The 4th Royal Welsh Fusiliers were attached to 47th Division and were to advance astride the Yser-Comines Canal.

At 3.10 a.m. on the morning of 7 June, the mines were detonated and a creeping artillery barrage began to support the advance of the infantry. The German General Erich Ludendorff described the effect of the British attack in his memoirs:

> The moral effect of the explosions was simply staggering; at several points our troops fell back before the onslaught of the enemy infantry. Powerful artillery fire raining down on the Wytschaete salient hindered effective intervention by our reserves and the recovery of the position... The 7th of June cost us dear, and owing to the success of the enemy attack the drain on our reserves was very heavy. Here, too, it was many days before the front was again secure.[37]

The 9th Royal Welsh Fusiliers were part of the first line of attack. They lost 15 other ranks killed and three missing. Four officers and 99 other ranks were wounded.

Among those killed was Private George Pullen from Acrefair, Wrexham. He had been awarded the Distinguished Conduct Medal in 1915: 'For conspicuous gallantry on 25th

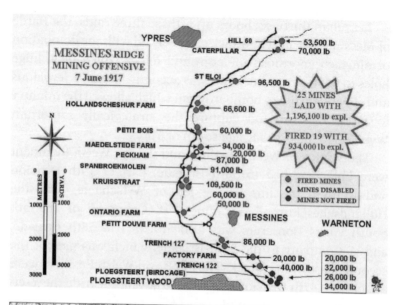

Map of the mines at Messines

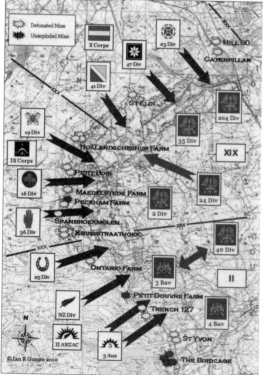

Plan of the attack at Messines

September 1915, at Loos, when, on his own initiative, he successfully carried a telephone wire to the German trenches, and in returning brought in some prisoners. Later he assisted to bring in a wounded man under very heavy shellfire. He was ultimately wounded when close to the trenches.'[38]

Pullen's last resting place is unknown and he is commemorated on the Menin Gate.

The 9th Welsh advanced through the line taken by the 9th R.W.F. and pressed on to the outer edge of Oosttaverne Wood. They lost 24 other ranks killed, four officers and 142 other ranks wounded. Captain E.B. Saunders was awarded the Military Cross, and Sergeants D. Price and W. Reeves and Corporal W. Cochrane the Distinguished Conduct Medal.

Price's citation described his deed: 'For conspicuous gallantry and devotion to duty. He entered a hostile dugout alone, found it full of the enemy, and compelled them to surrender. He subsequently collected a party which he led against a machine gun position, displaying the finest courage and initiative on both occasions.'[39]

Reeves' citation praised his leadership: 'For conspicuous gallantry and devotion to duty under continuous hostile fire. He rallied the men, got them well forward to the barrage, and in every way showed the finest possible example of leadership and courage at a time when it was invaluable to the success of the attack.'[40]

Cochrane's citation read: 'For conspicuous gallantry and devotion to duty. During an attack he reorganised and led his men and those of other companies under heavy fire, leading them well up to the barrage, and displaying the finest possible example of courage and fine leadership. He was finally wounded when the objective was secured.'[41]

The 5th Battalion of the South Wales Borders lost seven men killed. Amongst these was Private Henry Idris Thomas whose father was a minister at a church in Brynmawr. He was 20 years of age and was buried in Voormezeele Enclosure Number 3.

German shell embedded in a tree at Messines

Captain Simons received a bar to his Military Cross, Second Lieutenant Pink received the M.C., while Sergeant Apsden and Private Butcher were awarded the Military Medal.

Company Sergeant Major C.J. Hooper and Sergeant Rees were awarded Distinguished Conduct Medals.

Hooper's citation read: 'For conspicuous gallantry and devotion to duty in taking charge of his platoon after his officer was wounded, and carrying out the work of consolidation in the open under heavy machine gun fire and sniping. He showed total disregard of personal danger, and rendered invaluable service under very trying conditions.'[42]

Charles Hooper survived the war and was demobilised in February 1919.

Rees' citation read:

> For conspicuous gallantry and devotion to duty in leading his platoon forward to consolidate after his officer was wounded. He led a party against a strong point, containing twenty of the enemy with a machine gun, and captured fourteen of them, together with the gun. He kept perfect control over his men and set a splendid example of coolness and fine leadership.[43]

Arthur L. Rees was from Blaina in Monmouthshire and won a bar to his Distinguished Conduct Medal the following year:

For conspicuous gallantry and devotion to duty. After his platoon officer was killed he assumed command of his platoon and successfully held a strong point which was almost isolated owing to the enemy having broken through on both flanks. By his great determination and control over his men, he inflicted heavy losses on the enemy, and finally skilfully withdrew.[44]

Rees survived the war and was demobilised in February 1919.

Captain Robert Morgan Cox from Tonypandy was awarded the Military Cross for commendable work during the battle while serving with the 6th South Wales Borderers.

His citation read: 'For conspicuous gallantry and devotion to duty in superintending the laying of a trench tramway. Although under fire for four days, he pushed on the work with great rapidity in spite of many difficulties. Its completion proved invaluable to the forward troops.'[45]

Previously Mentioned in Dispatches, he had trained in the cadet corps attached to Exeter School and joined the Army in September 1914 as a second lieutenant.

Private Howard Clement Hooper was serving as a stretcher bearer with the 73rd Field Ambulance when he was killed on 10 June. Born in Penarth in 1886, he was employed as a teacher at Albert Road Council School in the town and was

married with a young daughter. Aged 32 when he died, he was buried in Dickebusch New Military Cemetery, Ypres. His officer, Captain G.W.R. Ridkin, said of him: 'He was universally liked and respected, and he always carried out his duties unflinchingly and with great

Robert Cox

45

cheeriness. I personally admired him for this, especially as I think I am right in saying that war was particularly abhorrent to his nature.'[46]

After the capture of the Messines Ridge there was a pause before the next offensive – the Third Battle of Ypres.

At the end of May 1917 the 38th (Welsh) Division was in the front line from Ypres to Pilkem Road to Boesinghe. The following month it switched from 8 Corps to 14 Corps and passed the Boesinghe sector over to the Guards Division, which included the 1st Battalion of the Welsh Guards. The various brigades of the 38th Division then marched to St Hilaire and underwent training for the forthcoming attack.

Second Lieutenant Harry Hill Bucknell of 114 Marlborough Road, Cardiff, was born in 1882 and educated at the Higher Grade Schools, Howard Gardens, in Cardiff. He was a clerk employed by the Cardiff Gas Company before becoming Cashier of the Swansea Gas Company. Having been in the Glamorgan Yeomanry before the war, he was called up on 4 August 1914. Commissioned in September 1915, he was killed on 22 July while serving with the 6th Welsh and was buried in Essex Farm Cemetery. His chaplain wrote: 'He was always a ready volunteer for whatever was taking place – fear was an unknown quantity. We have lost a brave comrade, and King and country has lost a gallant officer whom it could ill spare.'[47]

As British aeroplanes on observation patrols noticed that the Germans were withdrawing their guns to sites further back, Zero Hour was postponed from 25 July for three days, and finally until 31 July. The airmen also reported that the enemy front line was unoccupied, so patrols were sent out to establish the strength of the German forces.

Several days before the attack was due to be launched on 31 July, at just after midnight, a patrol of ten other ranks under the command of Second Lieutenant W.H. Jones of the 16th Royal Welsh Fusiliers was sent out to enter the enemy front line and reconnoitre. Jones described what happened:

Officers of the Welsh Regiment. Standing: Walter Charles Reynolds and E.T. Griffiths. Seated: H.C. James, Harry Hill Bucknell and Gwynne Lewis.

I posted my men about 25 yards in front of enemy wire. My Sergeant and I advanced to the lip of the trench when we were discovered by a sentry post. Revolver and rifle shots were fired at us and we opened fire. Six or eight bombs were thrown over our heads. We located the post, returned to our men and withdrew from his wire at 1.30 a.m... The post appeared to be in front of concrete.[48]

On 27 July information came through that the enemy was falling back, and further reconnaissance patrols were sent out.

At 5.00 p.m. the 15th Battalion Royal Welsh Fusiliers sent out two patrols of 1 platoon each, with the balance of two Companies in support to each. Our men could be seen advancing over no man's land, then over the German trenches, and they eventually disappeared. At 5.25 p.m. the enemy sent up several double red and double green lights from the region of Cancer Trench, and also further back. 5.30 p.m. – 5.40 p.m. sounds of rifle fire and occasional machine gun fire were heard. Lights were again seen from Cancer Trench at 9.00 p.m. These patrols met with considerable resistance, and eventually had to return to our front line. Casualties were considerable, and numbered at least 60 All Ranks.[49]

Amongst those killed was Lance Corporal Frederick Sheldrick. He was one of five children and his birth was registered in 1897. He was a clerk before he enlisted in the 18th Royal Welsh Fusiliers at Holborn in July 1916 at the age of 18, but added one year to his age on his Attestation Service Papers. After training, on Christmas Eve 1915 he was posted to the 15th R.W.F. at Folkestone and from there departed for France. Sheldrick gained promotion in July 1916 to lance corporal, but on 15 October that year he was tried by court martial for leaving his post on the night of 26/27 September without orders from a superior officer. He was found guilty and sentenced to one year's imprisonment.

Sheldrick was evacuated to Le Havre for imprisonment but after serving just one month he was released owing to his previous gallant conduct. He rejoined his battalion in the field and was promoted to lance corporal once more, on New Year's Eve 1916. He was killed in action on 27 July and was buried in

Welsh Cemetery (Caesar's Nose). Of the 68 men buried there, 23 are from the 38th (Welsh) Division.

Another casualty that day was Private David Owen Darley Davies, the son of a Wesleyan minister from Holywell. Born in Llanidloes, Montgomeryshire, in 1897, he attended Kingswood Wesleyan Public School in Bath before being employed as a bank clerk with the London City and Midland Bank in Flint. He enlisted in the 21st Royal Welsh Fusiliers on 6 December 1915 at Wrexham, claiming to be 19. The witness to his attestation was James Ayer, a draper, whose son Leonard was to die of his wounds after fighting at Mametz Wood in July 1916. Leonard had been a clerk in the same bank as David Davies.

Davies was posted to Kinmel Park Camp for training on 28 January 1916, transferred to the 3rd Battalion in August, and then spent a few days home on leave before he embarked for France from Southampton on 12 December 1916, after being posted to the 15th R.W.F. and qualifying as a signaller. He was admitted to a field hospital for a week in May 1917 suffering from a peptic ulcer disorder. After his death on 27 July his body was never recovered and he is commemorated on the Menin Gate Memorial to the Missing.

Private William Dawkins was employed as a tinman at the Beaufort Tinplate Works and lived in Martin Street, Morriston, Swansea. One of ten children, he had enlisted on 4 December 1915, aged 20, and was posted to the 12th R.W.F. After training at Kinmel, where he qualified as a bomber, he embarked at Southampton on 16 June 1917 and was posted to the 15th Royal Welsh Fusiliers. After just 41 days on the Western Front he was killed on 27 July and lies in Dragoon Camp Cemetery. His personal effects, a broken watch, a rosary and photographs in a case, were returned to his mother.

Owen Edwards of Bodwrog Farm, Swalchan Valley, Anglesey enlisted in the Royal Welsh Fusiliers on 21 February 1916. He landed in France on 24 May 1917 and was killed two months later. He was at first listed as missing and his death was not confirmed for two years. In March 1916 he married the mother of his two children; in May his third daughter was born. In January and April 1917 he went absent without leave and received 120 hours and then three days of Field Punishment Number 2, plus the forfeit of two days' pay.

Correspondence ensued when his death was confirmed to verify that he was the father of the three girls. A letter supporting this from an officer living in the same village as the widow stated: 'It was known that Edwards supported the mother but he was not a man of steady habits. The soldier always acknowledged that he was the father of the children named and seemed quite attached to the mother.'[50]

He is commemorated on the Menin Gate Memorial to the Missing.

Sergeant William Louis Williams had joined the Royal Welsh Fusiliers as a Territorial in 1912, aged 25. He was a timber foreman who was born in Machynlleth, Montgomeryshire. After serving in Gallipoli with the 1/7th Royal Welsh Fusiliers, he received a home posting until May 1917 when he was transferred to the 15th Battalion. He was killed on 27 July and is buried in Bard Cottage Cemetery. The father of three girls, his fourth daughter was born in January 1918, so never knew her father.

Despite these losses, information was gathered on the enemy forces and preparations continued for the opening day of the battle.

CHAPTER 3

The Battle of Pilkem Ridge:
31 July to 2 August

PILKEM RIDGE LIES to the north of Ypres and sits along the Boesinghe to Langemark road. In July 1917 elements of the German 4th Army occupied positions along its length and in the village of Pilkem itself. Their defences had been organised in three sections: a forward zone, a main battle zone and a rearward battle zone. Learning from their errors at the Somme the previous year, the Germans had determined that the forward zone would now be less heavily defended and that the majority of the fighting would occur in the main battle zone, supported by reserves situated in the rearward battle zone. This elasticity of defence would prevent the huge loss of life previously seen in the forward zone owing to Allied artillery fire.

British preparations for the coming attack were thorough. Based on intelligence gained from enemy prisoners and aerial photography, a replica of the 38th Division front, including enemy trenches and strong points, was constructed in the rear area between Enquin-les-Mines and Delettes and the various phases of the plan were marked out. These were designated as the Blue, Black and Green lines. The soldiers walked the course in slow time until they were familiar with their positions and objectives. Then timings were practised to fit in with the creeping barrage. A machine gun barrage was also rehearsed.

The Welsh battalions returned to the front line on 19/20 July, taking over the sector from the 29th Division. The Germans were by now well aware that an attack was coming, and British casualties from enemy artillery fire and mustard gas were heavy during this period. In return, British artillery fire continued, as it had done since the 38th Division left the line for training.

The plan of attack was that the 38th Division, with the 51st Division on its right, and the Guards Division on its left, would attack Pilkem Ridge and push on to capture Langemark on the far side of the Steenbeek stream. There would be four phases to the attack – the first as far as the Blue Line, the second to the Black Line, the third to the Green Line and finally to the Green dotted line. It was envisaged that the cavalry would ride through to capture further ground, which would then be consolidated by the infantry.

The 38th Division was made up of three infantry brigades. 113th Brigade comprised the following battalions:

13th Royal Welsh Fusiliers (1st North Wales)
14th Royal Welsh Fusiliers (Caernarvon and Anglesey)
15th Royal Welsh Fusiliers (London Welsh)
16th Royal Welsh Fusiliers

114th Brigade was formed of:

10th Welsh Regiment (1st Rhondda)
13th Welsh Regiment (2nd Rhondda)
14th Welsh Regiment (Swansea)
15th Welsh Regiment (Carmarthenshire)

115th Brigade consisted of:

17th Royal Welsh Fusiliers (2nd North Wales)
10th South Wales Borderers (1st Gwent)
11th South Wales Borderers (2nd Gwent)
16th Welsh Regiment (Cardiff City)
19th Welsh Regiment (Glamorgan Pioneers)

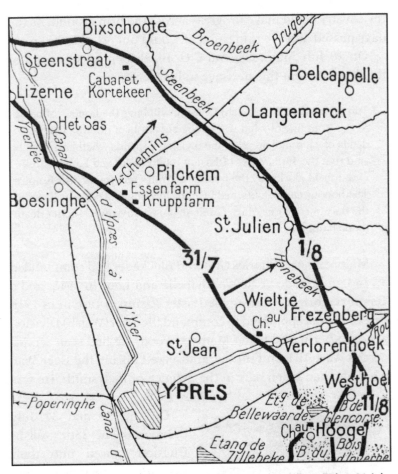

Map showing the advance of the 38th (Welsh) Division at Pilkem Ridge, 31 July to 2 August

The 113th Brigade would form the left flank of the attack, with the 114th Brigade on the right. They would attack up to the Green Line, after which 115th Brigade, in reserve, would push through them and secure the crossing of the Steenbeek, taking ground which had been captured by the British cavalry.

The operational order to use the cavalry to gain ground once the infantry had broken the German line was a sound one. The weather at this stage was dry, so it was entirely feasible that the cavalry could make progress across the firm ground. As the days passed and the rain came, it would not prove to be so.

On 30 July Major-General C.G. Blackader, in command of the division, sent this message to his troops:

> Tomorrow the 38th (Welsh) Division will have the honour of being in the front line of what will be the big battle of the war. On the deeds of each individual of the division depends whether it shall be said that the 38th (Welsh) Division took Pilkem and Langemarck and upheld gloriously the honour of Wales and the British Empire. The honour can be obtained by hard fighting and self-sacrifice on the part of each one of us. Gwell angau na chywilydd [better death than shame].[1]

Major-General Charles Guinand Blackader had commanded an Indian brigade at Neuve Chapelle and Loos in 1915, and a Territorial brigade during the Easter Rising in Dublin in 1916 before he was appointed to command the 38th (Welsh) Division a week after it had taken Mametz Wood. He had seen service on the West African Frontier and served during the Boer War, where he had taken part in the defence of Ladysmith. He was to retire owing to ill-health in May 1918.

On the 30 and 31 July the men of the 38th (Welsh) Division moved into their assembly positions and prepared to advance once the artillery had done its work.

The creeping barrage fired to launch the attack was the mightiest delivered during the war up to that point. Indeed, never again would

Charles Blackader

the British artillery deliver such a fireplan. The barrage was provided by 732 field guns firing at the rate of four rounds a minute, which equates to 24 tons of high explosive falling each minute, or 1,500 tons per hour. The standing barrage on the German second line was produced by 366 field guns and all the 4.5-inch howitzers in the sector. This lifted once the creeping barrage reached within 200 yards of it. In addition, back barrages by the 6-inch howitzers and 60-pounders were fired on the German second line to prevent counterattacks developing and to smash the long-range machine guns. At the same time the British machine gun barrage was launched, with 320 Vickers guns of the Machine Gun Corps sited 500 yards behind the British front line firing just ahead of the creeping barrage. One of the reasons for the failure of the division's attack on the first day of the battle for Mametz Wood was the underperformance of the British artillery. This was not going to happen this time, although the Germans were not slow in responding.

The German reaction to such enormous volume of fire was voiced by General Hermann von Kuhl:

Vickers Guns of the Machine Gun Corps

In the early morning of the 31st July a storm of fire broke out the like of which had never been experienced before. The whole Flanders earth moved and appeared to be in flames. It was no drum fire any longer, it was as if Hell itself had opened. What were the horrors of Verdun and the Somme in comparison with this giant expenditure of power? Deep into the farthest corners of Belgium one could hear the mighty thundering of battle. It was as if the enemy wanted to announce to the whole world 'We are coming, and we shall overcome'. At 6.30 in the morning the British and French troops rose from their trenches, following the heaviest drum fire, and moved into the attack.[2]

The method of attack for 113th Brigade was ordered to be as follows:

Two Companies 13th Battalion Royal Welsh Fusiliers on the Right, and 2 Companies 16th Battalion Royal Welsh Fusiliers on the Left, will attack the Blue Line, capturing it at Zero plus 45 minutes. Battle out-posts will be put out by each Company, who will also detail patrols to search the ground between the Blue Line and the Protective Barrage. The remaining 2 Companies of each Battalion will remain 50 yards behind Cactus Reserve and Cactus Avenue. A halt of 33 minutes will be made on the Blue Line.[3]

The 14th Battalion of the Royal Welsh Fusiliers was ordered to be in Brigade Reserve and to move forward when the Blue Line was secured. A second advance or 'bound' was then to occur: 'The rear Companies of the 13th and 16th Battalions Royal Welsh Fusiliers will come through the leading Companies and will capture the Black Line at Zero plus 2.10. Battle out-posts and patrols will be sent out as for the Blue Line.'[4]

With the capture of the Black Line, the 14th R.W.F. would move up to Villa Gretchen. The third bound would see the remaining battalion of the 113th Brigade, the 15th R.W.F., pass through the Black Line and capture the Green Line at Zero plus 4.50. All objectives were to be consolidated as quickly as possible, with an out-post line in front of these. Strong points were ordered in the remains of the three houses taken – House 10, Zouave House and Telegraph House – with the assistance of the 123rd and 124th Field Companies of the Royal Engineers. Three other houses were to be made into strong points by the infantry alone. Machine guns were to be moved into these.

The infantry attacks were to be supported by Stokes Mortars, two-inch mortars, six-inch Newton Trench Mortars and 9.45-inch mortars. Six brigades from the Royal Field Artillery would provide the artillery barrage, consisting of a creeping barrage and a standing barrage. In addition, a Heavy Artillery Bombardment Group of four 6-inch howitzer batteries and two eight-inch howitzer batteries would be in action. The creeping barrage would lift 100 yards every four minutes, and would remain on the German front line for six minutes. Intensive fire would fall on each objective and a protective barrage would fall 200 yards beyond each objective to prevent the Germans reinforcing it.

At Zero Hour plus three minutes the gas projectors would unleash their oil drums, pouring ignited oil onto the German second line positions and their line from Cariboo Trench to Telegraph House. Contact aeroplanes would be provided by No.9 Squadron. R.E.5s would fly over the line and call for green flares from the leading troops. The aeroplanes would be recognisable to the troops below as they would have black flags attached to the wings. Snipers would be sent forward during the period of consolidation for special duties.

The war diary of the 115th Infantry Brigade describes how on the night of 30/31 July, in preparation for the advance, one company of the 10th S.W.B. and one of the 16th Welsh laid ten complete bridges over the canal, though two of these were destroyed by shellfire.

On the right flank at 3.50 a.m. on 31 July, the 10th Welsh and 13th Welsh (the 1st and 2nd Rhonddas) led the way for 114th Brigade. The attack commenced in darkness to give the men the maximum amount of protection but it meant that it was almost impossible for them to see any of the landmarks they had focused on during their training. The Blue Line, the first German position, was soon captured as many of the Germans were still sheltering in their dugouts from the artillery barrage and gas shells.

An hour into the attack the battalions were moving towards the Black Line which encompassed the village of Pilkem, though as a result of the intense artillery barrage there was little recognisable still standing. As dawn broke the soldiers found themselves in a landscape of carefully sited blockhouses, pillboxes and dugouts. The Germans had made best use of what was left of the buildings after years of fighting. What appeared to be brick from the outside was reinforced by concrete and almost indestructible.

The 16th Royal Welsh Fusiliers met opposition at Cancer Avenue and Telegraph House and the 13th R.W.F. came under fire from a pillbox sited at a crossroads known as Corner House.

115th Brigade began its advance in support of the leading waves at 5.30 a.m. and began to suffer casualties as soon as it crossed the canal near its starting line. By 8.50 a.m. it had passed a position known as Iron Cross, halfway between Pilkem and the Steenbeek and was approaching the Green Line. 17th Royal Welsh Fusiliers were on the left and 11th South Wales

A blockhouse at Iron Cross in 1938

Borderers on the right. They waded through the river and by 9.53 a.m. had established a bridgehead on the eastern bank, near the position of an old inn called Au Bon Gîte.

They held this position until the early afternoon when communication with headquarters was cut owing to a telephone cable being destroyed by shellfire. The advance proceeded as planned and, by 12.30 p.m., a line had been established on the west bank of the Steenbeek. Patrols were sent across the stream.

> These patrols reported the enemy to be holding a line 100 yards from the Ridge on the Eastern Bank with Snipers and machine guns pushed forward in shell holes. Some enemy machine guns, observed firing from Wooden Huts by the Railway, were put out of action by the Light Trench Mortar Battery. By this time, the Commanding Officer Lieut. Colonel Taylor 17th Royal Welsh Fusiliers was wounded and the Battalion strength reduced to 4 Subaltern Officers and 200 Other Ranks.[5]

German aircraft flew over and opened machine gun fire on the troops manning the bridgehead. At 3 p.m. two large groups of Germans were seen massing for a counterattack which

The Steenbeek

eventually drove the 17th R.W.F. back, leaving the 11th S.W.B. exposed. The Germans recaptured some of their concrete blockhouses and opened fire on the Borderers, which forced them to withdraw back across the Steenbeek.

A second German attack commenced at 5 p.m.; it was repulsed but the battalion now came under constant rifle and machine gun fire from the Germans, some of whom were just 100 yards away. This continued throughout the evening and night. Fighting carried on the following day without any progress on either side and, on 2 August, the 11th S.W.B. was withdrawn, having suffered 350 casualties.

The attack had been a success; however criticism was reserved for those responsible for communications:

> Elaborate arrangements were made for communication by telephone, power buzzer, wireless, visual, pigeons, and runners. The party which had not been in the trenches and had had special training were late starting, and to this is attributed a good deal of the subsequent failure, and also to the fact that reconnaissance had not been sufficient either of our own trenches or of the ground on our front. The party got broken up, and parts of the wireless and power buzzer got lost. Added to this it was very difficult to find the way owing to the amount of damage done by the bombardment, and telephonic communication continually broke down. Runners took a long time to deliver messages. After 1st August matters improved, as the power buzzer and wireless were got going. More use might have been made of pigeons, but the tendency is, when communication is faulty, to reserve pigeons for any very important messages which might have to be sent.[6]

The change in the weather made conditions difficult for the infantry after the attack had paused:

> Rain fell steadily all through the night 31st July/1st August, thus preventing the troops from getting the sleep they required so much, and turning the shelled areas into regular morasses. The work of carrying was very greatly increased especially as the Mules were unable on subsequent nights to get beyond Villa Gretchen,

and all rations, ammunition, etc. had to be carried on from there by hand.[7]

The enemy shells and rain continued to fall and the ground was soon sodden. After the brigade was relieved on 4 August, the days that followed 31 July were summarised as:

Nothing of any great importance had occurred after the night 1st/2nd August. There was a considerable amount of shelling at times, and the 'S.O.S.' signal was sent up a few times, but no attack was made by the enemy. Company Commanders, however, found it difficult to be sure there was no attack owing to the smoke. During the 2nd, 3rd, and 4th August the weather had gradually improved and the ground was fairly dry for the relief. The men had, however, suffered a good deal from wet feet and loss of sleep, but kept remarkably cheerful the whole time, and the Officers did all they could for their men. Great difficulty was found in keeping Rifles and Lewis Guns in working order owing to the mud. It is estimated that this Brigade captured over 300 Prisoners.[8]

Brigadier-General Price-Davies recorded the casualties suffered by his 113th Brigade from 30 July to 4 August as: 'Officers: 9 killed and 25 wounded. Other Ranks: 101 killed, 589 wounded and 95 missing.'[9]

He recorded his thoughts on the events of 31 July in a letter:

New dugout made for a double battalion HQ was nearly knee deep in water. Some of the troops in trenches for 2 nights already, artillery fired away as usual. The German reply was not so serious as usual. At 3.30 a.m. the barrage and bombardment opened with a beautiful display of burning oil drums and some other fearful forms of frightfulness. I did see the fellows go over and anyway it was not too healthy outside my dugout. The line moved into Battle HQ at 2.30 a.m. All went well except signal communication which was a disaster. Eventually I got the message via the telephone. I went to the front line and everything was chaos though the concrete dugouts had withstood the artillery fire in a wonderful manner. Everything looked the same dull and uninteresting and many of my old landmarks have gone.

I reached the spot where I expected to form my new HQ but there was nothing there to be seen but another dugout. The telephone had moved on so on I went but we very soon found we were in a very unpleasant spot sitting in an open shell hole near the railway. I was close to Pilkem and a kindly subaltern told me of a good strong point to which I moved. All round us was the chaos of battle, equipment, rifles, ammunition and every conceivable thing lay in piles outside the door. And no dugout was complete without one or two corpses inside and a collection of wounded inside, all Bosche. I heard stories of the fight told to me by an excited subaltern. At some point a corporal had led two men and rushed a dugout whence MG's were firing, bayoneted the inmates and captured 2 MG's.

In the afternoon and evening shelling became more intense. Now men fell and conditions became very bad but nothing really dampened the spirits of the men. The officers too were magnificent. They seemed to have suddenly developed and have gained confidence in themselves and to have realised the power to command the men and help them in difficulties.

Subsequent days contained more of the glory of war but called for the highest military virtues, patience, endurance of the wet ground where little shelter existed and where the rain rapidly filled up the trench as soon as it was dug. Every day I inspected a collapse, numbers of men were falling exhausted but instead their spirit never flagged and with the return of the sun and the idea of relief they soon began to look more cheerful.[10]

The Brigade Major of 114th Brigade recorded in the war diary that: 'All objectives were carried within ten minutes of scheduled time and by 9 a.m. the 15th Welsh on the right and the 14th Welsh on the left were firmly established on the Green Line.'

By the following day progress was much less easy: 'Heavy rain having very serious effect on operations owing to state of ground and observation – great difficulty in carriage of stores and munitions to forward positions.'[11]

The difficulties in re-supplying the advance troops did not

ease until 5 August. The brigade war diary noted on that day: 'Ground dried up and activity easier. Duckboard tracks and railways being pushed on and are of great help.'[12]

The 38th Division had reached all its objectives, captured over 700 prisoners and inflicted severe casualties on the enemy. Opposite them were the German 3rd Guards Division, including the Guards Fusilier Regiment – the 'Cockchafers' – and from this regiment alone 400 prisoners had been captured. The regiment had earned this nickname in the 1830s. Raised in 1826 as two battalions, the 1st Battalion was stationed in Potsdam and the 2nd in Spandau. In May each year the 2nd Battalion marched to Potsdam to join the other battalion for joint exercises. As they marched they were jeered as the 'May Beetles', Cockchafers or *Maikafer* in German. This irritation soon became a source of pride when King Friedrich Wilhelm III used it when the regiment was being reviewed.[13]

The heavy rain now meant an end to this stage of the offensive and the 38th (Welsh) Division was relieved on 6 August. However, there was more fighting to come.

CHAPTER 4

The Welsh Guards

THE WELSH GUARDS was formed by Royal Warrant on 26 February 1915 and on 17 August 1915 they sailed for France. They fought in their first major action at the Battle of Loos, which began on 27 September that year, as part of the Guards Division. In July 1917 they were moved into the line north of the 38th (Welsh) Division and were to form the left flank of the advance on the first day of the battle.

In the path of their attack lay the Yser Canal. Various raiding parties sent to investigate the state of the canal reported that the water was deep in places. However, information arrived on 27 July that the enemy trenches were empty. Accordingly, at 5.20 p.m., four patrols of the 3rd Battalion Coldstream Guards crossed the canal on buoyant rigid mats and found the information to be correct. This advance indicated to the Germans that the British offensive was about to commence so their artillery stepped up their activity.

The Welsh Guards marched into the line on 29 July from their camp in Forest Area, near Woesten. The front line was now Baboon Support Trench and on the night of 30 July the Prince of Wales' No.1 and No.4 Companies crossed the canal and took up their battle stations.

The first wave consisted of two platoons of No.2 Company on the right flank, and two platoons of No.3 Company on the left. The remaining platoons of No.2 and No.3 Companies formed the second attacking wave, while the four platoons of No.1 Company made up the third assaulting wave. In reserve were

Recruiting poster for the Welsh Guards

two platoons of No.4, who were to be employed in mopping up any German resistance left behind as the attacking waves passed by.

Their orders were to take two objectives: the Blue Line, which lay on the far side of a wood known as Wood 15, and was to be taken by the first wave; and the Black Line, which would be captured by the second and third waves. When these objectives had been achieved then the 2nd Battalion of the Scots Guards and the 4th Battalion of the Grenadier Guards would advance through them and take the third objective, the Green Line.

Zero Hour was 3.50 a.m. but, owing to the bloodless advance across the canal on 27 July by the 1st Guards Brigade and the 201st French Regiment, it was decided to give the Guards Division an additional 38 minutes before their attack began.

Throughout the night gas shells were fired on the German artillery positions and when the attack began it was still dark. The barrage for the other battalions involved in the assault began at 3.50 a.m., with the Guards' batteries waiting their turn.

At 4.24 a.m. the Guards Divisional Artillery opened fire, its shells landing 200 yards in front of the first wave, which

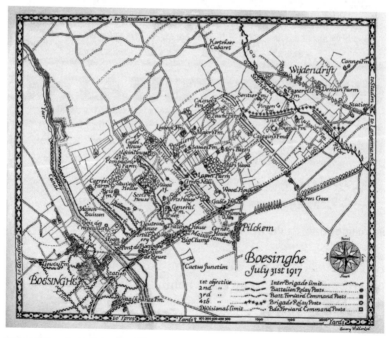

Map of the plan of attack
F.C. Grimwade

now advanced to within 50 yards of the exploding shells. The barrage advanced at a rate of 25 yards a minute, the first wave meeting no opposition until they reached Wood 15, where on the right of their line they were held up by machine gun fire from a concrete blockhouse which the barrage had failed to destroy. This was eventually outflanked and neutralised.

As a result of this delay, the soldiers had now lost distance from the barrage which continued its relentless progress. When they passed Wood 16 on their left flank, machine guns again opened fire and held up the advance for a second time until they were bombed. The line then continued its advance and reached its final objective, the Black Line.

This was the first time that the Welsh Guards had encountered blockhouses and several men distinguished themselves in capturing these. Sergeant Robert Bye was awarded the Victoria Cross (see page 220).

Second Lieutenant Reginald Rees Jones was 21 years of age when he was wounded on 31 July after attacking one of the German blockhouses. He succumbed to his injuries in a casualty clearing station on 25 August, having been unconscious for most of the time, and was buried in Mendinghem Military Cemetery. Mendinghem, like Dozinghem and Bandaghem, were the popular names given by the troops to the casualty clearing stations in this area.

At the time he was wounded, Jones had been leading his men in No.4 Company in the advance.

When the leading waves were temporarily held up by fire from a blockhouse, he pushed up to the obstacle and fired his rifle through the slits, regardless of the danger which confronted him. He then entered the blockhouse himself, dealt with the occupants and enabled the advance to continue. He was later wounded in the head, having acted throughout the operation with great gallantry and initiative.[1]

Colonel Douglas Gordon of the Welsh Guards wrote: 'He did

Reginald Jones

so well in the attack and he got the D.S.O. for wonderful bravery. I am unable to praise him too highly. He was loved by all the Battalion and no words of mine can give him too much credit.'[2]

His company commander, Captain Battye, wrote: 'He was very plucky and brave and I would also like to say that his conduct during the battle was splendid. He behaved with great coolness and gallantry and it gave me great pleasure to send in his name to the General for special mention. He certainly deserved the honour.'[3]

Prior to the joining the Army in January 1916, he had assisted his father in the family grocery business in Barry, south Wales. He was gazetted with the Distinguished Service Order on 26 September 1917.

In January 1920 his mother received a letter from Guardsman H.G. Davies, now working as a police constable:

Dear Mrs. Jones,

I am taking the opportunity of writing these few lines in regard to your son's death, Lieutenant R. Jones, who was wounded very badly in the head on 31st July 1917 on the Battlefield about 16 miles in front of Ypres called Pilkem Ridge. Well in the first instance I had been on the officer's staff for over 12 months before your son joined us on active service and that is why I know so much about Mr. Jones. On the day mentioned I was with Mr. R. Jones and the captain of our company: we went over the top as the first wave of our division. I was always employed as captain's orderly and was standing with him when a shell burst quite close to us and I saw Mr. Jones drop close by my side. I stopped with him and bandaged his head as I was a St. John Ambulance man. He was quite sensible at the time. He said to me, 'Davies I am hit so try and comfort me a little. Thank you old boy.' This was all he said, he gradually got worse. I lifted him in the shell hole close by and stayed with him until I could manage to get him away and then I carried him on my back about half a mile until I met the stretcher bearers.

In course of a time [*sic*] I heard that Lieutenant Jones was dead of wounds in a field hospital in a small town called Proven where he had been several times with the battalion for rest – later I had heard that he had won the D.S.O. I had been orderly to Lieutenant Jones on several occasions. I know that Mr. Jones liked to get me if he could as I had seen a good lot of fighting. I am glad to think today I had done all I could for him.

I was very fond of him, and his men also worshiped him because he was not only a good soldier but a thorough gentleman to his men and that was a great thing in those days. He had a very bad wound in his head. I know for sure he was buried in a proper manner for I know some of the officers were at his funeral.

Well Mrs. Jones I can sympathise with you and your family, with the hope of your gallant soldier who died a gallant soldier's death for the sake of his King and country. If there is anything you would like to know please let me know as I shall be glad to meet you at Pontypool. I am residing in the parish of Beguildy as police officer. I can feel for you as my own family suffered great losses. I was myself carried off the battlefield some time afterwards badly wounded. I must close now and must say I am only too pleased to give you this information.

I remain,
Yours truly
Police Officer Davies[4]

Herbert George Davies was a police constable at Beguildy, near Presteigne, Radnorshire. He had enlisted in December 1915 and served on the Western Front from 9 July 1916 to 22 May 1918, when he sustained a severe shell wound to the face which led to him being discharged in September of that year.

Another gallantry medal winner was Private William Hughes who killed or captured the occupants of a blockhouse in Wood 16, which was holding up the advance of the French troops on the left. He was awarded the Distinguished Conduct Medal, being gazetted on 17 September 1917. From Glasinfryn, near

Bangor, he was wounded three times during the course of the war, which led to his discharge in November 1919 after his right leg had been amputated.

His citation read:

> For conspicuous gallantry and devotion to duty when one of a liaison party with other troops. At a critical moment, when fire had been opened from a strong concrete emplacement upon the attacking troops, he charged the position himself, and was followed by the remainder, who were so inspired by his fearlessness and determination that they captured the post. His heroic action was heartily cheered by the troop with whom his party was cooperating.[5]

Just after 5 a.m., the Guards Division began their advance to their second objective. They encountered machine gun fire from Hey Wood and there was a break in the barrage at this point but, by 6 a.m., they had reached the Black Line. At 7.15 a.m. the supporting battalions deployed behind the Black Line began to move forward. The 3rd Battalion of the Grenadier Guards found its way impeded by the German blockhouses along the Ypres-Staden railway line. Eventually, the most serious obstacle was captured and three German officers, 52 other ranks and four machine guns were found inside and captured. By 8 a.m., all the reinforced farmhouses had been captured and the third line had been reached.

The 1st Guards Brigade was now detailed to continue the advance. They began their attack at 8.50 a.m. by which time the enemy resistance had noticeably stiffened. The rifle and machine gun fire from the farmhouses and blockhouses west of the Steenbeek slowed the British advance. After a determined advance, the Guards were soon in possession of most of their objective. The divisional artillery began to move forward at 8 a.m. on 31 July along smashed-up roads. The Guards had driven the enemy back 2.5 miles on a front of a mile wide. They had captured 15 officers and 617 other ranks.

The Welsh Guards' headquarters was established in Sauvage

House near the Blue Line and two companies of the 55th Field Company Royal Engineers began to erect barbed wire along the Green Line – the Welsh Guards having already consolidated their line in front of Wood 15. By 3 p.m. the Welsh Guards had been relieved and were moved back to Elverdinghe. They had suffered 138 casualties – 3 officers and 135 other ranks.

Among those killed was Guardsman Albert William Hallworth from Heckenfield, near Wokingham. A family story says that while on leave he did not want to return to the horrors of the front line and when the time came he instead concentrated on digging a vegetable patch in his garden. He was arrested and imprisoned in Wokingham Jail before being sent back to Flanders.[6] Albert's body was unable to be identified and his name is inscribed on the Menin Gate Memorial to the Missing.

A local newspaper carried the story of his death: 'Private A. Hallworth, Rose Street, Wokingham, killed in action, July 31st, aged 20. Before joining up last October he assisted his father in his business as baker and corn factor.'[7]

Private Joseph Knowles was also killed on 31 July. A resident of St Helens in Lancashire, he was employed by the St Helens Co-operative Society in the grocery department. He was described thus:

Welsh Guards in training

As a boy at School he showed marked ability, won a Scholarship and was awarded many prizes. He was very fond of music and played the cornet in the Ragged School Mission Band. He was a member of the Congregational Church and Sunday School and at one time was awarded a prize with honours for a Scripture Examination. He was fond of sport and liked a game of football. He was also the holder of two certificates for swimming.[8]

Joseph Knowles had enlisted in June 1916 and trained at Caterham Barracks. He arrived in France on Christmas Eve 1916 and was just 19 when he was killed. He is buried in Artillery Wood Cemetery.

Private Thomas Mansell died of his wounds on 31 July. His death was reported as follows:

Official news has been received by Mrs Mansell, 8 Mackintosh Terrace, Trelewis, that her husband, Private Thomas Mansell, Welsh Guards, was wounded in action and succumbed to his injuries on July 31st. Private Mansell was very well known in this district and had worked at the Treharris and Penallta Collieries.

He joined the Grenadier Guards in November 1914, a few days after he learned that his brother Private Sam Mansell, of the same regiment, had been killed in action. He was later transferred to the Welsh Guards and with them went to France. He was severely wounded in 1916 and spent several months in hospital at Eastbourne. He again went to France on his recovery and was home on rest leave in December last. Whilst home he was entertained to a smoking concert by the reception committee. Private Mansell, who was only 33 years old, leaves a wife and five children. This brings the Nelson death roll of soldiers in action up to 22.

Mrs. Mansell has received a message of sympathy from the King and Queen and the following letter from deceased's company officer: 'Dear Mrs. Mansell, With great regret I have to inform you that your husband, Pte. T Mansell, has died of wounds received on July 31st. I was with him myself just before the advance on that date and he was in high spirits and among his friends. His death is a great loss to the company. He was a very good soldier and set an excellent example to the younger men, both in smartness

Joseph Knowles   Thomas Mansell

when out of the line, and in courage when in it. He was wounded severely in both legs. Yours truly, B.T. Herbert, Lieut., Welsh Guards.'[9]

Thomas Mansell is buried in Dozinghem Military Cemetery.

William Haywood from Bargoed enlisted in March 1915 at the age of 34, despite being a married man with five children. He had taken part in the Battle of Loos and survived the attack on the first day of the Third Battle of Ypres. He was wounded later in the year, receiving a gunshot wound to the head. Invalided home for treatment, he was discharged in December 1918.

John Broom, a locomotive fireman from Barry, enlisted in the Welsh Guards in July 1915, aged 20. In September 1916 he won the Military Medal and was promoted to corporal for keeping his gun in action with great success against a party of German machine gunners. He wrote to his mother: 'It was in the advance on September 25th that I saw a German machine gun party roaming about. I just turned the gun on them – and they have stopped roaming now! One of my mates fetched in their gun.'[10]

Broom had been in the Army for 16 months and in France for about 13 months. In March 1917 he was presented with a certificate for courageous work with a Lewis Gun. He took part in the advance of 31 July but was killed on 1 December 1917 at Cambrai.

Thomas George Hill, a 19-year-old hairdresser from Barry, had enlisted in July 1915. Arriving in France in February 1916, he was shot in the head on 1 July 1916. After recovering at home he returned to the front in March 1917. He was awarded the Croix de Guerre on 25 September 1917 but was killed on 1 December 1917 at Cambrai.

Among those who had distinguished themselves was Captain David Lees who was awarded the Distinguished Service Order for five times passing through the barrage carrying wounded men back to safety. Lees survived the war but died after a short illness at the age of 53. His obituary ran:

> Dr. David Lees was educated at Ayr Academy and Edinburgh University. He had a distinguished undergraduate career, and on qualifying became a resident house surgeon in Edinburgh Royal Infirmary and later in the Royal Maternity Hospital and in Bangour Asylum. From 1909 till 1914 Dr. Lees was in general practice in Northumberland. In 1914 he joined the R.A.M.C. and served with the Guards Brigade in France. Dr. Lees was wounded, was twice Mentioned in Dispatches and was awarded the D.S.O. for conspicuous gallantry on the field.[11]

Corpl. John Broom, M.M.

John Broom   Thomas Hill   Thomas Hill's mother at his grave

His D.S.O. citation read:

For conspicuous gallantry and devotion to duty. He passed through an intense barrage in order to attend to the wounded who were lying exposed to heavy fire of every description. Single-handed and under heavy shelling, he dressed the wounds of an officer, a Sergeant, and a private, and carried each of them in turn to a place of comparative safety. To do this he had to pass through the enemy's barrage no less than four times, but with complete disregard for his personal safety he went forward a fifth time to attend to others, inspiring all ranks by his own splendid example of fearlessness and devotion.[12]

Private Edward John Miles was killed on the first day of the attack, leaving behind a widow. He lived in Roath, Cardiff, and had been employed by Messrs. Cox and Sons of City Road. His body could not be identified and he is named on the Menin Gate Memorial to the Missing. Edward Miles' brother Arthur served as Company Sergeant Major with the 16th Welsh, fought at Mametz Wood and Pilkem Ridge and survived the war.

Another casualty of 31 July was Private Henry Harold Hobday of Vine Cottage, Pontyclun. He was 29 and a married man. Before enlisting in the Welsh Guards he was employed at the Royal Stores in Pontyclun. His brother Wyndham served in Salonika. Henry Hobday lies in Artillery Wood Cemetery.

David Lees

Edward Miles

Henry Hobday

Sergeant Thomas W. Thomas fell on the same day. Born in Cwmavon, in civilian life he worked at the Cynon Pit and his brother Llew Thomas was a well-known Cwmavon Rugby Club forward. Thomas' body was lost and he is remembered on the Menin Gate Memorial to the Missing.

The rain now began to fall and did so continuously for four days and nights. The ground soon changed into a quagmire, with the Steenbeek and its tributaries overflowing their banks. The infantry were now up to their knees in water. Such conditions meant that a further advance was not possible.

Guardsman Norman Hadley Williams died on 5 August and was buried in Artillery Wood Cemetery. Originally from Cradley in Staffordshire, he was living in Kidwelly when he joined up in 1916, not long after getting married. In civilian life he was a furnace man at the Kidwelly Tinplate Works and had been a chorister at the local St Mary's Parish Church from boyhood. It was reported that his mother had a premonition of her son's death:

> It is reported that at his parents' house on the day of his death, his tennis racquet, which was standing on a shelf in the sitting room, burst three of its strings with a bang. The deceased soldier's mother and sister and another young lady were in the room at the time, and Mrs. Williams exclaimed, 'Oh, there's my poor boy gone – killed.' The news of his death did not reach Kidwelly till several days later.[13]

On 7 August the Guards Division was relieved by 29th Division and marched back to the Proven-Herzeele area. As was usual, the divisional artillery was left in the line and was in action throughout the whole of August. Despite the poor visibility owing to the mist and rain the batteries fired constantly on the area between Wijdendrift and the Broembeek stream.

Before they left the front line the Guards Division was ordered to salvage the unfired small-arms ammunition that lay strewn across the battlefield and it was reported that they retrieved over a million rounds.[14]

On 11 August the divisional artillery contributed to a barrage in support of a minor advance made by the right flank of 29th Division, and the next day it covered an attack made by a brigade of the 29th on Passerelle Farm. On 16 August they bombarded the enemy trenches east of Wijdendrift and the infantry drove the Germans out. The batteries then broke up several hostile counterattacks. From 21 August onwards, the 74th and 75th Artillery Brigades were subjected to bombardment from the enemy guns in Houthulst Forest and on the high ground near Poelcappelle. Few casualties were inflicted but considerable damage was caused to the guns, dugouts and battery positions. It appeared that the batteries were under the direct observation of the German gunners, and the battery commanders were instructed not to fire except in response to S.O.S. signals.

Amongst the ranks of these gunners was my grandfather, Ernest Cyril Hicks, of Phyllis Street, Barry Island, who had responded to the call for volunteers to enlist in the British Army to supplement the British Expeditionary Force at that time fighting the Germans in France and Belgium.

Ernest, who had been born in Truro, Cornwall, was employed as a blacksmith's striker at Barry Docks and a member of the 'Forward Movement', a religious group that met at Barry Island. He enlisted in Barry on 31 August 1914 when he was 19 years old. He was given the Service Number of 28420 and was posted to the Royal Field Artillery. Whether he volunteered for this

Thomas Thomas   Norman Williams   Ernest Hicks

branch of the service or whether his blacksmith's training seemed an appropriate background for the R.F.A. is uncertain. In either case, he was soon part of the Guards Divisional Artillery. He was gassed in August 1918, which contributed to his premature death after the war.

On the night of 27 August, the Guards came back into the line. The rain was pouring down and the infantry set to work to improve their positions. The Guards were now ordered to cross the Broembeek and advance into the Houthulst Forest. A divisional conference held on 4 September decided that the 2nd Guards Brigade would assault the line of the Broembeek, consolidate the far bank and use it as a starting point for the troops of 29th Division.The banks of the Broembeek were marshy and their width varied from eight to twenty feet. The depth was only some two to three feet but, below this, was a bed of thick mud.

Second Lieutenant George Christopher Serocold Tennant was killed by German shellfire as he came out of the line on 3 September, aged 19. He had only joined the Welsh Guards the previous month and was described as: 'a charming young officer... a clever youngster who had shown in the few days he had been in action the greatest contempt for danger.'[15]

Christopher Tennant was the eldest son of Charles and Winifred Tennant of Cadoxton Lodge, Vale of Neath, and was educated at West Downs School and Winchester College. He then progressed to Trinity College, Cambridge, before entering Sandhurst. Commissioned into the Welsh Guards on 30 April 1917, he arrived at the reinforcement camp at Proven on 17 August.

In October 2004, workers who were in the process of laying a new carpet in Elverdinge Church, near Langemark, moved a pulpit and underneath found a small brass plate from Mrs. Tennant in memory of her son.

His friend Basil Webb, who was later killed in December 1917, had joined the regiment at the same time. He wrote to Tennant's mother:

Brass plate in memory
of Christopher
Tennant[16]

Christopher Tennant

It was quite unavoidable, just one of those bits of bad luck which go to make up this business of war. The great thing is, he was doing his job up in the line, and did not get hit by a stray shell miles behind, which is the fate of many poor people. Also he was killed practically outright and suffered nothing. If he was going to be knocked out it could not possibly have happened in a better way. But even so, the whole thing is a horrible affair, and I can only express my sympathy with you.[17]

Tennant's last letter home was found on his body. It read:

All well, I come out tonight. By the time you get this you will know I am through all right. I got your wire last night, also your three letters. Many thanks for that little book of poems. It is a great joy having it out here. There is nothing much to do all day except to sleep now and then. It will soon be English leave, and that will be splendid! I got hit in the face by a small piece of shrapnel this morning, but it was a spent piece, and did not even cut me. One becomes a great fatalist out here.[18]

Second Lieutenant Thomas Harry Basil Webb was the only son of Lieutenant-Colonel Sir Harry Webb, M.P. of Llwynarthau, Castletown, Cardiff. He attended Winchester College and was known to be a good football and cricket player who had accompanied Tennant to the Western Front.

Another casualty of the German shelling on 3 September was Private James Sherwood from Roath in Cardiff. He wrote home:

I got wounded on Monday night last [3 September] by a shell which dropped right in our trench; it also wounded three others beside myself. I caught it in my left arm, and had the left side of my face burnt, and I am glad to say it is very much better. I hope that the next time I write I shall feel much better in my head, for I have a sore ear which has made me quite deaf, and gives me a nasty headache.[19]

The following day, 4 September, Corporal Percy John Marks, formerly of the Cardiff City Police, was killed in action. Standing over six feet tall, he was the son of Mr and Mrs E.F. Marks of the Priory Dairy, Taunton, and after leaving school he worked in the family business. He had joined the Cardiff City Police in 1914, but in 1915 had enlisted in the Welsh Guards. In that year he went to France and had served there continuously. He was buried in New Irish Farm Cemetery. A newspaper reported:

He went through 2 memorable charges at Hill 70 and was also actively engaged in the important action near Loos. The following letter was received from Sergeant D.J. Richards, one of his Comrades:

Dear Mrs. Marks,

Just a few lines to inform you of the death of your son. Cpl. Marks and myself were very good chums, because we belong to the same battalion and came together on the job. All the boys miss him because he was so cheerful. He always had a smile on his face and I miss him very much, because he was one of the best NCOs I had under me. The way he met his death was by a shell dropping right on top of the dugout killing one NCO and 3 men. They were killed outright, buried beneath the dugout. I was out digging for him last night and this morning and I shall do my best as a soldier and a pal to see that your son and the others are buried properly. If

Thomas Webb

James Sherwood

Percy Marks

there is anything you would like to know I shall be only too pleased to help you. Your son was a good soldier and a brave one as well. Please accept the sympathy of all the boys and myself in your great loss. D.J. Richards Serjt.[20]

One of the other men killed by this shell explosion was Private William John Jenkins of Glen View Terrace, Llanbradach. His captain described him as: 'a splendid worker, always cheerful and willing.'[21]

He was one of the original members of the battalion and is commemorated on the Menin Gate Memorial to the Missing.

Lance Corporal Reginald Norman Charlie Winn had joined the Grenadier Guards on 3 December 1914, and was transferred to the Welsh Guards when they were formed in 1915. He was wounded on 7 November 1916 and again on 4 September 1917, dying of his wounds later the same day. He was buried in Canada Farm Cemetery, aged 24.

His brother William Joseph Winn mobilised with the 1st Battalion South Wales Borderers as a reservist in August 1914 and sustained a serious wound at the Battle of Mons, and was wounded again at The Quarries in September 1914, where he was one of only 16 survivors. He received the Military Medal, and was promoted to Sergeant on the field for conspicuous bravery. He subsequently contracted pneumonia and was hospitalised in Aberdeen for four months. After recovering, he returned to France and was killed on 18 April 1918, aged 23. His death is commemorated on the Loos Memorial to the Missing.

The brothers were orphans, having been born in Stroud, and were raised by their uncle and aunt in Gilfach Goch.

Corporal John T. Crumb died of his wounds on 6 September and was buried in Dozinghem Military Cemetery. A married man, he had enlisted with the first batch of recruits from the Rhondda to join the Welsh Guards and had landed in France in August 1915, later taking part in the Battle of Loos. He had been awarded the Military Medal, and not long before he

William Jenkins   Reginald Winn   William Winn

was wounded had been recommended for the Distinguished Conduct Medal. He had been home on leave in Aberaman the previous April where he had been presented with a wristwatch and a cheque by the committee of the local 'Heroes Fund'.

A touching tribute to him was published a year after his death:

> In loving memory of our dear son, Corporal John Crumb, 1st Batt. Welsh Guards, who fell in action September 6th, 1917, age 28 years.
>
> Sleep on dear son, in a far-off land,
> In a grave we may never see;
> But as long as life and memory last,
> We will remember thee.
>
> Ever remembered by his father, mother, sisters, and brothers.[22]

It was accompanied by another from his widow:

> In proud and loving memory of my dear husband, Cpl. J.V. Crumb, Welsh Guards, who died of wounds received in action, September 6th, 1917, aged 28 years.
>
> I loved him in life, he is dear to me still,
> But in grief I must bend to God's Holy Will;
> My sorrow was great, my loss hard to bear:
> But angels, dear husband, will tend thee with care.
>
> Deeply mourned by his devoted wife and baby.[23]

During this latter period in the appalling terrain of the front line, spent wet to the skin in mud-filled shell holes, with the danger of imminent German counterattacks, four Guardsmen distinguished themselves. Private J. Lloyd Roberts from Denbigh was awarded the Military Medal, as was Private J. Lewis from Carmarthen (who held his post despite being wounded in seven places) and Privates T. Griffiths from Blaenporth in Cardiganshire and T. Evans from Flint.

Thomas Griffiths was 28 when he was killed at Arras on 10 March 1918. His final resting place was lost and he is remembered on the Arras Memorial.

Thomas Evans died of his wounds on 5 September 1917 and was buried in Mendinghem Military Cemetery. He was born in 1886 and baptised in Hope Parish Church. His father was a timber merchant and in 1911 Thomas was a student. His brother Frank joined up and was reported missing early in 1918 but was later declared a prisoner of war. Thomas Evans had previously been awarded the Military Medal.

(In 2016 I noticed that his gallantry award was not recognised on his headstone or on the Commonwealth War Graves Commission website and consequently I petitioned them on his behalf. This omission was quickly corrected and I thank the CWGC for doing this.)

On 4 September the Welsh Guards were relieved by the 2nd

John Crumb

Thomas Evans' family grave

Battalion of the Coldstream Guards, and spent the time until 21 September working on forward fatigues from their camps at De Wippe Cabaret and Eton Camp.

CHAPTER 5

The Royal Welsh Fusiliers

THE 16TH ROYAL Welsh Fusiliers went into the line during the night of 28/29 July and had to remain there while the other battalions in the brigade moved up. Heavy German shelling of the positions held by the 14th R.W.F. meant that Lieutenant-Colonel Hodson, commanding, had insufficient fit men to supply the 32 soldiers required to act as carriers for the six Lewis Gun teams and the 113th and 176th Machine Gun Companies.

The strength of the battalions of 113th Brigade on 31 July were:

13th R.W.F. : officers 15, other ranks 551
14th R.W.F. : officers 10, other ranks 294
15th R.W.F. : officers 12, other ranks 420
16th R.W.F. : officers 16, other ranks 456[1]

During the night of 30/31 July, the German artillery was subdued by the gas shells being fired on their positions. The 14th and 15th Battalions moved to the west bank of the canal, and the 13th Battalion crossed it at 10.30 p.m., the 16th Battalion being already in position.

The 13th R.W.F. formed the right flank, with the 16th R.W.F. on the left. They were to capture the Blue and Black Lines. Two companies of each were to take the Blue Line, at which point the other two companies in each battalion were to push through and take the Black Line. When this was accomplished, the 15th R.W.F. would advance through them to the Green Line.

The artillery barrage poured shells down on the German positions and, in darkness, at 3.50 a.m. the 13th and 16th Battalions advanced. Officers led the advance by compass, as it was impossible to pick out landmarks in the dark. They crossed the German front lines, with some firing coming from their left. A party of Germans was cleared from the railway cutting by the 16th Battalion and they soon reached the Blue Line.

The advance to the Black Line was more problematic as the enemy resistance increased. The 16th Battalion battled to clear Cancer Avenue and Telegraph House, and the 13th Battalion fought through to Pilkem village.

There were an estimated 280 concrete fortifications in the path of the advance of the 38th (Welsh) Division and

they presented a formidable obstacle to the advancing troops. Made of concrete with iron bar reinforcement, they were able to withstand everything bar a direct hit from a heavy calibre gun.

Three photographs showing Germans being captured at Pilkem

Corner House, a ruined building, had a pillbox built inside it. Close by it was another more conventional pillbox.

It was here that Corporal James Davies of the 13th Royal Welsh Fusiliers won his posthumous Victoria Cross (see page 222).

The Black Line had now been reached by the 113th and 114th Brigades. The 15th R.W.F. then advanced through the other battalions, accompanied by six Lewis Gun teams, and advanced to the Green Line.

Second Lieutenant William Lloyd Davies of 'C' Company, 13th Royal Welsh Fusiliers, was killed at this time, aged 23. A native of Carmarthen, he had attended the University of London and St George's College, London. He joined the Artists' Rifles Officer Training Corps in November 1915, obtaining his commission on 7 July 1916, and was sent to France in August.

His death was reported thus at home in Carmarthenshire:

> Another local officer who has made the supreme sacrifice was Second Lieutenant W. Lloyd Davies, Royal Welsh Fusiliers, official information in regard to whose death in action in France on July 31st was received on Tuesday by his parents, Mr. and Mrs. J.G. Davies, Coombe Park, Peniel, Carmarthen.
>
> He was the eldest son, and had been in France over a year.
>
> Twenty-three years of age, he was a former pupil of the Grammar School, Carmarthen, and had passed a Civil Service examination a day before he enlisted. His brother Lieutenant D. Vaughan Davies, of the same regiment, was gassed recently by a gas shell whilst on his way up, in company with his brother, to the front line trenches, and has come home on sick leave.[2]

William Lloyd Davies

His commanding officer wrote: 'We were all very fond of him, and his loss leaves a blank amongst us today.' Another officer wrote: 'I had known him for just twelve months; he had always been a most gallant officer in every way, and was most popular with his men. His death will be a great loss to the battalion. He advanced far into the German line, leading his platoon.'[3] William Davies was buried in Dragoon Camp Cemetery.

Second Lieutenant William Howard Martin, 29, was killed during the attack of the 13th R.W.F. Originally from Haverfordwest, he joined the 28th London Regiment as a private and was commissioned into the Royal Welsh Fusiliers in September 1916, embarking for France a month later. His body was lost and he is commemorated on the Menin Gate Memorial to the Missing.

Corporal Thomas Thomas of the 13th R.W.F. fought at Mametz Wood and at Third Battle of Ypres, only to be killed on 22 April 1918 when a British field gun burst and killed eight men.

Thomas was born in Rhosllanerchrugog in 1896 and, after leaving school at 12, joined the garden staff at Erddig Hall, near Wrexham. By 1914 he was working at Hafod Colliery with his father, before enlisting in November 1914. As part of the Machine Gun Section, he landed in France in December

1915 and was wounded by a gunshot wound to the head during the fighting at Mametz Wood and was awarded the Military Medal. He was in a Base Hospital in Dannes Camiers in France for six days and then came back to Britain on leave.

Thomas Thomas is buried in Bouzincourt Ridge Cemetery, north of Albert.

Thomas Thomas

The 114th Brigade had met fierce resistance at Marsouin Farm. A platoon of the 15th R.W.F. was sent in support and had attacked Rudolphe Farm, capturing 15 prisoners. The 15th Battalion subsequently came under heavy fire from Germans located in Battery Copse and the houses and pillboxes around the railway crossing. They lost contact with the creeping barrage and a smoke barrage fell amongst them, causing confusion.

Amongst those who fell here was Second Lieutenant Ernest Charles Derwentwater Radcliffe, aged 20, the only son of David Clark Radcliffe and Florence Mary Radcliffe, of Pen Dyffryn, Meliden, Prestatyn, Flintshire. He had joined the Inns of Court Officer Training Corps in 1915 and had gained his commission in the Royal Welsh Fusiliers in November 1916. Radcliffe was later buried in Artillery Wood Cemetery.

Second Lieutenant David King had been a partner in a firm of solicitors in Carmarthen before enlisting. He was killed on 31 July, aged 32, and is remembered on the Menin Gate Memorial to the Missing. King's death was reported in his local newspaper thus:

> Widespread regret was aroused in Carmarthen and district on Tuesday, when it became known that a telegram had been received from the War Office stating that Second Lieutenant David King, Royal Welsh Fusiliers, was killed in action on July 31st.

> Thirty-two years of age, he was a son of the late Mr. William King and of Mrs. King, Frondeg, Waterloo Terrace, Carmarthen, and was recently married to Miss Ethel Collins-Davies, daughter of Mr. Collins-Davies, tailor, Hall Street, Carmarthen. He was a solicitor in the town when he enlisted as a private, being a partner in the firm of Messrs. Ungoed, Thomas and King, and had a highly promising career. He was a former law student at Aberystwyth College.

David King

He had been in France for a couple of months, and had been in the front line trenches only a week. The young officer was very popular in the town, and was a prominent member of the local Free Church Council, and was the first secretary of the Carmarthen Young Liberal League, of which he was one of the founders. He took an active interest in the affairs of the English Baptist Church, where he was a deacon and superintendent of the Sunday School, and his loss will be keenly felt there. His brother is the Reverend W. Vaughan King, chaplain to the forces in France, who met with an accident some time ago.[4]

The war diary of the 15th Royal Welsh Fusiliers notes that although the barrage was excellent, owing to the dark it was very difficult to keep direction, though it was described as fairly easygoing until Pilkem, when a German barrage erupted and fire from machine guns and snipers opened up. Despite incurring casualties, the village was passed with the battalion still in good formation and they continued their advance supported by two companies of the 16th R.W.F. and the six Lewis Guns provided by the 14th R.W.F.

The Germans in the houses in Brierley Road opened fire, causing casualties, including Lieutenant-Colonel C.C. Norman, the officer commanding, who was wounded. He now ordered the battalion to consolidate on Iron Cross Ridge.

By this time there were no unwounded officers remaining, so Regimental Sergeant Major Jones organised the consolidation work. This was some way short of the Green Line, which was their objective, thus giving 115th Brigade an even greater task when they passed through.

At 9.45 p.m. on 1 August the battalion was ordered up to the Green Line and was taken over by Captain R. Bower. During the night he went round the outposts held by the battalion on the banks of the Steenbeek and was hit by machine gun fire and taken to the rear. Captain S.G. Fitzsimons took over command until they were relieved.

Private Edward Albert Jones was killed on 31 July, aged

24, and lies in Vlamertinghe New Military Cemetery. A local newspaper reported:

> Mrs. Margaret Jones of the neighbourhood known as the Rising Sun, Bagillt, has received information that her son, Private Edward Albert Jones, of the R.W.F. Machine Gun Section, has been killed in action. He took part in the recent heavy fighting in Belgium. Deceased, who was 24 years of age, is the second son Mrs Jones has lost in the war and the other being Private T.C. Jones who earned the Military Medal a few weeks before last year on the Somme. Private E.A. Jones was well-known and respected in the town, and was a member of the Tabernacle (C.M.) Church, and secretary of the Sunday School connection with that church.[5]

Also killed on the same day was Private George Griffiths Parry of the 15th R.W.F. He was 28 years old and had lived with his parents in Cemmaes, Montgomeryshire.

The 115th Brigade, with the 11th South Wales Borderers on the right and the 17th Royal Welsh Fusiliers on the left flank, was also advancing. The 17th R.W.F. fought their way forward from Iron Cross Ridge down to the Steenbeek. The houses on the road at the crest of the ridge had been fortified and the machine guns located within them exacted a heavy toll on the advancing troops.

The units on the flanks moved forward to encircle them and, in turn, each of the enemy positions was taken. The 17th Royal Welsh Fusiliers were reinforced by a company from the 10th South Wales Borderers and, after many losses, the Steenbeek was crossed at noon.

Algernon Stuart Edwards, the second son of John Stevenson and Kathleen Dora Edwards of Achnashean, Llandygai, Bangor, was

George Parry

serving as a lieutenant with the 17th Royal Welsh Fusiliers when he was killed on 31 July, aged 20. He studied at Friars School, and afterwards worked for the London and North Western Railway. He landed in France in 1915 and was wounded at Mametz Wood on 10 July 1916, whilst leading his platoon in a charge when he was struck by shrapnel, which inflicted a bad scalp wound and concussion. He was subsequently invalided home, where he remained until March 1917.

A fortnight before he was killed he wrote home saying that he had never felt fitter in his life and was eagerly looking forward to the battle which he thought was impending. A brother officer, writing to the parents, stated: 'He died a brave death fighting the enemy until the last moment. Death was instantaneous, so that he could have felt no pain.' Edwards was said to be 'one of the most popular officers in the battalion', and 'would never ask his men to do something he would never do himself.'[6]

A newspaper carried an account of his death by an eyewitness:

Particulars of the death of Acting-Captain A.S. Edwards, Royal Welsh Fusiliers, who was killed in action on the 31st of July, have been received. He was (says the writer) in charge of 'B' Company, which met in its advance one of the many farmhouses, all of which were converted, by means of concrete gun emplacements, into

miniature fortresses. They were momentarily in a tight corner, and Lieut. Edwards advanced himself as far as the door, when he was shot down from within. His death was instantaneous. He is buried just near the spot, about half a mile beyond Pilkem. Colonel, the Hon. Henry Lloyd Mostyn, who was the first Colonel of the 17th Battalion, in a letter of sympathy, said: 'I shall always, I assure you, have the

Algernon Edwards

pleasantest recollection of your gallant boy, who served under me in the Welsh Division for six months. He was a most promising and capable young officer, and devoted to his duties. All ranks will much regret his loss.[7]

His grave was subsequently lost and he is commemorated on the Menin Gate Memorial to the Missing.

His brother, Kenneth Grenville Edwards, also fought at the Third Battle of Ypres. He had enlisted in November 1914, and later took part in the fighting at Mametz Wood with the 13th Royal Welsh Fusiliers before falling in 1918.

A newspaper carried this account of his death:

We regret to record the death of Mr. Kenneth Grenville Edwards. He was educated at St. Deiniol's Preparatory School and Friars School, Bangor. At school he took a prominent part in games, and was a promising cricketer, particularly in the field. He was a member of St. James' Church Choir for several years. Upon leaving school he entered the service of the National Provincial Bank, his first appointment being to the Llandudno branch. Three weeks afterwards he was taken seriously ill with pleurisy, and subsequently pneumonia, and was confined to the house for some months. After his recovery, he was transferred to the Shrewsbury branch of the Bank, where he remained till war broke out. At Shrewsbury he took a prominent part in sports, occasionally assisting the town cricket club, and was also a member of

the Pengwern Rowing Club. In November 1914, as the Bank were unable to release him, he resigned his position in order to join the 'Pals' Company of the 16th Battalion Royal Welsh Fusiliers, at Llandudno (then being organised by Col. Wynne Edwards), with his brother, the late Captain A.S. Edwards. He gained his Sergeant's stripes, and in February,

Kenneth Edwards

1915, was gazetted 2nd lieutenant, receiving his promotion December, 1916. He married in August, 1915, Lucy E. Steward. He went to France in April, 1916, and fought at Mametz Wood, July, 1916, and Pilkem, August, 1917. In October, 1917, he came to England for six months' light duty, and returned to France on April 18th of this year. He leaves a daughter and a son. Later intelligence states that Lieut. Edwards was killed instantaneously in a communication trench by a shell about midnight on Wednesday last. On Friday the body was interred in a little village cemetery behind the lines, and the grave is marked by a cross.[8]

He was killed on 8 May 1918, aged 24, and was buried in Harponville Communal Cemetery.

Second Lieutenant Herbert Glyn Rhys Morgan of 'A' Company, 17th R.W.F., died of his wounds on 1 August, aged 21. Mentioned in Dispatches for his work, he is remembered on the Menin Gate Memorial. He was from Pontypridd and had enlisted in the 21st Royal Fusiliers (4th Public Schools) as a private and had landed with them in France on 14 November 1915, before being commissioned into the Royal Welsh Fusiliers in 1916.

One of the officers of the 15th R.W.F. who died was Second Lieutenant Clifford Jones who was killed in action on 2 August, aged 25. He is remembered on the Menin Gate. The only son of Mrs E. Jones of Bodlondeb, Whitland, in Carmarthenshire,

and the late Reverend Daniel Jones, the Baptist Minister for Whitland, he was a graduate of Wales and Oxon.

Thomas Glyn Williams was the eldest son of Thomas and Mary Williams of 33 Greenfield Terrace, West End, Bangor. He was educated at Friars School in Bangor and then studied at the University College of Bangor, where he graduated with

Clifford Jones

Thomas Williams

honours in French. Before joining the Army he taught French at Moreton House School, Cardiff.

Serving with the 16th Battalion of the Royal Welsh Fusiliers, he was killed on 2 August, aged 33. His body was never identified and he is commemorated on the Menin Gate Memorial to the Missing.

At 2 p.m. it was noticed that the enemy was massing for a counterattack, which commenced at 3.10 p.m. This was repulsed except for a bridgehead held at Au Bon Gîte, where the 11th South Wales Borderers were driven back across the Steenbeek. A second enemy attack was launched later that afternoon but artillery fire soon dispersed it.

The weather now broke and heavy rain began to fall. The Germans began to shell the newly won British positions and the casualties suffered by 115th Brigade meant they were relieved by 113th Brigade during the night of 1/2 August.

Captain Clifford Nichols of the 2/5th (Territorial) Battalion, R.W.F., was in command of the 164th Machine Gun Company. Born in Birmingham in 1890, he had attended Dudley Grammar School and King's Cathedral School in Worcester before becoming a chartered accountant in 1912. He was employed by Price, Waterhouse and Cooper before enlisting in November 1914. He was commissioned as a second lieutenant in December 1915, becoming Adjutant and then joining the 164th Machine Gun Company in 1917. After seeing action at Arras earlier in the year, he was killed on 31 July.

The Brigadier-General wrote to his parents:

He did splendid work in command of the company, and instilled in them a new spirit and discipline, with the result that during the battle they all behaved magnificently. He lived up to the tradition of the great regiment to which he belonged, and fell whilst actually firing a gun. He was a splendid fellow, and we all feel his loss very much.[9]

Nichols was a keen sportsman and was well known in Midlands hockey and golfing circles, and frequently represented the Midland Counties team. His body could not be identified later and he is named on the Menin Gate Memorial to the Missing.

At 9 a.m. on 31 July, Captain Irwin and Lieutenant Phillips of 'C' Company of the 9th Royal Welsh Fusiliers were sent forward to reconnoitre the ground near Hollebeke, south of Ypres. Two further companies of the battalion arrived in the front line around 4 p.m. that day and Irwin moved them forward to occupy the hedge line near Tiny Farm. 'D' Company was sent forward to support 63rd Brigade in trying to recapture Rifle Farm, but the Germans counterattacked and drove the advancing troops back. The battalion was relieved that night by the 9th Welsh Regiment.

Second Lieutenant Sidney George Davies of the 9th Battalion was killed on 31 July. Before the war he had been the English Congregational Church Minister for Stony Stratford and Whaddon in Buckinghamshire. He had set aside his ministry and enlisted in the Royal Welsh Fusiliers. His name is commemorated on the Menin Gate Memorial to the Missing.

His death was reported thus in a local newspaper:

Mrs. Davies, of Abergele, wife of Second Lieutenant G. Davies, formerly Congregational pastor at Stony Stratford, has received a letter from the Lieutenant-Colonel commanding his battalion of the Royal Welsh Fusiliers. It states: Lieut. Davies was with a party attacking the enemy, and was killed instantaneously by a rifle bullet, which hit him in the head. He was liked and respected by every man in the battalion, and his loss was a severe blow. His cheerfulness under all circumstances was amazing.

A letter from his Company Officer includes: 'The company was called upon to drive back the Germans who had surrounded another battalion, and it was on the way across that Lieut. Davies met his death, bravely leading his men forward. He had many friends in the battalion, and was popular with all. The battalion has lost a valuable and fearless officer.'

A sympathetic letter was also received from the Chaplain, saying that Lieutenant Davies was beloved by them all. Conducted by the Reverend Angel, of Potterspury, at Stony Stratford a memorial service was conducted on Sunday in the Congregational Church. A native of Ammanford, South Wales, Mr. Davies went straight from New College, Hampstead, to be pastor at the Stony Stratford Congregational Church, but this being at the outbreak of war, when the call came for volunteers under the Derby Scheme he joined the colours, despite ministers of religion being exempt from service if they chose.

In January 1916 he joined the Army as a private, and later received a commission in the Royal Welsh Fusiliers. Two weeks before leaving for France he had been married at Abergele, and it would be from Wales that his widow sent the sad news of his death to the Congregational Church secretary, Mr. W. Meakins, at Stony Stratford.[10]

Second Lieutenant Harry Kilvert of the 9th R.W.F., born in Clunbury, Shropshire, in 1884, was a former bank clerk

and a married man with a son. He was wounded during this action and died the following day. He was buried in Bailleul Communal Cemetery Extension.

Second Lieutenant David John Davies of the same battalion survived the attack. In 1914 he had

David John Davies

joined the 15th Royal Welsh Fusiliers and had risen to the rank of Warrant Officer 2nd Class before being commissioned. He had also fought at Mametz Wood and on 22 May 1917 was Mentioned in Dispatches. In 1918 he was awarded the Military Cross. His citation read: 'For conspicuous gallantry and devotion to duty. By his personal example and by the excellent fire control which he maintained he kept his front intact against repeated enemy attacks. At night he went out on patrol on three occasions, capturing a prisoner and killed a machine gun crew and bringing in the gun.'[11]

A newspaper article gave details of his career:

Lieut. Davies joined the London Welsh Battalion on its formation in 1914, and proceeded with his battalion to France in the following year. He saw much fighting during the years 1915–1917, and returned to take his commission in February 1917. He was gazetted to another battalion of the R.W.F., and was with a division which made a glorious stand in the great German offensive early this year. It was then Lieut. Davies gained his distinction. Educated at the National School, Aberystwyth, Lieut. Davies was in turn a pupil teacher there, and after proceeding to Carmarthen Training College where he passed for his headmaster's certificate, he has held various appointments, and was, on the outbreak of war, an assistant master at the Trinity-road Boys' School, Upper Tooting, London.[12]

Private Trevor Jones, also of the 9th Battalion, was 22 when he was killed in action on 31 July. From Llanelli, he was awarded the Military Medal and bar. A local newspaper reported: 'This young hero gained the medal for his gallantry in the Ypres fighting, but afterwards was killed in action. He was the son of Mr. W.J. Jones, Cilwrfa Row, and worked at the Old Castle Works. After his death it was announced that he had been awarded a bar to his medal.'[13]

He is commemorated on the Menin Gate Memorial to the Missing.

William Healey was a regular soldier who had enlisted at

17 in the Oxfordshire and Buckinghamshire Light Infantry in 1908. A native of St Mary's, Reading, he had deserted in 1910. He was subsequently transferred to the Royal Welsh Fusiliers in 1911 and spent the next three years in India. He qualified as a signaller and was described in 1914 as 'strictly sober, intelligent, hard working'.[14]

Sent to France in October 1914 with the 9th R.W.F., he spent three weeks at the 1st General Hospital with a sore on his left heel. Healey was promoted to lance corporal in December 1915 but was deprived of this rank in April 1917 for neglect of duty in the trenches. Killed in action on 31 July, his body could not be identified and he too is remembered on the Menin Gate Memorial to the Missing.

At 11.30 p.m. on 1 August, the 13th Royal Welsh Fusiliers moved forward to relieve the 10th S.W.B., 14th R.W.F. and the 17th R.W.F. at the Steenbeek Line and this was completed by 2.30 a.m. the following morning. It was noted in the battalion's war diary that: 'The excessive rain had rendered the ground almost impossible for progress and the going was extremely difficult.'[15]

Harold Madoc Jones was a lieutenant with 'C' Company of the 17th Royal Welsh Fusiliers. A resident of Cardigan, he was born in 1878 in Llangynhafal, Denbigh.

His death was reported in the local newspaper:

Lieutenant Harold Madoc Jones, R.W.F., killed on July 31st, was the son of the late Mr. J.R. Jones, J.P., of Bodfeirig, and of Mrs. Jones, of Bryn Cadnant, Anglesey. He was educated at Christ's College, Brecon, and afterwards gained a scholarship at the University College of Wales, Aberystwyth, where he graduated with classical honours. He took up teaching as his profession, and was successful and popular as a schoolmaster. At the outbreak of war he was on the staff of Cardigan County School and enlisted in a battalion of the Royal Welsh Fusiliers (University Company). In March, 1915, he obtained his commission in the same regiment, and left for the front early in December of the same year. Thenceforward he had been almost continuously in the line. He spent two winters in the trenches, and was mentioned in dispatches. His commanding officer writes: 'He died painlessly and gallantly.'[16]

His school magazine carried the following tribute:

Hostel, 1890–1892; Lieut. in the Royal Welsh Fusiliers. He came to school 'a small shock-headed freckled boy' some five and twenty years ago; he fell in France the other day – a tall, handsome man of commanding presence. 'Silent' was his nickname and well illustrates his calm, self-reliant character. He was an athlete and a scholar. Quite recently he distinguished himself in the Cross Country Race of his Division. Many years ago he won his scholarship and graduated with honours at Aberystwyth College. Teaching was his profession, and he held appointments as Classical Master at Llandudno, Llangefni, Porth and Cardigan. From the last post he volunteered as a Private on the outbreak of war, and took a Commission some months later at the desire of his friends. He saw much service at Neuve Chapelle, Laventie, Festubert, and afterwards in the Somme Push, winning promotion and a mention in dispatches for his share of the good work at Mametz. Another officer describes him 'as the calmest soldier I ever met in the face of danger; no man's land had no terrors to disturb the tranquility of his mind.' On July 31st he was on patrol duty, and in trying to save a badly wounded corporal he was shot by a sniper. He was buried almost where he fell, just by Langemarck. We quote again from a superior officer's letter: 'A more gallant gentleman I have never seen. Had he lived he would have had a decoration. No soldier faced battle so calmly and so bravely.'[17]

Harold Jones was, in fact, twice Mentioned in Dispatches. His medals were claimed by his sister but his body could not be found and his is among the names commemorated on the Menin Gate Memorial to the Missing.

Another officer of the 17th Royal Welsh Fusiliers who was killed on the opening day of the battle was Captain Ralph Picton Daniel. A report was carried in a national Welsh newspaper:

Information has reached Mrs. Daniel, of 17 Fenton Place,
Porthcawl that her son, Captain Ralph Picton Daniel was killed in
action on July 31. The captain belonged to the R.W.F. He joined
at the commencement of the war, and two and a half years ago, as
a sequence to devotion to duty, received his commission. He was
home on furlough a month ago, but knowing that his company was
to be engaged in the great offensive, he hurried back to his post of
duty. He was 35 years of age, and he leaves a widowed mother and
several sisters, one of whom is now at one of the Cardiff military
hospitals, and a brother, Lieutenant Jasper Daniel, is in the Royal
Flying Corps.[18]

Ralph Daniel was buried in Artillery Wood Cemetery.

After the 13th R.W.F. took up their new positions on the
night of 1/2 August, the German shelling became heavy,
concentrating on Battalion Headquarters. Around 9.15 p.m.
on 2 August three separate barrages were fired on the British
positions: one along the Steenbeek, one in front of Brierley
Road and one behind Brierley Road. An S.O.S. rocket was
sent up and a heavy British barrage was laid 100 yards beyond
the Steenbeek. This effectively broke up any attempts by the
Germans to mass for a counterattack. Intermittent enemy
shelling continued over the next few days until the battalion
was relieved by the 10th Welsh on the Steenbeek Line on 4
August.

Captain Richard Lloyd Williams of the 17th Royal Welsh
Fusiliers was born in October 1887 and was educated at
Llanrwst County School. He was a clerk on the staff of the
London City and Midland Bank, Denbigh, when he enlisted
on 7 November 1914. He obtained a commission and was
gazetted as second lieutenant on 25 February 1915, promoted
to lieutenant on 30 June and captain on 27 November 1915.
Williams had served on the Western Front since 1 December
1915 and died at No.12 Casualty Clearing Station, Proven,
on 2 August 1917 of wounds received in action at Iron Cross,
Pilkem. He was buried in the British Military Cemetery,
Proven. A soldier wrote: 'Captain R. Lloyd Williams had won

the confidence of his men and we would have followed him anywhere.'[19]

Six other casualties were recorded amongst the battalion during this period, three of them dying of their wounds and being buried in Dozinghem Military Cemetery. Corporal Frederick Davies had arrived in France in December 1915 and had fought at Mametz Wood the following year. He was unmarried.

Buried near him was Private Thomas Gordon Hall from Weaste in Manchester, who was living there with his parents before enlisting with the King's Liverpool Regiment and landing in France in May 1915. As a young trolley boy he had enlisted on 21 August 1914 and was considered fit for service by the recruiting officer – this, in spite of his declared age being 17 years and four days when, in fact, he was merely 16, and just five foot two inches tall. Nevertheless, he was accepted into the Manchester Regiment before being transferred to the King's Liverpool Regiment. He seems to have had some regrets regarding his decision however, as several times he was late returning from leave and suffered subsequent punishment. On 6 December 1915 his father, Charles, wrote the following letter to the Secretary for War:

Sir, I beg respectfully to apply to you for the release of my son (age 17) Private Thomas Gordon Hall 28166 – 16 section – 16 platoon – D Company – 1st King's Liverpool Regiment from duty in the trenches, at all events until he has reached a more suitable age. He enlisted shortly after the War commenced in the Manchester Regiment, and transferred to his present Battalion for duty in France. I have another son – Bernard Ritson Hall 1937 – 1st 7th Lancashire Fusiliers (Salford) who was wounded in the head at the Dardanelles. He is now in a serious condition, after an operation in Salford Royal Hospital, and is continually asking to see his brother Thomas.

I firmly believe the granting of this request will save his life, and put him on his feet again. Please understand that I have the highest and best possible opinion of Mr. A. Lund, the operating surgeon, and the nursing staff at the Hospital – Soldier patients confirm this. I have only two eligible sons, and both have done a bit.[20]

Charles Hall's request was partly successful. In January 1916 Thomas Hall was sent back to England for Home Duties. However, on 6 June 1916, he landed in France again, after being transferred to the 13th Royal Welsh Fusiliers. He took part in the attack on Mametz Wood, aged 18.

On 3 August 1917 Thomas Hall was admitted to No.4 Casualty Clearing Station at Lozinghem with a gunshot wound to his back that had penetrated his abdomen, but he died later that day, aged 19. His brother Bernard, who had served with the Lancashire Fusiliers, had succumbed to the effects of a head wound on 10 February 1916, aged 19. He was buried in Salford (Weaste) Cemetery.

The third man in Dozinghem Cemetery was Private Herbert Milligan who died of his wounds, aged 20. He was born and enlisted in Blackburn.

Private Richard Gladstone Hough, aged 28, was killed in action on 2 August and buried in Dragoon Camp Cemetery. He was born in Marchwiel in Denbighshire and was married to Elizabeth. They had lived in Liverpool before he enlisted in 1914, landing in France in December 1915 and taking part in the fighting at Mametz Wood.

Lance Corporal Thomas Thickens Oliver had won the Military Medal during the fighting at Mametz Wood the previous year when he succeeded in rescuing an officer and four wounded comrades under heavy fire. Serving with the 17th R.W.F., he died of his wounds on 3 August after being struck in the chest by a piece of artillery shell. He was from Ystrad Rhondda and had been employed as a miner at Bodringallt Colliery before enlisting, aged 28, in June 1915. Mrs Oliver of 23 Cross Street, Ystrad Rhondda, was presented with the medal awarded to her son by Lieutenant-General Sir William Pitcairn Campbell at the Prince of Wales' Hospital, Cardiff, on 24 January 1918.

The sixth casualty during this short period was Private James Treharne Howells, aged 31,who died of wounds on 4 August. He was buried in Bard Cottage Cemetery. He too had enlisted in 1914 and had taken part in the attack on Mametz Wood in 1916. Originally from Neath, his parents worked in the post office in Cilfrew.

Private John Carradus (who served as 'Carradice') was killed on 3 August and has no known grave so is remembered on the Menin Gate Memorial to the Missing. Born in Kendal, he was 35 and a married man who was employed as a bobbin mill machinist before the war.

The 14th Royal Welsh Fusiliers were in reserve on 31 July, but six of their Lewis Gun sections under Second Lieutenant G.E.J. Evans were attached to the 15th R.W.F. for the day under the command of Lieutenant-Colonel Norman.

Their Headquarters moved forward as the attack progressed and, by 6.30 a.m. on the morning of 31 July, they were at Villa Gretchen. Little hostile shelling was reported up to this point but at about 8 a.m. the German guns opened up in earnest and kept up a barrage all day, alternating between Pilkem, Villa Gretchen and Cactus Reserve. The battalion's duties during the day were to supply carrying parties, taking forward ammunition and supplies.

At 7.45 p.m. the battalion arrived at Battery Copse and three parties under Second Lieutenants J.C. Brommage, E. Roberts and L. Stephens set to work consolidating the front line. By 11.30 p.m. it was deemed that the strong points and advance posts had been dug to a sufficient depth, this taking place in the face of heavy rain and much hostile shelling.

It was around this time that Lieutenant Thomas Cyril Nicholls-Jones was killed, aged 30. Born in Pentraeth, Anglesey, he was an only son. He was educated at Oswestry Grammar School and at the Harper Adams Agricultural College in Newport, Shropshire, before becoming the land agent to the Rt Hon. Lord Boston. He joined the Duke of Cambridge's Public Schools Battalion of the Middlesex Regiment in October 1914, and was gazetted second lieutenant in January 1915. He arrived in France in November 1915 and was promoted to lieutenant in 1916. General Sir Owen Thomas wrote to his parents: 'I knew your son well, and I was proud of him when he served in my brigade.' Colonel David Davies wrote: 'Always so cheery and devoted to his work, always thinking of the welfare and comfort of his men.' His commanding officer added: 'There is no man who could have performed his duties with more conscientiousness or with greater efficiency. I most sincerely regret his loss for personal reasons and for the Army. His place in the Roll of Honour is no empty honour.' Captain Glyn Jones wrote:

> When I think of all the brightness he brought to my company, I am unable to dream that such a cheery, gentlemanly and brave man could have been cut off like this. Loved by all the men and officers – more, worshipped by the men – and such a fine comrade. The men can say best what a brave officer he was – sympathetic and so full of the ordinary common sense – always willing to do something for anyone in trouble.

The Chaplain stated: 'He did jolly good work, and his transport loved him and worked well for his sake.'[21]

Thomas Nicholls-Jones was buried at Villa Gretchen Cemetery, named after Villa Gretchen which was taken by the Division on the 31 July. It was later renamed Dragoon Camp Cemetery.

August 1 saw the 14th R.W.F. in position behind the 17th R.W.F. with the 11th S.W.B. to their right. Between 3 p.m. and 5 p.m., a large number of wounded men from 115th Brigade began

Thomas Nicholls-Jones

to come through their lines. It was noted that demoralization seemed to have set in amongst the front line battalions as considerable numbers of unwounded men from the 17th R.W.F. were seen retreating. The 14th R.W.F. were ordered to hold up these stragglers and defend the line at all costs.

The enemy bombardment was now intense and a counterattack was expected. Considerable difficulties were being caused by the large numbers of stragglers and no clear information from the front line could be ascertained, so Major Jesse Williams took out a patrol and went forwards some 800 yards. He returned and reported that there was no evidence that the Germans were massing for a counterattack.

At this point the battalion was informed that the front line had been abandoned and that they now constituted the front line. They were ordered forward and regained the ground lost. The line was held for the following days in heavy rain and under constant shelling.

Private George Varley acted as a guide during this period, guiding officers and men from other battalions forward. Born in Padiham in Lancashire, he had enlisted in Accrington. He was killed on 4 August and is buried in Cement House Cemetery, Langemark.

Such was the difficulty of getting supplies up to the advance posts that iron rations were ordered to be eaten. (These consisted of preserved meat, cheese, biscuits, tea, sugar and salt, and were carried by all British soldiers in the field for use in the event of being cut off from regular food supplies.) By 9 p.m. the battalion had been relieved under an extremely heavy bombardment and an hour later they had moved back to the Battery Copse-Iron Cross line where they set up nine posts, four of these being Lewis Gun posts. While this work was being completed Lieutenant Arthur Tryweryn Apsimon was mortally wounded, and Lieutenants G.E.J. Evans and L. Stephens were wounded.

Apsimon's father was from Bala and before the war Arthur was employed by his father, who was a commissioning agent for a warehouse firm in Manchester. He had enlisted in the London Irish Rifles and had then been commissioned into the Royal Welsh Fusiliers. He arrived in France on 1 December 1915 and fought at Mametz Wood in July 1916. After being wounded by an exploding German shell, he was taken to a dressing station but died two days later.

His death was reported in a local newspaper:

The very sad news has been received that Lieut. Arthur T. Apsimon, of the R.W.F., and the third son of Mr. T. And Mrs. Apsimon, of West Kirby, who are staying at Caergwrle, had been severely wounded and had succumbed to his wounds. The deepest sympathy is felt for the parents and family in their great bereavement. Mr. Apsimon has been in ill health for some time, but the bereaved parents, while acknowledging the kind sympathies of their many friends, feel proud and glad that they had a son who led such a grand life, and that he lived and died with so much self-sacrifice. He had 'the spirit of Christ,' and they feel happy to think that he is no further from them now than when he was in France. Mr. and Mrs. Apsimon have another son with the Expeditionary Forces, who is a doctor. The following is a brief encounter of the fallen officer: Lieut. Arthur T. Apsimon, Royal Welsh Fusiliers, third son of Mr. and Mrs. Thomas Apsimon, of West Kirby, was wounded on the 2nd August, and died of his wounds on the 4th inst. at an advanced dressing station. He was 34 years of age, and immediately on the outbreak of war enlisted in the London Irish Rifles, shortly afterwards being granted a commission in the R.W.F. He went to France in 1915. In a letter to Mr. Apsimon, Major Wheldon says that his son took part in the recent operations in Flanders, in which the Welsh Fusiliers distinguished themselves by defeating the famous Guards Fusiliers. He went into the

Arthur Apsimon

fight at a critical time, and in the words of Major Wheldon, 'he did the job.' Major Weldon says: 'I do not think you can believe how very sorry we all are to lose him. For some of us he was precious as one of the few survivors of the old Battalion. He was for all of us a most lovable man, who never spoke or thought unkindly of others, and of whom no one could speak or think except with affection. After he was hit I heard one of his men say, "Mr. Apsimon never seemed to mind shellfire." I know he did mind it – we all do, but his serene and quite courage left that impression on his men, and gave them confidence. I will miss him personally – more than any officers I have known. His quiet humour, gentle nature, and the sturdiness of his views were ever a comfort to me. He was honourably buried by the Rev. D.M. Jones in Bard Cottage Cemetery by the canal bank, leaving us much the poorer in his absence, and his country and his friends richer in the memory of a noble sacrifice.'[22]

Apsimon was Mentioned in Dispatches as a result of his work and was buried in Bard Cottage Cemetery, aged 34. He is commemorated on Ireland's Roll of Honour as 'Arthur Injwerm Apsimon', having been born in Belfast.

The line was held the following day and night. During the day every man had his feet rubbed and dry socks issued, as well as a hot drink. This was down to the good work of Regimental Sergeant Major Samuel Tucker.

Born in Martock, Somerset, Tucker had enlisted in Caerphilly in September 1914 and landed in France in December 1915. He was awarded the Meritorious Service Medal in 1917. A local newspaper reported his laudable service on the Western Front:

Regimental Sergeant Major S. Tucker of the Royal Welsh Fusiliers has a record of which he may well be proud and which commands the esteem and respect of his fellow townsmen. He enlisted as a private in the Royal Welsh Fusiliers and in less than six months he had received promotion to Sergeant Major rank. In addition to this he obtained the Meritorious Service Medal for valuable service in June of the present year, and last week he was informed

Samuel Tucker

by his Officers, with their congratulations, that he has been awarded the Military Cross for gallantry under an intense bombardment during the recent fighting on the Western Front. Sergeant Major Tucker, whose home is at St. Fagan's Street, has been home on leave for ten days and left for France on Sunday evening when a number of friends waved him good-bye and the best of luck.[23]

The citation for his Military Cross stated: 'For conspicuous gallantry and devotion to duty under an intense bombardment. He assisted to rally all available men at a time when part of the front line had been abandoned. By his courage and example in collecting stragglers, he was able to move forward and occupy the abandoned front line position.'[24]

Samuel Tucker was to die of his wounds on 8 September 1918, aged 38. He left a widow, Emily, and four children, the last of whom he never saw. He was buried in St Sever Cemetery Extension in Rouen. Before enlisting he had been a miner, and a chorister and bell ringer at St Martin's Church, Caerphilly.

The trenches were full of water and the shelling continued, but on 4 August there was a slight improvement in the weather. The 14th R.W.F. were relieved at 9 p.m. that evening and marched back to Elverdinghe Château where they were given a complete set of dry clothes, a hot meal and a hot drink.

CHAPTER 6

Hedd Wyn – The Soldier Poet

PRIVATE ELLIS HUMPHREY Evans, better known as the poet 'Hedd Wyn', served with the 15th Battalion of the Royal Welsh Fusiliers. He was killed on 31 July at around 11 a.m., aged 30. The son of Evan and Mary Evans of Trawsfynydd in Merioneth, he had worked on the family farm before joining the Army.

He was born on 13 January 1887 in a cottage called Pen lan in the village of Trawsfynydd, the eldest of eleven children. The family moved to a farm called Yr Ysgwrn when he was four months old. Welsh was his first language and he began to write poetry at the age of 11. He left school at 14 to work as a shepherd on the family farm.

Evans took part in his first local Eisteddfod poetry competition at the age of 12 and won his first Chair at the Bala Eisteddfod in 1907 with his ode 'Y Dyffryn' (The Valley).

In search of wages (his parents never paid him for working on the farm), he left Yr Ysgwrn soon after Christmas 1908 and began work at Abercynon Colliery

Pen Lan, Trawsfynydd

in south Wales, but after a few months he left this job and returned to life at Trawsfynydd. In 1910 he acquired his pen-name 'Hedd Wyn' which means 'Blessed Peace'.

In 1913 he won the Chair at the Pwllheli Eisteddfod with his poem 'Canol dydd' (Noon). The same year he entered his poem 'Fy Ngwynfa Goll' (My Lost Paradise) in the Llanuwchllyn Eisteddfod and won the Chair. In 1915 he won the Chair at the

Yr Ysgwrn

Royal Artillery at Trawsfynydd

Pontardawe Eisteddfod with his poem 'Cyfrinach Duw' (God's Secret), and the Llanuwchllyn Chair again with the poem 'Myfi Yw' (I Am).

The same year he wrote his first entry for the National Eisteddfod, and a year later he came second at the National Eisteddfod which was held that year in Aberystwyth. He resolved to enter a poem for the 1917 National Eisteddfod which was to be held at Birkenhead and began work on his poem 'Yr Arwr' (The Hero).

The impact of the war could not be avoided, however. A British artillery unit was training in the fields outside Trawsfynydd and conscription would soon be introduced.

In early 1917 Evans enlisted at Blaenau Ffestiniog and was sent for training at Litherland Camp, near Liverpool, on 29 January, travelling there with another Welshman, Simon Jones of Aberangell, mid Wales. According to Jones, during training Evans showed no aptitude as a soldier and he often heard officers shouting at him, 'Come on, you're not on your bloody Welsh farm now – wake up!'[1]

Ellis Evans was at Litherland Camp at the same time as another great poet – Siegfried Sassoon, but there is no record of their meeting. In March Evans was granted seven weeks' leave to return to Yr Ysgwrn to help with the ploughing and used this time to continue work on his poem.

Assigned to the 15th Royal Welsh Fusiliers, he returned to Yr Ysgwrn for the final

Simon Jones

time in June 1917 for a fortnight's leave. He then reported for duty at Litherland and by the second week in June he had arrived at a base depot at Rouen in France. On 1 July he joined the battalion at Fléchin, Nord-Pas-de-Calais. While here he completed his poem and posted it home on 15 July, just before the battalion left camp.

The 15th R.W.F. marched through Steenbecque, Saint-Sylvestre-Cappel, Proven and Saint-Sixtus Abbey until, by 20 July, they were at the Yser-Ypres Canal, in preparation for the coming assault on the German lines.

There are several accounts of the circumstances surrounding his death on 31 July. It seems certain that he was hit in the back by shellfire while advancing, but there are inconsistencies as to the timing of his death.

Simon Jones witnessed him being wounded. This is his account, as recorded in 1975:

It was the last day of July, you see. The first day of probably the biggest battle that ever took place. The Battle of Passchendaele. And we were going over the top at half past four. We started over Canal Bank at Ypres, and he was killed half way across Pilkem [Ridge]. I've heard many say that they were with Hedd Wyn and this and that, well I was with him, as a boy from Llanuwchllyn and him from Trawsfynydd. I saw him fall and I can say that it was a nosecap shell in his stomach that killed him. You could tell that. You couldn't stay with him – you had to keep going, you see.

Interviewer: When did you see him last, to speak to him?

Oh, it's difficult to say. Perhaps I spoke to him that morning, because if I saw him get killed, I must have been near to him. I remember well that we had an officer leading us called Newman, Lieutenant Newman. He was going in front of me, and I saw him fall on his knees and grab two fistfuls of dirt. Well there was nothing but dirt there, you see – the place was all churned up. He was dying, of course.

Interviewer: What did you do? Could you do something when you saw Hedd Wyn…?

Nothing at all. No. There were stretcher-bearers coming up behind us, you see. There was nothing – well, you'd be breaking the rules if you went to help someone who was injured when you were in an attack. Your business was to keep going.

Interviewer: How did you feel when you saw your friend fall?

Well I'll tell you straight. To be honest, you had no time to sympathise because you didn't know whether you'd be in the same situation as him in a couple of yards.[2]

Private Frederick Herbert Hainge, from the village of Arthog in Merionethshire, also served with the 15th R.W.F. and saw Evans fall. He survived the war and his account was reported in a newspaper.

A mad rush through the horrors of no man's land. Safe. Through the hell of the barbed wire. Safe again. Then they were met by a hail of bullets. And before the guffawing of the machine gun was silenced, there were many Welshmen who would never return to their own country. But Hedd Wyn was alive, and with him a small band of comrades and the first enemy line behind them. They pressed forward, towards the second line. Forward. But not far. A horrific explosion. A shell burst in their midst. And in the flash of the explosion, Fred Hainge saw the poet falling. The party went out the next day to fetch the dead. And Hedd Wyn was found lying dead exactly where Fred Hainge had seen him falling, and he was buried nearby.[3]

Private, later Acting Sergeant, Idwal Williams from Penmorfa, north Wales claimed to have seen Evans fall and gave an account in October 1917. Williams had served on the Western Front since December 1915 and had fought at Mametz Wood in 1916. He survived the war and was demobilised in February 1919.

Fred Hainge

After heavy fighting our objective was attained, but, at mid-day, as we were consolidating our new positions, and as we were being showered by enemy fire, the poet was struck in the back by a shell fragment, causing a deep wound. He fell down helplessly, and because the fighting was so fierce, medical assistance was not possible, and he could not be carried away to safety. But his comrades tried to treat his wounds and ease his pain in the midst of incredible danger. As he lay wounded on the battlefield, he neither groaned nor uttered a sigh from mid-day until three o'clock in the afternoon – and it was thus that the Hero of all Heroes lay on the Battlefield of all Battlefields for three hours. At three o'clock the stretcher-bearers arrived and carried him down the trenches, but they had not gone far before the wounded soldier breathed his last breath, his battle over.[4]

Evans' commanding officer, Captain Frank Louis Ratto, gave a different account: 'This soldier was in my platoon and went over the top with us on the 31st July. He fought extremely well and was always in the thick of the fighting. It was while consolidating on the Green Line that he was shot by a sniper and died instantaneously, the bullet entering his stomach and going right through him.'[5]

In September 1917 the Reverend R. Peris Williams, who served as the Senior Chaplain to the Royal Welsh Fusiliers, interviewed some of the surviving members of the battalion regarding the circumstances surrounding Ellis Evans' death. He concluded that he was killed by a shell while advancing towards Iron Cross and was taken on a stretcher by four comrades to a first-aid post sited in a German dugout called Corner or Cork House. His wounds were treated by a Doctor Day from Wrexham and Evans asked him, 'Do you think I will live?' Another soldier said, 'You seem to be very happy.' Evans replied, 'Yes, I am very happy.' He died at around 11 a.m.

Major J. Edwards of the battalion wrote: 'There is very little account of him whilst with the battalion, except that he was a very silent fellow and from what I hear his only friend was also killed. Also it would appear he could speak but little English, or at least if he could, he did not.'[6]

Another chaplain, the Reverend Abi Williams, wrote in November:

> Although much has been written in *Y Brython* about Hedd Wyn, I am certain that it will interest your readers to know that he was buried not far from the 'Iron Cross' on the Pilkem Ridge. The burial service was conducted in Welsh by my friend Chaplain D. Morris Jones, and although unaware at the time that he was paying his last respects to a master of his art, it is sad but interesting to remember that fact by now. Yes, the rhythms of our dear old language were heard above the grave of the poet from Trawsfynydd; and though buried in a foreign land, the atmosphere and the emotions at his funeral were essentially Welsh.[7]

His temporary wooden cross grave marker originally stated '41117 T. Evans 17th R.W.F.' There was no such soldier and this was later amended, with his correct service number (61117), initials and battalion when the body was reinterred at Artillery Wood Cemetery.

Ellis Evans

Six weeks after his death the National Eisteddfod was held at Birkenhead. On 6 September, the second day of the event, the ceremony of the Chairing of the Bard took place. The announcement was made that the entry with the pseudonym 'Fleur-de-lis' had won. It was then revealed that the winner had been killed on the battlefield. The empty chair was consequently draped in black.

The chair had been made by a Belgian refugee, Eugeen Vanfleteren, who had fled to England when war broke out; he had settled in Birkenhead. The chair was taken to the family farm on a cart draped in black. Until recently, Evans' nephew, Gerald Williams, the son of his sister Ann, still lived in the property.

In 1923 a statue of Ellis Evans as a shepherd was unveiled in Trawsfynydd. On 31 July 1992, on the 75th anniversary of his death, a commemorative plaque was unveiled at the Hegebos crossroads in Langemark and in August 2014 a memorial stone was unveiled to him on Pilkem Ridge.

Part of Ellis Evans' ode 'Rhyfel' (War) is here translated by Damian Farrow from the original Welsh:

Alas that I live in an age so dull,
That God has ebbed away to the distant horizon;
And Man the tyrant,
Now raises his ugly authority.

When he felt God depart,
He raised his sword to kill his brother;
The sound of fighting is now heard,
And casts a shadow on our homes.

The old harps that once were played
Are hung on the branches of the willows,
The scream of boys fills the wind,
And their blood mixes with the rain.

CHAPTER 7

The South Wales Borderers

WHILE IN THE Boesinghe sector the Germans had withdrawn over 3,000 yards; in the Pilkem sector they had only abandoned the front line. The reason for this was to spare their men from the artillery bombardment which churned the ground to such an extent that progress up towards the ridge was extremely difficult.

The two battalions of the South Wales Borderers who were involved in the attack on the first day were both part of 115th Brigade, which was to form the reserve. Both battalions moved up to the concentration area on 29 July, and then to the assembly area the following day, arriving before midnight.

The 10th S.W.B. assigned one company to lay bridges over the canal. The 11th S.W.B. arrived in their assembly area later, just an hour before the Zero Hour of 3.50 a.m.

The 11th S.W.B began their advance at 5.30 a.m. and came under long-range shelling until they reached Iron Cross Ridge at around 9 a.m., where they were met with machine gun fire from the pillboxes still in German hands. Two of their company commanders were wounded: Captain Jenkins of 'C' Company and Lieutenant Sayce of 'D' Company.

Cyril Frank Bingham Jenkins was commissioned as Temporary 2nd Lieutenant in the 11th South Wales Borderers in April 1915 and promoted to Temporary Lieutenant in July 1915 and Temporary Captain in November 1915. He died of his wounds on 13 October 1917, aged 23 years, and was buried in Wimereux Communal Cemetery.

Before enlisting in the Royal Welsh Fusiliers in October 1914, he had studied at University College, Cardiff. An unknown officer wrote to Jenkins' mother at 37 Conway Road, Canton, in Cardiff: 'I can assure you the sad news is deeply felt in the battalion, both by officers and men, especially by those of his own company, all of whom were so fondly attached to him.'[1]

Another officer wrote: 'You may be proud of him. In the line he always set a magnificent example of fearless courage to his officers and men, and I and the other officers and men who knew him will always remember him as one of the men who best exhibited the spirit of the regiment.'[2]

The Chaplain added: 'He was a fine officer, who took the greatest interest in his company, and knew almost every man in it personally. Danger seemed to have very little meaning for him, and he never asked a man to take a risk that he would not willingly undertake himself.'[3]

The battalion soon captured Iron Cross Ridge and swept down the slopes to the Steenbeek. Here they encountered severe opposition from German machine guns and rifle fire, and a number of men were hit. The left flank was held up by machine gun fire, so Lieutenant Vizer led his platoon against the German position, rushing it and capturing over 50 prisoners, including an officer, to enable the advance to continue.

John Henry Vizer from Wood Green in London had enlisted

in September 1914, aged 32, after serving with the 84th Yeomanry and fighting in South Africa during the Boer War. He joined the 17th Battalion Royal Fusiliers and was promoted rapidly: by March 1916 he was Colour Sergeant Major and was commissioned Second Lieutenant in the South Wales

Cyril Jenkins

Borderers in January 1917. For his actions on 31 July he was awarded the Military Cross. He was subsequently wounded and transferred to the Labour Corps as Lieutenant.

His brother, Private William Frederick Vizer, served with the 2nd Battalion of the Honourable Artillery Company and was killed, aged 37, on 15 April 1917. His body was never identified and he is commemorated on the Thiepval Memorial to the Missing.

Private Cuthbert Gordon Thomas of Brecon had been a schoolmaster before the war. He died on 31 July while serving with 'A' Company, 11th Battalion of the South Wales Borderers. He was 26 years of age and was buried in Duhallow Advanced Dressing Station Cemetery.

Cuthbert Gordon Thomas was born in Merthyr in 1891 to Arthur, a county court bailiff, and May Maude, a headmistress. The family had moved to Llangorse by 1901 and Cuthbert earned a scholarship to Brecon County Intermediate School, which he attended for six years until 1909. He then attended Carmarthen College and qualified as a teacher. He began his career as headteacher at Felindre School, leaving there to take a post in the Upper Rhymney School in Glamorgan.

He enlisted in Brecon in January 1916 and was initially posted to a reserve battalion but was mobilised in February 1917 and joined the Monmouthshire Regiment in March. He landed in France on 29 May 1917 and in June he was posted to the 11th Battalion of the South Wales Borderers. Initially he was listed as missing, believed wounded, on 3 August, but it was later confirmed that he had been killed in action on 31 July. These details were provided by Sergeant Ivor Rees (who was to win the Victoria Cross). He wrote to Thomas' mother and this is noted in the service record: 'Mother forwards letter received from Serjt. I. Rees 20002 SWB who talks about died of wounds received in action on 31.7.17 and was buried in a cemetery called Pilkem by some of his comrades. Passed to C.O. for his perusal. Letter returned to brother as requested by C.O.'[4]

His personal effects were sent to his father at Bank House, Llangorse, Brecon.

A newspaper carried this tribute to him:

Mrs. Thomas, Bank House, headmistress of the School, has received official communication, both from the Red Cross and the War Office, that her son, Pte. Cuthbert Gordon Thomas, made the supreme sacrifice while in action at Pilkem Ridge on July 31st 1917. It will be remembered he was reported wounded and missing last August. Pte. Thomas is the first and only one from this neighbourhood whose lot it has been to die for his country out of a large number who are serving in the ranks. Prior to his departure for the Army he designed the scroll of honour of those who volunteered their services from this parish in the early days of the war and presented it framed to St. Paulinus' Church, Llangorse, where it now hangs. Deceased was a member of a scholastic and much respected family, his mother having been a highly-successful headmistress for over 10 years, while five of her children entered the same profession, three of whom were college trained. Pte. C.G. Thomas was himself a most promising and successful schoolmaster, having teaching abilities of a high order. He was an old pupil of Brecon County School, where he matriculated, and afterwards gained admittance to Carmarthen Training College. Here he had a brilliant career, securing first-class honours, as well as proving himself extremely popular in the social life of the college. He began his profession as headmaster of Velindre School, Three Cocks, where his high ideals of duty and sportsmanship made him beloved by the children and won the sincere esteem of all who came in contact with him. He was presented with a handsome marble clock on his departure thence to take up a new appointment at Upper Rhymney School, Glamorgan, where he was doing service when he volunteered to join the colours. His loss will be deeply felt in Llangorse by a wide circle of friends and very deep sympathy is felt for the family in their bereavement. Mr. and Mrs. Thomas have also another son on active service in India, while the remaining son, Mr. T.C. Thomas, who completed his training at St. John's College, Battersea last year and is now appointed to Sirhowey School, has also done 18 months' service in the Army. Letters of condolence have been received from the staff of Upper

Rhymney School, the Teachers' Association, the Baptist Church at Llangorse and many others.[5]

Second Lieutenant Harold Otto William Moynan was 30 when he was killed in action on 31 July serving with the South Wales Borderers. He was the younger son of Dr Richard Moynan and his wife Emma of Llantrisant House in Llantrisant. He and his brother enlisted in the summer of 1914. Harold joined the Welsh Regiment and progressed to the rank of lance corporal. On 10 December 1915 he was discharged to a commission in the Brecknockshire Territorial Battalion of the South Wales Borderers. He has no known grave and is commemorated on the Menin Gate Memorial to the Missing.

His brother Richard had qualified as a doctor at the University of London in 1912. After joining the Royal Army Medical Corps at the outbreak of the war, he was commissioned as lieutenant on 2 September 1914. He landed in France on 11 October 1914 and later served at Gallipoli. Richard Naunton Ouseley Moynan survived the war and later qualified as a surgeon.

Second Lieutenant Gervas Frederic Bullock of the 3rd (Reserve) Battalion of the South Wales Borderers was the only son of the late Frederic D'Olbert Bullock, LL.B. Cantab, Sessions Judge, Bengal Civil Service, and his wife, Minnie

Weir, of 59 Mount Park Road, Ealing, London. He was born in the Punjab, India, in 1881 and educated at Temple Grove and Malvern, where he gained a scholarship and was Head of the School House. He then studied at Corpus Christi College, Cambridge.

Gervas Bullock

When war was declared he was in Ceylon, but returned home and joined the Inns of Court Officer Training Corps in July 1915. He obtained a commission on 30 December that year and was posted to the Western Front. Gervas Bullock was killed on 31 July while serving with the 11th South Wales Borderers during the fighting for Pilkem Ridge. A fellow officer wrote:

> He was killed instantaneously by a sniper. He was in charge of the company at the time, and by his gallantry and coolness won the admiration of everyone. He was very highly esteemed by all, and his men positively loved him, and would have followed him anywhere. He died doing his duty nobly and well, as he had always done. I never knew him do a mean or ungentlemanly thing. He was a delightful friend and companion. He was a thorough sportsman; it was the very essence of his character.[6]

His body could not be identified later and he is commemorated on the Menin Gate.

In contrast to the regimental history of the Royal Welsh Fusiliers, which claims that the battalions had not encountered pillboxes and blockhouses before, the historian of the South Wales Borderers states: 'The worst trouble came from machine guns in concrete shelters, in houses, or on the sites of what had once been houses. However, special attention had been paid during training to the tactical problem of these pillboxes and the 11th were ready to tackle them.'[7]

It was at this time that Sergeant Ivor Rees won his Victoria Cross (see page 224).

The Steenbeek was now crossed and, at around 12.30 p.m., 'A' and 'C' Companies reached Au Bon Gîte, with 'D' Company to their left and the 17th Royal Welsh Fusiliers next to them. All set about establishing bridgeheads in preparation for the anticipated German counterattacks, with rifle and machine gun fire harassing them from the direction of Langemark village.

In the meantime, the 10th South Wales Borderers had advanced to the old German front line positions, suffering casualties from German shellfire. Lieutenant W.H. Evans was wounded at this time. They arrived at Kiel Cottage at the appointed time of 6.50 a.m. where they waited in Caddy Lane for further orders.

When the expected counterattack began at around 3 p.m., the 11th Battalion's telephone wires had been cut and they were unable to call for support, so faced the Germans alone. They succeeded in driving the Germans back but the 17th Royal Welsh Fusiliers were forced to retreat and the Germans recaptured some pillboxes from which their machine guns were able to pour enfilade fire into the left of the position at Au Bon Gîte, the remains of an old inn. The 11th S.W.B. retired to the Steenbeek with heavy casualties. Captain B.E.S. Davies took command after Colonel Radice had been wounded by a shell at Battalion Headquarters.

Alfred Hutton Radice had served as a lieutenant during the Boer War and had been wounded at the first battle of Ypres in 1914. Awarded the Distinguished Service Order in 1916, he had taken command of the battalion in February 1917. Radice survived his wounds at Pilkem Ridge and retired from the Army in 1921, having been Mentioned in Dispatches four times.

Wounded by the same shell was Second Lieutenant Llewelyn Lloyd, the Signalling Officer. He died of wounds on 1 August, aged 32, and was buried in Dozinghem Military Cemetery. His parents lived at 41 Holywell Road in Flint, and he had landed in France in December 1915.

Second Lieutenant Griffith Christmas Owen of 'C' Company was killed on 31 July. Aged 30, he was the son of Mr and Mrs Owen of Bryngwenallt, Dolgellau, Merioneth. Although buried on Pilkem Ridge, his grave was not found until April 1927, when his body was exhumed and reburied in Sanctuary Wood Cemetery.

At about 5 p.m. 'D' Company of the 10th S.W.B. under Lieutenant Harry Cottam arrived, having been sent forward to reinforce the 11th S.W.B. after its battalion had reached Iron Cross Ridge and begun work on a support line running south-east from Iron Cross. The battalion had set off mid-afternoon, and the war diary notes:

> At 3 p.m. the Bn. was ordered to move forward to the western slopes of the IRON CROSS Ridge, which was now in British hands having been taken by the other Brigades of the Division. The march was commenced, moving in Artillery Formation in half platoons, but on reaching PILCKHEM such a fierce hostile fire was opened on the men that orders were given for columns to split into sectional columns, which was quickly done at a cost of only about a dozen casualties. The behaviour of the men while passing through the exceedingly heavy barrage which was put down by the enemy Artillery at this point deserves the highest commendation, especially when it is remembered that about 150 of them were recent drafts of reinforcements, and were for the first time under serious fire.[8]

Communication had been re-established with the artillery, and a second German counterattack launched by the 9th Grenadiers from shell holes in front of Langemark was broken up by a barrage and rifle and Lewis Gun fire.

Lieutenant Harry Cottam took command of men who had lost their officers and, though badly wounded, he refused treatment until the line had been consolidated. For his actions he was awarded the Military Cross, receiving a bar to it in March 1918 for leading a successful trench raid. He survived the war and settled in Ebbw Vale.

The change in the weather that afternoon caused problems:

> Rain was now falling heavily, and men were experiencing great difficulty in keeping their rifles and especially their Lewis Guns in good working order. The Lewis Gun difficulty was overcome when Battalion Headquarters moved next day to Rudolphe Farm, where there were four strong machine gun emplacements. There the 4 Headquarters Lewis Gun teams gave their guns a thorough

overhauling and cleaning, and exchanged with 4 teams in the line, which were again cleaned by HQ teams. In this way a continual supply of clean guns was maintained throughout the operations.[9]

Some comforts were available to the men too: 'Facilities were afforded at Rudolphe Farm for making hot tea, and the constant supply was greatly appreciated by the men.'[10]

The rain fell heavily during the night and the German artillery kept up heavy shelling, during the course of which shells fell on the First Aid Post at Rudolphe Farm. This resulted in the medical officer, Lieutenant G.L. Gall, being wounded.

George Lockhart Gall was born in 1891 in Lachute, Quebec. He was a medical student in Montreal when he enlisted as a private in the Canadian Army Medical Corps in February 1915. He arrived in England in May 1915 and the following month traveled to France. His time in the Canadian Army Medical Corps did not last long though as in December that year he was shipped home to Canada and discharged in January 1916 in order to resume his medical studies. Gall was determined to

S.W.B. Lewis Gun teams

do his bit and, after qualifying, he enlisted in the Royal Army Medical Corps. At the end of the war he was a captain working at No.53 Casualty Clearing Station at Bailleul, south-west of Ypres.

Despite the atrocious conditions Second Lieutenant David F. George, the Transport Officer of 10th South Wales Borderers, organised the supply of rations to the front line. When the pack animals were hit by shellfire, George helped to carry the rations himself and then proceeded to spend hours rescuing mules that had fallen into the shell holes, as well as assisting the wounded to the rear. For these actions he was awarded the Military Cross. He survived the war and afterwards lived in Hirwaun, near Aberdare.

One of these casualties was Lance Corporal Major Phillips. In 1916 he had been selected as batman for Lieutenant Raymond Barrington Parry. On 11 July that year, he followed his officer into action at Mametz Wood. In the fighting inside the wood Parry was badly wounded. Phillips picked him up and carried him back across the open ground, under enemy fire, to a dressing station before returning to the wood. Phillips did not receive any official recognition for this act of courage but as a token of his gratitude Parry presented him with a silver cigarette case.

Phillips, an ex-miner, was wounded at Mametz Wood but returned to action and was killed on 31 July 1917. His body was never identified and he is commemorated on the Menin Gate Memorial to the Missing. For many years after the war Phillips' widow Florence and young family at Torfaen Terrace, Pontnewynydd, received a basket of food every July from Parry.

At 5 p.m. on 1 August, a heavy German barrage began and Lieutenant Harry Cottam sent messages that he feared an enemy counterattack was imminent, and his ranks were very much depleted. Second Lieutenant W.T. Cobb led 'B' Company of the 10th Battalion forward to support Lieutenant Cottam's position and Captain Galsworthy ordered 'A' Company to consolidate their position forward of the line. Ammunition in the front line was now running low, so 'C' Company of the 10th took forward ammunition and bombs, as did Captain Kenward, the Adjutant of the 10th, who also supplied them with hot food as well as going forward under heavy fire to collect information. For these actions he was later awarded the Military Cross and Distinguished Service Order.

Frederick Robert Edward Kenward was educated in Cheltenham.

Arthur Galsworthy was a schoolmaster before enlisting. He survived the war, but his brother Edgar, also a schoolmaster, did not. Edgar Galsworthy enlisted, aged 21, in July 1915 in the Machine Gun Corps, and was commissioned into the Tank Corps in February 1918 and killed on 27 September that year during an attack on the Hindenburg Line.

Some 60 yards in front of the main line, three battle outposts were set up from which enfilade fire could be brought to bear on any attackers. A patrol was sent out to ascertain the position of the troops on the left. They reported that they had come across the remnants of 'A' Company of the 11th S.W.B., a Lewis Gun position of the 14th Welsh, and a post held by an officer and 50 men of the 17th Royal Welsh Fusiliers.

At midnight the enemy artillery fire slackened, but still

Major Phillips   Raymond Parry   Frederick Kenward

continued. The following day, 2 August, it increased again and that night constant patrolling was carried out to spot enemy activity until the 10th S.W.B. were relieved the next morning by the 15th Royal Welsh Fusiliers.

When the 10th S.W.B. reached Elverdinghe Château at 5.15 p.m. on 5 August, it was recorded: 'An excellent and much needed hot dinner was immediately served, and was very much appreciated by the men, as also were the hot baths which some were fortunate to get. Particular and necessary attention was paid to the men's feet.'[11]

Private Thomas Henry Basil Rigby of the 10th South Wales Borderers was not one of those men of the battalion who marched back to Elverdinghe Château; he had deserted earlier in the battle. Born in Nabb in Shropshire, he had been a labourer on the tramways in Manchester before joining the Army pre-war and had entered France on 29 September 1915 with the 8th S.W.B. Eight days earlier he had married Gladys May Lloyd Jones, living briefly with her at 13 St Helen's Place in Rhyl. He subsequently deserted for the first time and received a three-year suspended sentence. Transferred to the 10th Battalion, he was serving as a brigade runner when he deserted for the second time.

The court martial papers outlined the series of events:

At about 3 p.m. on the afternoon of Tuesday, 31 July 1917, when 10th (Service) Battalion, South Wales Borderers was at Kiel Cot [Old German Front Line], instructions were received that No.1 Platoon was to supply four men to act as Brigade Runners. Four soldiers from the Platoon were detailed for this task, including Private Rigby. He was last seen by the other members of this unit at 11 a.m. on Thursday, 2 August 1917.

At 11.20 a.m. on Tuesday, 7 August 1917, Lance Corporal Kirby of the Military Field Police was on duty in Boulevard Jacquard, Calais, when he had cause to stop and question Private Rigby. On being asked which unit he belonged to Rigby said, The King's Liverpool Regiment. He was not in possession of a Pass authorising him to be in the town, he also had no shoulder or cap badges on show. He was therefore arrested and taken to Rue Léonard de Vinci Police Billet, Calais.

When later interviewed Rigby gave his name as Private 28075 Thomas Lee, 19th Battalion, King's Liverpool Regiment. He stated that he was from St. Martin's Camp in Boulogne and had left there on Saturday, 4 August 1917. He was not in possession of a Pay Book, Identity Discs or Regimental Badges. Not being satisfied with his explanation, Rigby was detained at Fort Risban Guard House, Calais. When further interviewed he admitted that he had supplied false personal details, stating that he was in fact Private Harry Rigby of 10th (Service) Battalion, South Wales Borderers.

The Court Martial of Private Rigby took place on Monday, 22 October 1917. The President of the Court was a Major T.H. Morgan, with members Captain E.A. Singleton and Captain I.A. Morgan. Offence Charged: 'When on active service deserting His Majesty's Service, in that you Private No. 11490 Rigby, a Soldier of the Regular Forces, in the field on 2 August 1917, absented yourself from the 10th (Service) Battalion, South Wales Borderers, until apprehended by the Military Police on 7 August 1917.'

He pleaded 'Not Guilty'. Following the Prosecution case, Private Rigby elected not to give oral evidence but instead supplied a written statement which read – 'Gentlemen, I was detailed by Sergeant Green at about 2.30 p.m. on 31 July 1917 as a Runner for Brigade. This was at Kiel Cot. I went to Brigade along with Private Johnson and six other men. The Corporal in charge was Corporal Watling, but he was wounded in the wrist before he arrived at Brigade Headquarters. I do not remember anything which happened to me after about 12 noon on 2 August until I came to my senses on the outskirts of a town called Watou on the 6 August. I made my way towards the railway where I saw a freight car, with not knowing which way the line ran. I thought the train was coming towards Poperinghe. Whilst in the train I fell asleep, and when I awoke the train was in a siding at Calais. I did not know that it was Calais at the time until I got into the town. I am sorry this has happened but I must have been partially mad at the time through worrying about my wife. I was married on the 21 September 1915 and sent out to the front on the 29th of the same month, and I have not seen my wife since. Gentlemen, I remain your honourable servant. Harry Rigby.'[12]

He was found guilty of desertion and shot at dawn at Armentières at 6.40 a.m. on 22 November, aged 21. His wife died soon after the war. Harry Rigby was buried in Cite Bonjean Military Cemetery, Armentières.

In 2006, under Section 359 of the Armed Forces Act 2006, he was officially pardoned. The statement read: 'The pardon stands as recognition that Harry Rigby was one of the many victims of the First World War and that execution was not a fate he deserved.'

Percy Joseph Treloar was the youngest son of Joseph Treloar, headmaster of the Church Schools, Crickhowell. He served as a Rifleman with the 1/16th London Regiment (Queen's Westminster Rifles), landing in France on 3 November 1914. Christmas 1914 saw the battalion in flooded trenches opposite the Saxon 107th Regiment in the Rue-du-Bois near the French village of Festubert. This was the setting for one of the Christmas truces and Treloar was among the men who met with the Germans in no man's land on Christmas Day.

He wrote home to his parents to say:

> There was much firing the day before Christmas but it became more quiet in the evening. About six p.m. the Germans sang patriotic songs and lit up their trenches. Our fellows replied by giving them some of their choice tunes. Then the Germans cheered. One or two of them seemed to speak English fairly well and yelled their greetings. By about 9.30 things had become fairly quiet again and not a single shot was fired during the remainder of the night. When the morning broke on Christmas Day the Germans were running about the tops of their trenches.[13]

Percy Treloar

During the morning Rifleman Treloar and three companions walked to halfway between the opposing trenches and spoke to two German soldiers who were burying a dead comrade. They exchanged cigarettes and shook hands. He returned to his trench with a sample of German ammunition and a button as souvenirs. Not a shot was fired that day.

Treloar was commissioned into the South Wales Borderers on 17 December 1916 and survived the war, rising to the rank of captain. He won the Military Cross in July 1918 whilst leading a trench raid when he was wounded in 27 places by German bombs and bullets. Despite this he led his men to safety, taking all other casualties with them. He settled in Newport after the war.

On 31 July the companies of the 11th S.W.B. at Au Bon Gîte had lost contact with 'A' Company on their right, as it had retired about 200 yards from the river before reforming and holding the advancing Germans back. The Germans took up their positions about 100 yards from the Steenbeek and set up machine guns in shell holes, along with snipers. They did not attempt an advance and the accompanying artillery fire was irregular. In the light of this, orders were issued to the 11th Battalion to advance once more to Au Bon Gîte and re-establish the bridgehead. Captain Davies went forward to reconnoitre the ground and was killed by a sniper.

Benjamin Evan Stedman Davies was 24 years of age. He was the son of Peter and Mary Davies, of Caerllugest, Llangeitho, Cardiganshire. Enlisting in the 2nd County of London Yeomanry, he had later gained his commission in the South Wales Borderers. His grave was later lost and he is commemorated on the Menin Gate.

Benjamin Davies

133

Private James David Dallow fell on 31 July while serving with the 11th South Wales Borderers and his name is also inscribed on the Menin Gate Memorial to the Missing. He was born in 1895 in Abercarn, the eldest son of Charles and Margaret Dallow. By 1911 the family was living at 42 Celynen Terrace in Newbridge and Charles and his two sons were working as coal hewers in a local colliery. James Dallow is commemorated on the Newbridge War Memorial in the grounds of St Fagans National History Museum and on the Celynen Collieries Roll of Honour.

Private Charles Lancaster of the 11th South Wales Borderers was also killed on 31 July, aged 25. He was the eldest son of William and Maria Lancaster. Before the war he was living at home at 83 John Street in Biddulph and was working as a builder's bricklayer – probably for his father who was a builder and contractor. He married his wife Clara in February 1914. On 4 January 1916 he joined the Royal Engineers and was subsequently transferred to the South Wales Borderers.

His death was reported thus in the local newspaper:

Biddulph soldier falls in action. It is our sorrowful duty to record the passing of yet another local hero in the person of Private Charles Lancaster, South Wales Borderers, son of Mr. William

Lancaster, builder, of Whitemore Village, Biddulph. Each week one hears that another of our heroic lads has given his all so that we and our children's children may be spared the horrors of Belgium, and the news of the death of each one causes poignant grief among the soldier's erstwhile friends and associates.

His devotion to duty, his earnestness, and his sangfroid in times of danger, won for him the commendation of his officers,

Charles Lancaster

while his genial nature was a sure passport to friendship among the rank and file.

The news of his death in action was received by his friends in sorrowful silence – which is perhaps the best tribute that could be paid to one who had died for them – but the name of the dead soldier, who had no pretensions to rank, will ever remain green in the memory of the good folk of Whitemore Village; indeed, the name will go down to posterity, for the manner of his passing entitles him to be classed among the Immortals.[14]

Sergeant Robert Allen Blackwell of the 11th South Wales Borderers was killed on 31 July, aged 23. His body was never located and he is recalled on the Menin Gate Memorial. He was the eldest son of John and Annie Blackwell of 6 Pitt Street, Rock Ferry, Cheshire. He had been born in Denbigh in 1894 and was educated at St Paul's School in Rock Ferry. He was employed as a general dealer before enlisting in Birkenhead in August 1914. He had served in France since 4 December 1915.

The Chaplain wrote to Blackwell's mother:

I am sorry you have not been written to about your son. His platoon commander was killed and his company officer wounded, otherwise you would have heard. I regret that I cannot give you room to hope, but I think it will be wiser to tell you what actually occurred. His platoon went over the Steenbeek and were surrounded by the enemy, who intended to take them prisoner. Soon our men advanced, however, and the Germans retired. One cannot say definitely that your son is a prisoner, for the reason that others of his platoon came back and some say that your son was killed.[15]

Captain King, Brigade Major, was with him, and realised that the battalion was not strong enough to advance on the German positions, so the order was cancelled. Soon afterwards the enemy artillery launched a ferocious barrage along the Steenbeek and on Iron Cross Ridge, which seemed to indicate another counterattack was in the offing.

The German shelling now became so heavy that at around 6 p.m. Lieutenant B.H. Jones withdrew the 11th about 200 yards to a series of shell holes for shelter. Three hours later the shelling abated and the original line was reoccupied, Second Lieutenant Lancaster bringing up a platoon of 'B' Company in support.

The 11th S.W.B. had lost heavily and the front line was now thinly held. Only three officers remained: Lieutenant B.H. Jones and Second Lieutenants Treloar and Vizer. Jones was subsequently wounded but survived.

Lieutenant Cobb now set about consolidating the front line, setting up strong points and battle outposts and using the German barbed wire to good effect. He was assisted by Second Lieutenant L.G. Williams who, though wounded, refused to go back for treatment until the defences had been finalised. Patrols were sent out to reconnoitre the German positions. Both officers survived the war, with Williams being awarded the Military Cross for his actions at Pilkem and Cobb winning the Military Cross for his work during a trench raid in November 1917.

On 2 August orders were received for the 113th Brigade to relieve the 115th Brigade and most of this was achieved by the evening. Unfortunately, 'C' Company was not relieved until 4 August, as it was not realised that they were further forward at the Steenbeek.

The men of both battalions of the South Wales Borderers were exhausted and filthy. The rain had continued almost incessantly since the first day of the attack and they were covered in mud and soaked through.

The casualties of the battalions were:

10th S.W.B.:
41 other ranks killed and missing
6 officers and 159 other ranks wounded.
11th S.W.B.:
4 officers and 116 men killed or missing

10 officers and 220 men wounded, more than half those in action. (Captain Jenkins was to die later of his wounds.)

Military Medals were awarded to the following men of the 10th Battalion: Sergeant H.J. Williams, Sergeant Bull and Sergeant Hulbert; Corporal J. James, Corporal D.J. Morgan and Corporal E.W. Pleece; Lance Corporal R. Baker; Drummer Hales and Privates J. Bevan, T. Watkins, Hiscock and Foote.

Corporal Ernest Walter Pleece was killed on 27 August 1917. The son of Ellen Elizabeth Pleece, of 8 Commercial St., Ebbw Vale, he was 25. His body could not be identified and he is commemorated on the Tyne Cot Memorial to the Missing. Lance Corporal Richard Baker died of his wounds on 6 or 8 November 1917 and was buried in Erquinghem-Lys Churchyard Extension. He had joined the South Wales Borderers from the Welsh Regiment.

In the 11th Battalion, Privates O. Evans and P. Mahoney were awarded the Military Medal.

In addition to those battalions in action at Pilkem, other battalions of the South Wales Borderers who were attached to different divisions took part in attacks on 31 July. 'A' and 'C' Companies of the 5th South Wales Borderers took part in 56th Brigade's attack south-west and south of Hollebeke on 31 July. They attacked on a front 2,000 yards wide and were required to penetrate to a depth of 500 yards. 'C' Company came under such heavy shellfire that it could not continue. 'A' Company went forward to assist in consolidating the line taken, but heavy enemy counterattacks drove them back, though they did establish a defensive line. Second Lieutenant L.V. Kent and nine men were killed.

Brothers Lionel Victor Kent and Harold Kent of Holywell Lodge, St Albans, joined the Territorial Force on the same day in February 1909 and were given the service numbers 538 and 595 respectively in the 28th Battalion County of London Regiment (Artists' Rifles). They attended annual camps at Salisbury Plain, Minster Camp, Dover Camp and Aldershot over the following years and both progressed through the ranks to Sergeant.

They had been educated at St Albans Grammar School and Merchant Taylors' School, where they were members of the Officer Training Corps. Lionel was a stockbroker's clerk and Harold was a clerk at Lloyds. They were posted abroad with the British Expeditionary Force in October 1914 and, apart from two short periods home on leave, served on the Western Front until their deaths. Harold was awarded the Royal Humane Society's Bronze Medal for saving from drowning a French soldier in the Lock of Saint Bostin on 2 September 1915.

In February 1916 they were sent back to England for discharge as their time had expired. They re-enlisted with the 3rd Special Reserve Battalion of the South Wales Borderers and both were made lieutenant.

Lionel died of his wounds, aged 33, on 31 July 1917 and Harold was killed in action on 4 August 1917. Both men left approximately £3,000 each to their elder brother, Reginald.

Lionel Kent

Harold Kent

Lionel was buried in Ypres Reservoir Cemetery and Harold, who was attached to the 8th South Wales Borderers, was buried in White House Cemetery, St Jean-les-Ypres.

A report on their deaths was carried in a local newspaper later in August:

A sad war tragedy is associated with a well-known St. Albans family, two officer brothers being killed within a few days of each other. Mrs. Kent, their mother, died last year, and their father's death took place quite recently.

Lieut. Lionel Victor Kent, youngest son of the late Mr. and Mrs. Thomas Kent, Holywell Lodge, St. Albans, died on July 31 from wounds received on the same day. In August, 1916, he was gazetted to the South Wales Borderers and was promoted lieutenant in June, 1917. For several years he was secretary of the St. Albans' Hockey Club and was a regular player. He was also well known locally as a keen tennis player.

Second Lieutenant Harold Kent, South Wales Borderers, killed August 4 was the seventh son of the late Mr. and Mrs. Thomas Kent, and his scholastic and military career was almost identical with that of his brother. His commanding officer writes 'He was one of my bravest, best and most affable officers: beloved by all ranks and universally admired for his high moral character and magnificent courage.'[16]

The 6th S.W.B., Pioneer Battalion, was part of 25th Division and, though they did not go forward, they were employed working on roads, mule-tracks and communication trenches. The conditions they worked in were terrible as in places the mud was thigh deep. German aircraft attacked them with bombs and machine guns, and artillery fire was a constant menace. Second Lieutenants D. Jenkins and J.H. Richards distinguished themselves by bringing up stores and ammunition through a gas bombardment and artillery barrage.

On 10 August, Westhoek Ridge was captured and 'B' Company helped consolidate the position against repeated enemy counterattacks. During this work Major G.S. Crawford, the commander, was wounded. He died later the same day from his wounds at No.17 Casualty Clearing Station, aged 34. Born in London, he was educated at Malvern College and Pembroke College, Oxford, gaining his B.A. in 1902 and his M.A. in 1907. He then followed his father into the Army and was buried in Lijssenthoek Military Cemetery.

Private Lewis Frayne was awarded the Distinguished Conduct Medal. His citation read:

> For conspicuous gallantry and devotion to duty as a company stretcher-bearer. He attended to the wounded under very heavy shellfire, regardless of his own safety. He also found, and put in a place of safety, his company commander, who was severely wounded, and although wounded in several places, blinded in one eye, and buried on two occasions by shellfire, made his way back to Battalion Headquarters and reported that his officer was wounded.[17]

Frayne was born in 1884 in Treharris, Glamorgan. He was a married man living at 7 Railway Parade in Pontnewynydd before the war and was employed as a colliery hauler. He had landed in France on 24 September 1915 and was discharged

from the Army on account of his wounds on 15 January 1918.

The officer who owed his life to Frayne's courage was Lieutenant William Henry Hanna, a former schoolteacher, from King Edward's Road, Swansea, who had landed in France in October 1916. Commissioned

Lewis Frayne and his family

in 1916, he was Mentioned in Dispatches in December 1917 and was wounded three times during the war but survived.

Private F. Reacher, another stretcher-bearer, was awarded a posthumous Military Medal for staying with the wounded under heavy fire until he himself was hit, dying of his wounds on 29 August. He was 26 and from Derby. Reacher was buried in The Huts Cemetery, south-west of Ypres. This cemetery takes its name from a line of huts strung along the road from Dickebusch (now Dikkebus) to Brandhoek, which were used by field ambulances during the 1917 offensive.

In addition, Sergeant Sheppard, Corporal A. Williams and Privates Carter, Horrobin, Lipyeart, Price and Sargent were awarded Military Medals. Sergeant Quinton received a bar to his Military Medal.

Besides Major Crawford and Second Lieutenant Harold Kent, 11 other ranks were killed, and one officer and 94 men were wounded.

The 6th Battalion was removed from the line on 13 August but returned in September for a further seven days. During this period Second Lieutenant Kerley and one other man were killed, one officer and six men being wounded.

Bertram Fredrick Kerley, aged 22 and from Winchester, died on 10 September. He was buried in Belgian Battery Corner Cemetery, south-west of Ypres, which was used until October 1918 largely for burials from a dressing station situated in a nearby cottage.

***

After a fortnight's rest, the 38th Division moved back into the line on 16 August. The 115th Brigade was placed in reserve and set about improving their position between Pilkem and the canal, as well as moving supplies and ammunition forward and keeping the tracks in good repair.

They came under frequent attack from German artillery and aircraft and took casualties before being ordered into the line on the evening of 22 August. The 10th S.W.B. were in support near Au Bon Gîte, while the 11th S.W.B. were further forward at Alouette Farm, near Langemark. The 17th R.W.F. were on their left.

One of the company headquarters was hit by German shelling on 25 August and Company Sergeant Major Charles Francis Clissold, aged 30, of the 10th S.W.B. was killed, leaving a widow in Newport. He had been in France for nearly two years and was an only son. He was buried in Poelcappelle British Cemetery.

On the night of 24/25 August a patrol of the 11th S.W.B., under Second Lieutenant Pembridge, set out to reconnoitre Eagle Trench. They found it full of German dead, victims of an intense bombardment earlier that day. On 27 August, the 16th Welsh was ordered to seize the position but, after a clear morning, rain poured down in the afternoon and the soldiers found it difficult to traverse the sodden ground, so lost touch with the barrage.

A platoon of the 11th S.W.B. was sent forward on the right and captured White House, but the 16th Welsh failed to reach their objective. The 11th S.W.B. were soon severely shelled and took many casualties. Wire communication to them had been cut by the shelling, so runners, Privates Park and J.C. Williams, made their way forward through the barrage to Battalion Headquarters and returned. They were both awarded Military Medals for their conduct. The position at White House was reinforced.

Corporal John Trevor Williams of the 2nd South Wales Borderers was killed on 27 August near the Bronbeke stream. From Ogmore Vale, he had enlisted on 16 December 1915, served in Ireland during the Irish Rebellion in April 1916, and proceeded to France the following September. His commanding officer wrote: 'Corporal Williams volunteered for the duty... It was one of those bits of bad luck we have to contend with... He was a fine lad, and had tons of pluck,' and another officer wrote: 'We were in many scraps together, but

Trevor always turned up with a smiling face.' Another also wrote: 'He was a capable soldier, popular with his men, and a brave man,' and a comrade: 'I never knew a non-commissioned officer like him, he will be greatly missed.'[18]

Coincidentally, 100 years earlier, in 1815, Corporal Williams' great-great-grandfather, a Breconshire farmer, had also been drafted into the South Wales Borderers.

On the evening of 29 August, 115th Brigade was relieved by 113th Brigade. The 10th S.W.B. had suffered over 100 casualties, with 50 more being evacuated sick, most suffering from shellshock. The 11th S.W.B. had 20 men killed and 40 wounded.

Among those killed was Major William Orlando Jones, aged 24, who died when Battalion Headquarters was shelled with gas. He had been in France since December 1915. A native of Pontypridd, Glamorgan, he had obtained an M.A. and he was buried in Bard Cottage Cemetery.

His obituary read:

Captain W. Orlando Jones, M.A., A.R.I.B.A., killed in action in France, was one of the most brilliant scholars Wales has

John Williams   Orlando Jones

produced. He was the son of Mr. D.R. Jones. M.E., Tyvica Crescent, Pontypridd (late of the Fernhill Collieries), and gained his B.A. with honours when only 19 years of age. He had a brilliant career at Manchester University, where he took the course in architecture. At the age of 19 he lectured before the Manchester Society of Architects and the Manchester School of Arts. He left the University with a scholarship entitling him to a four months' tour in Italy. The following year he obtained his M.A. degree. All the designs required by the Royal Society of Arts were accepted, and he was to sit for their final examination in November 1914, but had in the meantime joined the Public Schools Battalion as a private. Five months later he was gazetted as second lieutenant to the South Wales Borderers, and a month later full lieutenant, and next month acting captain. He went to France two years ago, and at the time of his death was senior captain of his battalion. Captain Jones was a clever artist in oils, water-colours and pencil drawing. He was also a brilliant pianist, and was organist of a Treherbert church when 14 years of age. His brother was killed in action a few months ago.[19]

On 11 September, the 38th (Welsh) Division left the Ypres Salient for the last time.

CHAPTER 8

The Welsh Regiment

THE 114TH BRIGADE, commanded by Brigadier-General Marden, was on the right of the attack on 31 July; the 113th Brigade, under Brigadier-General Price-Davies V.C., was on the left. The total advance to the Green Line was a distance of about a mile and three-quarters. When this had been accomplished, 115th Brigade under Brigadier-General Gwyn Thomas was to pass through and establish bridgeheads over the Steenbeek about half a mile further on and within 600 yards of the village of Langemark.

Thomas Owen Marden was born in Bath and had entered Sandhurst before being commissioned into the Cheshire Regiment in 1886. He served in Burma and in the Second Boer War, where he was Mentioned in Dispatches. On his return from South Africa he studied at the Staff College in Camberley, and on graduating was posted to India. In 1908 he transferred to the Welsh Regiment and served in South Africa once more. During the course of the First World War he was Mentioned in Dispatches eight times.

Llewelyn Alberic Emilius Price-Davies was a career soldier who had served in the Second Boer War, winning the Victoria Cross there at the age of 23. Born in Chirbury, Shropshire, he was commissioned into the King's Royal Rifle Corps in 1898. The citation for his V.C. read:

At Blood River Poort, on the 17th September, 1901, when the
Boers had overwhelmed the right of the British Column, and some

400 of them were galloping round the flank and rear of the guns, riding up to the drivers (who were trying to get the guns away) and calling upon them to surrender, Lieutenant Price-Davies, hearing an order to fire upon the charging Boers, at once drew his revolver and dashed in among them, firing at them in a most gallant and desperate attempt to rescue the guns. He was immediately shot and knocked off his horse, but was not mortally wounded, although he had ridden to what seemed to be almost certain death without a moment's hesitation.[1]

The leading battalions of 114th Brigade were the 10th Welsh, led by Lieutenant-Colonel G.F. Brooke, on the right, and the 13th Welsh, led by Major G.S. Brewis, on the left. Their objective was the Blue Line, 1,000 yards from their starting positions. Once the battalions had gained the Blue Line, the 15th Welsh under Lieutenant-Colonel T.W. Parkinson on the right and the 14th Welsh, under the command of Major D. Brock Williams, on the left, were to pass through them and advance to the Black and Green Lines.

Brooke, born in 1878, was commissioned into the Connaught Rangers and served in the Boer War, being seriously wounded at the Battle of Colenso. He was awarded the Distinguished Service Order three times for his service during the Great War: in June 1917, December 1918 and February 1919. He was also Mentioned in Dispatches three times.

Thomas Marden   Llewelyn Price-Davies   Geoffrey Brewis

G.F. Brooke (left)

Geoffrey Sydney Brewis was later awarded the D.S.O. and saw service in India after the Great War ended.

Thomas William Parkinson and Dyson Brock Williams had both commanded their respective battalions at Mametz Wood a year earlier. Parkinson had begun the war as captain and Adjutant to the 5th York and Lancaster Regiment before being attached to the Welsh Regiment; he was also awarded the D.S.O.

Major Dyson Brock Williams survived the war and was subsequently awarded the Distinguished Service Order by the King at Buckingham Place. A Swansea cricketer, he had helped form the Swansea Battalion of the Welsh Regiment. Shortly after his mother's death in 1921, Williams told a friend he felt 'desolate' and was soon bankrupt. Not only had he business losses, but he also had interest on loans and gambling debts; he vanished soon after the bankruptcy hearing. His brother managed to trace him and sheltered him in his Maidenhead home. Afterwards, Williams worked with an old Army friend, Major Arnold Wilson, to promote the Georges Carpentier – Ted 'Kid' Lewis World Light Heavyweight boxing fight, but Brock Williams then suffered another relapse. He resumed gambling and his cheques bounced, including one for £200. He sailed for Belgium and began playing the casinos but, on the 18 April 1922, he committed suicide in London. The cleaner found his room filled with gas and his body on the floor. Major Wilson later blamed the war for his friend's sad decline.

The advance of the Welsh battalions was described by one of those present: 'It was still dark and all we had to guide us was our barrage moving forward like a living line of fire, from left to right as far as the eye could see.'[2]

The Blue Line was taken by the 10th and 13th Welsh with little difficulty. Twenty prisoners were captured in Caesar Support and Reserve Trenches, more in Mackensen Farm and in the other trenches. Fire now came from an enemy machine gun position in the direction of Hindenburg Farm. The 10th Welsh launched an attack and it was soon silenced.

During this time the 10th Welsh lost two officers and 44 other ranks killed or missing, while six officers and 100 other ranks were wounded. One of these casualties was Lieutenant Clifford Stanton, who was killed on 31 July, aged 23. He was the son of Charles B. Stanton C.B.E., J.P., M.P., and Alice Maud Stanton, of Tydraw House, Aberdare, and had joined the Welsh Regiment as a private before being commissioned. Prior to the war he had worked as an assistant cashier at the Tower Colliery, Hirwaun. He had first enlisted in the 5th Welsh, but just before the battalion left for Gallipoli, he was commissioned into the 10th Welsh.

Stanton had fought at Mametz Wood in July 1916 and a newspaper report told of his bravery:

From a wounded Sergeant of a Welsh battalion, whom I discovered somewhere in London this evening, I had some interesting sidelights regarding the great attack on the Mametz Woods. He told me, for instance, how the Aberdare boys in one battalion shook hands and said 'good-bye' just before they were to rush over the parapet of their trench for the big push. But what I heard about Lieutenant Clifford Stanton, eldest son of Merthyr Tydfil's M.P., was most thrilling of all. He described how young Mr. Stanton went out under cover of night to capture a German flag which had been sported on the enemy's trench for days, presumably as a boast of invincibility. It was a perilous adventure, but he brought back his prize all right, and it has passed into the colonel's keeping. Perhaps Aberdare will have that flag some day.[3]

He was Mentioned in Dispatches in 1917 and his conduct was described thus: 'Lieutenant Stanton and his platoon had taken refuge from the enemy's fire at a place called Irish Farm, when the enemy concentrated their fire upon the farm, utterly wrecking it. Lieutenant Stanton, immediately taking in the situation, realised the peril of retiring, and he gave the order to advance, and thus saved his platoon from being destroyed.'[4]

At the time of his death he was acting as bombing officer to the battalion.

The following year his father learnt of the circumstances of his son's death from an eyewitness:

Mr. C.B. Stanton M.P., has had with him in London as a visitor Pte. Jack Evans, a Rhondda miner, who acted as servant to Lieutenant Stanton in France, and so was able to tell the father the story of how the fine young officer fell. It is one of the most thrilling war stories related. The young lieutenant was absolutely fearless, and a few seconds before he led his men over the top he lit a cigarette, and told his men to follow suit.

'Come along, Rhonddas,' he shouted, as he led his men forward. But a shell came and severely wounded him in the leg. He was up again in a few seconds and placed himself at the head of the company, and led them forward until he fell fatally wounded into Private Evans' arms. 'We loved young Mr. Stanton,' remarked

Private Evans, when he told the story, 'and he was among the bravest.'[5]

Clifford Stanton was buried in No Man's Cot Cemetery.

With him that day was Colour Sergeant Major David Jones from Merthyr Tydfil who was awarded the Distinguished Conduct Medal for his work: 'For conspicuous gallantry and devotion to duty during an attack. Reorganising part of his company, which had become detached, he led them forward and regained touch with the main body, and afterwards with four privates he attacked and captured an enemy strong point and killed the garrison. He showed fine qualities of resource and initiative.'[6]

Buried in the same cemetery as Clifford Stanton was Second Lieutenant Joseph Francis Avery, aged 20, of the 10th Welsh who was also killed on 31 July. He was the son of Andrew James and Rosalea S. Pitre Avery, of Quinla La Primavera, Quilmes, Argentina. His death was described in a local newspaper by Lieutenant-Colonel S.F. Brooke who wrote:

Lieutenant Avery was killed while most gallantly leading his platoon in the attack, and up to the moment of his death had inspired his men with his courage and example. A letter from Captain Owen mentions that Lieutenant Avery was killed in the enemy lines by a German machine gun when taking a dugout. He was shot through the heart and instantly killed.[7]

Clifford Stanton   David Jones   Joseph Avery

Private Leonard George Allen of the 10th Welsh was killed on 31 July. He was born on 7 November 1895, the son of James and Mary Allen of 73 Walkern Road, Stevenage. After leaving school he worked as a hairdresser's assistant and later lived at 105 High Street, Stevenage, with his wife Constance, before enlisting in the Somerset Light Infantry. He was buried in the Welsh Cemetery (Caesar's Nose).

Corporal Raymond Jones was killed on 2 August, aged 20. He had been awarded the Military Medal for his gallantry on the night of 11/12 June 1917 when the 10th Welsh in trenches at Ypres were raided by a German officer and 50 men. The raid was beaten off and the enemy officer and two other men were captured, giving valuable identification material.

Jones' real name was Raymond Leyarza Goitia. Born in Belgium in 1897, he was living at 51 Loudoun Square in Cardiff and working as a clerk when he enlisted under an alias for four years' service as a Territorial in February 1915, aged 18 (though he claimed to be 19). During his period of training at Seaton Carew, he was absent from parade twice, from church parade once and from roll call on another occasion. Despite these misdemeanors, for which he was confined to barracks, he was appointed lance corporal on 8 July 1916 and embarked for France on 26 July, being promoted to full corporal on 12 March 1917. In November 1916 he applied for a discharge on account of his being of Spanish origin, but this request was denied. His body was unable to be identified and, like so many, his name is inscribed on the Menin Gate Memorial to the Missing.

Leonard Allen

In July 1918 his mother, Teresa Goitia, wrote to the War Office from her home at 164 Bute Road in Cardiff: 'Kindly forward medal to my home. I am not well to leave home. If you have found anything belonging to my son, please send it to me.'[8]

Company Sergeant Major Benjamin Bessant of the 10th Welsh was killed on 4

Benjamin Bessant

August. His wife and two children lived at Trealaw in the Rhondda. He had enlisted in September 1914 and was formerly a collier at Nantgwyn Colliery. He was 28 and just over two weeks before he died, he had met in France his brother George who was serving with the Somersetshire Regiment. He is also commemorated on the Menin Gate.

The 13th Welsh suffered 39 other ranks killed or missing, while five officers and 52 other ranks were wounded.

Captain Tom Stanley Richards of the 13th Welsh, son of an M.P., was awarded the Military Cross for gallantry which was reported in a Welsh newspaper.

> It was Captain Richards who led the gallant Welshmen of the Rhondda over the Pilkem Ridge on that memorable morning at the end of July when the 3rd Guards Division of the Prussians, known as 'The Kaiser's Own Cockchafers', were cut up and seven officers and 622 other ranks taken prisoners. The Welshmen rushed the ridge like forwards in a football match and hustled the Boche to the rear; but the full story has yet to be told. Captain Richards was highly complemented upon the excellent work done.[9]

In civilian life Tom Richards was employed as a surveyor at the Ebbw Vale Works and he was commissioned in 1914. He

Tom Richards

rose to the rank of major by the end of the war. Two of his brothers also served in the Army.

The 14th Welsh on the left and 15th Welsh on the right then advanced through the positions taken by the 10th and 13th Welsh and made for Pilkem Ridge. While waiting in the front and support trenches, they had endured the

Officers of the 13th Welsh Regiment

enemy counter-barrage and had suffered casualties, among them Captain Humphreys of the 15th Welsh.

Percy Lloyd Humphreys was the son of C.W. and Sarah Humphreys, of Tylissa Farm, Llanfair Caereinion, Welshpool. Aged 35, he was buried in Welsh Cemetery (Caesar's Nose). He had worked in a bank in Llandeilo before the war and gained his commission in November 1914. Tributes were paid to him in a local newspaper:

The Rev. W. RICHARD ROBERTS, Wesleyan Minister, Newtown.

The cost of the war in money and material becomes more staggering every day, but even more deplorable are the losses that cannot be tabulated; the loss to brothers and sisters of an idolised brother; the loss to parents of a noble son who never caused them a moment's pain or anxiety, and in whom so many bright hopes were centred; and the irreparable loss to the community of a man destined to play his part well and fill a wide sphere of usefulness. This is the nature of the loss sustained in the death of Captain Humphreys.

He was born in a happy Christian home at Llanfair Caereinion in 1882. His parents, Ald. C.W. Humphreys J.P., and Mrs. Humphreys, are natives of the parish, and belong to some of the oldest and most respected families in the county. After receiving a good education at the local elementary and intermediate schools, Percy Lloyd entered the service of the North and South Wales Bank, first at Liverpool, for a few months, then Denbigh, Pwllheli, Colwyn Bay, Llangollen, and Llandilo.

He would have excelled in almost any calling or profession; but his tact, courtesy, winsomeness, integrity, and his keen judgement of men seemed to qualify him in a special manner for the banking profession. This is verified by the fact that he became a member of the Institute of Bankers at an early age, and was appointed manager of a new branch of the London City and Midland Bank at Llandilo, being at the time one of the youngest managers appointed by the company. His subsequent success justified the appointment.

Soon after the war broke out he heard the stern call of duty to enlist, and joined the first band of volunteers to defend his Fatherland. He made his choice speedily and decisively. None who knew his chivalrous nature were surprised to hear of the step he had taken. We all knew that fighting was not congenial to him, except as a last resource of those who set honour and righteousness above a dishonourable ease when infamous injustice had been committed.

He joined the Welsh Army as a private, soon became second-lieutenant, and by the end of his training at Llandilo and Rhyl, had

been promoted to the rank of captain. He was drafted to France, and fought in many engagements on the Somme, Mametz Wood, and latterly in Belgium, in the neighbourhood of Ypres. Although he led in these bloody conflicts with a fearless calm that bordered on recklessness, he came through without a scratch.

Adjutant Lieut. Silk shall tell the story: 'In the first place, I should like you to know that your son was the idol of the men, and his death came as a severe shock to all. As a soldier, he was one of the coolest and bravest

Percy Humphreys

men I have ever met, and as a man a good thorough Christian.
He did excellent work, organising and getting things in order for
the attack we made on the morning of the 31st. For four days
previous to this we had a most trying time, and one of the best of
his subalterns and two other officers were killed on the 27th. The
battalion were in position ready for the advance on the morning of
the 31st, having taken up position overnight. At a fixed time just
before dawn, other battalions started to advance.

Twenty minutes afterwards our men were to go over. Just as
time arrived to start off, Capt. Humphreys, who was with his
company, was looking over the parapet to see where the enemy
barrage was falling, in order to avoid it if possible in the advance.
It was not imperative that he should do so. It was his care and love
for his men that prompted such an action.

While so doing, the end came. An enemy shell dropped quite
close, and death was absolutely instantaneous. When I think
of his sterling character, and his purity in thought, word and
deed, I have not the slightest doubt but that he rests in peace
in that little cemetery between the villages, that spot which is
forever Britain. What made matters worse was the fact that Capt.
Humphreys was to have been in charge of the battalion in one
phase of the attack.

The Colonel had to take supreme command, only one subaltern
remained in the company, and many of the men and Sergeants
were casualties. We have had scarcely any rest since your son was
killed. The second in command, Major Helme, intended writing
you, but he was wounded three days ago. Your son was given a
proper Christian burial, and his grave is marked by a cross. I hope
to place a bigger cross with a suitable inscription, if God spares
me. May God be with you all and comfort you.'

Major Rhydderch, who has since been put out of action, wrote:
'He was loved by all the officers and men, and admired as a brave,
conscientious, good-hearted soldier. He is missed by all, but his
death has only taken away his body; he still lives in the battalion,
and his fine spirit will never be forgotten. Yr oeddem yn ffryndiau
mawr iawn. Yr wyf wedi colli ffrynd annwyl a chydwladwr hoff.
Gymraeg oedd ein haith, a theimladau Cymreig oedd gennym ein
dau. [We were great friends. I have lost a dear friend and praise-
worthy compatriot. Welsh was our language and we both had
Welsh feelings.]

I trust God will comfort you in this hour of trial, and you can take it from me that all the old folk of the battalion, so few of whom are now left, join with me in this wish.'

Capt. D.H. Thomas, another officer of the battalion writes: 'I had the privilege and pleasure of acting as second in command under your son while in training at Rhyl and Winchester, and later for nine months in France (until I was wounded), and as such came to know him, perhaps, better than any other officer in the 15th Welsh Regiment. Our association was the happiest, and I valued him as my greatest friend. Thus it came to me as a great personal blow and loss to learn of his death, and I know I shall not be able to replace him by another. In his death, the county lost a most courageous, hard-working, and competent officer – an officer that was too valuable to lose. He knew no fear, and applied himself with the greatest energy and diligence to his work and duties. May God comfort you all.'

Rev. Arthur Hughes B.A., chaplain, writes: 'I was chaplain to his battalion for fifteen months, twelve of which were spent together in France. I was deeply grieved to hear of his death, for we were good friends, and I held him in great esteem. He was a good soldier, but, more than that, he was a good Christian. No officer was as faithful at my services as he was. I believe that his calmness and coolness in the trenches under heavy fire was the result of his Christian spirit. Yours was a fine son.'

The Rev. Richard Morgan, Swansea, said: 'For the last twenty years I have held him as a pattern of holy life, before my own sons; his charity and gentleness sweeten our tears today. I have seen three men from his battalion, who said that the glory of their battalion was gone. He was a king wherever he went. His body rests at the foot of Pilkem Ridge, and the gallant young captain will never return, but his remembrance of his noble life and heroic death will live forever in the thoughts of all who came in contact with him. He was continually receiving some promotion in the Wesleyan Church, in the Bank, in the Army; but on July 31st, on the dawn of the battle, described by one of the officers as the biggest battle in the history of the world, Capt. Humphreys received his divine promotion. His men had to fight and die and win without his aid that day; nevertheless, his victory was supreme. It was a grand finale to a harmonious and beautiful life.'[10]

The advance continued as dawn broke, but the objectives that the battalions had practised taking were almost unrecognisable even in the daylight, owing to their destruction by shellfire. The German machine guns inside the pillboxes had each to be taken in turn, through being outflanked. Stokes Mortars were moved forward by the Trench Mortar Battery and were employed in bringing down fire on these concrete structures. The 15th Welsh took Marsouin Farm and Candle Trench, capturing 48 prisoners and a machine gun. They then headed towards what they thought was Jolie Farm, their next objective, but it was in fact Stray Farm. The 14th Welsh had encountered only minor opposition and the two battalions linked up on the Black Line where they were met by the 13th Royal Welsh Fusiliers, who had taken Pilkem village after fierce fighting.

The pillboxes on the far side of this ridge were now seen in increased numbers. The advance to the Green Line continued, with the 15th Welsh outflanking another pillbox and capturing two machine guns and 16 prisoners. They now came under fire from Rudolphe Farm which was in the neighbouring 51st Division area. That division being held up some way back, a platoon under Second Lieutenant F.H. Jordan was dispatched to capture the farm, which it did, taking two machine guns and 20 prisoners. Stray Farm was also taken and with it ten prisoners.

Francis Henry Jordan ended the war as a captain in the Welsh Regiment, after a time with the York and Lancaster Regiment as a full lieutenant. He returned to the regiment as a major in time for the Second World War and won the Distinguished Service Order for service in Norway in 1940.

During the Great War he was awarded the Military Cross on two occasions. The first citation for his work at the Third Battle of Ypres read: 'For conspicuous gallantry and devotion to duty. He led his platoon with remarkable ability during a reconnaissance of the enemy's trenches, obtaining information which was most valuable in subsequent operations. In the

Francis Jordan

attack which followed he displayed the greatest gallantry and coolness, largely contributing towards the success of the operation.'[11]

His second citation in 1918 read: 'For conspicuous gallantry and initiative in an attack. He led his men with great skill and determination, and captured all his objectives, together with a whole company of the enemy. Though wounded he remained with his men until he had established them in their position.'[12]

At the end of the war he was just 21 years of age and went on to serve in Turkey.

Second Lieutenant George Elton Morgan of 'C' Company 15th Welsh was fatally wounded, dying of his wounds on 19 August, aged 31. He was buried at Dozinghem Military Cemetery. Morgan had served with the Artists' Rifles before joining the 9th Royal Welsh Fusiliers as an ordinary soldier. He had landed in France on 12 July 1916 and received his commission on 25 April 1917, later being Mentioned in Dispatches. He was the son of Rebecca Morgan, of 35 Park St, Rhosddu, Wrexham, and the late William Morgan.

Private John Henry Stagg was one of the other ranks of the 15th Welsh who died on 1 August. At the outbreak of war he was living in Abertridwr in Glamorganshire and working on a farm. He had enlisted in Caerphilly.

A newspaper report stated:

Private J. Stagg killed. The sad intelligence has been received by Mr. and Mrs. Stagg of West Street, that their son, Private J. Stagg of the Welsh Regiment, has been killed in action in France. Private Stagg, who was 22 years of age, was working in Wales until the outbreak of hostilities. As stated in a letter from his officer, he was a good lad and respected by all his officers and comrades.[13]

John Stagg is commemorated on the Menin Gate Memorial to the Missing.

Corporal Ernest Harry Richards of the 15th Welsh was also killed on 1 August and is also remembered on the Menin Gate. A newspaper reported on his death:

Following comparatively soon after a gallantry act which earned for him the Military Medal, the death on active service of Corpl. 'Dot' Richards, a well-known Lincoln figure, is especially sad. The news that he had been killed while asleep in a dugout has just been received by his relatives in Lincoln, and his brother, Mr. G. Richards, of 13, Albert-crescent, has received a letter from 2nd Lieut. R.G. Low of the 15th Welsh Regt., in France, in which he says: 'It was the afternoon of the big advance. He had done splendidly all day, and had done some very good work. When we had gained our objective we dug ourselves in and rested. Your brother was sleeping in the trench with a friend, and a shell landed in the trench and killed the two of them instantly, and wounded several others. He was in my platoon, and was always a very useful soldier, especially when under fire. He was awarded the Military Medal on his first tour in the trenches and created a great impression on every one.'

Corporal E.H. Richards first enlisted in the Cyclists' Battalion, Hampshire Regiment, in 1915. Formerly he was employed as a clerk in the G.N. and G.E. Railway office at Saxilby, and later at the Lindsey and Kesteven Chemical Works. He then removed to Lincoln to undertake a more important post with Messrs. A. and W. Hall, pea merchants, Lincoln, where he was engaged at the time of the outbreak of war. It was a particularly meritorious action which earned for him the distinction referred to. It was, as he subsequently said in a letter home, the first time he had been in such a 'strafe', but 'I was not nervous, only anxious that I should do well in doing my bit.' In that letter he described how a raid was made on an enemy trench. 'I was,' he said, 'in charge of a section of three men, and our part of their line was a concrete dugout and machine gun emplacement. We captured the gun, and took ten prisoners, and killed three men. I myself killed two of them, and so avenged the death of dear old Percy (his brother who had been killed earlier in the war) and Stafford.'

Public sympathy with the parents and relatives will be the greater, as this is the second death in the family during the present campaign.[14]

The 15th Welsh continued their advance and met no further opposition until they reached a house at Iron Cross; the Green Line was now 400 yards ahead of them. Here they captured a telephone exchange, three German officers and 67 other ranks. On their left the 14th Welsh had been held up by two enemy machine guns at Iron Cross. These were outflanked and taken; 20 Prussian Guards were killed and 40 captured. The battalion then advanced to the Green Line where they took a dressing station and 38 prisoners.

Captain David Aubrey Sandbrook of the 14th Welsh was killed here. Aged 34, he had been Mentioned in Dispatches. The son of Thomas and Harriette Sandbrook of Rhyd-y-Gors, Swansea, after the declaration of war he had returned from Rhodesia and volunteered for active service. He was married to Harriette Sarah Sandbrook and lived in De-La-Beche Road, Sketty in Swansea. It was he who had led the capture of the German dressing station. He was reportedly killed near Stray Farm a little while afterwards. Sandbrook's body could not be identified later and he is commemorated on Panel 37 of the Menin Gate Memorial to the Missing.

The *South Wales Weekly Post* carried a copy of his last letter home.

Keen regret will be expressed at the news of the death of Captain Aubrey Sandbrook of a local unit of the Welsh Regiment, who was killed in action on July 31st. He was educated at the Swansea Grammar School and had been in Central Africa and Rhodesia for some years. He came over to England with three friends as soon as war was declared. Finding, when they reached Capetown, that they were unable to obtain their passages to England, they worked it.

Aubrey Sandbrook

The dead officer joined the Welsh Regiment and had been in command of a company almost from the start. His mother resides at Sketty, and his brother, Mr. J.A. Sandbrook, a former Swansea journalist, who was attached to the old *Cambrian*, is now editor of the *Englishman* in Calcutta. Captain Sandbrook is a brother of Mrs. Major Perkins and Mrs. Charles Moxham. Another sister is 'Sister' Sandbrook, a hospital nurse. His last letter home was to his mother, and read:

'At dawn we go over the parapet to fight for all that is worth fighting for. When I travelled from Southampton to London in September 1914, in the perfect golden calm of a St. Martin's summer evening, and looked out of the windows at the gracious southland of England, the quiet villages and poppy-studded cornfields, the green pastures dotted with cattle – the perfect picture of England as I had always dreamed of her – I felt a sudden flush of anger at the idea that Germany had for one moment imagined that the owners of so fair a heritage would lay it down at the bidding of a military autonomy.

'To-morrow I have a chance of translating the emotions I then felt into deeds and if anything happens to me please do not grieve but rather be glad that my last thoughts of the England I may die for are so very bright.

'Ever since I was a little child I have always thought that no man could die more proudly than for England, and to-morrow when I take my men over the top, their thoughts, mingled with thoughts of you, will inspire me more than anything I can say to you.

'My colonel, when he said "Good-bye" to me last night, said "I know you will lead them well, and I know they will fight for you." My only thought of them, I who have now gained this precious privilege of leading Tommy Atkins into battle, is one of pity for what they have missed rather than of envy for their craze for glory.

'So darling, if I die, I die proud and happy. I dedicate my life to the England I have always loved, and my soul to Jesus Christ, who died for all the world, and whose example England, as a nation, is trying to follow.

'Wherefore mourn not for me, and please don't allow anyone to wear mourning for me.

With all my love, darling.

Your affectionate son,

Aubrey.'[15]

Second Lieutenant John Humphrey England of the 14th Welsh was also killed atthis time, aged 20. Mentioned in Dispatches for his work previously, his body could not be identified later and he is commemorated on the Menin Gate Memorial to the Missing. Before enlisting he had been employed at Messrs. Spillers and Bakers, Llanishen, Cardiff, and lived with his grandfather at The Knap, Barry. He had joined the Welsh Cyclists' Battalion at the start of the war and assisted in guarding the north-east coast of England for 12 months. He obtained his commission in August 1915 and went to Flanders a year later. His colonel wrote to the bereaved parents: 'He was a fine, brave boy and always did his work well. Your boy's company had fought their way to the final objective before he was killed.'[16]

His batman was Leonard George Selby who had enlisted in the Glamorgan Yeomanry in December 1915, before joining the 14th Welsh a year later. He was wounded on 31 July, sustaining gunshot and shrapnel wounds. After recovering, he was posted to the Machine Gun Corps and was wounded again on 16 October 1918, this time by shrapnel and gas.

After being wounded the first time, Leonard Selby wrote to John England's parents and received this reply from the father:

We were most thankful to have a letter from you who was with my dear boy when he fell. It was most kind and thoughtful of you to write. I am extremely sorry to hear that you have been wounded and do trust that your wounds are not serious. I shall be in the Midlands early in September and if you are still in hospital at the time I will call on you. If you should be moved in the meantime, please let me know where you go to. I should so much like to have a talk with you. As you say it is a very sad blow to my wife and myself but we rejoice to hear, as we have, from my boy's colonel that he was so brave and we feel that his sacrifice will not be in vain. I shall be glad to hear how you get on. With many thanks and a sincere wish that you may have a full recovery of your health.[17]

Private William John Powell from Tretower, Crickhowell, in Breconshire was killed during this time as well. Born at Cwmdu, he had enlisted in the Glamorgan Yeomanry; he was buried in Poelcappelle British Cemetery, aged 21.

Captain Leonard Powell Godfrey of 'B' Company of the 14th Welsh was wounded and evacuated from the battlefield to Mendinghem Casualty Clearing Station but died there of his wounds on 23 August, aged 27. He was buried in Mendinghem Military Cemetery. The son of Joseph and Mary Godfrey of Swansea, and the husband of Agnes Jean Godfrey, of Glantawe, Heathfield, Swansea, he had been appointed temporary second lieutenant on 10 October 1914 after enlisting in the 14th Welsh as a private. He was an assayer before the war and had formed a local debating society. Godfrey had also taken an active part in Sunday school and social work, and had been at home 12 months previously recuperating from wounds received at Mametz Wood.[18]

Further details were also printed in a Devon newspaper:

Capt. L.P. Godfrey (WR), who has died in France from wounds received in action, was and 'Old Boy' of Shebbear College, Devon. He was a native of Swansea, being a son of Mr. Joseph Godfrey, the assayer at the Docks. He was married in 1915. The *Cambria*

John England   Leonard Selby   William Powell

Daily Leader, recording the death of the gallant officer said, 'he was the very soul of chivalry and honour, sensitive and tender to a degree, and his gracious character will be a very cherished memory.' Capt. Godfrey was a well-known cricketer, and he more than once conducted a tour in North Devon. On leaving college he returned to Swansea to enter the profession of his father, that of an analytical chemist.[19]

Second Lieutenant (Temporary Lieutenant) Francis Roderick of the 14th Welsh was buried in Bard Cottage Cemetery. On 7 July 1916 he had been one of four officers of the battalion who were accidentally wounded by the explosion of a percussion bomb just before the battalion went into action at Mametz Wood. None of them was seriously wounded but a Court of Enquiry heard from Second Lieutenant J.A. Wilson who said that on the evening of 7 July the four officers who were subsequently wounded, along with Captain A.H. Dagge, Lieutenant John Strange and himself, were practising the throwing of Number 19 bombs. The four injured officers comprised one group and they were throwing the bombs to each other, about 30 yards apart. The bombs had been used for the same purpose earlier but this time one went off and injured the four men.

Roderick recovered from his wounds at Mametz Wood but was wounded again on 31 July 1917 before dying later the same day. He had enlisted in the 16th Royal Welsh Fusiliers before

gaining his commission on 26 January 1915 with the Welsh Regiment. He had landed in France on 2 December 1915.

His death was reported in August 1917:

The sad news was received on Saturday morning by Mr. and Mrs. David Roderick, Cross Hands, that their younger son, Lieutenant Frank Roderick had been killed in France. The late lieutenant died while soldiers were dressing his wounds. A former student of the Carmarthen Grammar School, and

Francis Roderick

of Aberystwyth College, where he took his B.A. degree, deceased was a teacher at Cefneithyn Council Schools, Cross Hands, before the war.

He enlisted as a Private in October 1914, and was granted his commission in February 1915 [*sic*]. He had served for a considerable time in France, where he was wounded in December 1916 [*sic*]. He returned to France in March last. Of him his commanding officer writes: 'He always did his duty well and conscientiously, and will be a great loss to his battalion.'

He was a very popular young man in the district, and his death has aroused widespread regret. Deceased was recently married to a lady from Rhyl. His only brother is also in the Army, Lieutenant D.J. Roderick.[20]

His widow resided at Addison Villa, The Grove, Rhyl; Francis Roderick is buried in Bard Cottage Cemetery.

Second Lieutenant Francis Nevil Wilson Fox, aged 23, was killed on 31 July and buried in New Irish Farm Cemetery. The only son of A. Denise Fox, of Southdown Lawn, Gownhill, Devon, and the late Francis W. Fox, of Uplands, Plymouth, he was gazetted as an officer in October 1914 and had landed in France on 6 September 1916.

His commanding officer wrote: 'He will be a great loss. He was a brave boy; he always did his work well, and under all conditions was cheerful, a very great asset under the present conditions.'[21] A fellow officer noted: 'He had an exceptionally fine nature, and was an excellent soldier, who was loved by officers and men. His chief good quality was his continual cheerfulness under all conditions, and he had kept us so many a time. He has left us all a great example of a soldier and a gentleman.'[22]

The 14th Welsh had six officers and 80 other ranks killed or missing.

Both the 113th and 114th Brigades had now taken their objectives so, at 9 a.m., the 11th South Wales Borderers and 17th Royal Welsh Fusiliers passed through them and began their advance to the Steenbeek. The enemy resistance began

Officers of the 14th Welsh

to increase and casualties amongst these two battalions were severe. Accordingly, a company from the 10th South Wales Borderers and 'B' Company of the 16th Welsh, led by Captain W.J. Foster, advanced to continue the attack, Foster being twice wounded.

News of Foster's wounds was reported thus:

Mr. William Foster, 51 The Parade, Cardiff, has received two telegrams from the War Office informing him that his son, Captain W.J. Foster, Welsh Regiment, has been wounded on July 31, and is now in hospital in France suffering from gunshot wounds in his left arm and left leg, but reported slight. This is the third time Captain Foster has been wounded in France, where he has served, except for periods in hospital, ever since his battalion went out under Colonel Gaskell. Before the war Captain Foster was in the Glamorgan Yeomanry, and served with them until he was granted a commission. Captain Foster was in the champion football team of his battalion.[23]

William James Foster had played rugby for the Old Monktonians and had served with the Glamorgan Yeomanry.

William Foster

He was subsequently awarded the Military Cross and survived the war, rising to the rank of captain.

Private Charles William Neal of the 16th Welsh was killed, aged 20, during this advance but it was not until April 1927 that his body was found; he was subsequently reburied in Sanctuary Wood Cemetery. Working as a warehouse boy in 1911, he had enlisted in Birmingham with the Worcestershire Regiment before being transferred, and his personal effects were claimed by Mrs Rosina Caddick, his mother.

Sergeant Brown of the 16th Welsh led a platoon across the Steenbeek and captured a German position. They held it for three days against repeated German counterattacks. Brown was unsuccessfully recommended for the Victoria Cross and died the day after he and his men were relieved. There were only four survivors and each received the Military Medal.

Sergeant Thomas Alfred Brown of the 16th Welsh was killed on the 5 August 1917, aged 35. He had been born in King's Kerwell in Devon and had subsequently married Beatrice Helena and settled at 24 Cenydd Terrace, Senghenydd, where he was a special constable and employed at the Universal Colliery. His

Thomas Brown

widow Beatrice was left with three small sons to care for. His body was lost and he is commemorated on the Menin Gate Memorial to the Missing. He had served on the Western Front since 4 December 1915.

The 16th Welsh lost 24 other ranks killed or missing, and the 19th Welsh nine other ranks killed or missing.

During the morning the weather had been dull and cloudy but now the rain poured down, continuing for three days, which turned the already difficult ground into mud. Pioneers laid duckboards to the top of Pilkem Ridge, as this was the only way to gain access. The Welsh soldiers were pounded by German artillery and machine gunned by enemy aircraft. Their artillery moved forward to new positions in the lee of Pilkem Ridge, and Brigade and Battalion Headquarters staff occupied the captured German pillboxes, ankle deep in water. With their entrances towards the German positions, they were exposed to shelling from the enemy batteries. The signallers and runners had great difficulty in maintaining contact with the advance troops, their telephone lines being regularly cut by the enemy shelling.

Captain Chapman, the Intelligence Officer attached to 114th Brigade, was wounded early in the day. Lieutenant Harris commanding Brigade Signals was wounded twice but continued with his duties.

The appalling weather restricted the effectiveness of the German counterattacks and the division held its positions, despite the heavy German shelling, until 6 August when it was relieved by 20th Division.

The British artillery had pounded the German positions prior to the attack and then supported it well as the infantry advanced. The taking of so many pillboxes had been a major success, and the Welsh Regiment historian commented: 'The 31st July was the day of the platoon commander.'[24]

Other Welsh battalions took part in the fighting which began on 31 July, albeit serving with other divisions. Second Lieutenant Osmond Whitlock Nicholl-Carne was serving with the 9th Welsh when he was killed, aged 28, on 1 August. He was born at Nash Manor

Osmond Nicholl-Carne

in Glamorgan and was the son of John Devereux Nicholl-Carne and Alice A. Nicholl-Carne, of Tresilian, Llantwit Major, Glamorgan. After attending Dean Close School, Cheltenham, he matriculated at Pembroke College, Oxford, in 1908. He is buried in Oosttaverne Wood Cemetery.

Second Lieutenant Meurig Owen of the 9th Welsh, the son of a builder, was from Llanfairfechan in Caernarvonshire. He was educated at Friars School in Bangor where he was said to have been one of the most brilliant pupils to pass through the school. He won the Meyrick Scholarship to Jesus College, Oxford, where he commenced his studies in October 1914. In January 1916 he joined the Welsh Regiment. After serving in France he was sent to officer training school and had only been at the front for three weeks when, aged 21, he was killed on 1 August by a shell whilst taking a party up the line. Lieutenant Owen is commemorated on the Menin Gate Memorial to the Missing.

Captain Thomas William Percy Herbert of the 21st Welsh, who was attached to the 9th Welsh, had enlisted in August 1914 after being educated at the West Monmouthshire School, Pontypool. Commissioned in December 1915, he was promoted to lieutenant on 21 May 1917 and captain the following June. He had served in France and Flanders from August 1916, and was killed in action at Wytschaete on 2 August 1917 and was buried there, south of Green Wood. His colonel wrote:

He was in charge of his company, and had taken over the outpost line, when he was shot by an enemy sniper through the head. I should like to tell you how fond we all were of him, and how very much I shall miss him in the regiment. I could always depend upon him, both in courage and work.[25]

Thomas Herbert

He had married Elsie Mary Parry at Caerleon on 29 November 1915.

The 115th Trench Mortar Battery was attached to the 16th Welsh and serving with them was Private Hubert Merchant, who was born in Llanhilleth in Monmouthshire in 1896. The family then moved to Cathays in Cardiff and Hubert was educated at Moorland Road Council School before being employed as a clerk. He enlisted in the 7th Welsh (Cyclists) in April 1915, aged 18 (though he stated he was 19), before being transferred to the Cardiff City Battalion and landing in France at the end of July 1916 as one of the replacements for those lost at Mametz Wood.

While in France he received minor punishments for having a dirty rifle, being dirty on parade, and using his water bottle without permission. He was also awarded ten days of Field Punishment Number 2 for distributing information via a letter.

Hubert Merchant was killed in action on 1 August. His captain wrote of him:

> He went into the fight with his usual cheerfulness, and went right over Pilkem Ridge, as far as the River Steenbeek, where he fought gallantly until he was hit by a sniper in the side. He was carried into a shelter, but never regained consciousness, and died soon after. What officers are left are all sad, because we have left our best boys sleeping their last sleep near the river; but they all died like gallant soldiers.[26]

Merchant's grave was subsequently lost and he is commemorated on the Menin Gate Memorial to the Missing.

The war diary notes two officers of the brigade who were wounded on the same day – 5 August. German artillery activity that day was considerable.

Hubert Merchant

Second Lieutenant Alfred George Davey from Upper Norwood in London had enlisted as a soldier in the Royal Welsh Fusiliers. He was commissioned into the 10th Welsh Regiment and had only just arrived on the front line.

Davey survived the war but the other officer wounded on that day was not so fortunate. Henry George Trott who was born in Cardiff 30 years earlier, was working as a wheelwright in Dinas Powys, Glamorgan, when he enlisted in the Royal Army Medical Corps. He rose to the rank of corporal before accepting a commission in the 10th Welsh Regiment in December 1916. Wounded on 5 August, probably by the German shelling, he was evacuated to the Casualty Clearing Station at Dozinghem where he lingered for a time before passing away on 16 August. His brother Frederick claimed his medals, he himself having served in France.

CHAPTER 9

The Monmouthshire Regiment

As soon as Pilkem Ridge was taken, 'B' Company of the 2nd Battalion of the Monmouthshire Regiment moved off at 8.30 a.m. and reached Boesinghe by 11 a.m., where they commenced work on the road running across the canal over the Pont de Boesinghe. Little enemy shelling was reported and, at about 2.15 p.m., the company was ordered to cross the canal and to make a track where a road had once been; this had been destroyed by the British artillery.

At 4 p.m. 'B' Company was relieved by 'A' and 'C' Companies and returned to camp. These two companies continued work on the track until 8 p.m. when they too were ordered back to camp. By this time the German shelling was more severe and several men were killed. They were Privates J. Bateson, H.C. Buxton, J. Pickford, T.H. Williams and Sergeant R.J. Powell, M.M. All these men were buried close to each other in Artillery Wood Cemetery.

John Bateson was living with his widowed mother and working as a loom sweeper in a cotton factory in Preston when he enlisted in the Monmouthshire Regiment in December 1915, aged 18. Posted initially to the 3rd Battalion as a reservist, he transferred to the 2nd Battalion and entered France on 26 March 1917. His body was buried in the grounds of Boesinghe Château before being exhumed and reburied in Artillery Wood Cemetery on 29 April 1920.

Alongside him lies the body of Sergeant Robert James Powell from Abertillery who had landed in France in October 1915 and was awarded the Military Medal for his conduct at Le Transloy. Aged 32, he had worked as a colliery labourer and lived with his wife and two daughters in Llanhilleth. A German shell fell near to him and he collapsed, wounded. John Pickford, who was acting as a stretcher-bearer, went to his assistance. A second shell fell close by and killed them both. Captain C. Comely was attending to Powell at the same time but he miraculously escaped unharmed. Comely was Mentioned in Dispatches in January 1916 and promoted to Major. Lieutenant H.Ll. Hughes described him as 'a splendid soldier, capable, and afraid of nothing'.[1]

John Henry Pickford was born in Bedwellty, near Ebbw Vale, and was working as a collier with the Ebbw Vale Coal Company and living in King Street, Cwm, when he enlisted, aged 17, in May 1912 in the 3rd Battalion of the Monmouthshire Regiment. He landed in France in February 1915 and was hospitalised for a week, later that year, after cutting his finger with an entrenching tool while chopping wood. He was awarded a gallantry card in July 1916 and posted to the 2nd Battalion the following month.

Captain C. Comely

Alongside Powell lies Henry Charles Buxton who was originally from Dymock in Gloucestershire. He was a married man living in Grange Cottage, Pontnewydd, Monmouthshire, and working as a gardener when he enlisted in Pontypool. His wife Josephine was from Mannevillette, near Le Havre. Aged 32, he attested on 30 November 1915 and was mobilised the following May. Henry Buxton was originally buried in the grounds of Boesinghe Château but on 29 April 1920, as with John Bateson, his body was exhumed and reburied in Artillery Wood Cemetery. He had been in France since March 1917.

Josephine Buxton suffered from mental illness and spent some time in Abergavenny Asylum in 1916. This was expanded upon in a letter written by Henry's mother to the War Office in November 1917:

> I have just received a letter from Mrs. Thickpenny, Talywain, Wales, saying that you have been inquiring for the address of my eldest son, Pte. H.C. Buxton 291337 1/3 Monmouth Reg. who was killed in action on 31/7/17. I was with them last summer twelve month when, after an illness she was put in an asylum at Abergavenny, Wales. On my son's enlistment he obtained a passport, she went back to France, her being a French woman. I have not heard from her and her home address is unknown to me and my son stated in his last two letters that he had not heard from her for some time and I fear she may have been put away ill again. If you have any property of my son I will hold it until such time as we may [hear of] her.
> R.A. Hollander[2]

Josephine Buxton died aged 76 in 1943 in Mougins, near Le Havre, leaving a daughter, Jeanne.

Thomas Henry Williams was born in Wavertree, Liverpool, and enlisted in the 5th Battalion of the King's Liverpool Regiment. He entered France on 12 October 1915 and was posted to the 2nd Monmouthshire Regiment. His widower father claimed his personal effects. Thomas had a twin brother who served in the Royal Army Medical Corps, and survived.

The battalion continued its pioneering work for the next few days, with 'D' Company working on constructing a light railway to enable supplies to be brought forward as the advance continued. The weather was still very wet and, on

6 August, German shelling accounted for four men killed and nine men wounded. The four dead men were buried side by side in Bleuet Farm Cemetery. They were Privates D.L. Davies, W. Downey and G. Rimmer, and Lance Corporal W. Jones.

David Llewellyn Davies was born in Pontypridd before the family moved to Gorseinon, near Swansea. His father worked as an underground repairer in the local colliery. Davies enlisted in Cardiff and was 20 years old when he was killed.

William Downey left a wife and children; he had enlisted in Brecon.

Born in Holmes Chapel in Cheshire and working as a hawker and greengrocer before the war, George Rimmer had enlisted with the South Lancashire Regiment in Warrington and had served on the Western Front since 5 August 1915. His personal effects were claimed by his wife Elizabeth. He was 21 years of age.

Lance Corporal Wyndham Jones was born in Newbridge near Newport and employed at the Celynen collieries before enlisting in the Monmouthshire Regiment in Pontypool. He

Wyndham Jones

was 19 and is commemorated on the Newbridge War Memorial which now stands in the grounds of St Fagans National History Museum.

The Steenbeek stream had originally been some ten feet wide but the shelling had obliterated its banks, meaning that it saturated the country either side of it to a distance of half a mile, turning it into a morass. After Langemark was captured, the battalion made duck-board tracks just two

175

boards in width, supported by piles driven into the cloying mud. This work continued for the remainder of the autumn, with a regular toll of casualties, until the battalion was ordered out of the line in November.

William Charles Leinthall of Chapel Road, Abergavenny, had joined the 3rd Battalion of the Monmouthshire Regiment on 2 September 1914. Posted to the 2nd Battalion the following year, he landed in France in February 1915. He was wounded in action in April that year and was killed at the Third Battle of Ypres on 18 August 1917; he was buried in Artillery Wood Cemetery.

Private Percy James Scannell was born in Newport in 1897, the son of a shoe repairer. He had enlisted in the 1st Battalion of the Monmouthshire Regiment as a reservist, entering France in 1917. Scannell died on 25 August 1917 while serving with the 2nd Battalion and was buried in Bleuet Farm Cemetery. Severely wounded while on his way to Elverdinghe Station to entrain for Proven, he was taken to Bleuet Farm Advanced Dressing Station but died the same day, aged 20.

Private Eli Phillips from Newport was killed on 23 October, aged 21. He was buried in Bard Cottage Cemetery.

Several officers with the Monmouthshire Regiment were attached to other regiments at the Third Battle of Ypres.

William Leinthall   Percy Scannell (front left)   Eli Phillips

Second Lieutenant George Williams Hastings was killed in action on 1 August, aged 34, and was buried in Brandhoek Military Cemetery. He was the son of Charles, a journalist, author and publisher, and Amelia Hastings, and was born in Kentish Town in London. In 1912 he had married Annie Jones, of Buckley in Flintshire, whom he had met while working as a teacher in St Matthew's School. Enlisting as a private in the Monmouthshire Regiment, he was commissioned as a second lieutenant in the 3rd Battalion in October 1916 before being transferred to the 10th Battalion of the Cheshire Regiment. He was one of 54 casualties in the battalion that day as they attacked Pilkem Ridge.

Second Lieutenant Stuart Ray Duncanson of the 1st Monmouthshire Regiment was also attached to the Cheshire Regiment. He was killed in action, aged 25, on 11 August and was buried in Tyne Cot Cemetery. Before the war he had worked as a clerk in a shipping office and lived with his parents in Clifford Crescent in Newport. Enlisting as a private, he had obtained his commission in October 1916.

Nevill Graham Newcome Hart Lewis served as a captain in the 3rd Battalion. He lived in Aberystwyth with his sister and, after attending Shrewsbury School, had joined the regiment as a private before being commissioned in October 1914 and entering France in August 1916. Attached to the Royal Sussex Regiment, he was engaged in preparatory work prior to the attack on Passchendaele Ridge when he was killed by a German shell on 17 September, aged 24. He was buried in Duhallow Advanced Dressing Station Cemetery.

Stuart Duncanson

***

Besides the Welshmen who served in the Welsh Guards and the other Welsh regiments, many Welsh soldiers fought in other regiments in what was commonly called the 'Battle of Mud'.

Joseph Beddow from Rogerstone, Newport, enlisted in the 20th Machine Gun Company. Born in 1897, he later served in Kurdistan, via Basra and Mesopotamia. His brother Percy served with the 7th South Wales Borderers at Salonika. They both survived the war.

Alfred George Morris served with the 18th Battalion of the King's Royal Rifle Corps. Born in Glyncorrwg in 1876, pre-war he was an assistant gardener and groom at Ganarew House near Monmouth in the 1890s, before working as a driver at the Llanvaches Waterworks. He had enlisted in the Army Service Corps, working on mechanical transport before being transferred to the King's Royal Rifle Corps to fill the gaps in their ranks.

At 3.50 a.m. on 31 July the battalion left their positions and attacked across the Ypres-Comines Canal. They were held up by German machine gun fire from the direction of Hollebeke

Church. Alfred Morris was killed during this period. He left a wife and three children living at Julian Street, Baneswell, near Newport, and was buried at Voormezeele Enclosure Number 3, south-west of Ypres.

Alfred Morris (front)

CHAPTER 10

The Royal Artillery

THE FIRST WORLD War was an artillery war, with the majority of its casualties being caused by shellfire, and during the course of the conflict artillery warfare made more technical progress in four years than it had done in the previous century. At the commencement of hostilities, gunners had fired over open sights, but as the war progressed artillery techniques were refined, with the development of observation by aircraft, sound ranging and flash spotting, the use of forward observation officers and the laying of communication lines back to the batteries, the development of the box barrage and creeping barrage, all designed to focus the destructive power of the guns onto the enemy.

At the First Battle of Ypres in 1914, each 18-pounder field gun in the British Army had a stock of around 300 shells. By the time of the Battle of the Somme in 1916, the same guns were firing 125 rounds each in 30 minutes. At the Third Battle of Ypres, over 3,000 guns of different calibres fired over 4,000,000 shells in the period leading up to the infantry assault on 31 July. By the end of the battle on 10 November, it has been estimated that the British artillery fired over 33,000,000 shells; the figure for the German artillery fire is approximately 18,000,000 shells.

Second Lieutenant Huntly Strathearn Gordon described the initial barrage:

Now we have really belted the daylights out of them. With a continuous roar, shells went screaming over our heads and burst in a flashing smoking line barely 200 yards away. Our fire was so accurate that many of the chaps were getting up on the fire-step and shouting 'That's the stuff to give the bastards!' and other quips: I was thrilled, and very proud to be a gunner. The Boche lines more or less disappeared some time ago, and I gather that they are thought to be occupying a line of big shell holes out there. But I doubt if there will be many occupants left by now... The roar of the barrage was deafening. We had to communicate by signs. Such flashing fireworks in the dark I have never seen before. It was the greatest thrill of my life, and I wanted to cheer and cheer again.[1]

Lieutenant-Colonel, the Hon. Ralph Hamilton, Master of Belhaven, commanded an 18-pounder battery with the Royal Field Artillery and gave an account of the effect of the German artillery fire on 1 August:

We had a quiet night, but kept up a very slow fire all the time. At 10 o'clock this morning the Hun really began to attend to us. From that time till 6 this evening, we have been simply deluged with shells. It has been one of the worst day's shelling I have yet known. C Battery was shelled out this afternoon, and Welch and his people took refuge with me. As my little dugout is exactly 6-foot square, and there were eight of us squatting in it, there was rather a crowd. The difficulty here is that if one is heavily shelled there is nowhere to withdraw to, as the shelling is promiscuously scattered over the whole district. We are still barraging slowly, but there is no news of what is going to happen. From all accounts we have done very well up to the north, and places like Pilkem and St. Julien are again in our hands after nearly three years. The Salient has not quite gone yet, but it is a very flat curve now. Meanwhile, the unfortunate batteries in this valley of death are slowly being smashed up.[2]

The German shelling continued the following day:

Another black day. We have been pounded by guns of all calibres from 10 o'clock this morning till now (5 p.m.). It got so bad at 11 o'clock, when they were actually dropping 8-inch among my guns, that I had to take the men away. At that time there was no shelling on the immediate right of the battery, and I took all the men there, about three hundred yards, away from the guns. I left them there and went to B Battery to tell the brigade by 'phone that I had had to leave the guns. On my return I found that poor Bath had been hit by a fragment of a high-explosive pip-squeak. It had gone in behind the right ear and at the top of his neck, cut his tongue badly and lodged in his left cheek. We got him over to the dressing-station, where fortunately we found Mortimer and another doctor doing nothing. So they set to work on him at once. He was nearly choking with the blood running down his throat, but Mortimer said that that would quickly stop. They can't tell how bad he is yet; it all depends if the wound becomes septic or not. He has a good chance of living but I am afraid he is very bad. He is a dreadful loss to me, as he has looked after me since just after Loos, and has been a devoted slave, anticipating everything I could possibly want. Now at 5.30 p.m. the shelling has become intense, and my office has just been hit. Several more men killed and wounded. I wonder how long we shall be able to stand this sort of thing.[3]

Acting Bombardier Arthur William Bath died of his wounds on 7 August, aged 26. He contracted bronchopneumonia as a result of the blood he had swallowed and was buried in Bard Cottage Cemetery.

Hamilton described the condition of the battlefield as a result of the rain and the gunfire by 4 August: 'The country is now a morass – it is almost impossible to move. We were shelled again last night, and Welch has lost another gun. A third man in my battery has gone off his head. I have been feeling horribly ill myself all day – very sick and a bad headache. It is all owing to the beastly gas.'[4]

The next day things were no better:

We got gas-shells again in the night, but only for an hour or so at midnight and a short time at dawn... Lissant and I went to the Observation Post this afternoon and had to pass through a heavy barrage going. We lost our way in the hopeless wilderness of shell holes and had to move about in full view of the enemy. The mud is simply too awful for anything. I really think it is worse even than in the winter. The ground has been churned up to a depth of 10 feet, and, before the rain, was like powder; now it has turned into a material of the consistency of porridge. It is only possible to get along by walking along the edges of the craters, which, as on the Somme, are so close that they touch each other for miles. It is really very dangerous, as the middle of the craters is so soft that one might easily sink over the head. As it was, I got stuck to-day and it was all the combined effort of my party could do to pull me out. I was quite alarmed as I felt myself sinking deeper and deeper and could not move either foot... The whole forward area is getting very unpleasant now it is wet, as there are numerous dead floating about in the shell holes and there must be hundreds, if not thousands, of German dead buried everywhere in ruined dugouts. Their own shells are now re-ploughing the district and turning them up.[5]

Ralph Hamilton was born in 1883 and commissioned into the Grenadier Guards in 1901. Two years later he transferred to the 3rd King's Own Hussars and served in India. Married at 21, he left the Army in 1908 and joined the Royal Horse Artillery, Territorial Force. At the outbreak of war he was appointed as an interpreter with the 7th Division and landed at Zeebrugge in October 1914. He saw extensive service on the Western Front but died on 31 March 1918 when a German shell burst under the horse he was riding. He was buried in Rouvrel Communal Cemetery, aged 35.

Ralph Hamilton

Second Lieutenant John Hubert Howells, attached to the

15th Brigade of the Royal Horse Artillery, was killed on 9 October, aged 24, and was buried in Canada Farm Cemetery. He was an architect and surveyor who was educated at Swansea Grammar School.

His parents received a letter from his colonel which stated:

> During the few months he had been with us, your son proved himself a most useful and efficient officer, and was liked by everyone. Alas, it is always our best that are taken. He was acting as forward observation officer for the brigade in the attack on the 9th, and he and his colleague were both killed by the same stray shell at this assembly place before they started.[6]

Sergeant Edward Boyle of the 113th Siege Battery, Royal Garrison Artillery, was killed on 15 October. His brother John served with the same battery and had been killed in August 1916. A well-known local boxer, 'Teddy' Boyle played rugby for Penarth Rugby Football Club and was in camp at Lavernock, outside Penarth, when war broke out. He had been at the front for 16 months and was home on leave just a few weeks before his death.

Frederick Joseph Noyes served as a gunner, then a bombardier, with the Royal Field Artillery and was attached to the 38th (Welsh) Division. Before enlisting, he had lived in Pontypridd and had been employed as a butcher's assistant. The

John Howells

Edward Boyle

Frederick Noyes

death of his younger brother, John Robert Noyes, at Mametz Wood the year before, had a profound effect on him, and he named his first son John Robert Noyes.

Frederick Noyes in training on Blackpool beach (fourth from the left)

CHAPTER 11

The Royal Engineers

THE INFANTRY WERE reliant on the Royal Engineers to enable their supplies to reach them via the Army Service Corps. The Royal Engineers built and maintained the roads, railways and water systems that allowed the passage of supplies of all descriptions. They built bridges where there were none, repaired the ones destroyed in battle, and dug the mines under the German lines that exploded with such catastrophic effect. The engineers maintained communication lines, the telephone wires, wireless and signalling equipment. They also maintained the weapons of war.

Lieutenant-Colonel Brian Surtees Phillpotts commanded the Royal Engineers serving with the 38th (Welsh) Division. He was wounded on 2 September and died of his wounds on 4 September, aged 42. Buried in Dozinghem Military Cemetery, he was the son of James Surtees Phillpotts, former headmaster of Bedford School. Educated at his father's school, he had attended the Royal Military Academy at Woolwich. He was commissioned Second Lieutenant in the Royal Engineers in 1895, promoted to lieutenant in 1898, captain in 1904, and major in 1914. Appointed Commandant Royal Engineers with the rank of lieutenant-colonel in 1916, he was twice Mentioned in Dispatches in June 1916 and made a Companion of the Distinguished Service Order in January 1917.

The following tribute was paid to him in a newspaper:

Born in 1875 and educated at Bedford School, he passed into

Brian Phillpotts

Woolwich in 1893. After leaving Chatham he specialized in submarine mining and was stationed successively at Plymouth, Bermuda, Halifax, N.S., and Hong Kong, and was in charge of the submarine defences of the Thames till these were transferred to the Navy. When war broke out he was at Fort Camden, County Cork. Shortly afterwards he was gazette major, having been appointed to train a field company, which he took to the front in September, 1915. In the Autumn of 1916 he was appointed C.R.E., of a Division with the rank of lieutenant-colonel, being present with them to the end. His General writes: 'Ever since his arrival on my staff he had endeared himself to everyone. He was indefatigable in his work, never sparing himself, and was the bravest of the brave. A finer character and a more lovable comrade I have never met, and the country is indeed the poorer through his early death.'[1]

On 15 September Major-General Blackader wrote to the grieving father at The Ousels, Tunbridge Wells:

I will endeavour to give you a short outline of your son's work and duties, though I am afraid the description will fall far short of reality, owing to my very indifferent powers of committing such description to paper.

As you surmise, this Division was successful in routing the Prussian Guard on the 31st July. For two months prior to this, preparations for this assault were commenced. In connection with them your son's work and responsibilities were especially onerous. He had to plan, and supervise the making of assembly trenches, for the assault troops within 150 yards of the enemy's position. The making of tram-way lines up to our front system for the purpose of forming dumps of R.E. material, ammunition, rations, water, etc. The making of roads to the same, so that these could at once be extended, as the advance progressed, for movement of guns, ammunition, etc. The extension of the tram-way lines into the enemy's position for the feeding of the troops with everything they required. The bridging of the canal, getting all the material ready so that the bridges could be blown on the last night, so that the enemy could not photograph them, and so destroy them by artillery fire before they were wanted.

These are only some of the many important things your son had to plan, foresee, and supervise, and the latter had to be done under constant shellfire. He always appeared to me to be perfectly oblivious to danger. No officer ever set a finer example of utter contempt of all danger, so much so that I frequently remonstrated with him, and on several occasions went further, and gave him definite orders that I would not have him exposing himself to the extent he did at times. All his work during the attack, and after, was beyond praise.

He showed to others what could be done in overcoming what appeared to be insurmountable obstacles. The weather, and the state of the ground were appalling. Yet he overcame them all, and in a very short space of time we had a tram-way and two roads up to our new front line in the captured position. This was over 2½ miles of Flanders mud, waist deep in most places. Mainly through his exertions, the Infantry in the front line had their full rations, and were kept supplied with everything. And this notwithstanding the physical difficulties, and that the whole area was swept with shellfire.

I had spoken to him only a short time before he was hit, as he was going up to look how his work was progressing. This was about 7 p.m. And to my great grief I was told at 1.a.m. that he had been wounded. The first reports were good, and that he was as cheerful as possible, and said it was nothing. The next day I went to see him at the Casualty Clearing Station. As soon as I saw him I feared the worst. The Sister told me I could see him but that he could not speak. He just managed to say to me, 'A little short of breath, that is all.' He was as brave then as he always had been and laughed to me...[2]

He added in a further letter on 3 October: 'The number of bridges over the Yser totalled 19, 8 of them were of a permanent structure, planned and made by your son's directions. The

Royal Engineers building a bridge

remaining 11 were floating foot-bridges which could be thrown across in a few minutes. These were also his idea, and made up under his instructions...'[3]

For his courage in building a bridge across the Yser at this time, Corporal (Acting Sergeant) Albert Lennox of Aberdare was awarded the Distinguished Conduct Medal. His local newspaper reported:

Aberdare D.C.M.
Sergt. A. Lennox Royal Engineers (Welsh Division), has been awarded the Distinguished Conduct Medal for conspicuous bravery at Ypres. He won the honour when a Corporal for putting a pontoon bridge across the Yser Canal after his Officer and Sergeant had been disabled. Previous to this he had been recommended for a distinction and mentioned in dispatches. Before enlisting Sergt. Lennox was employed as a gardener at Glandare. His wife resides at Maes-y-coed, Oxford Street.[4]

His citation gave a different account: 'For conspicuous gallantry and devotion to duty for many months, especially on one occasion when in charge of a demolition party in a raid.'[5]

Albert Lennox served with 151 Field Company of the Royal Engineers and was demobilised in March 1919.

Pioneer William Alfred Criddle from North Road, Cardiff, was hospitalised in September after being gassed. He survived,

but five other men who were with him at the time did not. Prior to enlisting at the age of 22 in January 1915, he had worked as a boot maker and first served with 122nd Brigade of the Royal Field Artillery before he was transferred to the Royal Engineers in June 1917.

His commanding officer wrote that he remained under heavy shellfire in the open for many hours and repaired telephone

William Criddle

lines, thereby enabling communications to be kept up during important operations.[6] Before the war he was employed as a shop manager in City Road, Cardiff.

Pioneer Arthur Cyril Jenkins was killed on 18 October 1917. Educated at the Board School, Porth County School and Porth Pupil Teachers' Centre, he was for some years assistant surveyor at the Crawshay Bailey Estate, Pentre, and afterwards on the engineers' staff of the Cardiff Railway Company. Jenkins had joined the Royal Engineers on 17 October 1916 and served with the Expeditionary Force in France and Flanders from 25 April 1917. He was killed in action between Langemark and Poelcappelle and buried where he fell. His commanding officer wrote: 'He had only been with this unit about five months, but we all thought very highly of him, and I had noted his name for promotion. He did his work thoroughly well, and was always cheerful and willing... I miss him very much. He was very capable and always willing and cheerful.'[7]

Several Welshmen were killed while serving with Tunnelling Companies.

Sapper Albert Richard Mallows died of his wounds on 1 August, aged 21. He was serving with the 254th Tunnelling Company and was buried in Brandhoek New Military Cemetery. His parents lived in Ystradgynlais, Breconshire, and his death was reported thus:

> Deep regret has been felt locally at the announcement of the
> death from wounds received in action of Sapper A.R. Mallows,
> of the Royal Engineers and son of Mr. and Mrs. George Mallows,
> Glan-y-dwr, who was badly wounded on August 1st, and died later
> in the day in a clearing hospital. Gunner Mallows, who wrote a
> cheerful letter to his parents shortly before being wounded, joined
> the Swansea Battalion in January, 1915, and was transferred in
> the course of six months to the Royal Engineers as a miner in the
> tunnelling corps. At an examination he was awarded the certificate
> for proficiency in the mine rescue school. Prior to joining he
> was employed for a few weeks at Seven Sisters, before which he
> worked at the Ystradgynlais colliery. He had been presented at

both Seven Sisters and Ystradgynlais. Mr. and Mrs. Mallows have had a letter from his captain, Captain H.N.W. Boyes, notifying them of the fact that Sapper Mallows had been wounded, and passed down the lines. His right leg was shattered but he bore his agony with fortitude. He was very popular at Ystradgynlais and much sympathy is felt for the bereaved parents and family in their sad loss.[8]

Also serving with the 254th Tunnelling Company was Sapper Reuben Jones who was 36 when he died of his wounds on 7 August. He was buried in Mendinghem Military Cemetery, leaving behind his wife Frances in Cefn Maur, Ruabon. Born in Stockton-on-Tees, he had enlisted with the Royal Welsh Fusiliers and had arrived in France on 25 May 1915.

Sapper George Edwin Richards served alongside these two men in the 254th Tunnelling Company. He was killed on 22 October, aged 35, and was buried in Ypres Reservoir Cemetery. His wife Ada lived in Pwllgwaun, Pontypridd.

Stephen Rees, a sapper serving with the 257th Tunnelling Company, was killed on 12 August, aged 29, and buried in Coxyde Military Cemetery. He was from Llannarth in Cardiganshire and had joined the Tunnelling Company when an appeal was made for miners to serve. In civilian life he lived at 111 Caerau Road in Caerau, and was employed at Caerau Colliery.

One tunneller wrote home of the morale of his peers:

Under the heading 'Somewhere in Belgium,' and dated August 1st, we have received communication from Cpl. John Thomas, 7 Harvey Street, Maesteg (checkweigher for 16 years at Maesteg Deep Colliery, and now on active service). The Corporal, who has relatives in Bridgend, writes: 'Dear Mr. Editor, – Having just had a chat with Cpl. Madley, of Ogmore Vale, in our billet of brass bedsteads and feather beds (I don't think), I felt in duty bound to write to you a few lines in appreciation of the *Gazette*. I can honestly say that I eagerly devour its contents as one of the best tonics. I have read it since a boy ten years of age. I am now 42, and am proud to say that I am fighting with my comrades from Wales in one of the two foremost Tunnelling Companies in this campaign. We are roughing it at times, but we are all right, and have the dogged spirit of our race – "Gwell angau na chwyllydd." We shall beat Kaiser Bill, as Gwilym Taf used to sing. I shall now conclude, with the best of wishes and every success to you and the *Gazette*, which is always welcomed by the boys of Maesteg, Garw and Ogmore. – I am, yours truly, Cpl. John Thomas.' Cpl. Madley, Rhiwglyn, Ogmore Vale, adds: 'Kindly express my best wishes and good luck to all Maesteg people.'[9]

Another Welsh tunneller spoke with a reporter when he was home on leave:

Heolycyw Officer Visits Home. Second Lieut. T.M. Evans, Tir Gwilym Farm, Coychurch Higher, who joined the colours on the outbreak of war in 1914, is the only soldier from this parish who has obtained a commission. As an officer he is entitled to leave twice a year. He was home in December last, and is again home at present, having arrived on the 22nd inst. His many friends here rejoice to see him looking so well, and gave him the heartiest of receptions. Lieut. Evans, who was wounded at Mametz in July, 1916, has been in charge of a tunnelling company for nearly a year, and meanwhile contributed substantially towards the result which so disconcerted the enemy at Messines. While admitting the strength and effective strategy of the enemy, Lieut. Evans has no misgivings whatsoever as to the result of Armageddon.[10]

Thomas M. Evans had enlisted with the Royal Munster Fusiliers before joining the Royal Engineers as a sapper. He had landed in France in October 1915 and served with a railway unit of the Royal Engineers before gaining his commission.

Corporal William Abraham Insley died on 13 August, aged 49, while serving with the 184th Tunnelling Company. His body was unable to be located and he is commemorated on the Menin Gate Memorial to the Missing. Born in St Luke's, Middlesex, he and his wife Susan and their 12 children lived at Caefelin Street in Llanhilleth, Monmouthshire, and he worked

William Insley

at Llanhilleth Colliery as a coal miner. His company was employed in the Ypres-Brielen sector in July, preparing crossings over the Ypres Canal for the Tank Corps.

Sapper William Evans served with the 250th Tunnelling Company and was killed on 24 August, aged 32. He was buried at Kemmel Château Cemetery and was the son of Thomas Evans of Myrtle Hill, Pwll, Llanelli. He had been employed in digging the deep-level mines under the Messines Ridge and had been with the tunnellers for 18 months after enlisting in the Royal Welsh Fusiliers in September 1914.

Sergeant Charles Butler was serving with the Royal Engineers when he was killed on 4 October 1917 as he was drilling for water in no man's land near Ypres. He had been awarded the Distinguished Conduct Medal the previous year while serving with Number 3 Railway Company, Royal Monmouthshire, Royal Engineers (Special Reserve). His citation read that it was awarded 'For conspicuous coolness and gallantry under

Charles Butler

fire, after being wounded.'[11]

Born in Cork, he had moved to Tredegar and settled there with his wife, Mary, in Iron Street. He had arrived in France in November 1914 and was 30 when he was killed. Charles Butler was buried in Hooge Crater Cemetery outside Ypres.

Sapper Philip Charles Wyatt was a packer in the engineering

department of the Great Western Railway before enlisting in the Royal Engineers and serving with the 262nd Railway Company. He had lived with his parents in Blanche Street, Roath, in Cardiff. Admitted to No.3 Canadian Casualty Clearing Station suffering from shrapnel wounds to the head, he passed away on 31 October and was buried in Lijssenthoek Military Cemetery, aged 22.

Two rows away in the same cemetery lies Sapper S. George Rendell of the Royal Engineers Railway Operating Division who died of his wounds, aged 29, in a hospital on 29 October. A married man with three children, he was born in Colyton in Devon and had been employed at the Biglis Pumping Station in Barry. He had enlisted 18 months previously.

Royal Engineers of the 38th (Welsh) Division

CHAPTER 12

The Tank Corps

TANKS HAD FIRST been used during the Battle of the Somme in September 1916 when they had been deployed at Flers-Courcelette with mixed results – only nine of the 32 which advanced made it across no man's land to attack the German lines. The Tank Corps took part in the fighting at the Third Battle of Ypres but the ground was wholly unsuitable for their use and many foundered in the mud. A number of these tanks were crewed by men from Wales.

Lieutenant Henry Paul Mainwaring Jones was killed on 31 July. His obituary appeared the following month:

Death in action on July 31 of Lieutenant H.P.M. Jones of the Machine Gun Corps. He was the elder son of Mr. Harry Jones, Parliamentary correspondent and member of the editorial staff of the *Daily Chronicle*, formerly of Llanelly and Cardiff. He had a brilliant career at Dulwich College, both in scholarship and athletics. He won a junior scholarship in 1909 and a senior in 1912, being the only student to achieve this distinction for 200 years. He was head of the Modern Side, a member of the First XV for three seasons, captain of football 1914–15 and editor of the college magazine from 1912 to 1914. At the athletic sports in March 1915, he won the mile flat race, the half-mile, and the steeplechase, and tied for the 'Victorludorum' shield. In December 1914 he won a Brackenbury scholarship in History and Modern Languages at Balliol College, Oxford.

He joined the Army in April, 1915. Refused in the infantry on account of short-sight, he received a commission in the Army Service Corps. He went to France in July 1915 as a requisitioning officer to the 9th Cavalry Brigade, and subsequently acted in the same capacity to the 1st Cavalry Brigade. At his urgent request he was transferred in February last to the MGC, heavies – in other words, Tanks, and as such, took part in the great offensive of last April and in the battle of July 31.

In his last letter home, written on July 29, he said: 'Have you ever reflected on the fact that, despite the horrors of the war, it is at least a big thing? I mean to say that in it one is brought face to face with realities. The follies, selfishness, luxury, and general pettiness of the vile commercial sort of existence led by nine-tenths of the people of the world in peace time are replaced by a savagery that is at least more honest and outspoken. Look at it this way: in peace time one just lives one's own little life – engaged in trivialities, worrying about one's own comfort, about money matters, and all that sort of thing – just living for one's own self. What a sordid life it is! In war, on the other hand, even if you do get killed, you only anticipate the inevitable by a few years in any case, and you have the satisfaction of knowing that you have pegged out in the attempt to help your country. You have, in fact, realised an ideal, which, as far as I can see, you very rarely do in ordinary life. The reason is that ordinary life runs on a commercial and selfish basis; if you want to "get on," as the saying is, you can't keep your hands clean.

Personally, I often rejoice that the war has come my way. It has made me realise what a petty thing life is. I think that the war has given to everyone a chance to "get out of himself" as one might say. Certainly, speaking for myself, I can say that I have never in all my life experienced such a wild exhilaration as on the commencement of a big stunt like the last April one, for example. The excitement for the last half-hour or so before, it is like nothing on earth. The only thing that compares with it are a few minutes before the start of a big school match. Well, cheerio!'

Lieutenant Paul Jones was born in May, 1896. He was a young man of great physical strength and remarkable intellectual gifts. He had a rare aptitude for languages and a passion for history. He was also a very gifted musician. His death on the threshold of a life very rich in promise extinguishes many high hopes.[1]

Paul Jones' body could not be identified and he is remembered on the Menin Gate.

Gunner Ernest John Buffin was also killed on 31 July. As a boy he had worked in the local colliery in Mitcheldean in Gloucestershire, leaving home at 16 to work in the south Wales coalfields. He was residing in Bargoed when he enlisted there in January 1915 in the Royal Army Medical Corps, before transferring to the King's Shropshire Light Infantry and landing in France in September 1915 where he served as a stretcher-bearer. He joined the Machine Gun Corps in January 1917 and is buried in Poelcappelle British Cemetery.

Private Charles L. Cook of Newport was killed on 2 August while serving with 'B' Battalion. Before the war he had been employed as a night operator at Newport Post Office. He had enlisted with the 2nd Monmouthshire Regiment and had served in France with them before transferring to the Heavy Brigade Machine Gun Corps – later the Tank Corps. He is buried in Railway Dugouts Burial Ground.

Gunner Edgar John Holwill of Neath had joined the 8th Welsh in 1914 and landed with them in the Balkans in September 1915. He survived the fighting and joined the Tank Corps. He died of his wounds on 7 August 1917 at a hospital centre at Le Tréport and is buried in Mont Huon Military Cemetery. He was aged 23 and the son of John and Elizabeth Ann Holwill.

On the night of 21/22 August, Lieutenant Ernest James

Paul Jones   Ernest Buffin   Charles Cook

Rollings was in command of a Pioneer tank, which was charged with assisting the fighting tanks across the Steenbeek. Under heavy, high-explosive shellfire and a gas bombardment, he helped ensure every tank in his section went into action and then returned to rescue a seriously wounded officer and his men. He was subsequently awarded the Military Cross for his actions. The citation read:

> T./2nd Lt. Ernest James Rollings, Tank Corps. For conspicuous gallantry and devotion to duty. He commanded his Tanks in difficult ground and under heavy shellfire with the greatest courage and perseverance, helping them out of many difficulties and keeping them in action by his splendid personal energy and fearlessness. After he had completed his duties, he went back to assist a seriously wounded officer and several men who were still under heavy shellfire.[2]

Raised in Knighton, Radnorshire, Rollings worked as a post office messenger boy and later as a postman before joining the Glamorgan Constabulary in 1913, serving at Caerau, Maesteg. He enlisted in the cavalry in November 1914 but soon transferred to the infantry and was wounded in 1915. He was commissioned into the Machine Gun Corps in January 1917 and volunteered for the 'Heavy Branch' in order to serve in

tanks. He was awarded a bar to his Military Cross for capturing extensive plans of the German positions of the Hindenburg Line in August 1918. Rollings was wounded in the head soon afterwards. After leaving the Army in 1920, he re-joined the Glamorgan Constabulary, serving at Gwaun-Cae-Gurwen and Ystalyfera. When the story of how he led an armoured car raid on the German Headquarters at Framerville on 8

Ernest Rollings

August 1918 and seized the German defensive plans emerged in the 1930s, he was described in the press as 'the man who ended the war'.

Sergeant Joshua Weeks was killed in action on 22 August 1917, aged 22. He has no known grave and his name is commemorated on the Tyne Cot Memorial to the Missing. Born in Ogmore Vale, he had enlisted in the 3rd Monmouthshire Regiment before joining the Machine Gun Corps Heavy Branch and winning the Military Medal on 3 May 1917 at Bullecourt.

On 3 May 1917 they had attacked a German machine gun position which was holding up an infantry attack. Armour piercing rounds had wounded four of the crew, five of the Lewis Guns had been put out of action and his officer, Lieutenant Tom Westbrook, had been wounded in the right hand. After evacuating the wounded crewmen, Weeks set up his Lewis Gun in a shell hole and continued firing at the German position until his gun was also put out of action.

His citation read:

At Bullecourt, May 3, 1917. When his officer was wounded he took his place in the brakesman's seat and was responsible for getting the car as far back as it did. When he left the car he looked after the wounded by placing them in safety in shell holes and getting them water. He also got a Lewis gun and ammunition out of the tank and helped to man a shell hole. All this was done under very heavy machine gun fire.[3]

At the Third Battle of Ypres his tank, 'Devil', took part in an attack near Bulow Farm alongside another tank named 'Dracula'. The report on the action tells what happened:

The action of the Tanks – Dracula (male) and Devil (female) as far as can be ascertained from officers who were on the spot, was as follows: (the mist and smoke made it difficult to observe the movements with great accuracy).

By Zero Dracula, which was leading, had reached the junction of the St. Julian-Poelcappelle and Winnipeg-Langemarck Roads, with Devil close behind. They advanced with the Infantry, but on getting to within 150 yards of the track leaving Poelcappelle Road for Bulow Farm, found the road blocked by fallen trees and were unable to proceed any further. They were then about level with Vieilles Maison upon which they opened fire for a short time. They then came back towards home. During their homeward journey, a direct hit was observed on Devil. This shell is reported to have killed the brakesman and wounded the gunner. 2/Lieut. Lawrie, commanding the Tank, then got out and commenced to bandage up the wounded man, when a second shell arrived and killed both him and the wounded man. Nothing further was seen of the Tank Dracula until the evening when it was located on the West side of the Poelcappelle Road.[4]

Second Lieutenant Andrew Ralph Lawrie is also named on the Tyne Cot Memorial. He was the eldest son of Andrew Lawrie, a J.P. The family home was at Dungoyne, Kirkintilloch, and he had just finished the first year of his studies for a degree in medicine at Glasgow University when war broke out.

Lance Corporal Edward George Williams served in the same 'D' Battalion as Joshua Weeks. Born in Ferndale in 1892,

he was initially employed as a schoolmaster at Tylorstown Boys' School, until he followed his father and became a winding engineer at the local colliery. He had enlisted in Coventry in the Machine Gun Corps and was killed in action on 9 October 1917, aged 25, whilst entering the village of Poelcappelle and is commemorated on the Tyne Cot Memorial to the Missing, as he has no known grave.

Andrew Lawrie

Edward Williams

His commanding officer wrote to Williams' father and stated that he had been recommended for a decoration for his bravery, and paid high tribute to his splendid character, as he had set a fine example to the rest of the crew; he had lost a man that would be hard to replace.

Williams had taken part in the tank attack on Flers in September 1916 and probably at Bullecourt where the tanks of his battalion were badly damaged. His tank D8 (Male) was ordered to attack north-west of Flers but it was damaged as it moved up to its starting point. The steering wheels were rendered useless but the commander, Second Lieutenant George Brown, pressed on and caught up with the infantry by 7.05 a.m. At 7.20 a.m. it moved forward again and reached its objective. It was soon targeted by enemy artillery and Brown and his driver were

Tanks stuck in the mud of Passchendaele

both temporarily blinded by glass fragments from the vision prisms when they were hit. Brown recovered his vision and the tank returned after being in action for around 20 hours.

Second Lieutenant Allan Everett Renwick served with 'F' Battalion of the Tank Corps. He was also awarded the Military Cross:

> At Ypres on July 31, 1917, when his tank ditched and six of his crew were wounded, he personally carried four of them into a trench under heavy shellfire. He then returned to his tank, and with the aid of a new crew which had been sent up, got his tank out and reached the final objective, eventually bringing his tank back to within a mile of the position of assembly. His fine example and cheerfulness inspired confidence in his crew and enabled them to bring back the tank successfully.[5]

Renwick was born in Cardiff in 1898 and had originally enlisted with the London Scottish in April 1915 before being commissioned into the Heavy Section Machine Gun Corps. His tank 'Firespite' was part of 16 Company. In November 1917 he was severely wounded by a bullet to the right thigh and was admitted to hospital. He served in the R.A.F.

THE TANK "EGBERT" AND ITS CREW

Allan Renwick, second from left

during the Second World War and rose to the rank of Wing Commander.

Captain David Taunton Raikes of the 3rd Battalion South Wales Borderers was attached to 'A' Battalion of the Tank Corps and won the Military Cross:

> For conspicuous gallantry and devotion to duty during the operations on July 31, 1917. He personally led his tanks to their objective near Surbiton Villa under heavy shell and machine gun fire. When progress became otherwise impossible, he got into a tank, which soon afterwards received a direct hit, killing the tank commander and wounding most of the crew. He then went forward, on foot, with the remaining tanks and directed them towards enemy machine gun emplacements and silenced the guns. When three of his four tanks were placed out of action, he organised a party and salvaged all the Lewis Guns, again under heavy fire.[6]

At Cambrai in November he was awarded the Distinguished Service Order.

> For conspicuous gallantry in action at Marcoing on November 20 and 21, while in command of a section of tanks. During the afternoon of November 20 this officer controlled the movement of his section of tanks under heavy machine gun fire with absolute disregard for his personal safety. He got out of his tank at least a dozen times to give instructions to the tank commanders, in spite of the fact that his tank was on most occasions subjected to machine gun fire and the intervening space between the tanks was entirely devoid of cover and in full view of the enemy. Again, on November 21, under similar conditions, he directed his own section of tanks and also nine others who were in need of confirmation as to the situation. Throughout the two days' fighting he never rested as long as his services could be of any use, and his utter disregard for danger and his great cheerfulness throughout set a fine example to all ranks.[7]

In 1918 he was awarded a bar to his Military Cross:

During the advance beyond Villers-Bretonneux on August 8 this officer displayed quite exceptional courage, initiative, and devotion to duty. He closely followed his company on foot, horseback, and bicycle, as he found the means, re-directing his tanks as the situation demanded.

On August 10, near Fouquescourt, he displayed the same high soldierly qualities in superintending the operations. Throughout the operations from August 8 to 15 this officer has been continually reconnoitring and doing good work in the front area with an utter disregard to danger, and frequently under very heavy machine gun and shellfire. His example to all has been quite exceptional, and his initiative and untiring energy have rivalled any in my recollection.[8]

David Raikes was brought up at Treberfydd House near Llangorse Lake in the Brecon Beacons. Born in 1897, he was educated at Radley School, Abingdon. Four of his five brothers served in the Great War, each winning the D.S.O.

The tanks deployed at the Third Battle of Ypres had mixed success. For the majority of the time they were deployed across ground that was wholly unsuited to them, yet in their actions against two German positons in particular they proved their worth.

On Sunday, 19 August, two tanks attacked the German position known as the 'Cockroft' and drove out the garrison. Eight days later tanks successfully attacked 'Springfield', a German fortified farm on the Langemark to Zonnebeke road, but this was only a portent of things to come.

CHAPTER 13

The Army Service Corps

THE SOLDIERS WHO fought at the Third Battle of Ypres required immense logistical support in the form of ammunition, equipment, fuel and food, amongst other things, brought to the front on horses, mules and in motorized vehicles, on railways and on waterways. It was the role of the Army Service Corps to ensure that these lines of support remained unbroken, even in the face of enemy fire.

The A.S.C. was divided into companies, with each allocated a specific role. The largest component was the Horse Transport section, but notwithstanding this, when the war began the British Army was the most mechanised in the world.

At the Third Battle of Ypres they faced enormous challenges in getting supplies up to the soldiers in the front line, owing to the state of the ground. Several Welshmen sacrificed their lives attempting to ensure that the infantry had the means to continue fighting.

Private John Llewellyn Morgans was born in Lampeter, Cardiganshire, before moving to Cardiff with his parents. Serving with the 406th Mechanical Transport Company, attached to II Corps Heavy Artillery, he was killed in action on 19 August, aged 20, and buried in Reninghelst New Military Cemetery, south-west of Ypres.

Theodore Godfred Harry Torgeson, the son of a Norwegian sailmaker, was a driver with the 8th Reserve Park when he died of wounds, aged 31, at No.32 Casualty Clearing Station on 19

August. He was buried in Brandhoek New Military Cemetery. Born in Swansea, he had lived with his parents in Cardiff.

Private Aneurin Weber Evans was serving with the 717th Mechanical Transport Company attached to IX Corps Heavy Artillery. Born in Llanfihangel Ystrad in Cardiganshire, he was 32 and had formerly served with the Worcestershire Regiment before joining the A.S.C. His wife Doris and he had lived in Moreton, Bromsgrove, Worcestershire, before he enlisted. He was killed in action on 30 September and was buried in Locre Hospice Cemetery, south-west of Ypres.

Sergeant Stanley Oswald John was attached to 11th Infantry Brigade Headquarters when he was killed on 5 October, aged 28. Originally from Sketty in Swansea, he was a lance corporal with the Welsh Regiment before being transferred to the Army Service Corps. He had served on the Western Front since December 1915 and had fought at Mametz Wood before being transferred to the A.S.C. in mid August 1916. He was buried in Bard Cottage Cemetery.

Driver Ernest Albert Perkins of the 151st Company, attached to the 56th Field Ambulance of the Royal Army Medical Corps, was killed on 21 October, aged 28. Born in Pontycymmer, he

Men of the Army Service Corps

was living with his parents at 76 Cardiff Road, Llandaff, in Cardiff, when he enlisted. He was buried in Duhallow Advanced Dressing Station.

Private Edward Harcourt Drowley from Abergavenny was serving with the 402nd Mechanical Transport Company, attached to the Heavy Battery of the Canadian Corps when he was killed in action on 10 November, aged 19. He was buried in Oxford Road Cemetery, north-east of Ypres.

Providing logistical support to the tunnellers of the Royal Engineers led to one Welshman being awarded the Military Medal:

> Honouring a Hero. A very interesting meeting was held at Zion Congregational Church Hall on Thursday evening of last week, to do honour to a war hero in the person of Driver Thomas Amesbury of the A.S.C., who has been decorated with the Military Medal for gallant conduct at the front.
>
> The official account says: 'For gallant conduct under shellfire. He delivered a wagon load of stores to a tunnelling company. Shelling commenced at 11.50 p.m. and continued for two hours, both gas and shrapnel. The working party was not to be found, and

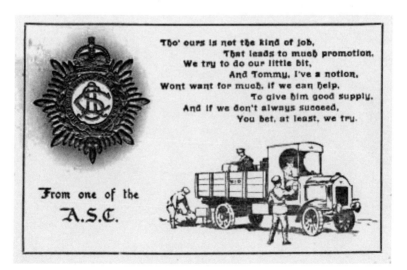

A greetings card from the Army Service Corps

Driver Amesbury, with the help of the guide, unloaded his wagon, working for two hours in his box respirator. The guide was gassed, and is now in hospital. Both horses were wounded, and Driver Amesbury returned to camp at 7.15 a.m. with difficulty, one horse frequently falling down. The remaining wagons of the convoy were turned back, and did not complete the duty.'[1]

Thomas Amesbury was born in Llangeinor, then in Glamorgan, in 1886, and was working as a haulier when he enlisted in the Army Service Corps, aged 28, in November 1914. He survived the war and was demobilised in February 1919, returning home to his wife in Caerau Road, Bridgend.

CHAPTER 14

The Field Ambulance Brigades

EVACUATION OF THE wounded to centres of treatment was vital if the soldier was to survive. Field Ambulance Brigades were established as mobile medical units situated near the front line, and comprised of men from the Royal Army Medical Corps. These brigades were attached to specific divisions, although this responsibility would naturally change in the thick of battle. Their full strength was ten officers and 224 men, although this varied under front line conditions, with a capacity for treating a maximum of 150 casualties. This was theoretical of course, as much depended on the ferocity of the fighting that ensued.

The Field Ambulance staff set up a chain of evacuation along a number of points from the Regimental Aid Posts, which were established in the front line, through the Bearer Relay Posts, which were up to 600 yards behind these, to the Advanced Dressing Station for each brigade, to the Main Dressing Station for each division.

An anonymous corporal left an account of the treatment of the wounded on the first day:

From the moment when the shell hit the ammunition behind the gun in the orchard, and woke me, to the moment when these lads reported 'all clear', it was one continuous struggle to keep pace with the stream of wounded that flowed remorselessly upon us like a tide. The Medical Officers above were so busy with the serious cases that they had to send on unexamined those who could walk; and these men came crowding in here by dozens and scores – wounded men always travel in gangs – panting with exhaustion, wild-eyed, often hysterical, sometimes speechless. Few of them had any reasonable idea as to how serious their injuries were, and it was this uncertainty that troubled them more than the pain. They looked like men who had discovered a plague spot on their skin. They watched my face anxiously while I cut off the foul dressing and examined the wound; they answered my questions tremulously; they called me 'Sir'. And when at last I told them, in a voice of delight and admiration, that it was an extraordinary lucky one; that it had just missed something extremely important and only injured something quite nugatory – inventing anatomical names if I could not remember – their relief and gratitude were pathetic.[1]

Three Field Ambulance Brigades were attached to the 38th (Welsh) Division: the 129th, 130th and 131st. The day before the attack began all ranks of the 129th Field Ambulance were posted to the Advanced Dressing Stations and Battle Aid Posts. The first casualties began to arrive at their Advanced Dressing Stations at 5 a.m. Two hours later the ambulance cars began to arrive to clear the casualties. The tramline to the Battle Aid Posts was broken by the enemy shelling and could not be used, so the stretcher-bearers were obliged to carry the wounded the full distance.

By the end of the day six, members of the 129th had suffered gunshot wounds, two of whom were to die the following day of their wounds: Private Stansbury and Private Williams.

John Henry Stansbury was 24 and was the son of Henry and Mary Stansbury of Tillicoultry, Clackmannanshire. Before the war he had been a miner with the Alloa Coal Company. Arthur Williams was 22 and had been born at the Garth Incline, Port Dinorwic, Caernarvonshire. They were both buried in Dozinghem Cemetery.

The war diary noted the change in conditions: 'Large numbers of casualties cleared during the day. Carrying becoming arduous owing to length of advance and to the

British wounded
© Imperial War Museum

broken up condition of the ground in the captured territory.'[2]

The 129th was to lose another man on 5 September when Lieutenant Arthur Gibson Dunn was killed, aged 36. His wife Ann lived with their two children at Eldon Place in Newcastle-upon-Tyne. He was buried in Cement House Cemetery. In the Newcastle Royal Grammar School Great War Memorial Roll it was noted:

> DUNN, ARTHUR GIBSON, M.D., B.S. ('95), had had a most promising career at the Medical College, Newcastle, and having qualified as M.R.C.S. and L.R.C.P. he became resident Medical Officer at the Newcastle Dispensary. After being for some time at the Northumberland War Hospital, he joined the R.A.M.C. in 1917 and was attached, as Lieutenant, to the 129th Field Ambulance. He was killed on September 5th, 1917, at Alouette Farm, near Langemarck, by a shell bursting near the dugout door. Only one hour before his almost instantaneous death he had taken the post of a Medical Officer wounded in action.[3]

The 130th (St John) Field Ambulance, which had seen such notable service at the battle for Mametz Wood the previous summer, was attached to 113th Brigade on 31 July. The wounded soon began to flood in and the Regimental Aid Post itself came under shellfire in the afternoon as the Germans launched their counterattack.

Captain Douglas Page described the conditions in the days leading up to the start of the battle:

Artillery bombardments were almost continuous up here, and our nerves soon became dreadfully jumpy. Aerial activity was great too. At nights our men were out in the open digging assembly trenches for the 'great push' which is to come off here someday. They went out with their faces and hands blackened and their feet and rifles wrapped in sandbags.

Nearly every day we got large numbers of wounded to attend to, and pass on to the Main Dressing Station by ambulance after dark, when the cars could come right up to the Canal Bank. Most nights I was never in bed and usually got my sleep in the afternoon.

Gas alarms and artillery bombardments made night hideous, and wounded trickled in all night and every night. It was a nerve-wracking life.[4]

Page also described the ground conditions leading up to 31 July and the work he undertook once the battle began:

The rain came on Sunday 29th. Soon all the roads and tracks were in a terrible state of mud and several wagons got stuck and had to be abandoned, or pulled out with extra horses and men.

Tuesday July 31st was the 'Great Day'. At 4.30 a.m. a terrific bombardment began. Every British, French and Belgian gun from the coast to Messines went full blaze. The din was terrific, and the Bosch line was a sight worth seeing. It was a mass of flame. I stood outside a dugout near the Canal Bank and watched the Hellish performance. As dawn broke one couldn't see the Pilkem Ridge for smoke. The ground trembled, and the air was filled with the shrieking and swishing of shells as they rushed along to deal death and destruction to the enemy.

I was detailed to report for duty to the Assistant Provost

Marshall at the prisoners of war cage at McMahon Farm. Here I was to attend to German wounded. Soon they came rolling in. During the day the 38th Division took about 800 prisoners, and about 300 wounded, some pretty badly.

Next day, August 1st, was very wet, and the wretched wounded were coming down soaked to the skin and covered with mud from head to foot. The attack was held up. As I only had seven wounded Germans to attend to during the day I was able to help in attending to our own wounded at Mordacq Collecting Post. August 2nd was another day of heavy rain. I helped at Robecq Loading Post all day, and also went down the 'cage' to attend a few sick and wounded Huns. My feet were painful and swollen owing to being unable to get my boots off for several days.

On August 3rd it rained all day and was cold and windy. We had lots of sick and wounded to attend to all day. It was pitiful to see the walking wounded coming down the road soaked to the skin, coated with mud and utterly exhausted. We were happily able to cheer them up a bit with hot cocoa, cigarettes, fresh dressing to their wounds, and a cheery word as we sent them off in the ambulance cars.[5]

Iron Cross from Page's diary. The caption reads: 'A fortified concrete German Pill Box captured by the 38th Division near Langemarcke. A ghastly spot mired by mud and shell holes full of filthy water and the bloated, stinking corpses of long-dead Germans.'

On 15 August the announcement was made of the award of three Military Medals to men of the 130th Field Ambulance:

Acting Sergeant Ernest Sweeting was 30 years of age when the war started. A married man with a son, he lived in Llantarnam. He had trained at Bangor Normal College and, after he was discharged from the Army, he became a teacher at Crindau Primary School. He had arrived in France on 4 December 1915.

His Military Medal citation read:

From 30 July to 5 August 1917 this NCO was in charge of an advanced stretcher-bearer party. He at once proceeded to discover a route to evacuate wounded, as the trenches allotted for this purpose had been completely destroyed. The NCO remained at duty to 5 August and showed great courage, coolness, judgment and determination, and proved himself to be a reliable leader of men.[6]

Lance Corporal David John Samuel had volunteered to help clear the Regimental Aid Posts of casualties when the German bombardment and counterattack of 1 August began.

Samuel's citation read:

From 30 July to 5 August 1917 while acting as one of the advanced stretcher-bearers, this Lance Corporal repeatedly made forages across the open, under intense shellfire to bring in wounded men, and exhibited the greatest coolness, endurance and courage and set a splendid example to all with him. He was the first to volunteer, after several days' heavy work, to clear the posts at Jolie and Stray Farms, and during the counterattack and barrage on the afternoon of 1 August, he guided stretcher squads conveying wounded, through his example and coolness, greatly encouraging other bearers.[7]

Lance Corporal William George Thomas' read:

From 30 July to 3 August 1917 while acting as one of the advanced stretcher-bearers, working from Jolie Farm to

Ernest Sweeting (standing)

Military Medal Winners.
Seated: Sgt Ernest Sweeting,
Col. John E.H. Davies, Sgt-Maj.
William Stroud. Standing:
L/Cpl William George
Thomas, L/Cpl David J.
Samuel, Pte Oliver Young,
Pte William J. Probert.

Regimental Battle Aid Post, this Lance Corporal showed conspicuous gallantry and devotion to duty in that he repeatedly made forages across the open to bring in wounded men. Under heavy enemy shellfire he worked, with but little rest, and that only at Advanced Regimental Aid Post, for 3½ days. He was one of the first always to volunteer, and showed great courage, coolness and determination.[8]

Although the 38th Division was now out of the line, the 130th Field Ambulance remained behind, running the Advanced Dressing Station facilities at Fusilier Farm and Sussex Farm. When the 38th did return to the line a new A.D.S. was set up at Cement House (Burnt Farm), close to the Pilkem-Langemark Road. This had previously been used by the Germans as an A.D.S. It was also used as a Regimental Aid Post by the Royal Field Artillery.

Sergeant Frank J. King from Ogmore Vale was awarded the Distinguished Conduct Medal. The citation read:

Wounded awaiting evacuation by ambulance

For conspicuous gallantry and devotion to duty. Learning that the medical officer in charge of an aid post had been wounded he went forward under very heavy fire, and discovered that the medical equipment had been destroyed, and that many of the stretcher-bearers were casualties. He then took up a party of bearers with fresh stores, and organised the collection of the wounded. He remained at this forward post for three days and nights, during the whole of which time he displayed exceptional gallantry and proved himself to be an able leader of men.[9]

Frank King

After the attack by 16th Welsh on 27 August, large numbers of wounded were brought to the Advanced Dressing Station as stretcher cases. They were made comfortable with food, hot drinks and blankets, and then moved on to Gallwitz Dressing Station. On 27 and 28 August the 130th, working alongside the other Field Ambulance units attached to the division – the 129th and the 131st – dealt with 213 casualties.

Private Herbert Charles Bills of the 130th died of wounds on 3 September, aged 25, and was buried in Dozinghem Military Cemetery. He had lived in Gillingham and was born in Stoke, Kent. Before the war he had worked as a hospital attendant and had been wounded in the chest and right arm on 2 September.

On 9 September Corporals William John Probert and Oliver Young were awarded the Military Medal. Young had landed in France in December 1915 and was discharged to the Reserve in January 1919. His citation read: 'He was one of a party of stretcher-bearers, working continuously from 31st July 1917 to 5th August 1917, carrying wounded from Stray Farm near Pilkem, often under heavy shellfire: he showed marked coolness and extraordinary powers of endurance.'[10]

The 131st Field Ambulance began to treat their first patients at around 6 a.m. on 31 July. From then until 12 noon on 1

August, they treated 52 British officers, 743 other ranks and 134 Germans.

For his work during this period Sergeant H.H. Dando was awarded the Military Medal, though, as the war diary noted: 'A Distinguished Conduct Medal was expected!'[11]

The war diary for 1 August read: 'A very wet day. Country is a quagmire. Very difficult for bearers to work.'[12]

Private David James Morris appears to have been the sole casualty the 131st suffered at the Third Battle of Ypres. He was killed on 31 July, aged 37, and was buried in Bard Cottage Cemetery. His wife Sophie Louisa Morris, lived at Queen Square, Aberdulais, Neath.

Private Albert John Price of the Royal Army Medical Corps served with the 55th Field Ambulance. Born in Llanfaes, Brecon, in 1884, he attended Brecon County School and after leaving was employed as a clothier's shop assistant in Tredegar. He married Mary Burch in Swansea in December 1915 and

A British soldier gives a cigarette to a wounded German
© Imperial War Museum

enlisted shortly afterwards. Sent to the Western Front in June 1917, he died of wounds at No.3 Canadian Casualty Clearing Station, Remy Siding, on 22 October, and was buried in Lijssenthoek Military Cemetery, aged 33.

The field ambulances would routinely treat wounded men of both sides and a vivid description was left of the injuries suffered by one German soldier:

> He could not have been more than sixteen, and he had been lying out in no man's land for four days in sun and shower, while barrage and counter-barrage roared over him, and the blow-flies defiled his wounds. His upper arm was smashed, and some great clod of steel had ripped through the muscle and sinew of his arm-pit, so that the bony hinge was exposed, and a mere strip of flesh held it in place. It seemed an inconceivable desecration of such a slim arm. Gangrene had set in, too, and he stank of death already. There was no reasonable hope for him.[13]

CHAPTER 15

The Welsh Victoria Cross Winners at Pilkem Ridge

THREE WELSH SOLDIERS won the Victoria Cross on the first day of the attack: Sergeant Robert Bye, 1st Battalion Welsh Guards, Corporal James Davies, 13th Battalion Royal Welsh Fusiliers and Sergeant Ivor Rees, 11th Battalion South Wales Borderers.

Sergeant Robert Bye was a miner from Penrhiwceibr in the Cynon Valley who had worked at the Deep Duffryn Colliery in Mountain Ash before enlisting in April 1915. He was 27 and the father of two boys and two girls.

The Welsh Guards formed part of the 3rd Guards Brigade which was on the left flank of the attack. They attacked from Baboon Trench at 4.28 a.m. and soon overran the initial German outposts. As they approached a small wood, known as Wood 15, they were held up by heavy fire from a blockhouse. The barrage advanced ahead of them, leaving them pinned down in shell holes.

Bye crawled from shell hole to shell hole to outflank the pillbox before throwing bombs into it through the openings. He then rejoined his men and the advance continued.

Robert Bye

Victoria Cross

As they passed Wood 16 on their left, more machine guns situated in another blockhouse opened fire. Once again Bye moved forward to attack. He tripped and fell several times, his men thinking each time that he had been wounded or killed, but he again managed to outflank the blockhouse and silenced it with Mills bombs.

In total that morning Bye accounted for over 70 Germans dead, wounded or captured. His Victoria Cross citation read:

For most conspicuous bravery. Sergeant Bye displayed the utmost courage and devotion to duty during an attack on the enemy's position. Seeing that the leading waves were being troubled by two enemy blockhouses, he, on his own initiative, rushed at one of them and put the garrison out of action. He then rejoined his company and went forward to the assault of the second objective. When the troops had gone forward to the attack on the third objective, a party was detailed to clear up a line of blockhouses which had been passed. Sergeant Bye volunteered to take charge of this party, accomplished his object, and took many prisoners. He subsequently advanced to the third objective, capturing a number of prisoners, thus rendering invaluable assistance to the assaulting companies. He displayed throughout the most remarkable initiative.[1]

Bye was the first Welsh Guardsman to be awarded the Victoria Cross. The newly-formed regiment had seen its first significant action at the Battle of Loos in 1915 and he was promoted to lance corporal in March 1916, made full corporal in September that year and Sergeant in April 1917. He survived the war and died in 1962.

221

James Llewellyn Davies had been a miner from Ogmore Vale and was 31 in 1917. On 31 July the 13th Royal Welsh Fusiliers were on the right flank of the attack as one of the leading battalions which were to attack south of the Ypres-Staden railway. Before moving into the assembly trenches he had written to his wife:

> You will see by the address that I have been made a corporal – two stripes instead of one. If I am spared I hope to be made a Sergeant soon. We are about going over. Don't vex, as I hope to go through it all right, and if I do not you will know that I died for my wife and children and for my King and country.[2]

Before the war Davies had been employed at the Wyndham Colliery. He married in March 1906 and had three sons and one daughter. He enlisted in the Royal Garrison Artillery on 12 October 1914 but had transferred to the Royal Welsh Fusiliers on 5 June 1915. Posted to Gallipoli with the 53rd (Welsh) Division, he was evacuated to a hospital in Alexandria in December 1915, suffering from enteric fever. He arrived back in Britain in January 1916 and spent the next few months in a hospital in Scotland. After recovering he was posted to the 13th Battalion R.W.F. in October 1916.

James Davies

The ground that the battalion was to attack across on 31 July 1917 had already been churned up by intensive artillery fire. Facing them were a series of German strongpoints – blockhouses and pillboxes. Some estimates put the total number facing the division as a whole at 280.

Attacking in darkness, the first attacking wave of the 13th R.W.F. crossed the German front line with little difficulty, and by 4.40

a.m. they had succeeded in taking their first objective. 'C' and 'D' Companies then pushed through the first wave to push the advance past Pilkem. Davies was a member of 'C' Company.

Near Corner House, sited at a crossroads near Pilkem, was a German pillbox which held up the advance of the 13th R.W.F. Corporal Davies moved forward alone and burst into it, bayoneting one man, capturing a second and returned to his men carrying the captured machine gun. When the attack was held up once more, Davies formed a bombing party and led them in a charge that broke the garrison of another pillbox.

By 6 a.m. they had pushed through Pilkem but were struggling to consolidate their position owing to the number of Germans still occupying the numerous shell holes in the area. Davies, by now wounded twice, stalked one of the German snipers and killed him with one shot.

Accounts as to what happened next differ. The regimental history states that Davies died of his wounds in the field after killing the sniper, but Davies' platoon commander, Second Lieutenant C.W. Coulter, wrote to Davies' widow with a different version:

> I regret to inform you that your husband Cpl Davies has died from the effects of a wound received on 31st July. He entered the attack with the others, and having passed through the most violent stage, had the ill luck to be struck by a bullet in the side. He was conveyed to hospital where all possible aid was rendered, but unfortunately he passed away next day at 6.30 p.m. Before he was wounded he did some wonderful work which consisted in capturing single-handed an enemy gun which three others had been shot down attempting to reach. The full details of this act I cannot give you. It is sufficient to say that he has been recommended for the V.C. The officers and men of the battalion regret their loss deeply, but I miss him most of all, he was easily the best NCO in the platoon.[3]

Davies was buried in Canada Farm Cemetery, near Elverdinghe, which was the location of a casualty clearing station during the battle. The official date of his death is given as 31 July, which is at odds with Coulter's version.

The citation for his Victoria Cross read:

> For most conspicuous bravery during an attack on the enemy's line, this non-commissioned officer pushed through our own barrage and single-handed attacked a machine gun emplacement, after several men had been killed in attempting to take it. He bayoneted one of the machine gun crew and brought in another man, together with the captured gun. Corporal Davies, although wounded, then led a bombing party to the assault of a defended house, and killed a sniper who was harassing his platoon. This gallant non-commissioned officer has since died of wounds received during the attack.[4]

Ivor Rees was born in Felinfoel, Carmarthenshire, in 1893 and when war broke out he was working as a crane driver at the South Wales Steel Works. He enlisted in the 11th Battalion of the South Wales Borderers in November 1914 and was promoted to corporal in December 1915. He survived the fighting at Mametz Wood but was sent home in February 1917 suffering from trench fever. By now he was a Sergeant and he spent seven weeks being treated at the Cardiff Red Cross Hospital before returning to the front.

Rees was 23 years old in 1917 and on 31 July his battalion was charged with seizing the third objective of that day's advance. The artillery barrage was moving on and the infantry were pinned down by machine guns firing from Battery Copse and in fortified positions near the railway crossing to their left. The 11th S.W.B. fought their way across the ridge and then advanced down the other side towards the Ivor Rees Steenbeek, which they reached at

10 a.m. Across the river at Au Bon Gîte, the Germans had constructed a blockhouse which was further supported by two large pillboxes. Fire from these halted the advance of the three companies of the battalion. Sergeant Rees led his platoon forward and they worked their way round to the rear of the strongpoint. He charged the last one, 20 yards ahead of his men, shot one of the defenders dead, bayoneted another and captured their machine gun. He then launched a bombing attack on the blockhouse, killing five Germans. The survivors, two officers and 30 men, surrendered.

Rees wrote home to his parents on 2 September:

> I am very pleased to say that I came out of the last 'push' quite
> safe and sound, and I have been recommended for the V.C. I hope
> I shall get it, mother. What do you say? It will mean some weeks
> leave for me, and possibly a commission in the Army. How would
> you like to see me an officer?[5]

Rees never received a commission but was promoted to Company Sergeant Major on 5 September 1917. His citation for the Victoria Cross appeared in the *London Gazette* on 14 September 1917:

> For most conspicuous bravery in attack. A hostile machine gun
> opened fire at close range, inflicting many casualties. Leading his
> platoon forward by short rushes, Sergeant Rees gradually worked
> his way round the right flank to the rear of the gun position.
> When he was about twenty yards from the machine gun he rushed
> forward towards the team, shot one and bayoneted another. He
> then bombed the large concrete emplacement killing five and
> capturing thirty prisoners of whom two were officers, in addition
> to an undamaged gun.[6]

Ivor Rees survived the war and returned to civilian life, dying at home in March 1967.

Two other Welshmen were awarded the Victoria Cross for their actions at the Third Battle of Ypres. Second Lieutenant

Frederick Birks served with the 6th Battalion of the Australian Imperial Force. Born in Buckley, Flintshire, on 31 August 1894, after leaving school he worked at the steelworks in Shotton before emigrating to Australia where he worked as a labourer and a waiter. He enlisted at Melbourne in August 1914 and was posted to 2 Field Ambulance. Birks was wounded at Gallipoli on 26 June 1915. After recovering, he was posted to the Western Front and, at Pozières, in July 1916 he won the Military Medal: 'At Pozières, France, on the 26th July 1916, L/Cpl. Birks continually led his squad of stretcher-bearers through Pozières Wood and village from the front line, many of the Regimental stretcher-bearers being out of action. He was exposed to heavy shellfire the whole time.'[7]

He was sent for officer training in February and was commissioned in May. As he was not a doctor, he had to leave the Field Ambulance and was posted to the infantry.

The 1st Australian Division took part in the Battle of Menin Road which began on 20 September. Birks was in command of 16 Platoon of 'D' Company which was in action at Glencorse Wood. It was here that he won his Victoria Cross:

For most conspicuous bravery in attack when, accompanied by only a corporal, he rushed a strong point which was holding up the advance. The corporal was wounded by a bomb, but Second

Lieutenant Birks went on by himself, killed the remainder of the enemy occupying the position and captured a machine gun. Shortly afterwards he organised a small party and attacked another strong point which was occupied by about twenty-five of the enemy, of whom many were killed and an officer and fifteen men captured. During the consolidation this officer did magnificent work in reorganising parties of other units which had been disorganised during the operations. By

Frederick Birks

his wonderful coolness and personal bravery Second Lieutenant Birks kept his men in splendid spirits throughout. He was killed at his post by a shell whilst endeavouring to extricate some of his men who had been buried by a shell.[8]

Frederick Birks was killed on 21 September and was buried in North Perth Cemetery, Zillebeke; he was 23.

Lewis Pugh Evans was born on 3 January 1881 in Abermad, Cardiganshire, the son of a barrister, Sir Gruffydd Humphrey Pugh Evans, and Lady Emilia Savi Pugh Evans. Educated at Eton and Sandhurst, he joined The Black Watch in 1899 and served in the Second Boer War in South Africa. He came from a distinguished military family, being the great-nephew of two V.C. winners in the Indian Mutiny. When the Great War began he joined the Royal Flying Corps as an observer but after a few months he rejoined The Black Watch.

He was awarded the Distinguished Service Order in 1915: 'For conspicuous gallantry and devotion to duty on June 16th, 1915, at Hooge, when, after troops had become much mixed up, he continually moved up and down the firing line under heavy fire from 10 a.m. till midnight reorganising units and bringing back their reports.'[9]

In 1917 he was appointed to command the 1st Battalion of the Lincolnshire Regiment. On 4 October 1917, near Zonnebeke, he won the Victoria Cross.

For most conspicuous bravery and leadership. Lt.-Col. Evans took his battalion in perfect order through a terrific enemy barrage, personally formed up all units, and led them to the assault. While a strong machine gun emplacement was causing casualties, and the troops were working round the flank, Lt.-Col. Evans rushed at it himself and by firing his revolver through the loophole forced the garrison to capitulate. After capturing the first objective he was severely wounded in the shoulder, but refused to be bandaged, and re-formed the troops, pointed out all future objectives, and again led his battalion forward. Again badly wounded, he nevertheless continued to command until the second objective was won, and, after consolidation, collapsed from loss of blood. As there were numerous casualties, he refused assistance, and by his own efforts ultimately reached the Dressing Station. His example of cool bravery stimulated in all ranks the highest valour and determination to win.[10]

Returning home in November 1917, thousands gave him a hero's welcome at Aberystwyth railway station.

After Evans had recovered from his wounds, he returned to duty and on 9 April 1918 he and his men came under attack during the German Spring Offensive. His conduct over three days led to the award of a bar to his D.S.O.

For conspicuous gallantry and devotion to duty in a three days' battle. On the first day he was moving about everywhere in his forward area directing operations, the next day he personally conducted a reconnaissance for a counterattack, which was carried out on the third day. It was largely due to his untiring energy and method that the enemy were checked and finally driven out of our forward system.[11]

He married Margaret Dorothea Seagrave Vaughan-Pryse-Rice on 10 October 1918 and had one child born in 1920. Margaret died suddenly in 1921 at the age of 26. He inherited the Lovesgrove Estate upon the death of his brother in 1945.

Lewis Pugh Evans

Lewis Evans retired from the Army in 1938 but returned to service at the start of the Second World War in 1939, serving as a military liaison officer at the Headquarters of the Wales Region. He achieved the rank of brigadier and, between October 1947 and January 1951, Honorary Colonel of the 16th Battalion, the Parachute Regiment.

He died of a heart attack at Paddington Station, London, on 30 November 1962, aged 81, and now lies buried in the churchyard of St Padarn's Church, Llanbadarn Fawr, in a private section which is used exclusively for burials by the Evans family, owners of the Lovesgrove Estate.

One Welshman won the Military Medal at Passchendaele and was later awarded the Victoria Cross. Sergeant Samuel George Pearse was born on 16 July 1897 in Penarth, one of five children. In 1911 his family moved to Victoria in Australia. He joined the Legion of Frontiersmen's Unit in 1911 and the Australian Army in July 1915, aged 18, and served at Gallipoli, the Battle of the Somme and at Passchendaele.

Pearse had a chequered military career: being court-martialled and reduced to the ranks after going absent without leave on several occasions; being wounded on the Somme and yet, as part of the 1st Machine Gun Battalion of the Australian Imperial Force, he won the Military Medal during the fighting around Passchendaele:

On the night of 18 September 1917, this man, while on outpost duty in a post on the western edge of Glencorse Wood East of Ypres, saw a light shine momentarily in a German post some distance in front and, after warning comrades, crept forward alone and dropped bombs into the position causing casualties to the enemy who vacated the post.[12]

He was discharged from the Army in July 1919 but joined the 45th Battalion of the Royal Fusiliers who were then ordered to Russia. The North Russian Relief Force had been formed to protect Allied supplies which were being sent to the White Russian forces then engaged in a struggle against the Russian Revolutionaries of the Red

Samuel Pearse

Army. It was during this campaign that he won the Victoria Cross. His citation read:

> For most conspicuous bravery, devotion to duty and self-sacrifice during operations against the enemy battery position north of Emtsa [north Russia] on 29th August 1919. Sergeant Pearse cut his way through the enemy barbed wire under very heavy machine gun and rifle fire and cleared a way for the troops to enter the battery position. Seeing that a blockhouse was harassing our advance and causing us casualties, he charged the blockhouse single handed, killing the occupants with bombs. This gallant non-commissioned officer met his death a minute later and it was due to him that the position was carried with so few casualties. His magnificent bravery and utter disregard for personal danger won for him the admiration of all troops.[13]

Samuel Pearse married Catherine Knox on 1 June 1919, who was at that time an ambulance driver with the Women's Army Auxililary Corps. She emigrated to Australia with the child he never met in 1920. Pearse is buried in the Obozerskaya Burial Ground in Russia. He is also commemorated on a special memorial in Archangel Allied Cemetery and on the St Cyres School Memorial, a precursor of the National School in Penarth which he attended.

CHAPTER 16

The Royal Flying Corps

BY JULY 1917 the Royal Flying Corps was emerging from the dark days of 'Bloody April' when it had suffered catastrophic losses at the hands of the German Air Service. While the R.F.C. was able to carry out good observation work for the artillery prior to 31 July, the badweather which then ensued reduced the plans for co-operation. One new air tactic was used – the bombing and strafing of enemy aerodromes prior to the German aircraft taking off. Several Welsh officers of the Royal Flying Corps were killed during the Third Battle of Ypres.

On 11 August Lieutenant David Beynon Davies, aged 30, of 52 Squadron, the son of John and Nancy Davies of Esgereinon, Cross Inn, Cardiganshire, took off at 12.40 p.m. on an artillery observation mission in an RE8 with Lieutenant Sawlor, a Canadian, as his observer. Davies had attended university and gained a B.A. before enlisting. Ray Haliburton Sawlor, who was born in Nova Scotia in 1886, was a wireless engineer before enlisting in the New Brunswick Regiment of the Canadian Army and later being attached to the Royal Flying Corps.

Their aircraft was attacked at 1.15 p.m. by *Vizerfeldwebel* Julius Buckler of *Jagdstaffel* 17 and shot down. Both men were killed. Davies was buried in Ramscappelle Road Military Cemetery; Sawlor was buried in the grave alongside.

Julius Buckler had won the Iron Cross 2nd Class as an infantryman in 1914, been severely wounded and invalided out of the Army. He volunteered for flying duties and won the Iron Class 1st Class in 1916, before being wounded four times in 1917 and a fifth time in May 1918. Surviving the war and registering 35 confirmed kills, he was also awarded the *Pour le Merite*.

The following day Second Lieutenant Griffiths Ifor Gibson died of his wounds, aged 22. He served with 6 Squadron and had previously been an officer in the 11th Battalion of the West Yorkshire Regiment (Prince of Wales' Own). He was the only son of Frederic and Mary May Gibson of 22 Llantwit Road, Treforest, in Glamorgan.

Born in Pontypridd, he had attended Colston School, Stapleton in Bristol before being articled as an architect to his father. Enlisting in August 1914 in the 5th Welsh, he had served at Gallipoli where he took part in the landing at Suvla Bay and a further eight months of fighting before being wounded by a bullet through the chest. He was invalided home but recovered to join the recruiting staff at Pontypridd. Commissioned in January 1916, he served with the British Expeditionary Force in France, and Flanders with the West Yorkshire Regiment before volunteering for the Royal Flying Corps in June 1916.

Gibson underwent training at Hendon and returned to France the following month and was wounded once more

David Davies   Julius Buckler   Griffiths Gibson

on 10 August 1917. He was the observer in an RE8, number A4293, which took off at 6.15 p.m. on an artillery patrol. His pilot, Lieutenant Pickett, survived and sent an account of what happened to Gibson's parents:

We had gone up to do a shoot rather a long way over the lines, and low clouds and bad visibility made the target very difficult to see. While we were busy we were suddenly attacked from above by nine Albatross scouts. Their machines were twice as fast as ours, and they simply made rings round us. I knew that it was useless to attempt to fly straight for even a second. I don't know how long the scrap lasted, but your son got off 100 rounds. I don't know how the machine managed to get home – the propeller, wings and engine were shot through, and so badly wrecked, that it had to be 'walked off'.[1]

The victory was claimed by *Leutnant* Ernst Hess of *Jagdstaffel* 28, who was shot down himself and killed on 23 December 1917 after 17 confirmed and four unconfirmed victories.

Pickett crash-landed the aircraft at Abeele aerodrome and Gibson was evacuated for treatment at No.3 Canadian Casualty Clearing Station but died two days later of gunshot wounds to his chest and right leg; he was buried in Lijssenthoek Military Cemetery.

Two days later, on 12 August, Captain Rodric Mathafarn Williams was reported missing. He had been flying a DH5 single-seater fighter on patrol when it was brought down north of the Houthulst Forest.

Born in 1894 in Liverpool to Welsh parents, he attended University College Wales, Aberystwyth, and served in the Officer Training Corps. He enlisted as a private in the 13th Royal Welsh Fusiliers in October 1914 and was later commissioned. Williams served in Egypt with the 2nd Battalion of the Royal Welsh Fusiliers before being struck down with pyrexia and then haematuria. He requested a transfer to the R.F.C. and, after a bout of severe diarrhoea, he was invalided home in November 1916.

Julius Schmidt

Williams had taken off from 32 Squadron's aerodrome at Droglandt at 4 p.m. and was last seen at 5.20 p.m. at around 5,000 feet over Houthulst. He was shot down by *Leutnant* Julius Schmidt of *Jagdstaffel* 3 – the 11th of his total of 15 victories. Schmidt survived the war, dying in 1944.

Four days before his death, Captain Williams had attacked two German Albatross scouts and driven one of them down to the ground, out of control.

The circumstances surrounding his death were reported in a Liverpool newspaper:

Mr. Richard Williams of Bryn Celyn, Llangoed, Anglesey, ophthalmic surgeon, formerly of Rodney-street, Liverpool, on Friday received from the War Office the following telegram: 'Regret to inform you that Captain R.M. Williams, R.F.C., reported missing August 12th. This does not necessarily mean that he is wounded or killed. Further news sent when received.'

On Saturday morning, Dr. Williams received the following letter from Major T.A. Cairnes, commanding the squadron in which Dr. Williams' son Captain R.M. Williams was engaged, dated August 13, 1917: 'Dear Sir, I very much regret to have to inform you that your son, Captain R.M. Williams is missing. He was on patrol duty yesterday and did not return. From evidence from a ground observer it is thought he attacked an enemy machine, and was in turn attacked by another, as one of our scouts – type unknown to the observer – was seen going down out of control in the afternoon. I very much fear that this was his machine, as no other was missing about this time, although, of course, it is not certain. As to his fate, I am afraid I can surmise nothing. He may have regained control lower down. He is a very great loss to me and my squadron. He was a thoroughly gallant fellow, and doing extremely well, and was universally liked and respected. I only hope he may be all right. Please accept all our sympathies in your great anxiety.'[2]

It was not until September 1919 that his burial at Veldhoek, north-east of Ypres, was confirmed but by this time the grave marker had been lost and he is commemorated on the Arras Flying Services Memorial.

John Lawrence Hughes from Swansea had been studying dentistry before the war but terminated his studies and joined the Royal West Kent Regiment. In August 1915 he was commissioned as a second lieutenant in the 17th Welsh. He served in France from May 1916, but in June 1917 he joined the R.F.C. and trained as an observer, being promoted to the rank of lieutenant and joining 25 Squadron. On 1 October his aircraft, a DH4 piloted by Second Lieutenant Charles Oliver Rayner, a Canadian, was returning from a bombing raid to Carvin when it was shot down near Burbure and both men were killed. They are buried alongside each other in Lapugnoy Military Cemetery. John Hughes was 25.

Second Lieutenant Edward Pugh Lewis from Tregynon near Newtown died on 6 October 1917, aged 20. He was serving with 9 Squadron and on an artillery observation flight when his RE8 aircraft was hit by a British shell. It was seen to come down in a spin, lost its tail at 2,500 feet and crashed near the Yser Canal one mile south-west of Pilkem.[3] Lewis and his observer, Lieutenant Hubert Granville Holt M.C., aged 23 from Manchester, were both killed. They were buried alongside each other in Mendinghem Military Cemetery.

A week later, on 13 October 1917, Second Lieutenant Thomas Penrose Heald died. He was 25 and the son of George and S.J. Heald. The family owned a wastepaper company and lived at 181 Cathedral Road in Cardiff.

Born in May 1892, by 1911 Thomas was in Ulverston with his brother learning how to make paper. He was a keen motorcyclist and in October 1914 wrote asking to enlist in the newly formed Welsh Army Corps as a motorcyclist. The proud owner of a 3.5 H.P. Rudge, he stated that he wanted to do something useful for the war effort. He may have served as 2911 Sergeant Heald in the Royal Engineers, obtaining a commission on 12 August 1917.

He took off for an artillery observation mission in an RE8 of 6 Squadron at 6.20 a.m. and was claimed to have been shot down by *Leutnant* K. Gallwitz of *Jasta* 2 at 6.42 a.m. Heald was killed but the pilot, Flight Sergeant G.W. Halstead, survived.

Thomas Heald left £116 to his widow, Sarah Jane, and £308 to his sister, Esther Mary Levers. He was buried in Ypres Reservoir Cemetery. Karl Gallwitz recorded ten victories before being injured in a crash the following year.

Captain Alwyne Travers 'Button' Loyd served with the 5th Battalion of the Buffs (East Kent Regiment) before joining the Royal Flying Corps. Born in Hawkhurst, Kent, in 1894 of Welsh parents, he was educated at Eton. He was commissioned Second Lieutenant in the East Kent Regiment

on 23 August 1914, and was granted a commission as Temporary Second Lieutenant Flying Officer on 19 June 1916. Between 7 September 1916 and 20 September 1917, Loyd claimed six 'victories' (three shared), including four during the Third Battle of Ypres. During this period he served with 25, 22 and 32 Squadrons. He entertained his fellow officer with his excellent voice for burlesquing operatic arias – male or female.

On 28 September 1917, Loyd took off on patrol at 1 p.m., flying a DH5 of 32 Squadron. His aircraft was hit either by a shell from an anti-aircraft gun or by fire from an aircraft flown

Alwyne Loyd

by *Oberleutnant* Rudolph Berthold of *Jagdstaffel* 18. He was buried in Lijssenthoek Military Cemetery, aged 23.

Peter Carpenter attended the National School at Grangetown in Cardiff where he stood out as a rugby player. He enlisted in the Royal Fusiliers in 1915 but broke his leg during a rugby game and served for a time on Home Establishment. He applied for a transfer to the R.F.C. and was posted to 45 Squadron in September 1917 after 84 hours of training.

Flying a Sopwith Camel, he recorded 24 victories, including four German Albatross aircraft during the Third Battle of Ypres. He survived the war, having flown 190 combat patrols and nine bombing raids.

Peter Carpenter was twice awarded the Military Cross. His first citation read: 'For conspicuous gallantry and devotion to duty. Within a period of the last three months he has brought down six enemy machines, four of which were observed to crash to the ground, the remaining two being shot down completely out of control. The offensive tactics pursued by this daring and skillful officer have produced most successful results.' [4]

He was awarded the bar to his M.C. just a month later:

For conspicuous gallantry and devotion to duty. He led an offensive patrol against seven of the enemy; three were destroyed. Again he

led a patrol of three machines against six of the enemy; two of them were destroyed and one driven down out of control. Later, with two other pilots, he engaged twelve hostile machines, of which three were destroyed and one driven down out of control. He shot down several machines himself.[5]

Carpenter was subsequently awarded the Distinguished Service Order:

Peter Carpenter

For conspicuous gallantry and devotion

to duty. He has destroyed nine enemy machines, and driven three down out of control. He has led forty-six offensive patrols. On one occasion twelve enemy aircraft were attacked, and on another he led two other machines against nineteen of the enemy, destroying six of them. He has at all times shown a magnificent example.[6]

Posted to the Italian front at the end of 1917, he was subsequently awarded the Italian Bronze Medal for Military Valour, rising to the rank of Flight Commander of 66 Squadron in January 1918.

Richard Aveline Maybery was born in Brecon in 1895. He was educated at Connaught House, Weymouth; Wellington College and Sandhurst, where he passed out fifth in his class. Gazetted Second Lieutenant in September 1913 in the 21st Lancers, he was promoted to Lieutenant in February 1915 and reached the rank of captain. Maybery served in India where he was seriously wounded during the fighting at Shabqadar in September 1915.

Unable to sit on a horse owing to his wound, on recovering he helped a nearby R.F.C. unit with their spotting. He transferred to the R.F.C. in 1916 and served as an observer and then a pilot. After joining 56 Squadron, he brought down an enemy machine on his first patrol in July 1917. He quickly became one of the best pilots in the squadron and during the

Third Battle of Ypres he shot down 13 enemy aircraft.

Maybery subsequently won the Military Cross and Bar. His first citation stated:

For conspicuous gallantry and devotion to duty. After attacking two aerodromes in succession at very low altitudes, and inflicting considerable damage,

Richard Maybery

he attacked and dispersed a number of mounted men and then attacked a goods train. He next attacked and shot down a hostile machine at 500 feet, and before returning attacked a passenger train. On numerous occasions he has attacked, single handed, large hostile formations and set a fine example by his gallantry and determination.[7]

The citation for his second award read:

For conspicuous gallantry and devotion to duty as leader of offensive patrols for three months, during which he personally destroyed nine enemy aeroplanes and drove down three out of control. On one occasion, having lost his patrol, he attacked a formation of eight enemy aeroplanes. One was seen to crash and two others went down, out of control, the formation being completely broken up.[8]

On 19 December 1917 he followed his last victory down and was hit by anti-aircraft fire, crashing near Bourlon Wood. His commanding officer wrote to Maybery's mother with a different story:

Your son had just crashed down his 20th Hun in flames, when his own machine was seen to be going down. It was very misty and the fighting was severe, and in the mist another German came from behind and above, and shot him down. Captain Maybery was, I think, the bravest and most dashing air fighter I have ever come across, and of course his career here has been brilliant. To this squadron his loss is a terrible blow; he was so brilliant, so popular, and always so cheerful. He set a wonderful example to the newer pilots; he was almost too brave.[9]

Another R.F.C. officer wrote: 'I don't think I ever met a man so capable – he was good at absolutely everything. He has done a tremendous lot of good in the war. I always say that he and Captain Ball and Lieutenant Rhys Davids did more harm to the morale of the German Flying Corps than any other 15 pilots we have ever had. They all, always, took on any odds – they were too brave and reckless.' The General of his Cavalry Brigade in India also wrote: 'He was one of the keenest youngsters I have ever met, and there never was a braver.[10]

Richard Maybery lies in Flesquières Hill British Cemetery.

Captain Arthur Gordon Jones-Williams scored eight victories flying Nieuport scouts with 29 Squadron in 1917, and three more with 65 Squadron in 1918. During the Third Battle of Ypres he shot down two Albatross aircraft. He had transferred from the Welsh Regiment in August 1916.

Jones-Williams won the Military Cross and bar. His first citation read: 'For conspicuous gallantry and devotion to duty. He has continuously shown the utmost dash and gallantry in attacking superior numbers of hostile machines. On one occasion he attacked twelve hostile scouts and succeeded in destroying one and driving down another.'[11]

The citation for his second award just a few months later stated: 'For conspicuous gallantry and devotion to duty when engaged in combat with hostile aircraft. On several occasions he attacked enemy formations although they were in superior numbers, fighting them in more than one instance single-handed, and showing the finest offensive spirit. He drove

Arthur Jones-Williams (left)

several machines down completely out of control, fighting until his ammunition was expended.'[12]

He survived the war and, as a squadron leader, he and Flight Lieutenant N.A. Jenkins made the first non-stop flight from England to India in 1929. A year later both men were killed when their Fairey-Napier monoplane crashed in the Atlas Mountains during a non-stop flight from England to Cape Town.

Captain Robert Leslie Chidlaw-Roberts was born in Towyn in 1896 and joined the Royal Flying Corps in May 1915 after serving with the Hampshire Regiment. He received his Royal Aero Club Aviator's Certificate in January 1916. For several months he flew combat missions over the Western Front as an observer. After flight training, he was assigned to 60 Squadron and began flying as a pilot. He shot down five enemy aircraft during the Third Battle of Ypres, and doubled his total before the war's end.

In an historic dogfight on 23 September 1917, he was almost shot down by the famous German ace Werner Voss shortly before Voss was himself shot down and killed.

He was awarded the Military Cross the following year: 'For conspicuous gallantry and devotion to duty. He constantly attacked superior numbers of enemy aeroplanes. On one occasion he repeatedly attacked five enemy machines, driving among them and attacking each in turn at short ranges. On three other occasions he brought down enemy machines. He showed great skill and courage.'[13]

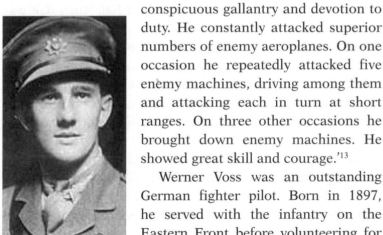

Robert Chidlaw-Roberts

Werner Voss was an outstanding German fighter pilot. Born in 1897, he served with the infantry on the Eastern Front before volunteering for the air service in August 1915. By the commencement of the Third Battle of

Werner Voss

Ypres he had shot down 34 enemy aircraft. He was killed south of Roulers having accounted for another 14.

On 23 September 1917 over the Third Ypres battlefield he attacked seven British S.E.5as, driving two to the ground and damaging the rest (including the aircraft of Chidlaw-Roberts and Maybery). However, his silvery-blue Fokker DR.1 Triplane was hit and the engine cut out. He was finally shot down by Arthur Rhys Davids.

Lieutenant Arthur Percival Foley Rhys Davids was of Welsh ancestry. Born on 26 September 1897 in south London, he was a top scholar at Eton, where he became a member of the Officer Training Corps and won a scholarship to Oxford. He reported for duty as a second lieutenant in the Royal Flying Corps Special Reserve on 28 August 1916 at Oxford. In April 1917 he joined 56 Squadron on the Western Front. On 7 May he was flying with the famous ace Albert Ball when Ball was killed. Davids' machine guns jammed and his engine cut out, but he made a forced landing and survived.

In July 1917 the announcement of his first Military Cross was made: 'For conspicuous gallantry and devotion. On many occasions he has shot down hostile machines and put others out of action, frequently pursuing to low altitudes. On all occasions his fearlessness and dash have been most marked.'[14]

Davids carried a book of poetry by William Blake with him into combat every day in case he was shot down and captured. He would confess to his mother that once in the air he became a different man and that people could not understand the nature of aerial combat. Two months after his first Military Cross he was awarded a bar:

Arthur Rhys Davids

For conspicuous gallantry and devotion to duty whilst on offensive patrols. He has in all destroyed four enemy aircraft, and driven down many others out of control. In all his combats his gallantry and skill have been most marked, and on one occasion he shot down an enemy pilot who had accounted for twenty-nine Allied machines. His offensive spirit and initiative have set a magnificent example to all.[15]

Davids was awarded the Distinguished Service Order in October 1917: 'For conspicuous gallantry and devotion to duty in bringing down nine enemy aircraft in nine weeks. He is a magnificent fighter, never failing to locate enemy aircraft and invariably attacking regardless of the numbers against him.'[16]

Twelve of his 25 victories took place in the skies above the battlefield of the Third Battle of Ypres. On 27 October 1917 his SE5 aircraft was shot down by *Leutnant* Karl Gallwitz of *Jasta Boelcke*. The Germans returned his personal effects but his grave was lost and he is commemorated on the Arras Flying Services Memorial.

CHAPTER 17

The Battle of Langemark: 16–18 August

THE 38TH DIVISION was relieved on 6 August and withdrew to Proven for rest and refitting, remaining there until 19 August. It received congratulations from the Prince of Wales, from Sir Hubert Plumer of Second Army, from General Lord Cavan of 14 Corps and from General Sir Hunter-Weston of 8 Corps. The Welsh battalions had taken over 6,100 prisoners and 25 German guns.

On 15 August the 10th (1st Rhondda) and 15th (Carmarthenshire) Welsh of 114th Brigade were sent from Proven to the reserve area. There they spent a sleepless night awaiting orders until they were moved forward on the morning of 16 August – the 10th Welsh to Marsouin Farm and the 15th Welsh to Jolie Farm, passing through the batteries of artillery guns firing the barrage on Langemark. While they awaited orders to move forward, the 10th Welsh were employed on carrying party duty, and the officers of the 15th Welsh went forward to reconnoitre the ground around the Steenbeek.

Killed during this relief was Private Reginald Jones, the son of Hopkin and Elizabeth Jones of 73 Commercial Street, Tynant, Pontypridd. Born in Pontypridd, he lived in Tonyrefail and had enlisted in Porth, Glamorgan. Aged just 18, he should not have been serving overseas with the 10th Welsh. His body could not be identified and he is commemorated on the Tyne Cot Memorial to the Missing.

Lieutenant-General Gough had planned his next attack to commence on 14 August, but heavy rain caused a postponement. He was anxious for the assault to continue, so permitted a delay of only two days. The Battle of Langemark therefore commenced at 4.45 a.m. on the morning of 16 August. The French forces on the left, supported by a heavyweight of artillery fire, achieved all their objectives. The British 20th and 29th Divisions were charged with capturing the heavily fortified village of Langemark, which they valiantly achieved but their artillery support was less successful than it had been in the taking of Pilkem Ridge. There was insufficient time to prepare properly and the fireplan was incomplete. Owing to the intense smoke over the battlefield, when the forward battalions asked for artillery fire against the enemy counterattacks these signals could not be seen. Only one spotter aircraft was employed, despite the weather conditions being favourable, and no gas shells were used against the pillboxes and strongpoints.

The 2nd South Wales Borderers moved up to the front line on the evening of 14 August. The following day there was some enemy shelling but counter-battery gas shellfire stopped this. At 9.30 p.m. the battalion followed its covering parties across the Steenbeek. 'A' and 'B' Companies were set the objective of a line halfway between the village of Wijendrift and Montmirail Farm, while 'C' and 'D' Companies in the second line were allocated an objective just past Craonne Farm.

German artillery fire commenced just before Zero Hour at 4.45 a.m. on 16 August but was ineffective and the battalion advanced through ground that was so wet that men sank in mud over their knees. The British barrage was extremely effective but the men only recognised their objective when the barrage halted. The Germans emerging from their dugouts were dealt with and a strongpoint and blockhouse were captured. For their actions here Captain Pierson and Second Lieutenant Gibbon received the Military Cross, and Lieutenant Mayger a bar to his.

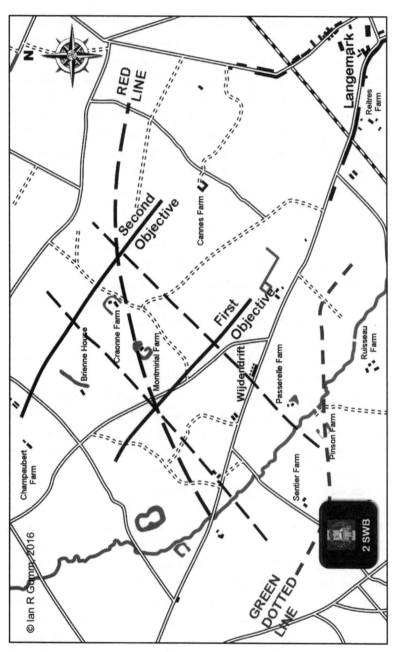

Map of the 2nd South Wales Borderers at Langemark

William Henry Maxwell Pierson was 36. From Norwood in London, he was the eldest son of John Clarence Hay Pierson and the Stuart Mary Pierson. He was educated at Rottingdean and Wellington College, and in December 1915 he returned from Brazil to enlist as a private in the Sportsmen's Battalion, Royal Fusiliers, obtaining a commission in the S.W.B. in June 1915. Pierson landed in France on 16 July 1916. The announcement of his Military Cross stated: 'He and another officer rushed an emplacement and captured its garrison single-handed.'[1] He was also awarded the Croix de Guerre.

He was killed in action at Cambrai on 21 November 1917 and buried in Marcoing British Cemetery. His brother, who served in the Royal Field Artillery and had been awarded the Distinguished Service Order, claimed his medals.

Frank James Lanham Mayger was educated at Giggleswick School and had represented Wales at hockey. He was working as a motor engineer in Sydney, Australia, when war broke out. After enlisting in the 1st Battalion of the Australian Brigade, he had boarded the troopship *Afric* on 18 October 1914. A single man of 23, whose family lived in Llandudno, he was discharged from the Australian Army on 19 April 1915. He subsequently joined the South Wales Borderers and fought at Gallipoli and on the Somme, where he won his first Military Cross. After the Third Battle of Ypres he took part in the Battle of Cambrai, where he was wounded.

He survived the war and was awarded the bar to his M.C. at Tanglin Barracks in Singapore on 21 May 1919 and the Governor read out the citation: 'For conspicuous gallantry and devotion to duty during an advance. Having reached his objective, he led a party forward and cleared a blockhouse which was still holding out, thus enabling the supporting company through. Previous to this attack he had carried out a very successful personal reconnaissance over a wide area of front.'[2]

After being discharged, he worked for the Borneo Company Limited in Penang, a mining and forestry business, and died in 1942.

Montmirial Farm was cleared and the line was consolidated. At 4 p.m. the German counterattack began. It was beaten off by a combination of artillery, rifle and machine gun fire. The casualties included seven officers and 36 men, with 127 men wounded.

The officers killed were Captains Robertson, Ross and Haydon, Lieutenant French and Second Lieutenants N.V. Evans, D.C. Phillips and Reid. Five of the officers lie in Artillery Wood Cemetery (Phillips and Evans lie next to each other) and two, French and Reid, who died of their wounds, are buried in Dozinghem Military Cemetery.

George Arthur Norris Robertson was promoted to captain on 10 March 1915 and appointed Adjutant of the 2nd Battalion in June 1915. He served at Gallipoli from September to December 1915 before proceeding to France. His medals were claimed by a Mrs Frodsham who was living in Peking, China.

Willie Ross had been Mentioned in Dispatches in May 1917.

Geoffrey Miles Haydon was 22 when he was killed. His parents lived in Midsomer Norton, Bath, and he had served in Salonika before being transferred to the Western Front.

Neville Vernon Evans was the son of the Reverend J.D. Evans of The Vicarage, Treherbert, Glamorgan, and was born

Neville Evans

in Pontypool in 1897. Educated at St John's School, Leatherhead, and Christ College, Brecon, he had enlisted on 28 August 1916 in the South Wales Borderers. Transferred to the 12th Officer Cadet Battalion on 1 December that year, he obtained a commission in the S.W.B. on April 1917 and landed in France on 28 May 1917. He was initially buried in a shell hole near Forick Farm, west of Langemark. His colonel wrote: 'He was a most promising officer; he was leading his men most gallantly when he was killed.'[3]

The Chaplain added: 'There are many officers and men who will remember his cheery manner, his encouraging smile, to the end of their days. In order to find and bring in his body, his men worked continuously under great difficulties for nearly nine hours – a tribute of affection more significant than any words could ever be.'[4]

The school magazine, *The Breconian*, printed the following tribute:

> School House, 1913–16; eldest son of the Rev. J.D. Evans, Vicar of Treherbert. Killed in action in August, 1917, while serving as 2nd Lieut. with the S.W.B. in France. He came to Brecon from Leatherhead and soon won a genuine popularity for his sterling qualities and cheery good nature. He worked his way steadily up the School and was in Va, when the time came for him to serve his country. He took a keen share in the School games and was not far from winning his place both in the XV and Hockey XI. But above all he will be remembered as 'dear old Neddy,' who was everyone's friend and nobody's enemy. He was in the ranks for some months, but then accepted the offer of a Commission, and had not been more than few weeks abroad before the last call came.[5]

In December 1917 his sister Dorothy died, and on 12 August 1918 his brother, Lance Corporal Arthur Trevor Evans, was killed, aged 22, while serving with the 4th Battalion of the Australian Infantry. After completing his formal education at King's College, Taunton, Arthur Evans had emigrated to Australia to study farming and enlisted there in October 1915. Their younger brother, Kenneth Gwynne Evans, served as a wireless operator in the Merchant Navy and survived the war.

David Charles Phillips was 22. His parents kept the Albion Inn in Llanelli. On 16 August he was in command of 'C' Company when the 2nd S.W.B. launched an assault on the German positions at Langemarck. Phillips was killed that day, leading

David Phillips' headstone

his men near Fourche Farm. He was 22 years old, and was buried by the Rev. Kenelm Swallow at Artillery Wood Cemetery, Belgium.

In the cemetery there are two small private memorial stones placed in front of the graves of soldiers. One of these is in front of his headstone. The inscription reads: '2nd Lieut. D C Phillips. In Loving Memory of our dear son and brother who died Aug 16 1917, we place this tablet. Mother, Father, Bessie, Herbie, Ethel, Eric. June 192–.' The last digit of the year is not visible as the stone has broken there.

The Hon. Ernest Aloysius French of the 2nd South Wales Borderers was 22 when he died of his wounds on 16 August, and was buried at Dozinghem Military Cemetery. He was the son of Arthur, 4th Baron De Freyne and Marie, Lady De Freyne, of 48 Queen's Gate, London; and French Park, County Roscommon, Ireland. His brothers, The Hon. Edward Fulke French, The Hon. George Philip French and Arthur Reginald, 5th Baron De Freyne, were also killed during the Great War.

John Shute Reid was also serving with the 2nd Battalion South Wales Borderers and was attached to the 8th Trench Mortar Battery. He died of his wounds on 17 August, aged 20, and is buried in Dozinghem Military Cemetery. He was the son of Major Edgar Reid (Territorial Force, Royal Army Medical Corps), of 164 St Helen's Road, Swansea. He was educated at Wells House School, Malvern, and Sedbergh School, Cumbria, where he played cricket for the First XI.

A report of his death was carried in a local newspaper:

Sec.-Lieut. John Shute Reid, South Wales Borderers, attached T.M.B., the only son of Major Edgar Reid, R.A.M.C. (T.) and Mrs.

John Reid

Reid, of St. Helens Road, Swansea, died from wounds received while leading his gun team into action on August 16th. He had only passed his 20th birthday by a few days.

Educated at Wells House, Malvern Wells, and at Sedbergh School, he obtained his commission within two days of leaving school in December 1915, and entered on his military training with a battalion of the South Wales Borderers. In November 1916 he joined another battalion at the Front, and was lately attached to a T.M.B. At Sedbergh he got his school colours in Rugby football and cricket, and was head of Sedgwick House during his last term. He also played a very strong game at golf for a boy of his age.

The officer commanding his battery writes: 'He was one of the most fearless soldiers I have ever met, and was loved by us all.'[6]

The 2nd South Wales Borderers were relieved on the night of 16/17 August but were back in the front line from 22 August to 27 August before being relieved again and entraining for the Proven area. Langemark was captured on 17 August by 20th Division and 114th Brigade was assigned to 20th Division to hold the village and part of the German trenches about 800 yards beyond it.

During 16 August the 10th Welsh and 15th Welsh were employed in carrying party duties, a difficult task given the state of the ground. At 7.40 p.m. that evening, the 15th Welsh were ordered forward and they crossed the Steenbeek. 'A', 'B' and 'D' Companies, under the command of Major Rhydderch, dug in and 'C' Company under Captain Daniel, M.C., advanced into the outskirts of Langemark.

Aneurin Rhydderch was the son and grandson of ministers of the church. He attended Aberdare County School before

Aneurin Rhydderch

studying for a degree in science at Aberystwyth College. He was commissioned into the Welsh Regiment in November 1914 and was appointed Temporary Lieutenant-Colonel while acting as commandant of a school of instruction. He arrived in France in December 1915 and fought at Mametz Wood. He was wounded in August 1917 and returned home to convalesce. Whilst there he married Lilian Pritchard in January 1918. Rhydderch was Mentioned in Dispatches in January 1917 and acted as Adjutant for the 15th Welsh. After leaving the Army in May 1918 owing to ill health, with the rank of Major, he settled in Sheffield where he worked as a metallurgist before emigrating to Australia and founding 'Quality Castings' in 1938.

James Alfred Daniel had been educated at Sandhurst and was commissioned into the 2nd Welsh Regiment in

James Daniel

September 1912. He served at the First Battle of Ypres in November 1914, as well as in Macedonia later. After joining the 15th Welsh he won the Distinguished Service Order and the Military Cross, being wounded on the Somme in August 1918. He was also Mentioned in Dispatches. During the Second World War he was the Brigadier in command of the Lucknow area in India.

German shelling had greeted their advance and it was at this stage that Captain P.H. Davies and two other ranks were killed.

Percy Hier Davies of the 17th Welsh was attached to the 15th Welsh when he was killed, aged 24. His body was lost and he is commemorated on the Tyne Cot Memorial to the Missing. He had landed in France on 28 March 1916 and was the son of Percy Llewellyn Davies and his wife Mary who lived at 75 Claude Road in Cardiff. Before the war he had been a solicitor's clerk. He left £229 to his mother, now a widow, who in the early 1920s was living at Mount Pleasant House in Kendal, Westmoreland.

Davies was the nephew of Sir Reginald Brade, the Permanent Under-Secretary for War, and had been born in Chepstow. Colonel Parkinson wrote of him: 'He was always a most cheery little man, and always had a smile ready, no matter what was going on. Your son will always be to me and to all of us an example of the most cheerful and unselfish devotion to duty at all times and in all places.'[7]

Killed alongside him were Private William Selby Hughes and Private Thomas Clee. Hughes and Clee are both commemorated on the Tyne Cot Memorial.

William Hughes, 22, the son of John Hughes of 64 Lamb Street in Swansea, had enlisted in the 14th Welsh and then

been transferred to the 15th Welsh. He had landed in France on 2 December 1915 and left £7 to his father in his will.

Thomas Clee was born in Diddlebury in Shropshire, and had enlisted in the Monmouthshire Regiment at Ludlow before being transferred to the 15th Welsh Regiment. He left £2 in his will to his father at Bishop's Castle in Shropshire.

Percy Davies

At this stage Langemark was in

Langemark in ruins

ruins, its church and château merely piles of rubble. There were German corpses strewn all around.

On 17 August Brigadier-General Thomas Marden, Lieutenant-Colonel Hayes who commanded the 14th Welsh, Captain Wilson and Captain Jones Williams, the Company Commanders, and Major E.E. Helme, Second in Command of the 15th Welsh, went to the Headquarters of 61st Brigade at Periscope House, situated on top of Pilkem Ridge. Periscope House was a small cottage with just two rooms which had been fortified with concrete to the British side, but was more lightly protected towards the German side. There were two exit doors.

When the meeting ended, Captain Parry, the Brigade-Major of 61st Brigade, Lieutenant Caskie, the Trench Mortar Battery Officer, and their two runners, left by one exit, while the others, apart from Marden, left by the other. At that moment a German shrapnel shell exploded. Both the runners were killed and all the officers apart from Lieutenant-Colonel Hayes were wounded.

Helme survived his wounds and was awarded the Distinguished Service Order in 1918. He was a pre-war Territorial who was made a staff captain in 1914. Jones-Williams was wounded again on 19 August.

During the night of 17/18 August, the 15th Welsh took over the left front line from 61st Brigade. Their charge was a series of unconnected shell holes which ran from the Ypres-Staden railway to the Langemark-Poelcappelle road. The 14th Welsh were pushed forward in support and, on 19 August, the 10th Welsh took over the right of the line, which included White Trench, with Eagle Trench still occupied by the Germans. The 16th Welsh were held in reserve across the Pilkem-Langemark road on the ground between Pilkem and the Steenbeek.

The 10th Welsh were under the command of Major Joseph Edward Crawshay Partridge, who had served with the Welsh Regiment in the Boer War. A prominent rugby player, although born in Monmouth, he had represented South Africa and the Barbarians. He was Mentioned in Dispatches during the Great War and had fought at Mametz Wood.

On 19 August Brigadier-General Marden was promoted from command of 114th Brigade to take over command of the 6th Division. He was succeeded by Brigadier-General Alexander Ramsay Harman, from Hartley Witney in Hampshire, who had commanded the 7th Battalion of the Worcestershire Regiment since November 1914. Harman had fought at the Battle of Khartoum and in the Second Boer War, and had been awarded the D.S.O. for gallantry at Ovillers, France, in

Joseph Partridge

Alexander Harman

July 1916. His citation read: 'For the excellent handling of his battalion, notably when clearing the enemy's trenches with great determination during several consecutive days.'[8]

Harman was Mentioned in Dispatches four times during the war.

The 114th Brigade held their sector of the line from 17 to 23 August. Each of its four battalions served three days in the front line. During this period the 10th Welsh lost seven other ranks killed, the 13th Welsh one officer and 23 other ranks, the 14th Welsh one officer and 12 other ranks, and the 15th Welsh 18 other ranks. The 16th Welsh of 115th Brigade lost four other ranks killed.

Among the 10th Welsh casualties was Private Francis W. Bayson of Chirbury Road, Montgomery, who had enlisted in the 3/1st Montgomery Yeomanry as a Territorial on 22 November 1915, aged 18. He was subsequently posted to the 4th Welsh (Reserve) Battalion before being transferred to the 10th Welsh on 8 August 1916 as one of the replacements for the casualties suffered by the battalion at Mametz Wood. Bayson lost his cap badge on 14 March 1917 and his pay was docked. He was gassed on 22 July 1917 but recovered to re-enter the line. Posted as missing on 20 August, his body was later identified and he was buried in Cement House Cemetery.

Private George Thomas Chadwick was another of the replacements brought in to fill the gaps in the ranks of the battalion post-Mametz Wood. He was from Rochdale and was 19 years of age when he was killed on 19 August. Probably hit by shellfire, he was never seen again and is commemorated on the Tyne Cot Memorial to the Missing, as is Private Reginald Jones from Commercial Street, Tynant, Pontypridd, who was killed on 17 August, aged 18. On the same memorial are three other soldiers of the battalion killed during this period, two of them being just 19 years of age.

Private William Duthie Grassick of the 15th Welsh was the son of the headmaster of Craigievar Public School in Aberdeenshire and was employed in the accountants' department of the Royal Insurance Company, Aberdeen, before enlisting on 9 October 1916. He served on the Western Front from 19 May 1917 and was killed in action at Langemark on 22 August. His Commanding Officer wrote: 'He fell in action on the 22nd inst., during the advance. Although he had not been with us long, yet he proved to be a brave and excellent soldier. He was always cheerful, and did his duty willingly and well.'[9]

Captain Thomas Thomas of 'C' Company of the 13th Welsh was killed in action, aged 24, on 23 August and was buried in Bard Cottage Cemetery. He was the son of John and Mary Ann Thomas, of Stradey House, Llwynhendy, Llanelli.

In the same cemetery lie two of the men of his battalion. Private George Churchill, who had enlisted in the Duke of Cornwall's Light Infantry before being posted to the 13th Welsh, was from Sydling in Dorset and died of his wounds on 18 August, leaving £11 and six shillings to his mother. Private William Henry Williams died of his wounds on the same day. Born in Weston-super-Mare, he had enlisted in the Hertfordshire Regiment as a Territorial before being transferred to the 13th Welsh. The Tyne Cot Memorial to the Missing panels commemorate the names of the other 13 men from the battalion who have no known grave.

Of the 12 other ranks of the 14th Welsh who were killed

Patrick O'Brien

during this period, eight have no known grave and are named on the Tyne Cot Memorial. One of these was Sergeant Patrick O'Brien of 'B' Company, whose parents lived in Oak Terrace, Brynhyfryd, in Swansea. Aged 26, he had won the Military Medal before he was killed on 22 August, having fought at Mametz Wood after landing with the battalion in France on 2 December 1915. Pre-war he had worked in the Cwmfelin Steel Works. The local newspaper reported his death as follows: 'An officer, in a letter, conveying the sad information, writes that deceased was a thoroughly reliable N.C.O. and a credit to the company.'[10]

The fighting around Langemark continued as a series of smaller attacks. One of the casualties was Private William John Holmes of the 10th South Wales Borderers, who was born at Crendall, near Farnham, in Surrey on 31 March 1898, and was the son of a gamekeeper. He himself was an assistant gamekeeper when he enlisted in the Royal Sussex Regiment in November 1914. Later transferred to the South Wales Borderers, he was killed on 24 August and buried at the ridge north-east of the village. The Rev. W.T. Havard, Chaplain, wrote: 'He went into action with his battalion, and, taking shelter for a moment under cover of a house during the intense hostile bombardment, he was instantly killed by shellfire, the shell striking and exploding, bringing down most of the ruined house. We recovered his body next day.' Lieut. C.A. Lundy wrote: 'Every officer and man in D Company loved and respected him, and all feel his loss keenly. I do especially, as he was in my platoon.' Sergeant G. Parsons also wrote: 'Your son was one of the very best boys in my platoon: a strong, fearless and gallant lad was he, and respected by all. I am sure it will be a great loss to his platoon and to the company.' Corporal J. Mathews also wrote: 'I lost a good little chum in him. He was a good boy, always ready to do any one of us a good turn. I may say Sergeant Parsons would never allow a man to speak rough to him, as he thought so much of him.'[11]

Holmes won a silver medal in a competition for bayonet fighting while on service in France, which he sent home to his parents only a few days before his death.

Private William Thomas Hugglestone was born in Cardiff on 17 August 1895 and educated at Crwys Road Council School before being employed at the Park Hotel, Cardiff. He enlisted on 16 January 1915 and served with the 16th Welsh. He was killed in action on 27 August during the subsidiary fighting around

William Hugglestone

Langemark. His officer wrote: 'He was a good and faithful soldier, and officers, N.C.O.s and men wish me to express their great sorrow at the loss you have sustained.'[12] He was a prominent member of the Miskin Street Chapel, Cardiff.

Also killed in action on 27 August at Langemark was Corporal Wilfred James Howells of the 16th Welsh. The son of a blacksmith from Briton Ferry, he was born on 28 September 1891 and educated at Neath Intermediate Schools before enlisting in the 38th (Welsh) Divisional Cyclists' Company on 10 October 1914. He underwent training at Llandudno and Winchester and served with the British Expeditionary Force in France and Flanders from November 1915. Howells took part in the Battle of Mametz Wood and other operations on the Somme in 1916, and won a silver medal in the musketry

competition held in France. He was shot in the head by a sniper while leading his platoon into action.

Sergeant Ernest Harold James from Roath in Cardiff was another soldier of the 16th Welsh to be killed on 27 August, aged 28. He left a widow, Florence, and a child; he is commemorated on the Tyne Cot Memorial. A member of the Roath Road Methodist Church, tribute was paid to him in his church magazine:

Ernest James

On 27th August last the 23rd of our brave 'Roamers' was killed in action at the Front, Sergeant Ernest H. James, Cardiff City Battalion, 16th Welsh Regiment. The sad news came the same week that our old friend was expected home on his second leave from France. For many years had we known Sergeant James and we can testify that he was a straight, splendid, manly fellow. With pride we followed and recorded his promotion from time to time, and took every opportunity of telling him so and cheering him on. But alas our last letter to him was posted on the very day he fell. In the old days he was a member of Mr. C.H. Thomas' Class. One of his own gallant comrades, a well-known 'Roamer' pays tribute to him, and we join with him in the touching words with which he closes. Bandsman Lance-Corporal James Chorley (16th Batt. Welsh Regt.) writes: 'I have sad news to relate as to the death of Sergeant Ernest James, a "Roamer" who was killed in our last offensive. No doubt you will have heard of it before this, but I can assure you, that he was a true, brave Soldier, who died heroically for his Country. He was greatly liked and respected by all his comrades, who miss him very much. God bless his Wife and Kiddie is our prayer from France.'[13]

The 38th Division held these positions at Langemark until 11 September, in atrocious conditions and amidst heavy German shelling. Casualties were also caused by enemy aircraft flying low over their positions and opening up their

machine guns. The captured pillboxes gave some cover, but their entrances were prime targets for enemy snipers and there was the occasional unexploded shell lying half-buried in the floor, which was often ankle deep in water.

Bunker at Pond Farm

David Williams

David Jenkin Williams of 5 Llewellyn Street, Pontygwaith, Rhondda, died of his wounds on 20 September, aged 27. After joining the Army, he underwent basic and officer training with the Inns of Court at Berkhamsted. Commissioned into the 1st Monmouthshire Regiment, he had served in France since 11 January 1917, and was attached to the 6th Battalion of the King's Shropshire Light Infantry at the time of his death. He was buried in Cement House Cemetery in Langemark. A newspaper report stated:

> Second Lieutenant David Jenkin Williams B.A., only son of the Rev. W. Williams, Sion C.M. Church, Pontygwaith, and Mrs. Williams, was killed in action on September 20 in France.
>
> The fallen officer received his elementary education at Pontygwaith Mixed School, and won a scholarship at Porth County School. Afterwards he proceeded to Cardiff University College, where he obtained his B.A. (Honours) Degree, and received another year for secondary training in education. He served for a period at Ystalyfera County School, but before was an assistant master at the Brynmawr County School. He was a brilliant scholar, and excelled in Welsh literature, and was also a fine athlete.
>
> One sister is a missionary in India and another, Miss Olwen Williams, is at Cardiff University College.

***

Private David Westacott was born in Grangetown, Cardiff, in 1882. Educated at Grange National School, he excelled at rugby and played for Cardiff R.F.C. at the age of 20, and in 1905 played against the New Zealand All Blacks in the same Glamorgan team as Richard Thomas and Johnny Williams

David Westacott

(who would both be killed at Mametz Wood in 1916). Westacott gained his only cap for Wales in the 1906 game against Ireland.

He enlisted in November 1914 at the age of 32, leaving his wife and four children. Posted to the Gloucestershire Regiment, he fought in the Battles of Aubers Ridge and Loos in 1915, and the following year at the Battle of the Somme. He was wounded in both legs in August near Guillemont and was evacuated back to Britain. After recovering, he returned to the Western Front in 1917 and was killed on 28 August at Wieltje when a German shell landed in the support trench the 6th Gloucestershire Regiment were occupying. He was buried the following day but the grave marker was lost and he is commemorated on the Tyne Cot Memorial to the Missing.

Not all the casualties during the Third Battle of Ypres were caused by the enemy. Lieutenant-Colonel James Robert Angus

James Angus

was the second-in-command of the 16th Welsh (Cardiff City). He had been Mentioned in Dispatches for his work at Mametz Wood in July 1916 for: 'Showing a fine example of leadership and disregard of danger by constantly exposing himself to fire.'[14]

After serving in the Boer War with the Grenadier Guards, he became a police office in Barry. A former member of the Glamorgan Police rugby team, he was accidentally drowned, aged 45, while bathing in the Lys Canal on 17 September 1917.

James Angus' original grave marker

By this time he was attached to the 11th Battalion of the South Wales Borderers. He was buried in Erquinghem-Lys Churchyard Extension and left a widow, Edith, who was living at Vaynor House in Treharris.

A Court of Enquiry into his death was held on 18 September 1917, Major Evan Thomas Rees of Barry being one of the members. Angus, several witnesses reported, had swum across the water with some difficulty, before resting for ten minutes and then attempting to swim back. He got into difficulties once more and went under. Three or four times rescuers dived below the surface to try to rescue him but his body was swept away before being recovered over an hour later.

CHAPTER 18

The Battle of the Menin Road Ridge: 20–25 September

By 22 August it was clear that if further progress towards the Broodseinde Ridge was to be made then the Gheluvelt Plateau would have to be taken. Sir Douglas Haig gave the task to Sir Herbert Plumer, who at Messines had demonstrated his grasp of the 'bite and hold' tactic. Haig agreed to Plumer's request for three weeks to prepare.

At the end of August Plumer submitted to Haig his plan for a step-by-step advance, insisting on an initial advance of up to 1,500 yards. This ground would then be consolidated before the next attack was begun. Opposing the British infantry were 550 German artillery guns which were in position behind the Gheluvelt Plateau. These needed to be dealt with first.

Fortunately for the British, the first three weeks of September were mostly dry and sunny which gave the ground a chance to dry out. Shells were brought forward and guns were moved to new sites to allow them to focus on the task in hand. Each objective for this attack was to be supported by 1,295 guns and howitzers which would fire the creeping barrages. In addition, 1,830 guns were allocated for the other tasks in the artillery plan. The ratio of field guns to medium/ heavy guns was 1:1.5 – the highest proportion at any stage of the war thus far. One gun/howitzer was assigned just five yards of front. Around 3,500,000 shells were allowed for the preliminary bombardment, and the same number for the first day of the attack alone. A newly designed five-line creeping barrage and huge counter-battery bombardments would make for a highly effective assault. In addition, 250 Livens Projectors were to launch flammable oil drums on the Germans in Eagle Trench.

The Livens Projector consisted of a metal pipe set in the ground at a 45-degree angle. Originally designed to fire gas shells, it had a maximum range of 1,500 metres.

The artillery bombardment began and inflicted enough damage on the enemy guns to allow the attack to take place.

Though the 38th (Welsh) Division had been relieved by 20th Division on 11 September and moved out of the front line, Welsh soldiers continued to take part in the subsequent battles which made up the Third Battle of Ypres, including the Battle of the Menin Road Ridge.

Second Lieutenant William James Williams of the 16th

Livens Projector

William Williams

Royal Welsh Fusiliers was killed while the bombardment was taking place. He was born on 26 November 1896 in Nantymoel, Glamorgan, and was an only son. Educated at Llandovery College, he was employed as a clerk with the Glamorgan County Council in Cardiff. He was commissioned in December 1916 and, after his death, his commanding officer wrote:

> W.J., as he was known to us, was one of the best of fellows, and appreciated by officers and men. He was a most promising officer and thoroughly distinguished himself during our fighting at Ypres on the 31st of July and subsequent days – it was then more than at any time that his sterling good qualities were shown. He was unassuming, but had been noted down as a good and willing young officer, and would have soon found promotion.[1]

Williams was posthumously awarded the Military Cross, the official record stating: 'On the 31st of July he took command of his company immediately his Company Officer was wounded, shortly after the commencement of the action. He rallied his men, kept them well in hand under heavy fire, and showed a splendid example of steadiness to his men throughout.'[2]

Weather conditions at Zero Hour of 5.40 a.m. on 20 September were misty, with a light drizzle falling. The tremendous artillery barrage opened up, with concentrated machine gun fire accompanying it as the infantry left their positions and advanced.

Private George Leonard Davies from Plassey Street in Penarth, serving with the 248th Company of the Machine Gun Corps, was killed on 20 September, aged 20. His body was unable to be identified later and he is commemorated on the

Tyne Cot Memorial to the Missing. Prior to the war he was employed as a pointsman at Penarth Dock. He enlisted in the Welsh Regiment and was assigned to the bombing section. Injured in the knee when a bomb exploded, he underwent two operations during a two-month stay in hospital. A third operation was suggested but he declined to have it performed and a fortnight later was sent to France as a machine gunner.

Among the battalions crossing the ground towards the well-prepared German positions was the 9th (Service) Battalion of the Welsh Regiment. The 9th Welsh was raised at Cardiff on 9 September 1914. Assigned to 58th Brigade, 19th (Western) Division, they moved to Salisbury Plain for training and thence into billets in Basingstoke in November 1914. In January 1915 they moved to Weston-super-Mare and then to Perham Down in May 1915 for final training.

The 9th Welsh landed at Boulogne in July 1915, the division concentrating near Saint-Omer. Their first action was at Pietre in a diversionary action supporting the Battle of Loos. In 1916 they were in action during the Battle of the Somme, capturing La Boisselle and being involved in the attacks on High Wood, Pozières Ridge, the Ancre Heights and the Ancre. In 1917 they were in action in the Battle of Messines.

At 5.40 a.m. on Thursday, 20 September, the 9th Welsh attacked alongside the 6th Wiltshires and the 9th Cheshires; the 9th Royal Welsh Fusiliers were in support. Heavy German fire came from the south-west of Hessian Wood, Jarrocks Farm, Pioneer House, Hollebeke Château and the railway embankment and the attack stalled. At 6.24 a.m., the advance resumed and, though the 9th Welsh were held up for a time in Hessian Wood, they pushed on to take the northern edge of it.

Major John Angel Gibbs D.S.O. was killed in action, aged 37, on 20 September, while serving with the 9th Welsh. He was buried in Kemmel Château Military Cemetery. Educated at Queen's College, Taunton, after undergoing a period of commercial training with the London and Provincial Bank

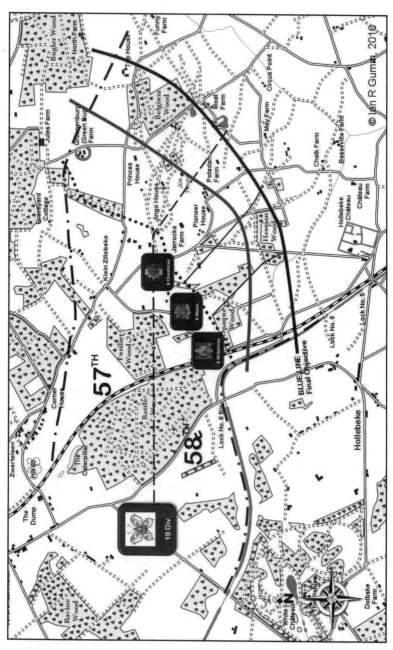

Map of the advance of the 9th Welsh at the Menin Road on 20 September

in London, he moved to Cardiff to work for Messrs. Pyman, Watson and Company, ship-owners. He later joined his brothers in the firm of Messrs. Gibbs and Company, ship-owners, of Merthyr House, Cardiff. He and his wife, the daughter of Sir Thomas Morel and Lady Morel, lived in Penarth. He was particularly fond of sport, playing hockey, cricket and football for clubs in Penarth. He was also a member of the Penarth and Southerndown golf clubs.

At the start of the war Gibbs enlisted in the Glamorgan Yeomanry, stating at the time, to a friend, that he would rather die in France than be thought of as a 'slacker'. He was transferred to the Welsh Regiment and underwent training at Kinmel Park. In 1916 he was sent to France, where he was made a lieutenant, and then a captain, before rising to major and command of the battalion. He was Mentioned in Dispatches and awarded the Distinguished Service Order for meritorious service, and in June 1917 was invested by the King at Buckingham Palace.

Four months before he was killed, he came home on sick leave, suffering from an illness he had contracted whilst in the trenches. He underwent an operation at King Edward VII's Hospital in Cardiff and endowed a bed at the hospital in the name of his only son, at the cost of a thousand guineas.

Gibbs returned to France and in his last letter to his wife, written an hour before he went over the top, he wrote: 'This will be the proudest moment of my life, as I know my battalion will live up to its reputation.'[3]

According to his grandson, Gibbs was known as 'Uncle' to the

John Gibbs

269

Llewellyn Price Jones

junior officers in the battalion. After the war his wife set up a children's home in Penarth in his name.

Second Lieutenant Llewellyn Price Jones was the son of William Price Jones and Gertrude Jones, of 12 The Parade, Barry. He was educated at Barry County School, The Cathedral School, Llandaff, and Llandovery College, and is commemorated on the Barry County School and the Llandovery College memorials. Price Jones had joined the Royal Navy and was an assistant paymaster before resigning in October 1916 to enlist in the 2/28th London Regiment. At the age of 24 he was killed in action on 20 September while serving with the 9th Welsh when attacking the German positions in Hessian Wood. His body was never recovered and he is commemorated on the Tyne Cot Memorial to the Missing.

His brother, Hugh Price Jones, had been serving in France since the early days of the war. Their father, Mr. W. Price Jones, was associated with the well-known Cardiff Docks firm of Trechmann, Carrick and Co., and had been secretary of the Barry Golf Club for a considerable period, whilst Mrs Jones had worked for the Red Cross for some time.

Frederick Jukes

Second Lieutenant Frederick Jukes of the 9th Welsh died on 20 September, aged 26. The son of George and Elizabeth Jukes of 126 Cathedral Road in Cardiff, his body could not be located and he too is commemorated on the Tyne Cot Memorial to the Missing.

Second Lieutenant John Arllwyd Jones of the same battalion also fell on the same day. He was 34, held a B.A. and was on the staff at Wrexham

County School. Jones is also among the names commemorated on the Tyne Cot Memorial. His widow Winifred lived at 56 Alexandra Street in Wrexham.

Second Lieutenant William Llewellyn Griffith of the 9th Welsh died on 22 September, aged 22. He was buried in Locre Hospice Cemetery, near Ypres, after being evacuated from the battlefield by field ambulance and dying of his wounds. Originally from Port Talbot he had lived at 12 Brookfield Terrace in Caerphilly.

Forty-nine other ranks were also killed on the first day of the attack. Among them was Company Sergeant Major James Morris. Born in Hereford, he was the adopted son of James and Elizabeth Morris of 4 King Street, Cwm, in Monmouthshire, and had enlisted at Ebbw Vale. He was presumed dead on 20 September as his body was never identified and he is commemorated on the Tyne Cot Memorial.

Morris was posthumously awarded the Distinguished Conduct Medal for his part in the fighting for Hessian Wood, and his citation read:

> For conspicuous gallantry and devotion to duty. All the officers of his company became casualties early in the attack, and he took command of the company, although wounded, and led them on to the final objective until put out of action by a second wound. His initiative and devotion to duty at a critical stage largely contributed to the success of the operations.[4]

Ernest Worth was born in 1893 and brought up in the Prescot Union Workhouse in Lancashire. By the age of 18 he was working as a labourer in a coal yard. He joined the King's (Liverpool) Regiment but was transferred to the 9th Welsh in time for the Third Battle of Ypres. He fell on 20 September and his body was lost and thus his name too is inscribed on the Tyne Cot Memorial to the Missing.

Private Arthur Ludgate's brother James had been killed at Gallipoli in August 1915 serving with the Border Regiment, aged 27. Born in Gorton, Lancashire, in 1895, Arthur had enlisted at Ashton-under-Lyne. He had served in the Royal Welsh Fusiliers, the 16th Welsh and the 115th Trench Mortar Battery before being assigned to the 9th Welsh. The 115th Light Trench Mortar Battery was formed from infantry personnel, and attached to the 115th Infantry Brigade of the 38th Welsh Division. It was responsible for manning Stokes Mortars and Ludgate would have worn a small 'flaming grenade' cloth badge on his arm to denote his status.

Arthur Ludgate was killed on 20 September, aged 22. Sadly, neither brother has a known grave; James is commemorated on the Helles Memorial and Arthur on the Tyne Cot Memorial.

Corporal George N. Games from Roath in Cardiff served with the 9th Welsh and was one of the survivors. Wounded, he wrote home from hospital in Leicester to say:

> I have great pleasure in being able to write to you once again in England. I am in a splendid hospital and am getting on all right, but I am suffering great pain with my thigh. I have a very severe

Menin Road, September 1917

wound in my right thigh, it is the size of my opened hand, but I am glad to say that there are no bones fractured and that is one good thing. During the operation I had two large tubes placed in the wound, they were exactly like two large gas tubes, but they have saved me from having my leg off. I shall never forget the day that the Offensive started, it was something terrible, one hardly can describe such a scene. I was hit just an hour after we started to advance, and there I lay for two solid hours in a shell hole, not able to move, shells bursting all around me and machine guns sweeping up the ground. I then tried to move and, with great difficulty, I succeeded in crawling to an old enemy gun emplacement where I rested for an hour and a half. All of a sudden the place was shelled and pieces of shrapnel were flying about and I was hit again but no damage done, so I trusted to Providence that I should be able to get to the dressing station which I succeeded in doing with the aid of a friend, after having a rough time in doing so. I managed to get my wound dressed and then I was moved out on a stretcher to a Casualty Clearing Station where the shrapnel was taken from the wound. I am glad that I am once again in England, and hope that I may have the pleasure of seeing you again soon.[5]

George Nash Games was born on 31 December 1891. He survived the war and married Edith Jane Yendle. They had two children during their marriage. He died 1 October 1971, at the age of 79.

In the aftermath of the action on the Menin Road Ridge, the 9th Welsh was awarded three Distinguished Service Orders, two Military Crosses, three Distinguished Conduct Medals and 12 Military Medals.

Lieutenant Dennis Kemp Bourne's D.S.O. citation appeared in *The London Gazette* on 22 March 1918:

For conspicuous gallantry and devotion to duty. He took command of his battalion and led them with conspicuous ability and fearlessness to the attack on an enemy position, and captured and held it under very heavy machine gun fire. His leadership and initiative while in command of the battalion were of the greatest value during a most critical period.[6]

Bourne was Mentioned in Dispatches on 21 December 1917.[7] He was born in Kenilworth in 1895 and educated at Lancing College. On 11 March 1915 he was commissioned as a second lieutenant in the 15th Welsh, but was transferred to the 9th Welsh with whom he landed in France on 27 September 1915. He was appointed adjutant and promoted to acting captain.

On 25 March 1918 he was shot in the right elbow and admitted to the 6th British Red Cross Hospital at Étaples before being evacuated back to England. Bourne was later appointed as Staff Captain in the Connaught Brigade. After the Armistice he volunteered for the Army of Occupation and was posted to the 53rd (Welsh) Division. By November 1920 he was working at the Herald Chambers in Carl Street, Coventry. He married Zillah Marion Rochfort Garrard in 1922 in Warwickshire. He died of typhoid at the age of 57 on 2 June 1952 at the RAF Hospital, Mauripur, Karachi 13, Pakistan.

Lieutenant I.T. Evans (5th South Wales Borderers, attached to the 9th Welsh) had landed in France on 17 July 1915. He was Mentioned in Dispatches on 14 December 1917 and was awarded the Distinguished Service Order and Military Cross. On 10 April 1918 he was wounded during the German Spring Offensive but survived the war.

Second Lieutenant Rees John Williams was Mentioned in Dispatches and awarded the D.S.O. He survived the war, being promoted to the rank of captain. His citation read:

> For conspicuous gallantry and devotion to duty. During an attack on an enemy position he took command of the whole front line. Regardless of danger, under the heaviest machine gun fire, he passed from place to place collecting his men, organising the defence, and clearing up the situation for his commanding officer. He went under heavy fire to report on the situation personally, and subsequently reorganised the whole line. His cheerful courage set an excellent example to all ranks.[8]

Military Crosses were awarded to Captain A.W. Young, the

I.T. Evans

Rees Williams

Medical Officer, and Second Lieutenant H.T. Horsfall of the 38th Trench Mortar Battery.

Alexander Waugh Young of the Royal Army Medical Corps had served in Gallipoli from 30 April 1915 until the evacuation. He lived at Fishbery Road, Boxmoor, Hertfordshire.

Herbert Trevor Horsfall was a pre-war Territorial who was born in 1893 and lived at 23 Gee Street in Hull. He rose to the rank of captain before being transferred to the 4th Welsh and survived the war.

A year after Herbert Horsfall won his Military Cross his younger brother, Laurence Joseph Horsfall, died. Born a year after his brother, before the war he was an apprentice carpenter and ship builder at the Red Cross Fishing Company, St Andrew Dock, in Hull. He enlisted in the Royal Army Medical Corps in September 1914 and was awarded the Military Medal for rescuing wounded. Taken prisoner by the Germans on 27 May 1918, he was repatriated but died on a British ambulance train on 23 September 1918, aged 24. He was buried in Terlincthun British Cemetery, Wimille, near Boulogne.

One of the other casualties of 20 September was Private Griffith Thomas of the same 38th Trench Mortar Battery as

Herbert Horsfall. From Penygroes, Llanllyfni, Caernarfon, he was 37 years of age. A bricklayer, he was married with three children. He had enlisted in the 9th Battalion of the Cheshire Regiment on 1 September 1914 and had served on the Western Front from June 1915. He was shot by an enemy sniper whilst trying to rescue a badly wounded comrade. Horsfall wrote to Thomas' widow:

> Words cannot express my appreciation of your husband's gallant conduct on that morning: cool, calm, collected under deadly fire; helping me invaluably with the guns which he took over the top. He was a hero of heroes, and what more can be said of any man? He gave his life for another, while performing an act of mercy. He was a man to be proud of, a heart of gold, and a worthy comrade of any officer or man. His loss will be felt throughout the whole battery.[9]

Distinguished Conduct Medals were awarded to Company Sergeant Major James Morris (above), Lance Corporal T.J. Green from New Tredegar and Private H. Davies.

Green's citation read:

> For conspicuous gallantry and devotion to duty. When the advance was held up by a group of enemy strong points, he led a party forward and captured them, together with two machine guns and a large number of prisoners. Later he located an enemy post, and singlehanded compelled the enemy to retire from it. He set a magnificent example to his men.[10]

Corporal Hiram Davies from Maesteg had fought at Mametz Wood a year earlier. His citation described his gallantry at the Menin Road Ridge: 'When the advance was checked by the fire of three machine guns, he at once organised and led a bombing party, which he skilfully manoeuvred to within short distance of the nest of machine guns. Shortly afterwards the advance progressed without opposition. His determined and gallant behaviour was worthy of very high praise.'[11]

During the fighting on 20 September, the 5th South Wales Borderers assisted in consolidating the new front line and digging communication trenches in their role as a Pioneer Battalion. Eight of their Lewis Guns under Lieutenant Runham were set up in Battle Wood, Ravine Wood and near the canal where they were engaged in anti-aircraft duties. They successfully brought down two German aircraft, for which Privates Hitchings and Brown were each awarded the Military Medal, and Runham the Military Cross.

Walter Keith Runham survived the war, rising to the rank of captain and winning the Military Cross and bar. He was from Hemel Hempstead and was Mentioned in Dispatches. He later practised as a solicitor in London.

During this period the 5th S.W.B. lost four men killed, and four officers and 30 men wounded.

Private Joseph Thomas Buckley was killed on 20 September. Born in Cannock Chase, he was living in Argoed, Monmouthshire, but enlisted in Basingstoke. He was buried in Perth Cemetery (China Wall), which is east of Ypres and named after a communication trench.

Wounded on the Menin Road

Lance Corporal Charles Henry Stringer and Private Michael Byrne were killed on 23 September and are buried close to each other in the same row in Spoilbank Cemetery. Stringer was 34 and was born in Caldicot, Monmouthshire. He was the husband of Mary M. Stringer, of 5 Richmond Parade, Nelson Street, Chepstow. Byrne was born in Dublin and had enlisted in St Helens, Lancashire. He had previously served with the Monmouthshire Regiment.

Private Peter Holden was born in Sheffield and was killed on 27 September, aged 28. He was buried in Bus House Cemetery, named after a nearby farm called that by the troops. He was the son of John and Margaret Holden, of 220 Savile Street, Sheffield.

Captain Ivor Thomas Evans of the battalion was temporarily attached to the 9th Welsh and took part in the attack of 20 September, where he was wounded. He led his company in the face of heavy German machine gun fire and refused treatment for his wound until the objective was taken and consolidated. He was awarded the D.S.O.

Throughout October, the 5th S.W.B. were occupied in maintaining the communication trenches in the face of enemy shelling and appalling weather. Eight other ranks were killed during this work. Two of them lie in the same row in Spoilbank Cemetery.

Andrew Hinds was 27 when he was killed on 2 October.

He was the son of Edward and Ann Hinds of Over Ross Street, Ross, in Herefordshire, and lived in Canon Street, Newport.

Just a few graves away lies Edward J. Mepham who was

Andrew Hinds

killed, aged 32, on 13 October. He lived in Nettlestead in Kent with his wife Edith and had enlisted in Maidstone.

Three Welsh Guardsmen were killed around 3 a.m. on 20 September when German shells began to fall on their positions at Eaton Camp. The three men were asleep in a dugout when it received a direct hit. The three were: Private Thomas Henry Grimshaw, Private William William Owen and Private James Newton Roberts.

Thomas Grimshaw was born and lived in Barrowford, Lancashire. He had enlisted in Nelson and was aged 34 when he died. He was survived by his widow, Effie, and three children.

William Owen's wife was named Asneth and they lived at 2 Sea View, Llandwrog, Caernarvonshire. He was 41 and had been born in Llandwrog. His regimental chaplain wrote to Asneth Owen:

September 20/17.

Dear Mrs. Owen,

It is with deep regret that I write to tell you that your Husband, Pte. W.W. Owen 3134 Welsh Guards, was killed by a shell which fell among the Bivouac as the troops were sleeping about 3 a.m. this morning. Death was instantaneous so that your Husband did not suffer any pain. The Commanding Officer wishes me to express to you his great appreciation of the way in which your Husband carried out his duties at all times, and his sympathy with you in your great loss. Your Husband was buried in a Military Cemetery, a cross with his name and regiment is being erected to his memory and a service was held at the funeral, attended by the Commanding Officer and several Officers and men of the regiment. Your Husband's personal belongings will be sent to you in due course by the authorities. For information as to the place of burial, or for a photograph of the grave, you should yourself apply to Directors of Graves Registration and Enquiries who has full particulars. May God our Heavenly Father guide and comfort you in your time of sorrow.

Yours sincerely,

G.M.S. Oldham[12]

Oldham had attended Christ Church, Oxford, and died in France in 1919.

The translation of the poem on William Owen's memorial card reads:

He was a friend to all who remembered him,
And loyal;
He did all he could without hesitation
He was strong.

An honest worker,
Was William Owen;
He was a spiritual brother
And light shone through his charming smile.[13]

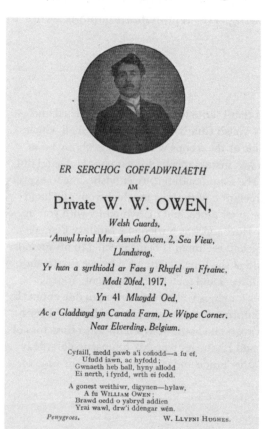

ER SERCHOG GOFFADWRIAETH

AM

Private W. W. OWEN,

Welsh Guards,

Anwyl briod Mrs. Asneth Owen, 2, Sea View,
Llandwrog,

Yr hwn a syrthiodd ar Faes y Rhyfel yn Ffrainc,
Medi 20fed, 1917,

Yn 41 Mlwydd Oed,

Ac a Gladdwyd yn Canada Farm, De Wippe Corner,
Near Elverding, Belgium.

Cyfaill, medd pawb a'i cofiodd—a fu ef,
Ufudd iawn, ac hyfodd ;
Gwnaeth heb ball, hyny allodd
Ei nerth, i fyrdd, wrth ei fodd.

A gonest weithiwr, digynen—hylaw,
A fu WILLIAM OWEN ;
Brawd oedd o ysbryd addien
Yrai wawl, drw'i ddengar wên.

Penygroes. W. LLYFNI HUGHES.

William Owen's Memorial Card

James Roberts was born in Broughton, Denbighshire, and had enlisted in Brymbo. He had arrived in France in October 1915 and before enlisting had worked as a coal cutter.

His death was reported in the local newspaper:

The death in action was announced this week of Private James Newton Roberts, son of Mr. William Roberts and Mrs. Roberts of 1 Cross-lanes, Pentre Broughton. The deceased, who joined in the early months of the war, had served several months with the Welsh Guards in France, and experienced some of the heaviest fighting on the British front. A popular lad, both in civilian life and in his battalion, his death is mourned by a large circle of friends.

His regimental chaplain writes to his mother as follows: 'Dear Mrs. Roberts – it is with the greatest regret that I write to inform you that your son, Private James N. Roberts, Welsh Guards, was killed by a shell which fell amongst the bivouacs where the troops were sleeping. Death was instantaneous. The commanding officer wishes me to express to you his great appreciation of the way in which your son carried out his duties at all times, and his deep sympathy with you in your great loss. Your son was buried in a Military Cemetery. A burial service was held, and a cross bearing his name and regiment has been erected to his memory. His funeral was attended by the Commanding Officer, several other officers, and men of his regiment. May God guide and be among you in your sorrow.'[14]

The three men are buried in adjacent graves in Canada Farm Cemetery.

During the evening of 21 September the relief by the 29th Division began and the Guards were withdrawn to the Herzeele-Proven area once more. The divisional artillery was also relieved at the same time. All its batteries had suffered severely, especially 74th Brigade. During the night of 17 September, an enemy 17-inch shell had landed near 'C' Battery and had buried the gun and its detachment without causing a single casualty. The brigade had fired over 30,000 rounds during September and had lost three officers and 32 other

German prisoners on the Menin Road, September 1917

ranks killed and wounded; six guns and five howitzers had been put out of action.

At this time a change was made in the personnel of the divisional artillery. One hundred and sixty men of 7th Bn. British West Indian Regiment arrived to replace the gunners when they went out of the line. These men were employed in salvage work and in collecting materials, as well as bringing up ammunition.

***

Welshmen also served with other regiments during this battle. Private Arthur Worthy Boobyer was killed during this period while serving with the 2/5th Battalion of the Lancashire Fusiliers. Born in Nantymoel, Glamorgan, in 1888, he was employed as a clerk at the Co-operative Stores, Ogmore Vale, and living in Bridgend before enlisting. He had last answered roll call on 19 September and was found dead some days

Arthur Boobyer

later in a shell hole. Boobyer had previously been wounded on two occasions, the first time being nearly buried by the explosion of a German shell and being so severely bruised that he was in hospital for some time; the second time he was injured in the thumb by a piece of shrapnel. He left a widow and a child.

The 2/5th Lancashire Fusiliers had lost over 50 per cent of their strength in an attack on the German lines south-east of Saint-Julien on 20 September. Though his body was recovered, his grave was subsequently lost and he is remembered on the Tyne Cot Memorial to the Missing.

Private Frederick May, originally from Cardiff, served with the Australian Light Horse after he joined up early in 1915 and was at Gallipoli for nine months, during which time he was shell shocked and contracted enteric fever. He was transferred to England and thence posted to France.

During the Battle of Pozières on the Somme in 1916, May was one of a bombing party in company with a lieutenant and a corporal. After descending into a German dugout which

they had bombed, they found at the far end of the dugout 64 Germans in hiding and these were taken prisoner. Private May was to have been recommended for the Military Medal but both corporal and lieutenant were killed before

Frederick May

his brave deed had been notified. Wounded by shellfire, he was evacuated to England but returned to France in April 1917.

On 20 September, he was part of the 20th Battalion of the 2nd Australian Division. At 5.40 a.m., the battalion was in the first attacking wave and soon met resistance from Germans sited in a line of old concrete artillery shelters. Frederick May was killed, aged 24, along with four other men by an enemy shell. He was buried in Birr Cross Roads Cemetery.

The Battle of the Menin Road continued until 25 September with the Germans launching ferocious counterattacks. The tactic of 'bite and hold' had proved successful, albeit that it had resulted in approximately 21,000 Allied casualties.

CHAPTER 19

The Battle of Polygon Wood: 26 September to 3 October

THE PLAN FOR this phase of the Third Battle of Ypres was that the 33rd Division would cover the right of the 5th Australian Division as they advanced through the remainder of Polygon Wood but, at 5.15 a.m. on 25 September, the Germans launched a counterattack along the whole front from the Menin Road to Polygon Wood. A feature of this battlefield was the German defensive position known as the 'Quadrilateral', which was to the south of the Menin Road. Despite being the subject of a heavy bombardment, the enemy were so deep underground that they took few casualties.

On that day the 2nd Battalion of the Royal Welsh Fusiliers marched to the south of Ypres to the area of Shrapnel Corner. At 8 p.m. that evening, they moved through Sanctuary Wood to Stirling Castle, arriving there after midnight. At 10 a.m. on 26 September, the 2nd R.W.F. crossed the Menin Road, advancing behind a creeping barrage. Enemy machine gun fire opened up when they were near Blackwatch Corner from a crescent-shaped line of concrete pillboxes.

Captain John Charles Mann, the Adjutant of the 2nd Battalion, was shot through the throat and died almost immediately. He was 23 and his parents lived in Sutton in Surrey, his father being an accountant. Educated at Bedford Grammar School, Mann was a member of the Officer Training

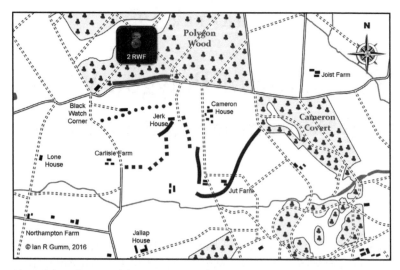

Map of the advance of the 2nd Royal Welsh Fusiliers at Polygon Wood on 26–27 September

Corps for three years. After leaving school he was employed as a clerk. Enlisting in the London Rifle Brigade on 7 August 1914, he was subsequently sent to France in November of that year and received his commission in the 2nd Royal Welsh Fusiliers in September 1915, becoming Acting Adjutant in December. He was awarded the Military Cross in January 1917 for his conduct during the Battle of the Somme, and was hospitalised in May 1917 after taking part in the Battle of Arras. Posthumously Mentioned in Dispatches in December 1917, his body could not be located after the battle and the Tyne Cot Memorial to the Missing bears his name.

His brother, Second Lieutenant Robert Leonard Mann, had been killed in October 1916, aged 19. He served with the 3rd R.W.F. but was attached to the 16th Battalion at the time of his death. Robert Mann was buried in Essex Farm Cemetery.

Captain Ernest Coster died on the same day. He was 34 and had married Marjorie Alice Burrell in June 1916. During the advance he was shot through the head whilst entering an orchard north of Jerk Farm. He was awarded the Military

Cross and is commemorated on the Tyne Cot Memorial. Coster, a musician and vocalist, is pictured here in the middle of the back row of the group. Lieutenant Ralph Charles Johnstone Greaves, on the left, was a brilliant pianist who had studied with Ralph Vaughan Williams. He was wounded by a grenade and lost an arm at Arras on 23 April. In the front is Lieutenant Thomas Conning who was killed four days later. Siegfried Sassoon is the officer on the right of the back row. This photograph was taken earlier in the month, the morning after the four had enjoyed an evening out at the Godbert Restaurant in Amiens.

The battalion was then held up in front of a wooded slope near Polderhoek Château by heavy enemy fire. The living took cover amongst the dead lying in shell holes.

The most senior officer killed during this advance was Major Roger Alvin Poore. He was 47 years old and had been awarded the Distinguished Service Order. His widow lived at Fernyhurst, Rownhams, in Hampshire. Poore had been sitting in a shell hole conferring with Second Lieutenant Casson, the Assistant Adjutant, and Second Lieutenant Colquhoun,

John Mann

Four officers: Ralph Greaves, Ernest Coster, Siegfried Sassoon and Thomas Conning (seated)

about 250 yards behind Polygon Wood when a German shell fell, killing all three men.

Poore was educated at Sherborne School where he played in the rugby and cricket teams, as well as boxing. He attended Hertford College, Oxford, before following his father into the Army and fighting in the Boer War, where he was Mentioned in Dispatches and awarded the D.S.O. He was buried in Poelcappelle British Cemetery.

His colonel wrote to Mrs Poore:

> There is one thing that you will hear with pride, and that is that the battalion under your husband's command behaved most gallantly in the action and has covered itself with glory. Your husband had endeared himself to everybody in the battalion, and his loss will be most acutely felt. He had helped and supported me most loyally; indeed, I do not know how I will get on without his wise advice. He was one of the most gallant gentlemen I have ever met.[1]

Poore was also described thus: 'He was a very big man, about fifty years of age, slightly deaf, and his favourite expression was "What, what!" He was a very decent officer.'[2]

Second Lieutenant Randal Alexander Casson was buried in the same cemetery as Poore. He was 24 and the only child of Randal and Lucy Casson of Bron-y-Garth, Porthmadog, and of Betchton House, Cheshire, though he was born in Chelsea. His father was a solicitor in Porthmadog with the firm of Breese, Jones and Casson (to whom the young David Lloyd George was articled). He was educated at Winchester College and later at Christ Church, Oxford. He obtained a commission in the Royal Welsh Fusiliers in 1915, later being promoted to Assistant Adjutant. His cousin was Sir Lewis Casson, the famous actor, and husband of Dame Sybil Thorndike, the noted actress.

A vignette of Casson was written in Frank Richards' famous autobiography, *Old Soldiers Never Die*:

Roger Poore

Randal Casson

A tall, slender young lieutenant who had just returned from leave
was made Assistant Adjutant for the show. I believe he was given
that job because he was an excellent map-reader... Mr. Casson was
said to be a first-class pianist, but trench warfare did not give him
much opportunity to show his skill at that. If he was as good a
pianist as he was a cool soldier, he must have been a treat to hear.[3]

Second Lieutenant Ernest Forbes Campbell Colquhoun
was 28 and from Clathick, Perthshire. He had emigrated to
Rhodesia but travelled back to Britain to enlist. The three
men lie side by side in Poelcappelle British Cemetery.

Acting Captain Norman Harold Radford received the
Military Cross in 1916 and the French Croix de Guerre a
year later. Owing to the heavy casualties on 26 September, he
assumed command of the battalion for the following few days
and was awarded the Distinguished Service Order. His citation
stated: 'For conspicuous gallantry and devotion to duty. On
two occasions he took command of his battalion when the

commanding officers became casualties, and displayed the greatest ability and courage under heavy fire throughout the operations. He contributed largely to the success achieved.'[4]

Norman Radford was born on 10 May 1891, the son of William Harold and Annie Radford, and survived the war.

Also killed in action on 26 September was Sergeant Ernest Courtney. Born in Roath in Cardiff, he enlisted in the 2nd R.W.F. in 1907, aged 18, giving his occupation as that of a labourer, and served in India for three years from 1911 until he was discharged to the Reserve in February 1914. Mobilised at Wrexham on 5 August 1914, he landed in France a week later. He was promoted to corporal in the field in August 1915 and made Sergeant in March 1916. On 25 July 1916 he was shot in the chest and thigh and invalided back to England to recover. Awarded the Military Medal in October 1916, he returned to France in June 1917. He was buried in Tyne Cot Cemetery.

Thomas Jones was a brickyard labourer in Rhyl when he was called up in March 1916, aged 35. He had been born in the town and lived with Matilda, the mother of his three young children, at Tynewydd Terrace in Rhyl. He stated his preference to join a naval battalion but was instead posted to the Royal Welsh Fusiliers and sent to Kinmel Park Camp. He said that he had previously had training in the Royal Engineers, so his training was foreshortened and he landed in France in July 1916. Prior to this he had delayed his return to camp on 6 June to marry Matilda, for which he received the punishment of three days confined to barracks. Later that same month he went absent without leave for five days and, on his return, was punished by being given 168 hours' detention and forfeiting 13 days' pay. He was killed on 26 September 1917 and is commemorated on the Tyne Cot Memorial to the Missing.

Private Arthur Mules was born in 1891 in Maughan Terrace, Penarth, and later worked as a coal tipper at Penarth Dock. When his half-sister Amy lost her husband and was left with

Arthur Mules

six children, Arthur moved in with her to provide financial support for the family. He volunteered for the Army in December 1915 and was posted to the 2nd Royal Welsh Fusiliers on 14 June 1917.

Arthur Mules was shot and killed on 26 September near Polderhoek Château. Amy Martin was named as his next of kin and Lieutenant T.H. Williamson wrote to her later:

British Expeditionary Force. 1st October 1917.

I regret to have to tell you that your brother, Private A. Mules, was killed in action on the 26th September during a successful attack by his battalion on that date. He was sniped, and his death was painless and instantaneous. He had been in my platoon since he joined the battalion in France, and I have always found him a very brave and willing soldier.

I and my platoon wish to send you their sincere sympathies. He will be very much missed by all who knew him. I hope it will give you some consolation to know that he died while taking part in one of the biggest battles of the campaign, and it is he and his comrades who made the great sacrifice that we have to thank for such a great victory.[5]

Also killed in action on that day was Allan Lloyd, who had enlisted at Llandrindod Wells in May 1915, aged 27. His preference was to serve in the Royal Army Medical Corps, but instead he was posted to the Royal Welsh Fusiliers. His occupation was that of a stoker and he was married to Alice; they had no children.

After training, he embarked on the SS *Princess Victoria*

from Southampton on 11 October 1915 and joined the 2nd Battalion R.W.F. in France on 15 October. He was appointed lance corporal in May 1917 and two months later notification of his award of the Military Medal appeared in *The London Gazette*. Lloyd was granted home leave from 7 September to 17 September, and died nine days after returning to the Front. His belongings were returned to his wife: a purse, his Military Medal ribbon, a notebook and pencil, a linen bag, two books of Psalms, a photograph, an identity disc and a distinguished conduct card. Allan Lloyd's body was unable to be identified and he is commemorated on the Tyne Cot Memorial.

William Norman Walker of 71 Woodhouse Street, Walton, Liverpool was an insurance clerk who had enlisted in the Royal Welsh Fusiliers in November 1915, aged 24. He lived with his cousin, Elsie, and his younger sister, Emily. He and Emily had been orphans since 1911. He was posted to the 3rd Battalion and was promoted to lance corporal in June 1916 and corporal six weeks later. However, later in August 1916, he was reprimanded for exchanging regimental duties without permission. A week afterwards he was admitted to hospital with severe eczema and spent the next 30 days undergoing treatment. He married his cousin Elsie on 24 April 1917 but his period of service in Britain ended when he disembarked in France on 15 August 1917 and was posted to the 2nd Battalion, reverting to the rank of private. When he was killed in action on 26 September 1917, his possessions were returned to his widow. They consisted of his wallet, some letters and photographs, and a knife.

On 21 November 1917, the Reverend A. Abraham of St Mary's Church, Anfield Road, Liverpool, wrote to the Infantry Records Office:

> I am writing on behalf of Mrs. Walker in reference to the official notice of her husband's death. The notice runs as follows 'On the 26th Sept. 1917 or shortly after, the report is to the effect that he was killed in action or died of wounds.' You will I am sure recognise that this is very indefinite, had it said 'killed in action

on the 26th Sept. or shortly after' that could have been understood but when the report says 'killed in action or died of wounds' on or about the date given, then the doubt remains as to whether he is dead. This uncertainty has been further emphasised by the fact that whilst at the Post Office drawing her allotment she overheard a woman say that she had found her husband after twelve months in Warrington Hospital and that there were many more there in the same condition viz. loss of memory. Do you know if there are any of the R.W.F. in hospital in that condition, and would it be possible for Mrs. Walker to visit the hospitals at Warrington or others near here to see if her husband was there. I am sorry to trouble you but you will understand Mrs. Walker's anxiety, and I shall be glad if you can help her.[6]

Sadly, a reply was received a week later stating that the initial report was correct.

Further correspondence ensued in December 1917 between the Liverpool Local War Pensions Committee and the Officer in Charge of Infantry Records, Shrewsbury, as to whether Emily had been a dependent of William's before he enlisted. The pension for both Elsie and Emily was eventually awarded on 23 January 1919. William Walker is commemorated on the Tyne Cot Memorial to the Missing.

Captain E. Howell Evans of the 2nd R.W.F. was struck on the helmet by a bullet in Polygon Wood but survived. From Aberdare, he had enlisted in the Pembroke Yeomanry in October 1914 and served in Egypt before being commissioned into the R.W.F. in March 1917. The following year he was promoted to captain and won the Military Cross. His citation read:

During the attack on the south-eastern outskirts of Englefontaine and Forêt de Mormal, on the 4th November 1918, he was commanding a company, and showed marked gallantry and skill throughout those operations. Under the heaviest machine gun fire and trench mortar fire he led his company successfully from the kicking off point to the final objective, capturing many machine guns.[7]

Harry Essery was born illegitimately in Barnstaple in 1894. His mother moved to Penarth and married a James Hookway and started another family. He joined the Royal Field Artillery in September 1914, aged 19, after working as a shop assistant, and served in Salonika before being transferred to the Western Front. Harry Essery was wounded on 26 September and died shortly afterwards. His personal effects were his pocket book, his wristwatch and pipe, some letters and cards, a match box cover and some photos. He was buried in the Divisional Collecting Post Cemetery and Extension.

His half-brother, Eddy Hookway, was just 15 when he enlisted with the 15th Battalion of the Royal Welsh Fusiliers. He took part in two fierce battles at Gallipoli with the 8th R.W.F. before he was 17, but he should not have served abroad before he was 19. Before the war he had worked at the golf course in Penarth. He had been killed on 4 August in the fighting around Pilkem Ridge. Reporting his death, his obituary stated: 'About the time Pte. Hookway died, his mother (Mary) dreamt he had been shot in the shoulder and killed.'[8]

His body was never found and he is commemorated on the Menin Gate Memorial to the Missing.

Harry Essery   Eddy Hookway

On 27 September the companies of the 2nd R.W.F. advanced again and an hour later had captured Jut Farm, taking 14 prisoners, and occupied a line of shell holes along the Reutelbeek, facing Polderhoek Château and the Reutelbeek Spur. The battalion was relieved that night. During the two days they had been in action, seven officers and 31 other ranks had been killed, and three officers and 122 other ranks had been wounded, with 27 other ranks missing.

Company Sergeant Major Victor Wallace Ward was awarded the Distinguished Conduct Medal for his actions at Polygon Wood on 26 and 27 September. His citation read:

> For conspicuous gallantry and devotion to duty. He took command of his company when all the officers were casualties. Later in the day, when the supply of ammunition in the front line gave out, by his personal example and influence he held his position until the arrival of a fresh supply. His courage and example were undoubtedly responsible for maintaining the front-line position.[9]

Ward was from Blackpool and had enlisted aged 18 in 1899. He served in China and India before being wounded in 1914. Mentioned in Dispatches in April 1917, he was commissioned as a second lieutenant in March 1918. He survived the war.

Another gallantry medal winner of this action was Sergeant Ernest C. Troman of the 2nd R.W.F. who was awarded the Military Medal for his courage at Polygon Wood. He had been born in Birmingham and brought up in Sir Josiah Mason's

Victor Ward (left)

Orphanage. In 1918 he was awarded the Distinguished Conduct Medal. His citation for this read:

> For exceptional good work as platoon commander during the last seven months. He has at all times displayed great courage and initiative, and has set a very fine example to the remainder of his men whenever his platoon has been in action. During the operations north of Albert on the night of 23rd/24th August 1918, he led his platoon against an enemy machine gun post with great skill and determination, and succeeded in capturing the post.[10]

Ernest Troman had joined the Army in 1905; he landed in France on 13 August 1914 and fought at Mons. He survived the war and was discharged in 1920.

On 29 September the 2nd South Wales Borderers came back into the line after nearly a month in rest and having received substantial reinforcements. During this period General La Cappelle of the French Army presented the Croix de Guerre to Major Garnett, Captain Pierson (see page 247), Sergeant Mason and Private Swift.

Harold Gwyer Garnett was killed on 3 December 1917, aged 38, during the Battle of Cambrai and is commemorated on the Cambrai Memorial, Louverval. The son of a J.P. from Liverpool, he had enlisted in 1914 and had been wounded with

the 1st S.W.B. at Givenchy in December 1914. He was wicketkeeper for Lancashire Cricket Club and also played for Argentina. In 152 first-class cricket matches, he scored 5,798 runs and made 203 dismissals.

His obituary in *Wisden* read:

Harold Garnett

Garnett will be remembered as a distinguished member of the Lancashire eleven. Tried twice for his County towards the end of the season of 1900, he jumped into fame the following year, playing so finely that he seemed likely to become the best left-handed bat in England. His style was attractive and his hitting very brilliant. Against Sussex at Manchester he scored 110 and 89, and in two other matches – against Leicestershire at Leicester and Middlesex at Lords – he made over a hundred, his scores being 139 and 114. As the result of his season's work he came out second to Tyldesley in the Lancashire averages. On the strength of this performance he was chosen to go to Australia with Mr. McLaren's team, but he failed, doing next to nothing during the tour. He was so obviously out of form that he was given few chances. For several seasons, till business took him to the Argentine, Garnett batted exceedingly well for Lancashire, but he never quite equalled his efforts in 1901. Returning to England in 1911 and again in 1914 he renewed his connection with the Lancashire eleven. In 1914 he had developed into a first rate wicket-keeper, and strictly on his merits he was picked for Gentlemen v. Players at Lords. He proved fully worthy of the distinction, and had no small share in winning the match. The way in which he stumped Hitch in the Players' second innings would have been wonderful even if done by Blackham at his best. Garnett volunteered at the outbreak of the War, and soon obtained a commission.[11]

Harry Leslie Mason had joined the 10th East Yorkshire Regiment in September 1914, landing in Egypt in December 1915. He was wounded in 1916 and transferred to the 2nd S.W.B. in March 1917. He was awarded the Military Medal for his actions on 16 August 1917 and later won a bar.

Thomas Edward Swift had enlisted in Sheffield in February 1916 in the York and Lancaster Regiment. Born in Pitsmoor in Sheffield in 1898, he was employed as a clerk. He rose to the rank of corporal and won the Military Medal and bar. Shot in the leg in October 1918, he was discharged in February 1919, afterwards applying for a pension on the grounds of a tubercle of the lung attributable to his military service.

The soldiers of the 2nd South Wales Borderers were situated

around Craonne, Cannes, Montmirail and Denain Farms. They were in the front line for four days, during which time they were intermittently shelled. Second Lieutenant Joyce was a casualty on 29 September.

Frederick George Joyce was 33 and from Dublin. The son of Stephen and Marie Flora Joyce, of 85 Boulevard Militaire, Brussels, Belgium, his four brothers all served in the war. Joyce was commissioned on 22 January 1916. He was buried in Artillery Wood Cemetery.

The Battle of Polygon Wood ended on 3 October but the battalion was back in the line on 4/5 October, taking over a section of the new front which stretched from Japan House on the left to 19-Metre Hill. The ground was unknown, so a patrol was sent out to reconnoitre during the night. Second Lieutenant Lowe was killed by enemy shelling and his body was lost.

Arthur Denis Worsley Lowe had been awarded the Military Cross for his actions on 27 January 1917. His citation read: 'For conspicuous gallantry and devotion to duty. When the attack was temporarily held up by machine gun fire, he led his party to this place and successfully bombed the enemy gun team, thus enabling the attack to push on. Later, he himself captured six prisoners.'[12]

His death was reported in the local newspaper:

Arthur Lowe's medals and plaque

Second Lieut. Denis Worsley Lowe, South Wales Borderers, elder son of Mr. and Mrs. Worsley Lowe of The Plas, Dolwyddelan, previously reported missing, is now reported killed. He had seen much fighting on the Western Front, and had been wounded two or three times. His younger brother Lieut. G.W. Lowe, Royal Welsh Fusiliers, was severely wounded in April last year.[13]

Lying next to each other in Bleuet Farm Cemetery are Corporal Holloway and Private Griffiths. Two graves away lies Private Stevens.

Griffiths and Stevens were killed on 5 October. D.G. Griffiths was the son of Robert Lewis Griffiths and Ellen Griffiths, of 3 Water St., Abergwynolwyn, Towyn, Merioneth. He was 27. Tom Alban Stevens was born in Risca and enlisted in Abertillery. He was 20 and the son of Arthur John and Emily Stevens, of 38 Grove Road, Risca.

Arthur Frederick Holloway was born in Deptford, London. He was a pre-war Regular who, on 23 September 1914 landed at Lao Shan Bay in China, and took part in the attack on the German territory of Tsingtao. In April 1915 he landed at Cape Helles and took part in the Gallipoli campaign. In March 1916 the battalion landed at Marseilles. He had been awarded the Military Medal.

The 2nd S.W.B. spent the period from 5 to 8 October in the line until being relieved and leaving the Salient for the last time. During October they lost two officers and 12 other ranks killed or missing, and one officer and 50 men wounded.

While the 2nd Royal Welsh Fusiliers were in action at Polygon Wood, the 10th Royal Welsh Fusiliers were part of the force attacking towards Zonnebeke.

The 10th Battalion had spent ten days training on the area of the old Somme battlefield. Here they practised assembling at night on taped positions and attacking strongpoints during the daytime. After moving to Watou on 17 September, they further rehearsed the attack at Brandhoek on 23 September. On the night of 25 September they passed through Ypres and moved forward along duckboard tracks until they reached the line of shell holes that constituted their starting positions.

The 10th R.W.F. was ordered to advance through the leading battalions when they reached the first objective, the Green Line, and press on to capture the village of Zonnebeke.

The attack began in a heavy ground mist at 5.50 a.m. on 26 September. The Green Line was soon occupied and the battalion was ordered forward. The soldiers had difficulty crossing the Zonnebeke as they met heavy machine gun fire coming from Zonnebeke Station. The company on the right under Captain A.W. Fish reached the centre of Zonnebeke village and entered the church but, by this stage, Fish had only 14 men of his company with him. On the left the advance was held up 200 yards short of the station. The following afternoon an attempt was made by the enemy to wrest Zonnebeke Church from Fish's party but it proved unsuccessful.

The ground between the two flanks of the battalion was a swamp and the ground in general was so wet that it severely hindered the progress of the troops. The men now dug in amidst the shell holes and awaited the German counterattack. This commenced at 2.30 p.m. but was driven off. A second, much heavier, enemy attack was launched at 6.35 p.m. On the right it was stopped by artillery and rifle fire, but on the left it was more successful, and the men of the 10th R.W.F. were forced to retire.

The Commanding Officer, Lieutenant-Colonel Compton Smith, was suffering from shell shock and Major A.J.S. James assumed command.

Geoffrey Lee Compton Smith was born in 1889 in Kensington. He was six times Mentioned in Dispatches in 1917 and twice wounded. He was awarded the Distinguished Service Order and French Légion d'honneur. The citation for his D.S.O. read:

> For conspicuous gallantry and devotion to duty. He commanded his battalion with the greatest skill and determination.

Immediately the objective was gained he moved forward to supervise consolidation and cover the advance of another brigade. Although wounded, he remained in the position, and his personal example was of the utmost value to all.[14]

After the war he served with the 2nd Royal Welsh Fusiliers in Ireland. He was captured by the I.R.A. on 16 April 1921, about a mile from Blarney, County Cork while on a sketching trip and was held hostage for four members of the I.R.A. who were due to be executed later that month. When the four men were executed he was taken to Barracharing Wood and shot in the forehead.

His captors allowed him to send two letters before he was executed. These were found after a raid on one of Michael Collins' offices in Mary Street in Dublin. The first letter was to his wife and read:

I am to be shot in an hour's time. Dearest, your hubby will die with your name on his lips, your face before his eyes, and he will die like an Englishman and a Soldier. I cannot tell you sweetheart how much it is to me to leave you alone – nor how little to me personally to die – I have no fear, only the utmost, greatest and tenderest love to you, and my sweet little Anne. I leave my cigarette case to the Regiment, my miniature medals to my father – whom I have implored to befriend you in everything – and my watch to the officer who is executing me because I believe him to be a

gentleman and to mark the fact that I bear him no malice for carrying out what he sincerely believes to be his duty. Goodbye, my darling, my own. Choose from among my things some object which you would particularly keep in memory of me, and I believe that my spirit will be in it to love and comfort you. Tender, tender farewells and kisses... your own Geof.[15]

Geoffrey Compton Smith

The second letter he sent was to his Regiment and read:

Dear Royal Welsh Fusiliers, – I am to be shot in an hour's time. I should ask you fellows to know that the sentence has been passed on me (two lines erased here) and that I intend to die like a Welsh Fusilier, with a laugh and forgiveness for those who are carrying out the deed. I should like my death to lessen rather than increase the bitterness which exists between England and Ireland. I have been treated with great kindness, and during my captivity have learned to regard the Sinn Feiners rather as mistaken idealists than as a murder gang. My cigarette case I leave to the mess. I carried it with the Regiment throughout the War, and shall die with it in my pocket. God bless you all comrades.[16]

The situation on 26 September was now critical – some men had just five rounds of ammunition left. Had the Germans pressed home their attacks, the line would have collapsed, but the night passed quietly except for a fierce enemy bombardment around 3 a.m., and no counterattack ensued. As the other men were still in a series of shell holes, communication via runners was dangerous during the daylight. Nevertheless, four men were ordered to attempt it – two were hit but two made it unharmed.

The battalion was relieved that night. The casualties were: three officers and 39 other ranks killed, nine officers and 202 other ranks wounded, with 38 other ranks missing. The three officers killed were Lieutenant Jenkins, Second Lieutenant Rowlands and Second Lieutenant Jones.

David Lewis Jenkins, 31, was from Llanon near Aberystwyth and was the son of a Master Mariner, Captain David Jenkins, and Anne Jenkins of Enkrateia House, Llanon. He was commissioned into the 5th Battalion of the Welsh Regiment, but instead of joining them in Palestine he was posted to France on 14 May 1917, joining the 10th Battalion Royal Welsh Fusiliers. He is commemorated on the Tyne Cot Memorial.

Charles William Rowlands was 22 and had been awarded the Meritorious Service Medal. His parents lived in Broughton,

Manchester. He was a clerk and had two brothers and three sisters.

Thomas Stephen Jones was 26 and from Cardiff. He was born on 15 September 1892 at 7 Coed Cae, Tir-Phil. After attending Tirphil Primary School and Lewis School for Boys in Pengam between 1906 and 1911, he enlisted in the Army at Easter 1915, and on 1 December 1915 he was posted to France as a private with the Royal Welsh Fusiliers. In 1916 he was wounded on two successive days, 10 and 11 July, during the fighting at Mametz Wood. He later attended Officer Training School and was commissioned as Second Lieutenant in the 3rd Battalion, Royal Welsh Fusiliers, on 27 March 1917.

All three officers were killed on 26 September and their bodies lost. They are commemorated on the Tyne Cot Memorial to the Missing.

Private Benjamin Colbert had enlisted, aged 30, in the Special Reserve of the 3rd Leicestershire Regiment in August 1914. During recruit training he exhibited conduct to the prejudice of good order and military discipline, struck his superior officer and attempted to escape confinement. He was court-martialled on 27 October and was sentenced to 56

David Jenkins   Thomas Jones

days' detention. The medical officer stated that Colbert had pulmonary tuberculosis and in his opinion was not fit to serve this punishment. Colbert was consequently discharged as not likely to become an efficient soldier on 4 December 1914.

In October 1915, at Holborn in London, he enlisted once more, this time in the 14th Royal Welsh Fusiliers. A cabinetmaker by trade, he lived at 50 Aubert Buildings, Hoxton Market. He was unmarried and had great loss and decay of teeth, many scars on his neck, and tattoos on his chest. He claimed not to have served in the Army previously and to be 37 years of age. Later that month he went absent without leave and was forfeited two days' pay. In the first two months of 1916 he went absent without leave once more and was given 144 hours' detention, and then refused an order which led to a further 168 hours' detention. In April he went absent again and forfeited three days' pay.

Three days later he embarked at Folkestone and by May was in action. He was wounded accidentally in Mametz Wood on 11 July but it was decided he was in no way to blame. Nevertheless, he spent ten days in hospital with a contusion to his left leg. After recovering, he was transferred to the 10th Royal Welsh Fusiliers. He was home on leave for 11 days in August 1917 but after returning to the front he was killed on 26 September. He has no known grave and is commemorated on the Tyne Cot Memorial. His personal effects were sent home to his niece. These consisted of part of his Army Book, a religious text, a postcard and a registration card.

Lance Corporal James Hill's name is also commemorated on the Tyne Cot Memorial. He was born in Newbridge, Monmouthshire, and was a coal miner when he enlisted in the Army Reserve. In October 1913, aged 20, he joined the Regular Army but deserted for 91 days in April 1914. He suffered 28 days' detention as a result and, after being released, was sent to France.

Within a week of arrival, he had been shot in the hand and was hospitalised. After recovering, he was sent to Gibraltar

The remains of Polygon Wood

where he was treated for syphilis. He was also confined to barracks for seven days for urinating in the barrack room. He remained at Gibraltar for a year before being transferred back to Flanders and was made a lance corporal on 13 September, but was killed 13 days later. His death was witnessed by Lance Corporal Johnson of Cathays Terrace in Cardiff who wrote from his hospital bed in Bradford: 'I saw L/Cpl Hill killed. I was close to him at Zonnebeke, Ypres. We were in a shell hole. I knew him well. Came from Gibraltar together. I think he was a single man.'[17]

Hill's sole effects were some photos and a press cutting. In 1922 his mother wrote to the War Office asking for details of her son's grave.

William Howarth was an orphan from Leigh in Lancashire. He was a coal miner before enlisting in August 1915. Arriving in France in May 1916, he underwent training as a machine gunner and attended an anti-aircraft course. He was killed on

26 September and his grave was one of the many lost as the ground continued to be shelled. He is commemorated on the Tyne Cot Memorial to the Missing.

Private Charles William Edwards is also remembered on the same memorial. Killed in action on the same day, aged 19, he was originally from Bath. He had joined the Army Service Corps before being transferred to the 10th Royal Welsh Fusiliers.

On 30 September, the Germans made further attempts to recover the ground that had been lost to the British advance. Two attacks were made north of the Menin Road using *Flammenwerfer* or flamethrowers. The following day they made five attacks in the same area and a sixth took place south of the Ypres-Roulers railway. All of these attacks were repulsed, and the Germans suffered heavy losses.

Private William Hugh Owens was born in Caernarfon and had enlisted in Liverpool in the Royal Welsh Fusiliers. Subsequently transferred to the 237th Company of the Machine Gun Corps, he was killed in action on 6 October and was buried in Tyne Cot Cemetery.

Charles Edwards

William Owens

Gunner Colin H. Beynon also served with the Machine Gun Corps and was wounded at Polygon Wood, aged 19. From Barry Island, he was treated in hospital in Manchester. He had enlisted two years previously and related the following story to a reporter:

His brother, who was not eighteen, first walked into the recruiting office, and said that he was nineteen. Colin followed, and the officer in charge became suspicious. 'Was that your brother who just went out?' he asked. 'Yes, sir,' was the reply. 'But,' said the officer, 'you say you are nineteen, and that is the age he gave.' Instantly Colin replied, 'Yes, sir, we are twins.'[18]

CHAPTER 20

The Battle of Poelcappelle, 9 October

AT THIS STAGE of the Third Battle of Ypres the rain and shelling had turned the battlefield into a quagmire and movement was limited. However, it was decided to attack once again in the hope that the weather would be drier in October. Haig was aware of the lateness of the season but decided to renew the advance on 9 October. The Guards Division was to advance across the Broembeek and then to push on to the southern edge of the Houthulst Forest. It was decided to repeat the structure of the advance of 31 July by using two brigades in the frontline of the attack – the 1st Guards Brigade on the right and the 2nd Guards Brigade on the left. The men took up these positions on the evening of 8 October in heavy rain and spent an uncomfortable night, wet and cold, in muddy shell holes.

By an enormous effort the guns were brought forward to cover the advance of the Guards. The 75th Brigade of the Royal Field Artillery was located in the valley of the Steenbeek on the right of Ruisseau Farm. As previously, all the ammunition had to be brought forward to the guns by packhorse.

At 5.20 a.m. on 9 October the artillery barrage opened up, 200 yards north of Broembeek. The creeping barrage was highly effective. The rain had ceased and four minutes later the infantry began to cross the Broembeek all along the line. They met little resistance and by 6 a.m. the first objective had been reached. The Guards paused for three-quarters of an hour

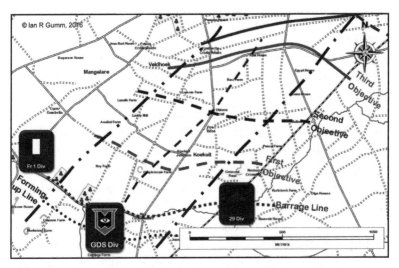

Map of the advance of the Guards Division at Poelcappelle on 9 October

then the creeping barrage came down again and the advance was resumed. The only resistance to this advance to the second objective was found in blockhouses near Vee Bend, but these were outflanked by the Coldstream Guards and 35 Germans surrendered along with their three machine guns.

By 8.15 a.m. the Guards were in position at the second objective and they lost no time in pressing on with their advance, again with the cover of an artillery barrage. This proved more difficult and involved some hard fighting for the Irish Guards on the right. By 10.15 a.m. the task was virtually finished. The enemy snipers continued to cause casualties from the direction of the Houthulst Forest and the Coldstream Guards suffered casualties when an artillery barrage by the British heavy guns fell short.

At dawn on 10 October a number of Germans were observed crawling about in the mud opposite the line held by the Coldstream Guards; they surrendered when fired upon. The rain poured down all day and it seemed fit to continue for some time but Haig was determined to press on and seize the ridge, so he ordered an attack for 12 October. The Guards, having already achieved their objectives, were to play only a small part.

Zero Hour, at 5.25 a.m., saw a barrage begin to cover an advance by the 1st Bn. Grenadier Guards on the right. The infantry was held up and it was not until nightfall that they were able to drive out the Germans manning blockhouses at Angle Point and Aden House. The guns of the 75th Brigade searched the ground for 500 yards beyond the final line reached. The British advance had been halted by the rain and from now on the fighting was to establish tactical positions while the strategic focus was on the surprise attack in the Cambrai area the following month. The Guards were required to improve their defensive positions, no easy task while the enemy artillery bombarded them continuously and the rain continued to fall, breaking the banks of the Broembeek and flooding the area.

Private Robert Christmas Jones died of his wounds on 9 October, aged 19, while serving with the motor transport section of the York and Lancashire Regiment. He was buried in Poelcappelle British Cemetery.

At the start of December 1917 his mother, Annie Jones of Blaenau Ffestiniog, Merionethshire, received a letter from an army chaplain:

Headquarters, New Zealand Discharge Depot.
Torquay, November 29th 1917.

Dear Mrs Jones,

I am writing to express my deep sympathy with you in the loss of your son, 33349, Robert Jones. He was wounded in action in an attack upon a strongly fortified ridge that barred the way to Passchendaele, and was brought to the Dressing Station at a place called Waterloo Farm, where he passed away.

   I laid him to rest, and his grave has been marked, and will receive every attention.

Unfortunately I cannot tell you how he was wounded. It was before I arrived on the scene with the New Zealand troops. There were a number of wounded in the Dressing Station when we arrived, and your son was one of them. Owing to the fact that I have been moving about in France and England till now, I have not been able to write sooner. I have been transferred here, and this is my first opportunity of writing.

Your sorrow will be very great, but you have the memory of a noble death in a great cause. May God have you in His care and keeping, comfort you and give you peace. Especially may He comfort you in the Blessed Hope of Life Immortal, and the glad prospect of one day meeting again all those you have loved long since and lost awhile.

Yours, In sorrow and sympathy.

W. McLean

Chaplain[1]

Private Harold Johnson of the Welsh Guards was killed on 12 October. He was born in 1892 in Wymondham, Leicestershire, and was employed as a grocer and draper and was residing in the family home together with his parents and sister, Louisa.

ER COF ANWYL

AM

Robert Christmas Jones,

Anwyl fab Mr. a Mrs. Gough Jones, 11, Maen-offeren Terrace, Blaenau Ffestiniog,

Yr hwn a glwyfwyd ym mrwydr Passchendael, yn Ffrainc, Hydref 9, 1917, ac a fu farw dranoeth.

Pe cawsai fyw buasai yn 20 mlwydd oed Nadolig, 1917.

Ymunodd a'r Fyddin ym Medi, 1916, gyda'r Motor Transport, a pherthynai i'r York and Lancashire Regiment.

Robert Jones' memorial card. In translation it reads: In Dear Memory of Robert Christmas Jones, Dear son of Mr. and Mrs. Gough Jones of 11, Maenofferen Terrace, Blaenau Ffestiniog, Wounded in the battle of Passchendaele in France on October 9, 1917, and died the following day. Had he lived he would have been 20 years old at Christmas 1917. He joined the Army in September 1916, with the Motor Transport, and was attached to the York and Lancashire Regiment.

His death was reported in a local newspaper:

It is with regret we learn that on Sunday morning Mr. Johnson,
grocer and draper, received a letter informing him, that his son
Private H. Johnson, was killed in action on October 12th when
the Battalion attacked and successfully took their objective. A
subsequent letter from the chaplain stated that Pte. Johnson was
killed instantaneously by a shell while up in the trenches, and
did not suffer any pain. He was buried on the field of battle in a
soldier's grave. Had deceased lived he would have been 26 years of
age on the 5th November. It will be remembered Mr. Johnson, had
a son (Fred) killed in action on September 18th 1916, yet another
(Jack) is wounded and prisoner of war.[2]

Harold Johnson's grave was lost and his name is
commemorated on the Tyne Cot Memorial to the Missing. His
brother Alfred had been killed, aged 30, while serving with the
14th Durham Light Infantry and he too has no known grave,
his name being inscribed on the Thiepval Memorial to the
Missing.

Second Lieutenant Nigel Newall, Welsh Guards, was killed,
aged 22, on 12 October in a long-range duel with a German
sniper. He is also commemorated on the Tyne Cot Memorial.
His parents lived in Redheath, Croxley Green, Hertfordshire,
and his elder brother Leslie had been killed, aged 23, in
September 1915 while serving with the Royal Fusiliers as a
second lieutenant.

Captain Arthur Gibbs M.C. of the Welsh Guards wrote
home:

Larrey Camp Oct. 14, 1917.

Dearest Mother,

Dear Nigel Newall was killed the day before yesterday. It is an
awful shock to me as we had been such tremendous friends, and
he was one of the dearest fellows in the world. It will be terrible for
his people as they all loved him so. All the men loved him: he was
so splendid with them and always played games with them, and

Welsh Guards officers in 1915

worked with them. The finest young officer in the regiment and his loss makes a gap that can never be filled. I miss him awfully as we had been such a lot together, and always did things together. Thank goodness he was killed instantaneously, shot through the forehead by a sniper. It will be awful for his mother, as she was only just getting over the loss of the other son.[3]

During the advance by the rest of the Guards Brigade on 12 October, Private Uriel Vincent Williams was killed. He too is commemorated on the Tyne Cot Memorial, as his body could not be identified. His death was reported in a newspaper:

An intimation has been received from the War Office that Private Uriel Williams, of the Welsh Guards, was killed in action in France. A letter has also been received from the Rev. G.M.S. Oldham, chaplain attached to the 1st Batt. Welsh Guards, expressing the sympathy of the officer commanding on the loss of such a good soldier, and testifying to the excellent character borne by him, and his deep appreciation of how Pte. Williams at all times carried out his duties. Pte. Uriel Williams was 28 years of age, and had been in France since January. He resided at Ivy Cottage, Frampton-road, Loughor. He was also a cadet officer in the Loughor company of the Church Lads' Brigade Cadets, and was for years a chorister, and before enlisting was the organist at the Parish Church at

Welsh Guards boxing

Loughor. Whilst in training at the Guards' depot at Caterham he won the light-weight boxing championship of the depot last November.[4]

Private Benjamin Smith, Welsh Guards, died of his wounds on 7 November 1917 and was buried in Wimereux Cemetery. Born in 1882 in Anstey, Leicestershire, he had previously worked in the boot trade. In April 1911 Benjamin was a cab proprietor, and residing in the family home at Church Lane, Anstey, together with his wife of three years, Elsie. It was reported in a local newspaper on 14 September that he had been wounded.[5]

On the 17 October, the Guards were relieved by the 35th Division.

During the night of 8/9 October, patrols from the 1st Royal Welsh Fusiliers were sent out to ascertain the enemy positions. They reported that the village of Reutel was clear but that an enemy trench containing a machine gun was situated in front of the cemetery. Judge Copse was occupied but Lieutenant

D.M. John thought that two companies would be enough to take it. Lieutenant I.R. Cartwright was sent towards Judge Cottage but did not return.

At 5.20 a.m. the British artillery opened fire. The Germans replied with a barrage that landed on the front and support lines, causing a number of casualties. The 1st R.W.F. waited in support for the attacking waves to take their objectives, which they did.

Of the 16 men killed during this period of the battle, no fewer than 13 have no known graves and are remembered on the Tyne Cot Memorial to the Missing. One of these is Private David Davies who had previously won the Military Medal and bar. Born in Pontygwaith, Glamorgan, he had enlisted in Ferndale and had served on the Western Front since February 1915. His personal effects were returned to his mother.

Another one of the missing is Private Philip Maurice Chapman who was 22 and from Clarence Hill, Wimbledon, London. He had formerly served with the Suffolk Regiment and wrote a last letter home two days before he died:

Dear Mum,
Thank you and Sid very much for your letters received this morning. We have just returned from up the line. Once again things were pretty bad but we managed to pull through. The weather has been very bad and seems as if it is going to continue so, which makes life away from civilisation bad.

I suppose Sid will be going soon but I hope that he will not see things out here. I hope it will all be over by that time. I expect he wants to come out but so did I and you want to get back again jolly quick too.

Thank Poll very much for the reg. letter and tell her that the fags and tip were A1.

Well then, I must close now with very best love to all.

Phil xxx

P.S. toad seems to be training for one game of chess next.[6]

Private Launcelot Bridges Shipton of the 14th Welsh

Launcelot Shipton

Regiment died at No.54 Casualty Clearing Station on 18 October 1917 of wounds received in action the previous day. His father was from Roath in Cardiff and his mother from Bristol but Shipton himself was born in Marianna, Jackson County, Florida, U.S.A., on 4 October 1889. Educated at Monkton House School, Cardiff, he was employed on the staff of the *Western Mail* before joining the 7th Cyclists' Battalion of the Welsh Regiment on 10 December 1915. Subsequently transferred to the 14th Welsh, he was employed as a Runner and served in France and Flanders from 28 July 1916. He was buried at Estaires.

Second Lieutenant Harold Spear Knapp, whose family lived in Roath, Cardiff, had enlisted in the 16th London Regiment as a rifleman. Commissioned into the 14th Welsh on 29 June 1917, he later transferred to the Royal Air Force and survived the war.

Signaller William Kent of 'B' Battery, 58th Brigade, Royal Field Artillery, died on 20 October. He had been born in St Nicholas, near Cardiff, on 3 April 1899. Educated in the village school, he was subsequently apprenticed on a merchant ship before joining the Royal Fleet Artillery on 23 November 1914. He served with

Harold Knapp

the Mediterranean Expeditionary Force at Gallipoli from April 1915 and was there until the evacuation in January 1916, during which he was nearly drowned by being capsized into the sea. Kent then proceeded to Egypt, where he took part in several engagements before being drafted to France in June 1916 after having been in hospital for some time, suffering from trench sores and septic poisoning. He died at No.3 Canadian General Hospital from wounds and gas poisoning received in action at Poelcappelle. He was buried in Boulogne.

On the same day Private Alfred E. Mundy of the Royal Army Medical Corps, from Morel Street, Barry Dock, was killed while on duty in one of the wards when the No.37 Casualty Clearing Station was bombed by German aircraft. He was buried in Godewaersvelde British Cemetery, south-west of Ypres. Twenty years of age, he had served in France and Flanders for two years and had only recently returned there after ten days' leave. Prior to the war he was employed by the Barry Railway Company as a trimmer at the commercial pumping shed.

Alfred Mundy

CHAPTER 21

The Second Battle of Passchendaele: 26 October to 10 November

THE FIRST BATTLE of Passchendaele had taken place on 12 October when the Second Australian and New Zealand Army Corps had attacked the German positions, without success. The weather had now improved but the mud remained sticky, deep and cloying. Herculean efforts were made to bring the artillery guns forward along plank roads, with all their ammunition. Gas lay heavy in thick clouds across the area, and the Germans adapted their defensive tactics to force the British guns to come even further forward in order to be effective. The Second Battle of Passchendaele commenced on 26 October with the British artillery opening fire with gas shells, neutralising the enemy batteries. The creeping barrage and infantry assault then followed and the village of Passchendaele was finally taken before the battle ground to a halt on 10 November.

One of the casualties on the opening day of the battle was Private William Biddle from Cardiff, who was serving with the 14th Battalion of the Royal Warwickshire Regiment. Wounded, he was evacuated back to Albany Road Military Hospital in Cardiff and wrote home:

> I got hit at Ypres, some warm shop I can assure you, in the left forearm and left leg, flesh wounds. We went over the top on the

Passchendaele Ridge

26th October, at 5.30 a.m., with the best of luck. I was also in it on the 6th and 11th October. Well these three trips were quite the roughest anyone could be in. It started drizzling rain when we went over. Talk about mud. I cleaned my rifle two or three times during the early hours of the morning. I had 5 kilos to walk after I got hit, and you never saw such a picture in all your life. Soaking wet to the skin, up to my knees in mud, only had shorts on. Well I had a bit of a smile to myself. When I got to the Dressing Station, hot cocoa. It went down all right I can tell you.[1]

On 26 October the 1st Royal Welsh Fusiliers were in the front line south of the Menin Road. There was considerable

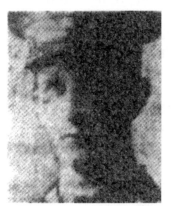

enemy sniping that day and this resulted in the death of Second Lieutenant Idris Rees who, after being hit, died of his wounds the following day. His grave was lost in the subsequent fighting and he is commemorated on the Tyne Cot Memorial. He was the son of a Presbyterian minister

Idris Rees

319

from Tredegar and had been employed as a bank clerk before enlisting as a private.

Second Lieutenant Thomas William Lewis was born at Llantwit Fadre, Pontypridd, on 14 May 1888, and educated at Pontypridd County School, Carmarthen Preparatory School, Hackney College, London, and at University College, Cardiff, where he was a Ministerial student. He was in charge of the Y.M.C.A. at Pembroke Dock. Gazetted Second Lieutenant in the R.W.F. in October 1917, he was killed in action on the Menin Road on 27 October. His Captain wrote:

> We loved him too. We had grown to like him immensely, and I am speaking for the N.C.O.s and men, not only of his platoon, but of the whole company, when I say that they mourn his loss very, very much. His was a quiet but steady influence, his sympathy was always with his men, and his actions as an officer were tempered accordingly.[2]

Lieutenant Albert Stanley Gabriel Williams died at Poelcappelle on 28 October, of wounds received in action the same day, while superintending the construction of a road. He was buried in Nine Elms British Military Cemetery. Born in Cardiff on 16 September 1890, he was educated at Lewisham School, Weston-super-Mare, and went to Canada in 1912, as

a mining engineer. He volunteered for active service at the outbreak of war and joined the 1st British Columbia (Duke of Connaught's Own) Rifles. Williams was wounded and gassed on 24 April 1915. He received a commission and was gazetted Second Lieutenant in the Royal Engineers on 11 September that year. In accordance with his

Thomas Lewis

background, he joined the 171st Company, R.E. (Tunnelling Section) and was promoted to Lieutenant on 29 July 1916. Wounded again on 14 March 1917, he was invalided home, rejoining his section in September. His commanding officer wrote: 'It is a great loss to my company; he was a very promising officer. I have known him since January, 1915, and he has done some excellent work. To be killed after seeing so much service, having been out in 1914 in the early stages of the war, is more than sad. Myself and his brother officers will miss him very much after such long association.' Lieutenant V. Hardy wrote: 'As you know, he had not been long with this company, but he had made himself very popular, and rendered most useful assistance lately in giving the men anti-gas respirator training, in his resting period.'[3]

On 28 October the 1st Royal Welsh Fusiliers were relieved and took no further part in the battle. The 10th Battalion of the R.W.F., which had been relieved on 29 September, also took no further part, and after being withdrawn on 11 September, the 38th (Welsh) Division moved down to the Armentières-Laventie sector between 13 and 15 September.

The 2nd and 9th R.W.F., however, remained in the Ypres area. For the remainder of the battle they manned the front line trenches and experienced the full horror of life in the trenches in the Salient: decomposing bodies built into the walls of trenches, constant enemy shelling, food sodden with muddy water, sniping, a waterlogged country of shell craters, cold nights, and death from exposure.

William Henry Hodges had joined the 2nd Royal Welsh Fusiliers prior to the war. Born in 1892 in Nantymoel, he was the son of a coal miner, and when he was old he enough he followed his father down the pits. He joined up in 1913 and took part in the attack on the German-controlled port of Tsingtao in China which began on 31 October 1914. He later served at Gallipoli, where he was wounded, and while recovering at home he met a young widow of 20 with two small children; her first husband had been killed on active service. They married in February 1916 and, while William was on the Western Front, he became a father. He never met his daughter as he was killed on 10 November 1917. His body was never found and he is commemorated on the Tyne Cot Memorial to the Missing. His widow threw his medals into a coal bunker when his daughter, Martha, was five, so upset was she by the death of a second husband. Martha retrieved them and kept them safe, hidden under her mattress, and would take them out and polish them when nobody was around.[4]

The 1st South Wales Borderers took part in the final attack on 10 November in the area around Passchendaele village. By now, the ground was so churned up by the shelling and heavy rain that to step off a duckboard would usually result in death by drowning. In places the duckboards themselves were underwater and the men laboured forward to the start line encumbered by three days' worth of ammunition and supplies.

Zero Hour was 5 a.m. and the objective was a line from Vocation Farm to Vox Farm, but the advance was held up by heavy German machine gun fire and sniping. At 7.15 a.m. the

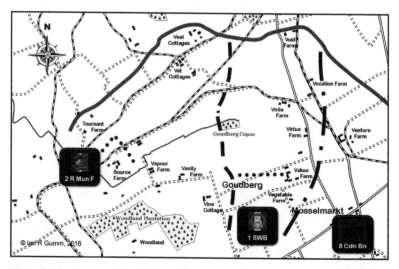

Map of the advance of the 1st South Wales Borderers at Passchendaele on 10 November

enemy counterattacks began. Casualties were heavy but the battalion clung on despite Lewis Guns and rifles being put out of action by the mud. German aircraft and shellfire now harassed them and they were running low in bombs, having used many of them to neutralise enemy pillboxes. By 1 p.m. the situation was untenable, so the survivors fell back. That evening they were relieved, having lost three officers killed, with seven others wounded, and 372 casualties amongst the other ranks.

Lieutenant Cyril Gordon Phillips was 25 and the son of Thomas and Clara Anne Phillips of The Vicarage, Kerry, Newtown, Montgomeryshire. He had enlisted as a private in 19th Royal Fusiliers before obtaining a commission in the South Wales Borderers. His body was never identified and he is commemorated on the Tyne Cot Memorial to the Missing, as is Second Lieutenant Harry Harding Davies. Davies was 21 and the son of William and Sarah C. Davies, of Bryn Celyn, Ruabon, Wrexham. He had arrived in France on 14 April 1917.

The third officer killed, Second Lieutenant Derrick Cecil Mason, is remembered on the same memorial. He was 20 and his death was reported in the local Burnley newspaper:

Destroyed German pillbox on the Passchendaele Ridge

Hapton Officer Missing. From the War Office a telegram was received on Friday by Mr. and Mrs. John Mason, 91, Manchester Road, Hapton, as follows: 'Regret to inform you that Second-Lieut. Derrick Cecil Mason, South Wales Borderers, is reported missing since November 10th. This does not mean killed or wounded.' Previous to his enlisting in the R.A.M.C. before he attained his 18th birthday, he had been at the Burnley Grammar School for three years. After serving in the R.A.M.C. he was transferred to the South Wales Borderers, and gazetted second-lieutenant last February. He was drafted out two months later, and obtained a short leave in September. He was much respected in the village, being a member of the choir of the School-Church. He was formerly in the Boy Scouts, and also St. John Ambulance Brigade.[5]

Of the 115 men of the 1st Battalion S.W.B. who died that day, no fewer than 99 have no known graves and are remembered on the Tyne Cot Memorial to the Missing. One of these men is John Charles Caveill, who was the husband of Winifred Caveill, of 17 Amherst St, Grangetown, Cardiff. In 1911, he was a bobbin winder at Gripoly Mills, Sloper Road, Cardiff. He was 31 years of age.

Patrick Murphy was 47 when he was killed in action and he is another who is commemorated on the Tyne Cot Memorial. He

Derrick Mason

John Caveill

had been awarded the Distinguished Conduct Medal in 1916. His citation read: 'For conspicuous gallantry in action. Pte. Murphy and another man volunteered to lead a bayonet attack. On reaching a block of wire and buried bayonets forming a kind of *chevaux de frise*, they climbed the parapet and removed the obstacles. They led the attack with great bravery and dash and utter contempt of danger.'[6]

Bertie Hughes was 22 and was also killed on 10 November. Born in Bristol, he was the son of Thomas and Ada Hughes who were living at Llewelyn Street, Cadoxton, Barry. Hughes worked at Ranks Mill on Barry Docks. He was buried at Poelcappelle British Cemetery.

Captains Lochner and W.J. Manley, and Second Lieutenants G.W. Massey and C.W. Nott received the Military Cross. Lieutenant Wales received a bar to his M.C., Private Burgess won the Distinguished Conduct Medal and Private Lomas a bar to his D.C.M.

Rupert Gordon Lochner was commissioned on 5 October 1910 and saw service in France and Belgium from July 1915 to July 1916, and again from January 1917 to November 1918. He commanded the 18th Indian Brigade during the Second World War and was twice Mentioned in Dispatches. He retired as an Honorary Major-General in January 1946. His son was declared missing, presumed drowned, while on active service in Ceylon in June 1945.

C.W. Nott had enlisted as a private in the South Wales Borderers and landed in Aden on 3 July 1915. He was discharged to a commission on 25 January 1917. Though wounded twice on 10 November, he refused to go back for treatment and led his men in repulsing the German counterattacks.

Owen Murton Wales served as a lieutenant in the Royal Flying Corps before joining the South Wales Borderers. Post-war he served with the 2nd S.W.B. in India and was a brigadier in that country also during the Second World War. He was awarded the O.B.E. in 1945.

Private G. Burgess' citation for his D.C.M. read: 'For

conspicuous gallantry and devotion to duty. Although himself wounded, he continued to bring in wounded under very heavy fire for four hours, at the end of which time he was in a state of collapse.'[7]

Private L. Lomas had first won the D.C.M. in 1916: 'For conspicuous gallantry. After being himself buried by the effects of a shell he dug out two comrades who were also buried. One of them was again buried, and Pte. Lomas tried but could not rescue him. On his report, however, the man was rescued by a party the same night.'[8]

The citation for his second D.C.M. read: 'For conspicuous gallantry and devotion to duty throughout two days' operations. He brought in wounded on several occasions under heavy fire. The company runners having become casualties, he volunteered to take a message to Battalion H.Q. He also volunteered to retrieve a Lewis Gun about 60 yards in front of the trench and did so under heavy sniping.'[9]

Leonard Lomas had arrived in France in November 1914 and was a native of Banbury. However, he later forfeited his medals for a breach of the King's Regulations, namely misconduct.

Private Henry Cottier (alias Cocolo) from Cardiff was killed in action on 26 October while taking part in the advance of the 2/5th Loyal North Lancashire Regiment. The attack was launched at 5.40 a.m. and immediately confronted an impassable morass, so bad was the condition of the ground, and the advance was halted.

Henry Cottier was, for two seasons, the captain of the Grange Wanderers Association Football Club in Cardiff. He was an excellent shot with a rifle and was selected as a sniper. Before enlisting he was a crane driver at the Dowlais

Henry Cottier

Fred Griffiths

Works. He is commemorated on the Tyne Cot Memorial and was 19 years of age.

Another former footballer, Sergeant Frederick John Griffiths from Presteigne, was killed in action on 30 October, aged 44, while serving with the 15th Sherwood Foresters (Nottinghamshire and Derbyshire Regiment). Before enlisting he worked as a bar manager in Shirebrook, Derbyshire, and ran his own pork butchery business. He had become a professional footballer at the age of 21, playing in goal for Tottenham Hotspur, Blackpool, Preston North End, and West Ham United, and winning two Welsh caps in 1900. He left a widow and six children and was buried in Dozinghem Military Cemetery.

On 10 November the 2nd Welsh Regiment took part in the final part of the battle – an attack on a low rise called Vat Cottage Ridge. The advance began at 6.05 a.m. but the swampy ground and an effective German counterattack saw the battalion driven back to its starting position by 4 p.m. Lieutenant G.L. Vawdrey was killed and, in total during their three days in the line, the battalion suffered 127 casualties.

Gilbert Lloyd Vawdrey was 20 and was buried in Duhallow Advanced Dressing Station Cemetery. He was

Gilbert Vawdrey

the son of Llewelyn Brookes Vawdrey and Louisa Maria Vawdrey, of Tushingham Hall, Cheshire. He had been educated at Colet House in Rhyl, then at Radley College and was a cadet at the Royal Military College, Sandhurst, in 1916. He was killed serving as the Battalion Intelligence Officer while carrying a message back to Brigade Headquarters.

The battalion had been heavily shelled on 8 November as it moved into the front line and this had continued the following day. Of the 40 men killed during this period, only eight have known graves.

One of these casualties was Lance Corporal Charles Penhorwood. He was formerly employed by the Swansea Harbour Trust and his mother was a widow who lived at 48 Watkin Street in Swansea. A month later she received the news that another of her sons, William, had been killed in action while serving with the King's Hussars. Worse was to follow on 28 March 1918 when a third son, Sergeant Thomas Penhorwood (served as Penharwood), also serving with the Hussars, was killed.

Charles Penhorwood

Another of the men commemorated on the Tyne Cot Memorial to the Missing was Private William Frederick James Rodd, who was killed on 9 November. His parents lived at Havelock Street in Cardiff and he worked in the publishing room of the *Western Mail* newspaper before leaving to work as a driver for Richard England potato importers. He had joined up with his brother George.

The German shelling on that

day also claimed the lives of two men from Stockport. Lance Corporal Ernest Heavyside was 23. His family had lived near Lichfield in Staffordshire before moving to Stockport some time before the war. He had served with the Cheshire Regiment was a Territorial and was married with a child. His platoon officer wrote:

> Your husband was killed at 8 o'clock in the morning. It may be some small comfort to you to know that his death was instantaneous and painless as he was killed outright by a shell. He was a very gallant soldier who always did his best and his loss is felt by all in the Company. Please accept my deep sympathy and may the consolation that he died a true soldier's death comfort you and your child in your great loss.[10]

Ernest Heavyside is remembered on the Tyne Cot Memorial.

Private Arthur Bentley was conscripted in Stockport in 1916 and served on the Western Front from early 1917. Fatally wounded by a shell fragment on the same day, he was buried

in St Julien Dressing Station Cemetery. He was 19.

Private John Thomas Forster was also killed in action on 9 November, aged 31. He was buried in Buffs Road Cemetery near Ypres. He left a widow, Emily Jane, and a son who lived at 2 Walter Street, Frodsham, Warrington. Prior to enlisting he was a carter working for Messrs. Joseph Ashworth and Sons of Frodsham Bridge and

John Forster

Charles Taylor

was described thus: 'A very steady and conscientious workman and was greatly esteemed.'[11]

Private Charles Richard Taylor served as a stretcher-bearer with the 2nd Welsh and was awarded the Military Medal. He was a member of the Roath Road Methodist Church in Cardiff and was later promoted to Lance Sergeant.

Three Welsh nurses returned home to Cardiff as the battle ended. Agnes Sooley Johnstone and Emma Hardy had each gained an efficiency stripe. The third nurse was Alice Davies. All three had undergone a course of training at the Ninian Park section of the 3rd Western General Hospital, Cardiff, and had subsequently served at one of the largest base hospitals in France from July 1916 – 26 General Hospital at Étaples.

Agnes Johnstone lived at 3 Morlais Street in Cardiff and was born in April 1879. She served as a Voluntary Aid Detachment nurse at Ninian Park from 7 October 1915 until 7 July 1916, then served at 26 General Hospital from 8 July 1916 to 6 November 1917. She gained a second efficiency stripe on 5 November 1917. She died in June 1972.

Emma Hardy lived at 10 Australia Road, Cardiff, and had joined the 3rd Western General Hospital in Cardiff as a Voluntary Aid Detachment nurse on 7 October 1915, serving there until she was sent to France on 8 July 1916 where she too worked at 26 General Hospital until 6 November 1917. She also gained two red efficiency stripes and was mentioned on Queen Alexandra's Roll of Honour.

Agnes Johnstone

Emma Hardy

Alice Davies

Probable photograph of Alice Davies (centre)

Alice Davies of 3 Partridge Road, Cardiff, joined the V.A.D. on 7 October 1915 and served at Ninian Park until 7 July 1916. On 8 July she landed in France and was also stationed at 26 General Hospital until 7 November 1917. She too was mentioned on Queen Alexandra's Roll of Honour.

The 3rd Western General Hospital in Cardiff was comprised of various requisitioned school buildings which were converted into hospitals to treat the flood of wounded men returning from the battlefields. These were: Howardian, King Edward VII, Albany Road, Splott, Lansdowne and Ninian Park schools.

Another nurse who worked at the 3rd Western General Hospital was Beatrice H.T. James who had enlisted in the Voluntary Aid Detachment on 26 February 1917, aged 22. At the time of her enlistment she was living with her parents at 88 Monthermer Road, Cathays, Cardiff. She worked at the 3rd Western until 25 September 1918, so would have treated many casualties from the Third Battle of Ypres. She subsequently transferred to the Military Hospital in Exeter on 28 October 1918 and was still serving there in August 1919.

Another Welsh nurse who treated the casualties from the battle was Rose Crowther of Miskin Street, Cathays Park, Cardiff. She had enlisted as a Voluntary Aid Detachment nurse on 3 June 1916, aged 23 and served at military hospitals in Devonport, Leicester, Oswestry, and Birmingham, before leaving the Voluntary Aid Detachment in March 1919.

The wounded at Ninian Park Hospital

Beatrice James   Rose Crowther

The fighting at the Third Battle of Ypres ended with the attack of 10 November and final preparations began for the Battle of Cambrai which commenced just ten days later.

CHAPTER 22

Other Survivors' Accounts

SOME OF THE Welsh survivors of the Third Battle of Ypres left diaries, letters or other accounts which give an insight into their time at the front in the summer of 1917.

Second Lieutenant Stephen Glynne Hughes served with the 173rd Siege Battery of the Royal Field Artillery and left the following description of the role that artillery played in the battle:

> The guns were placed in the farm orchard and one section (two guns) about 80 yards behind the other. An unsound method but necessary if we were to get any 'flash' cover. The farm was not too badly knocked about because up to a week or two previously this part of the front was held by the Belgians who had adopted a 'live and let live' attitude with the Boche in front of them. As things were now beginning to liven up, our sleeping quarters were in another farm a mile to the rear, this one being still occupied as a home by the family.
>
> Our officers and men on duty remained at Pelissier Farm, a wise precaution as our opponents soon realised another 'do' was about to take place and began to bring up additional artillery to counter our build up. Pelissier Farm was between Vlamertinghe and Elvertinghe west of the Canal at Ypres. We were now requiring sand bags and Elephants [small circular corrugated iron sheeting] for our command post, etc. The digging of dugouts was impossible because although the weather was dry – water was just beneath the surface. In a matter of days a terrific concentration of Batteries began. We fixed up a screen about 50 yards in front of the foremost two guns made of leaves and khaki cloth. This as it turned out

did us well because there was no natural flash cover from rising ground that we had on the Somme. The Boche was now heavily searching the area.

A number of shells fell in the orchard and on the Farm but our luck had returned to us. The 60-pounder battery in front of us had many casualties and they complained that every time we opened fire they got the return! One gas shell fell at the opening to the command post but fortunately we had the masks at the ready and had them on in seconds. I had a narrow shave from a 5.9 one morning. Walking across the road from the command post to the Farm, the shell pitched just where I had been. I flattened and was covered with dust and debris.

Our A.S.C. [Army Service Corps] Corporal leaving the battery position one night during heavy shellfire overturned his lorry at the curb by the farm entrance and was killed instantly by the lorry engine falling on him. As usual my duties were again chiefly observation post work – unsavoury as usual. The group observation post was in the trenches north-east of Ypres being a concrete 'Pill Box' in full view of the ridge near a place called Essex Farm. As it was always being shelled, no more than three were allowed to cross at a time.

We had to line up 20 yards or so short and then make a run for it. Some were lucky and some were not. The final stretch to Gowthorpe was a nightmare also. Gaps were blown in the parapets and snipers were trained on them. One morning two telephonists and myself were crawling past one when a bullet thudded in the back of the trench between me and the man in front. Another day two telephonists were killed and an officer wounded at the entrance to Gowthorpe. When inside the O.P. [observation post] you were safe from light shells and 4.2s often landed on the roof without penetrating the concrete. The 5.9s often landed near and the whole place shook. Apart from Gowthorpe we had another O.P. One the Major found. An isolated shattered tree stump on a little hillock standing in the midst of the flat country in full view of the Germans on the ridge. On our first visit we took a hammer and wedges and crawled on our bellies to the base of the tree. Here one of the telephonists hammered in the stakes at intervals up the trunk. The Major was first up and shouted down that he had a splendid view and could see our target perfectly – a ruined farm on Pilkem Ridge [north-east of Ypres]. He then came down and

Stephen Hughes (seated, extreme right) and his fellow officers

sent me up to conduct a shoot whilst he prepared to return to the battery. At that moment 5.9s began to arrive in salvos. A naval gun also opened up on us – the first intimation of this was a feeling the tree was being sucked away. Swaying back – with the shell bursting about 50 yards behind us – I could just about hear the Major shouting at me to get on with the job but it was useless and we had to run for it.

In subsequent visits we always arrived just before dawn and got into position before daylight, the signaller lying flat on the ground and I trying to hide myself behind the trunk up aloft. As, however, the whole area was being heavily shelled observation work became hazardous in the extreme. The German Air Force was also out in strength, machine gunning the roads, making our trip to Gowthorpe more trying than ever. One day I was out with the Major in Ypres when a large splinter landed between my feet from a shell burst nearby.

The Batteries were now literally wheel to wheel in the front and behind us. Shells of heavy calibre were falling among us, night and day, and still our luck held, but many of the other Batteries were suffering badly. Observation balloons were being set on fire all day and every day, and the occupants descending by parachute became a common event. Often you could see the German planes turning and shooting up the falling parachutist. Just before 31st July we moved up to an advanced position nearer the Canal – here

the ground was very swampy and the wooden boxes in which
we rested inside the 'Elephants' floated about – our clothes and
blankets became saturated. Again, I was chosen to be the group
observation officer and reached Gowthorpe overnight after a
hazardous journey. I shared the work with another Lieutenant
from a neighbouring battery. It was a steady drum fire all night
and the sky was lit with hundreds of Very lights – continuous gun
flashes – then just before dawn the barrage proper started. I had
been in several but this was the Mother and Father of them all. The
noise was so terrific that my partner and I couldn't hear each other
shout as loud as we could, although we were sitting shoulder to
shoulder.

At daylight we could see Pilkem Ridge literally heaving up and
down – the whole ridge was boiling – we saw the Guards leave
the trenches – walking slowly and laboriously over 'no man's land'
– one moment you would see a number of men – then a blanket
of an exploding shell would hide them – clear away – and the
stragglers marching on. Then German prisoners could be seen
struggling and splashing through the shell holes – some being hit
by their own Batteries. As usual communications broke down and
we had no means of finding out how things were going.

Then he started to shell Gowthorpe, 4.2s were literally
bouncing off the top – our vision would be blotted out by exploding
5.9s in front of us – we could hear them pitching all around us
and now I saw a sight not often seen at this stage of the war – an
18-pdr battery came into action right in front of us – the horses
struggling through the mud – the gunners unhitching the gun
teams, which were ridden to the rear – the gun trails slung round
and five opened on open sights in a matter of minutes – all this
with shells dropping among them with casualties. They were so
close to the O.P. that we could see nothing of the firing line. My pal
and I mutually decided that no useful purpose remained for us to
stay, so gathering our gear we trudged off and back over the Canal.
On the way I met an old friend leading a 60-pdr. battery forward.
When I reached our Battery I flopped into my box bed still floating
in the water and passed out. The following day I was taken to the
advanced dressing station near Eoson Farm, by ambulance to the
Field Hospital where I was given hot rum and milk and slept for 24
hours. I have very vivid memories of that drink. From Hospital to
Calais, from Calais by Hospital Ship – full of guardsmen wounded

on the 31st – landed at Folkestone – then by hospital train to London and hospital at Clapham Common and so ended for ever my active service. Trench Fever and general debility had taken its toll. Several months in hospital finishing at Harrogate and discharge from the Army with a disability pension which I finally capitalized.[1]

Captain Paul J. Campbell also served with the Royal Artillery and described the morning of the battle:

The morning was cold, there was a feeling of wetness in the air, but whether it was just the mist before dawn or a sign that rain was coming I could not tell. All the men were up; I could see them moving about behind the guns. Some of them were carrying shells from the pit where ammunition was kept and putting them down besides the guns in readiness. I heard the clink of the brass cases, one against the other, as the shells were put down. We went to speak to the Number Ones. Frank had the big battery watch in his hand and he gave the correct time to each of them. We were going to fire a creeping barrage, that is to say we had to increase the range of our guns by a hundred yards every four minutes, so that our attacking infantry could follow closely behind the curtain of fire, and each N.C.O. was responsible for firing the correct number of rounds in every minute and adding to the range at the right time. There was very little talking. Everyone was alert, each man had his work to do and he was doing it; he did not want to be distracted.

Then we took up our position in the centre of the battery and about fifteen yards behind the guns. My eyes had grown accustomed to the darkness by this time. I could see the line of poplars on the canal bank behind us; by daylight you could see they were all dead, there was not a green leaf among them, but some were still standing at their full height or nearly, others had been split in half, a few had completely gone. And on the other side in the east, over the German trenches, the sky already looked lighter.

It was still very quiet, the quietness gave a sense of unreality to the morning. How could so great an occasion be unheralded! But I could feel the palpitation of my heart.

Men of the 124th Siege Battery, R.G.A., manhandle a 9.2-inch howitzer at Pilkem, 14 September 1917
© Imperial War Museum

One gun behind us on the other side of the canal fired a second too soon. Then Frank blew a loud blast on his whistle, but I only heard the first note, the bombardment began as he was blowing, all the guns in the Ypres Salient opened fire and the roar of artillery drowned every other sound. All the guns in the Salient! It sounded like all the guns in the world. It sounded as though the sky was falling, as though the thunder of the guns had cracked it, as though the world itself was breaking into pieces. Our shells were breaking it. Low down, all along the eastern horizon, I saw their red flashes as they burst, spurts of fire in the darkness.[2]

Major Milbourne Bransby Williams had fought at Mametz Wood as a captain in the 14th Welsh. He was present at Pilkem and left an account of the battalion's actions:

In the last week much of the vigour acquired during training at Elstree Blanche had been lost. The Germans had gas shelled almost continuously at night, much heavy, carrying work had been done to supply artillery ammunition for the final bombardment and creeping barrage, and the hostile counter bombardment had never allowed much sleep. This last week had been perhaps the most trying that the battalion had ever experienced, but the spirit for the fight remained and the 31st was looked forward to with eagerness.

At dusk, the battalion moved up by platoons at 100 yards distance, to the assembly trenches. Marching across the open and avoiding communication trenches, the whole battalion assembled in its allotted position, without casualties, by midnight... (no gas at this time and shelling not as heavy as usual).

The battalion suffered a few casualties, among them 2nd Lieut. Fox, who was killed by a shell within 5 minutes of Zero Hour. This particular shell exploded right in the trench among a section of Lewis Gunners, and all except the corporal were killed or wounded.

The morning was dull. The smoke of the shells made it impossible to see more than about 100 yards, and in the first advance it was necessary to use compasses. The havoc wrought by the artillery was so great that even trench lines and old buildings could not be distinguished and a certain amount of mixing and loss of direction inevitably occurred.

The first stage had been completed well to time. The 13th had taken the Blue Line without difficulty, killing or capturing the few Germans who remained alive, and the 14th was in line close up to the creeping barrage, waiting to attack Pilkem Ridge some 300 yards away. As soon as the barrage advanced again, C and D Companies advanced behind it, keeping very close to it. It was soon evident that the opposition was weak, as there was practically no rifle fire. The enemy were seen to be hurriedly leaving their trenches.

The supporting artillery fire was perfect, too perfect perhaps from an infantry point of view, because the enemy simply could not remain alive in their trenches, and so no opposition was put up. The Germans were in very strongly built concrete forts, which could not be shattered except by a direct hit from a heavy shell. These little forts were held by machine gunners who could fire at the advancing troops unharmed until each was rushed. The fighting was hand to hand, and casualties were considerable, over twenty Germans were killed with the bayonet, and forty prisoners and three machine guns captured.[3]

Private Douglas Myers Anderton served with the 15th Royal Welsh Fusiliers. He wrote to his parents on 5 August 1917:

It is with a feeling of great thankfulness that I sit down to write you these few lines, as many a time during the last five days I have thought that I had written my last letter. I daresay you have seen in the papers about the big attack on July 31st. Well I went over the top at dawn last Tuesday and today Sunday we have just come out of the line, all that is left of us, for a thorough rest. We went right through the three German lines and well beyond into open country, capturing the village of Pilkem on the way. When we could get no further, we dug a rough trench and had to hold our position against counterattacks night and day for five solid days.

It was hell, especially when the rain started on the second day. The ground is very low and our trench was up to the waist in water all the time we held it, just in front of Langemarck. The Germans attacked us time after time, they shelled us, gassed us, bombed us and sniped us, but we held it like grim death until we were relieved yesterday. Our losses in this battalion are awful and there are only about 140 of us left out of a full battalion. I am in a bombing section and am the only one left in the section. I have come through without a scratch and it was just as though someone was watching over me, for chaps were knocked out all round me and yet it seemed as if I could not be hit.

When we got to the third German line, I was just going into a dugout with my rifle levelled when two Fritzs came out, both armed. I just managed to pull the trigger on one and the other one threw up his hands. I took him prisoner and took his cap, belt, cigarette case and two or three souvenirs off him and shoved them in my haversack, but unfortunately I lost my haversack the next day or I would have sent them home. We were held up by several machine guns but we bombed the Fritzs out of their concrete places and out they ran shouting 'Kamerad'. One of them took all the stuff out of his pockets and ran up to me, saying 'Me poor Fritz. Kamerad'. He gave me a whole pile of rubbish, cigarettes and letters and cigars, which I threw away. All our officers were killed or wounded except two, and we had a second lieutenant in command of the battalion at the finish.

We had to collect rations off the dead at night while we were holding our position as supplies were difficult to get up, so you can see that after living on dead men's bully and biscuits for a few days, some decent grub will be a treat, so send it as quick as you can. Also send a couple of newspapers with the big advance in, dated August 1st or 2nd. My feet are all swollen with standing in water and I can hardly walk about but that's all right so long as I am still alive.[4]

He wrote another letter home on 16 August:

We have had a lot of rain lately, and it makes all the difference here between 'comfort' and misery. It is not half so bad when you are dry, even if Fritz is strafing you, but when you are soaked through, and up over the knees in it into the bargain, it makes you feel rather tired of life. Still, however bad a time we are having, we always have the consolation that our friend across the way is having a jolly sight worse, because although he sends thousands of shells over to us, our artillery send over three or four to his one.

It is a terrible sight the devastated country round here. You can look for miles and see nothing but one long stretch of shell holes and battered trenches, not a tree nor a bush standing, except a few jagged stumps which look as if they have been struck by lightning. Bits of barbed wire, a heap of bricks which was once a house, some tangled ironwork once a railway, and a few tufts of scorched grass, and you have a picture of no man's land. The only living things are the rats and there are scores of them.

When you think that these lines have been held for close on three years, with continual bombardments and previous attacks, it is not surprising that everything is razed to the ground. You can imagine what it is like at night, pitch dark except for an occasional Very light.[5]

Douglas Anderton was born in Keighley in Yorkshire in 1898 and had begun his war service with the Royal Warwickshire Regiment before being transferred to the Royal Welsh Fusiliers, where he served with the 14th and 15th Battalions. He survived the war, dying in 1967.

Signaller Private Harold Diffey of the 15th Royal Welsh Fusiliers, along with a friend, Corporal Pugh, became separated during darkness from the rest of their battalion. They found a dry trench and took shelter in it.

> Of course, it had been an old German trench. Even at this stage there were a few stretches about that you could call by the name of trenches. But we were suspicious as soon as we dropped into it, because the Germans were always very careful when they retired – they never left anything behind but empty tins and ashes of fires – and, lo and behold, we saw this new equipment and a rifle at the entrance to this dugout. We immediately suspected that there were Germans about, keeping very quiet. I still had the signal lamp with me, so I pulled it round off my shoulder and shone a beam of light down the concrete stairs, and there at the bottom of the steps sat a German soldier, apparently asleep. We get down – shine the lamp – no German to be seen. Pugh sees a candle end. We light it and then we see a pair of boots sticking out under a lot of sacks, so we pounce on it and haul out this German. Just a little bloke and frightened as hell. Jabbering away in German, which we don't understand a word of. We search him. You're supposed to search all prisoners, but what we're after is cigarettes. We're dying for a smoke. He doesn't smoke. No fags. But he pulls out photographs of his wife and children and points to himself and says, 'Saxon, Saxon.' We take him to mean that the Saxons are friends of the British. I say to Pugh that we're supposed to escort him back to the transport lines. Pugh says, 'Well, I'm bloody sure I'm not going back with him, with all this iron flying about the sky!' Then he has an idea. 'Keep him here,' he says. 'If any Jerries counterattack, he can shout up the stairs to them. If any of our fellows come along, we can shout up the stairs. We're safer here than in London!' We sit down on the floor and after a bit the little Jerry relaxes. We go to sleep, all three of us huddled together for warmth.[6]

Emlyn Davies of the 17th Royal Welsh Fusiliers had fought at Mametz Wood the previous year. He wrote in his memoirs of the attack on Pilkem Ridge:

> The firing of a huge gun gave the signal both to the infantry to leave their trenches and to all calibres of artillery to open fire to the limit of their capacity. Amazed, I then saw some tanks crawl

slowly forward. Instantly the thought occurred to me 'We are going places this time.' But that was not to be the case. Although the Division forged forward, they captured Pilkem Ridge, advancing to a depth of three miles. They too were bogged down. A violent counterattack pressed them back a distance. Lying beside a machine gunner in a shell hole on the Ridge, I asked him why he was not firing. Cryptically he replied, 'Mud has blocked it.'

The Division's Commander, General Blackader, issued the order 'Every man must stick to his trench or shell hole. There must be no retirement.' 'Stick it Welsh,' was the attitude. The counterattack was foiled. They had overcome the elite German regiment known as 'The Cockchafers'. Enclosed in our cages they were not so cocky.

My next station was about three-quarters of a mile forward. The best shelter we could spot looked like two dislodged Stonehenge slabs. Its past use by the Germans was apparent. Of course it was filthy with used first aid remnants lying about. The cervices of the boarded floor teemed with red lice. Stinking black water oozed from beneath. We cleaned it up. There were two entrances, one the result of a direct hit and the roof had suffered similarly.

A row of high trees began about fifty yards away. In line and extending each side of the pillbox, our guns lay wheel to wheel to an unseen distance. They were being engaged by the enemy gunners. Once I witnessed an extraordinary sight. It was the perpendicular rising to a height of fifty feet of one of our pieces. A heavy German shell had exploded exactly underneath. It came down, disintegrating as it fell. I saw nothing of the poor gunners manning it.

Every afternoon, about 2.30, a heavy barrage sparkled along the track. A signaller at Red House 1 and I had to collect rations and batteries from the Canal Bank daily. I called upon him one day one hour earlier than usual. He had hopped off before noon, omitting to call upon me. The attraction was his Regimental Canteen on the Canal Bank. Left with a lone journey, I made a number of attempts to make the passage, but could not face it, the barrage having commenced an hour in advance of the usual time. Six gunners came running from laying new gun sites up front in preparation for the attack which was soon to be launched. I determined to follow them. The journey had to be made. I made it.

A shell burst five yards beside me. I felt a hell of a bang on my left foot and was knocked silly. The shell had burst in soft ground and most of the contents went skywards. I picked myself up and limped after the gunner hares. They took me into their small elephant shelter and tried to remove my boot. It declined movement. They slit further along the toe cap and it responded. It was most painful; I began to think this was my Blighty. Disappointed, it proved otherwise. The fragment had struck the side of my boot but had not pierced it. The swelling rose, but the injury was only slight.

Deciding to risk the shells bursting on the road, we made a dash towards the remains of Pilkem, consisting now only of one short low wall, and rested again. Now we were free of the fan-like barrage and could continue at a steadier pace and made it. I was to make three more journeys along that two-mile track in quieter circumstances. But I was disappointed by my non-Blighty.

The final attack on the enemy positions, so far as concerned the Welsh Division, emerged as their stiffest assignment. During the past twelve months they had become hardened to stiff engagement. They had held their sector in the Salient over a more extended period than any other unit. They had notched up a record toll of day raids and night raids on their opponents. Raids were invariably costly in lives lost. Indications of their activities appeared in a notice I read on passing through the old German lines: 'To the memory of 198 Welshmen killed in a raid.' It seemed to have been erected by the enemy.

The assault was launched in the face of a furious enemy bombardment. Curtains of falling shells descended upon the area in dispute, mushrooming on explosion to give a picture of schools of whales spouting upwards their excess of water. But this was a heaving uprise of liquid mud and earth and smoke and fire. Gaps appeared in the advancing waves, far too numerous. But the attackers moved forward, tottering about like Andean torrent ducks. On they went.

They reached Iron Cross, the outskirts of Langemarck and of Poelcappelle and consolidated their hard won ground. It was a great performance. The Germans had constructed their defences in depth, studded with concrete pillboxes arranged in diamond shaped groups. I was in an isolated canvas wigwam in front of Langemarck. The Church Tower was known to harbour enemy observers. It suffered intense shattering by a naval gun firing eighteen-inch shells. I could hear its firing from back of beyond. Moments later they thundered overhead, crashing into the village, leaving as evidence mountains of rubble. The King point and King conquest was in the form of a huge pillbox at Gournier's Farm. Walls and roof consisted of yard-thick concrete; built like the turret of a dreadnought, with embrasures for rifle and machine gun fire; it was a formidable obstacle.

In 1968 I toured the Salient; the Burgomaster of Ypres informed me the Memorial to the 38th Division was this same pillbox at Gournier's Farm. Examining it with redoubled interest, I could not imagine how this seemingly impregnable fortress could have been overcome by a handful of infantrymen. On it there were no signs whatsoever of its having suffered damage by shellfire. How on earth it had been successfully stormed only God in heaven could know. The Taffies had done it with bomb and bayonet.[7]

Emlyn Davies was hospitalised in early 1918, suffering from Trench Fever. He was treated for 14 months until he was eventually demobilised from the Army. On his return to the battlefield in 1968 he wrote: 'Bidding a final farewell, I paused awhile on the fateful Passchendaele Ridge in contemplation. I recalled the mud, the fire and brimstone sprouting everywhere, the sound of the guns, of mangled and rotting bodies, of men smothering in the sucking morass, helpless to save themselves or of being saved.'[8]

William Thomas Evans from Newport served with the 16th Welsh before being transferred to the Machine Gun Corps early in 1917 and fought at Passchendaele. He was wounded in the lower leg in 1916 and gassed several times which affected his health for the rest of his life – he suffered periodic bouts of pneumonia. Born on 14 June 1893, he emigrated to Canada in 1912. When war was declared his patriotism saw him pay for his own passage home to Wales and, on a Sunday lunchtime late in 1914, he walked into the Cardiff recruiting office. It was empty apart from a young Jewish man named Morris Cowan (who later ran a tailor's shop in Queen Street, Cardiff). Evans had every intention of enlisting in the Welsh Guards as he

Emlyn Davies

William Evans

stood 6' 2", but Morris produced a half-bottle of whisky and offered him a drink. A while later the Recruiting Sergeant returned from his lunch and when asked which regiment he would like to join, William replied, 'The same one as my mate here, the 16th Welsh!'[9] William Evans survived the war and was discharged as a Company Sergeant Major.

Sergeant William J. Collins of the Royal Army Medical Corps left a graphic account of the nature of his work at the Third Battle of Ypres:

A stretcher squad consists of four men and you lift the stretcher up and on to the shoulder, and each corner had a man. Now that's the only way you can carry a man properly. But, my God it was hard work, really hard. I mean, the road there was all lumps and bumps. It was being fed with every stone and every old brick that you could think of, and there was no steam-rolling it down flat,

347

you know! It was being knocked down with mauls. And carrying over that rough ground is very hard. And of course it's hard on the shoulders. When the conditions got really appalling, it required twelve men to a stretcher, but they couldn't get on the stretcher all at the same time... you could get six... one in the middle one side, one the other, and then they would stop and another six men would take over. You see, you're being dragged down in the mud and, of course, you're plastered in mud yourself. And not only that, they're not fed up like boxers for a contest, they're living on bully beef and water and dog biscuits. No hot meals! Hot meals? Never heard of them.

What we had was stretchers and the field surgical haversack with the usual bandages, morphia, quarter grain tablets, scissors, plaster, dressings. If I came across a casualty, and it could be dealt with, I always used to use the first field dressing out of the uniform pocket. You ripped the waterproof covering and there was a pad of gauze and an ampoule in it, and all you had to do was to press the ampoule and it crumbled immediately, and the iodine was released

German prisoners assisting British stretcher-bearers
© Imperial War Museum

all over the pad. And then you put the pad to the wound and bound him up. Every soldier carried one in his jacket so, naturally, to save my dressings in the surgical haversack, the first thing I used was the soldier's own field dressing.

If a fellow was bad, a man who'd lost all colour and was pallid and cold and was perhaps breathing heavily, you'd give him a little morphine. It dissolved immediately. You put it under the tongue, and it was in the blood stream in seconds. And there was always a little bottle of them in the surgical haversack.[10]

William Collins had been Mentioned in Dispatches in January 1916 and had first landed in France on 16 October 1914.

Major D.F. Grant, one of the artillery officers of a battery brought up to support the next stage of the advance, left an account of his time in the Salient:

The great 31st July, 1917, came, and the Guards Division did splendidly. After firing 28 lifts in the attack, the battery advanced at 8.30 a.m. to a position close to the Yser Canal, west of Boesinghe. We had orders to advance to the canal first, and perhaps later in the day to cross it and take up the advance. But the Fates willed otherwise, and we remained in the canal position for a week. The great breakthrough had not taken place, but the High Command hoped it might yet, if the attack was pressed. And so, on 7th August, 1917, we advanced to a position on the north-east of Artillery Wood, by the ruined village of Pilchem. The guns were got along the badly smashed-up roads by our splendid 'hairies', the help of drag-ropes, and much hectic language!

Ammunition was brought up by pack animal, and it was an unhealthy job coming up the road past Steam Mill. The wagon line moved up to Elverdinghe, and suffered casualties from heavy guns; whilst the Brigade Ammunition Column behind our lines, were worried even more. The gun line began to suffer severe casualties. Corporal A.F. Bethell, M.M., and Fitter Wetten were killed, and many went down with wounds. Poor Bethell had his thigh fractured by a splinter, and died at the Casualty Clearing Station at Canada Farm, behind Elverdinghe, being buried at the cemetery there. Though he must have been in frightful pain, he smiled as he was being carried away to the dressing station on a stretcher, and told us 'not to worry about him'. The very efficient and reliable signalling staff the battery had always possessed was chiefly due to his untiring hard work, and his death was a sore blow to his fellow-signallers and many friends.[11]

Donald Farquharson Grant was Mentioned in Dispatches in May 1917 and was later awarded the Military Cross. Corporal Archibald Francis Bethell died of his wounds, aged 23, on 11 August, and was buried in Dozinghem Military Cemetery. His parents lived in Bruce Road, Harlesden, London. Fitter Frederick Edward Wetten had been born in Harlesden and died on 13 August. He has no known grave and is remembered on the Menin Gate Memorial to the Missing. Bethell's service number was 40091 and Wetten's was 40093, so they probably enlisted together.

Lieutenant Douglas Wimberley of the Machine Gun Corps described conditions at the Battle of the Menin Road Ridge:

I spent the night before the battle in a concrete pillbox... It had very thick concrete walls but it was a curious sort of place to have a headquarters. It had been built by the Germans, and so the entrance faced the German lines. Inside it was only about five-foot-high and at the bottom there was about two foot of water. This water was simply horrid, full of refuse, old tins and even excreta. Whenever shells burst near it the smell was perfectly overpowering.

Luckily, there was a sort of concrete shelf the Boche had made about two foot above ground level. It was on this shelf that four officers and six other ranks spent the night. There wasn't room to lie down, there was hardly room to sit upright, and we more or less crouched there.

Outside the pillbox was an enormous shell hole full of water, and the only way out was over a ten-inch plank. Inside the shell hole was the dead body of a Boche who had been there a very long time and who floated or sank on alternate days according to the atmosphere.[12]

Francis Philip Woodruff of the 2nd Royal Welsh Fusiliers, who wrote an autobiography under his adopted name of Frank Richards, described his arrival at Polygon Wood:

I expected to find a wood but it was undulating land with a tree dotted here and there and little banks running in different directions. About half a mile in front of us was a ridge of trees, and a few concrete pillboxes of different sizes. The ground that we were now on and some of the pillboxes had only been taken some hours previously. I entered one pillbox during the day and found eighteen dead Germans inside. There was not a mark on one of them; one of our heavy shells had made a direct hit on the top of it and they were killed by concussion, but very little damage had been done to the pillbox. They were all constructed with reinforced concrete and shells would explode all round them but the flying pieces would never penetrate the concrete. There were small windows in the sides and, by jumping in and out of shell holes, attacking troops could get in bombing range: if a bomb was thrown through one of the windows, the pillbox was as good as captured.[13]

He later described the hazards of being a company runner:

During the afternoon the Major handed me a message to take to A Company, which consisted of the survivors of two companies now merged into one under the command of a young platoon officer. They had to advance and take up a position about two hundred yards in front of them.

The ground over which I had to travel had been occupied by the enemy a little while before and the Company were behind a little bank which was being heavily shelled. I slung my rifle, and after I had proceeded some way I pulled my revolver out for safety. Shells were falling here and there and I was jumping in and out of shell holes.

When I was about fifty yards from the Company, in getting out of a large shell hole I saw a German pop up from another shell hole in front of me and rest his rifle on the lip of the shell hole. He was about to fire at our chaps in front who had passed him by without noticing him. He could never have heard me amidst all the din around: I expect it was some instinct made him turn around with the rifle at his shoulder. I fired first and, as the rifle fell out of his hands, I fired again. I made sure he was dead before I left him. If he hadn't popped his head up when he did no doubt I would have passed the shell hole he was in. I expect he had been shamming death and every now and then popping up and sniping at our chaps in front. If I hadn't spotted him he would have soon put my lights out after I had passed him and if any of his bullets had found their mark it would not have been noticed among the Company, who were getting men knocked out now and then by the shells that were bursting around them. This little affair was nothing out of the ordinary in a runner's work when in attacks.[14]

Frank Richards was born in Monmouthshire and was orphaned at the age of nine. He was brought up by an aunt and uncle in the industrial area of Blaina and worked as a coal miner before enlisting. He served throughout the war and died in 1961.

Private Tom Davies was an ex-miner who served with a Field Ambulance unit. He committed his recollections of his wartime service to paper in a poem:

We then formed an Aid Post in Méteren
And another at Caistre close by.
At Méteren we treated the wounded,
At Caistre, to cure Scabies we tried.

Very soon we were moved up to Ypres,
Just a wilderness of shell holes and mud.
Many wounded were drowned in the trenches
As heavy rain caused the whole area to flood.

It was there that I caught my Blighty,
My right leg fractured quite bad.
But the pal who was with me, poor devil,
Had big gash right through his head.[15]

His brother Ivor was killed at Cambrai, but Tom Davies survived the war.

Frank Richards

Tom Davies in Cheltenham Hospital in 1917

Corporal Samuel Arthur White joined the 10th Welsh in November 1914. He was born in Penarth but was living in Fryatt Street, Barry Dock, and working as a labourer when he enlisted. He fought at Mametz Wood and Pilkem Ridge and survived the war, rising to the rank of Company Quartermaster Sergeant. He wrote a poem describing his experiences entitled, 'The Noble 38th':

The modern Attila, foul Hun, set forth with flag unfurled,
To ravage Belgium, conquer France, to terrorise the world.
Doubtless, he thought his vaunted troops would vanquish any foe,
And History proves those stricken lands sustained a fearful blow.
But Britain's 'Old Contemptibles' quick crossed the sea's highway.
And stemmed the tide of conquering, the Germans held at bay,
And soon 'One Hundred Thousand', at Kitchener's behest,
Were marshalled in Battalions, Britain's bravest, Britain's best.
From English counties, Erin's Isle, from Scottish moors and dales,
In quick response rushed volunteers, and SOME from Gallant Wales.
From Canada's far shores, from Australasian Seas,

From Africa, from India, from world-wide Colonies.
They came, some war-worn, some untried, but eager every one,
To stay the furious onslaught of that brutal beast, the Hun.
And well they proved their mettle, through seas of mud they toiled,
Till by superhuman bravery, the German plans were foiled.
The Welsh Division grandly led, shock after shock withstood,
Till the very hills were ringing, of their deeds at Mametz Wood.
Then came the crowning effort, famed Pilkem Ridge the scene,
Where the Welsh Division faced the foe, with wits and weapons keen.
Where the Kaiser's pets were beaten; his redoubtable 'Cockchafers',
Failed to withstand the Cymric band, and crumpled up like wafers.
Here the Hun, sore shaken, gamely rallied, vainly tried,
To pierce the line hard won by lads, from Taff and Tivyside,
By lads from every hamlet, 'twixt Rhyl and Barry Dock,
From Menai Bridge to Milford, and the Beacons in Brecknock.
Well handled by their officers, they nobly held the line,
And helped to drive the Butcher and his hordes towards the Rhine.
Aye, up the line and down the line, from Ypres to the Somme,
The sturdy little Cymros faced the gas, the shell, the bomb.
All valiantly their blood was shed, again, and yet again,
Trusting, believing, hoping it was not shed in vain.
They taught the foe a lesson, not to hold in false derision,
The brilliant gallant 38th, the famous Welsh Division.[16]

Samuel White

Captain James Churchill Dunn, the Medical Officer of the 2nd Battalion of the Royal Welsh Fusiliers, wrote of his experiences at the Third Battle of Ypres:

> The Staff had settled in a bit of trench behind our line of deployment: it was probably a relic of October-November 1914 because digging had exposed a rusted rifle barrel. When I got near, Sergeant Hogben shouted, 'Look out,' and pointed to the Fokker which was coming round for the second time. It was not a hundred feet up, and fewer yards away by then. 'Get down,' he shouted again, 'the bloody thing's hit me.' Very soon he was showing me the nose of a German bullet sticking out between two of his ribs in front... He did not feel ill, but septic pneumonia was to set in. Ten days later he died close to Beachy Head.[17]

Lance Sergeant William Willis Hogben of the 2nd Battalion R.W.F. died on 15 October and was buried in Kingston Cemetery, Portsmouth. He was 30 and was awarded the Distinguished Conduct Medal posthumously in April 1918: 'For conspicuous gallantry and devotion to duty. He has carried out his duties in a most gallant and efficient manner during a very long period, and has always shown great courage and resource.'[18]

The son of George and Sarah Hogben of Portsmouth, he was born at Sandgate in Kent. Formerly with the Worcestershire Regiment, he had served on the Western Front since August 1914.

Of the artillery duels Dunn wrote:

> Each time the gunners on both sides opened promptly on their night lines, firing their rapidest as though frenzied to add to the stupendous tempest of sound, it was as a rending of our part of the firmament. The staccato of the machine guns filled the intervals of the larger reports and of the shell-bursts, and the overhead rush of bullets through the nearly still, crisp air was like the whistle of a great wind. A veil of acrid smoke drifted over us, tainting the freshness of the autumn night.[19]

James Dunn

James Dunn was born in New Zealand, where his parents were killed in a Maori uprising when he was just a few months old. Raised in Scotland, after qualifying as a doctor he volunteered for service in the South African War, where he won the Distinguished Conduct Medal. He was awarded the Military Cross in 1916 and won a bar to his M.C. in the middle of July 1917.

CHAPTER 23

How the Press
Reported the Battle

REPORTS OF THE battle soon began to be published in the
British newspapers and the early press coverage of the success
of the 38th (Welsh) Division included reference to French
reports, which, given the fog of war, contained some errors
which were later corrected:

> Paris, Thursday. M. Andrew Tudesq, telegraphing from the British
> front in Flanders to the *Journal*, says: 'One of the most striking
> events in the attack was the battle between the Welsh troops and
> the "Hannetons". This nickname was once used to designate the
> regiment of Fusilier Guards which enjoyed the special favour of
> the Kaiser. I say "was used" advisedly, and not "is used," because
> this "markoefer" famous corps in the German Army, noted for
> its tenacity and success when in action, was wiped out to the last
> man. Surprised by the Welshman not far from Pilkem, the three
> battalions of Guards, marching in echelon formations, were cut to
> pieces and decimated. Machine guns, grenades, bayonet-fighting,
> all came into play, and the Kaiser's favourite Guards learnt to their
> cost every form of massacre in this desperate battle of Flanders.
> The Welsh regiments covered themselves with glory.' – Exchange.

> ONLY TWO LEFT ALIVE Paris, Thursday
> The 'Petit Parisian's' correspondence pays homage to the
> magnificent heroism of the Welsh. It was about three in the
> afternoon, says the correspondent, when the Welsh, having cleared
> all the enemy trenches by means of grenades, penetrated into St.

Julien from three sides, and after fierce fighting in the streets had to lay siege to each house in turn. The carnage was frightful, but the Welsh covered themselves with glory. The Prussian Guards obeyed their orders to die on the spot and no prisoners were taken. One young German prisoner declared, 'They had promised us that we should not participate in this fighting and that we were to constitute the last reserve and remain in the fourth line trenches. But as things were going badly we had to go forward. Out of a hundred and fifty of us only two were left alive.'[1]

A day later further French press reports appeared in the British press:

HEROES OF PILKEM. How the Welshmen Crushed the 'Cockchafers.' The French correspondents on the British front single out as one of the most glorious episodes of Tuesday's fighting the smashing of the Kaiser's favourite 'Cockchafers' (Guards Fusiliers) by Welsh troops.

The Cockchafers, celebrated in the German Army for their determined fighting and successes, writes M. Andre Tudesq in the *Journal*, exist no more. Surprised by the Welsh not far from Pilkem, their three battalions were cut to pieces, and every one slain with machine gun, bomb, bayonet, or knife. The Welsh gained their spurs against them in this Flanders battle. The 'Petit Parisien' correspondent says: 'Like La Basseville, and perhaps to a still greater extent, Pilkem was one of the principle points of the enemy's resistance. Every house round the village and in it had been transformed into a fort defended with revolver guns and machine guns. A double belt of trenches with ferro-concrete dugouts guarded the outskirts of the place. The Prussian Guard had been quartered there for a fortnight. At three o'clock in the afternoon, under a torrential downpour, the Welsh troops, after having quickly cleaned up the enemy trenches with bombs, entered the village from three sides. Street fighting was followed by a determined onslaught on each house. The onset was terrible and the carnage frightful, and the Welshmen covered themselves with honour and glory. As to the Prussian Guard, they obeyed their order to die where they stood: there was not a single prisoner taken. Elsewhere also, notably at Hooge, the fighting was stubborn. Here were found quite young men of the Bonn and Heidelberg student type. A few of them who had escaped the artillery fire were taken prisoners. "We were told we should not take part in the battle," one of them said bitterly. "We were to constitute the extreme reserve and to hold ourselves in readiness in the fourth line of trenches now being built, but as things went badly we were thrown in. We were 150, now we are only a handful." Speaking of the new tanks, which he had seen for the first time, another young German said: "Our newspapers pour ridicule on them, but when you see them at work you soon change your mind."

'Describing the work of the tanks in glowing terms, the *Matin* correspondent says: "Their principal triumphs were at Inverness Copse and Pommern Redoubt. One attacked a concrete redoubt and all its defenders surrendered. Another went from spinney to spinney hunting out machine guns, another tank went wallowing through the village, smashing everything. The Germans have formed special engineering sections to fight the tanks, which they attack with twelve-pound bombs."'[2]

Philip Gibbs was a war correspondent who had reported events on the Western Front since the early days of the war, one of only five reporters who held this official title. Although he wrote primarily for *The Daily Chronicle*, his reports received a wide circulation amongst a range of British newspapers. He later became frustrated at the degree to which his reports were amended by official censorship.

Philip Gibbs

In his first report on the capture of Pilkem he wrote:

WELSH WIPE OUT KAISER'S FAMOUS REGIMENT
In a graphic description of the fighting, Mr Philip Gibbs, the
special correspondent of the *Daily Chronicle*, says: 'The success of
the day is shared by English troops, including the Guards, with the
Welsh, who fought abreast of them with equal heroism, and with
Scottish and Anzacs. The Welsh have wiped out the most famous
German regiment of the Third Guards Division, known as the
"Cockchafers". Fighting with us the French troops kept pace with
their usual gallantry, carrying all their objectives according to time
table. In one great and irresistible assault, these troops of the two
nations swept across the enemy lines and have reached heights on
the Pilkem Ridge, as I hope to tell tomorrow in greater detail. For
today it is enough to say that our success has been as great as we
dared to hope.'[3]

A second, more detailed report soon followed:

The Song of the Cockchafers

August 8

One of the most bitter blows to Germany, if she has heard the news,
must be the destruction of the famous regiment of 'Maikaefer' or
Cockchafers, by our Welsh troops. The Kaiser called them his brave
Coburgers. In Germany the very children sang in the streets about
them. And proud of their own exploits, they had their own soldier
poets who wrote songs about the regiment, to which they marched
through Belgium and France and Galicia. I saw one of these songs
yesterday, picked up on the battlefield near Pilkem. It was written
by one Paul Zimmermann of theirs, and was printed in a leaflet sold
at ten pfennigs (a penny). It tells how the Cockchafers come out
in the spring and how the children sing when they come. They are
ready for battle then, wherever it may be. The call comes for them
wherever there is the hardest fighting, so the Cockchafers swarmed
through Belgium, and taught the French a lesson, and pressed after
the wicked English, who – so the lying legend goes – used dum-
dum bullets, and swept back the Russians through Galicia. Old
Hindenburg calls for them every time when there are brave deeds to
be done. I have copied out two verses for those who read German:

'*Der Mai der bringt uns Sonnenschein,*
Er bringt uns Bluhtenpracht;
Der Mai der bringt uns Kaeferlein
Viel tausend uber Nacht;
Und von der Kinderlippen klingts:
"Maikaefer, fliege, flieg"
Und durch den Fruhlingesjubel dringts:
"Dein Vater ist im Krieg."
Uns Garde Fusiliere nennt
Maikaefer jeder Mund,
Weil unser stolzes Regiment
Im Mai stets fertig stand.'

('The month of May brings us sunshine,
It brings us sumptuous flowers;
The month of May brings us little bugs
Many thousands overnight;
And so it sounds from children's lips:
"May bug, fly, fly"
And through the spring joy one hears:
"My father is at war."
Every mouth calls us Guards Fusiliers
May bugs,
As our proud regiment
Has always stood ready in May.')[4]

Well, old Hindenburg will call in vain now for his Cockchafers, the Guard Fusilier Regiment of the 3rd Guards Division, for nearly six hundred of them are in our hands and others lie dead upon the ground near Pilkem. They had relieved the 100th Infantry Reserve Regiment on the night of July 29, and lay three battalions deep in their trench systems across the Yser Canal north-east of Boesinghe, scattered thinly in the shell-craters which were all that was left of the trenches in the front lines, more densely massed in the support lines, and defending a number of concrete emplacements and dugouts behind. The 9th Grenadier Regiment and a battalion of the Lehr Regiment reinforced the Cockchafers and lay out in the open behind the Langemarck-Gheluvelt line, and in the support lines a battalion of the Lehr of the 3rd Guards Division had already relieved a regiment of the 392nd Infantry Reserve Regiment. Some sections of the 3rd Battalion of the 9th Grenadier Regiment had been sent forward from Langemarck to act as sniping posts, and two special machine gun detachments were also pushed up to check our assault. They were enough to defend this part of the Pilkem Ridge, and the ground itself was in their favour as our men lay in the hollow with their backs to the Yser Canal, across which all their supports and supplies had to pass.

What was in favour of the Welsh was that they knew the ground in front of them in every detail from air photographs and from night and day raids, having lived in front of it for several months, digging and tunnelling so as to get cover from ceaseless fire, and storing up a great desire to get even with the enemy for all they had suffered. They had suffered great hardships and perils, intensified before the battle because of violent shelling by high explosives and gas-shells, so that when the hour for attack came they had been hard tried already. It made no difference to the pace and order of their assault. Our bombardment had been overwhelming, and the heavy barrage which signalled the assault was, according to all these Welshmen, perfect. They followed it very closely, so closely that they were on and over the Cockchafers before they could organize any kind of defence. Many of the enemy's machine guns had been smashed and buried. Those still intact were never brought into action, as their gunners had no time to get out of the concrete shelters in which they were huddled to escape from the annihilating fire.

German Garde Infanterie

It was in these places that most of the prisoners were taken – there and in a big trench, ten feet wide and twelve deep, on the outskirts of Pilkem village, where there is no village at all. The Cockchafers came out dazed, and gave themselves up mostly without a show of fighting. In some of their concrete shelters, like those at Mackensen Farm – don't imagine any buildings there – and Gallwitz Farm and Boche House and Zouave House, there were stores of ammunition, with many shells and trench-mortars.

So the Welsh went on in waves, sending back the prisoners on their way, through Pilkem to the high ground by the Iron Cross beyond, and then down the slopes to the Steenbeek stream. On the left were the Royal Welsh Fusiliers, who took the ground of Pilkem itself. On the right were men of the Welsh Regiment. In the ground beyond Pilkem they found the regimental headquarters in finely built dugouts, but the staff had fled to save their skins. There was another big dugout nearby used by the enemy as a dressing-station. It had room enough for a hundred men. There were fifty men. The Welsh swarmed around it – thirty wounded and twenty unwounded Germans. The doctor in charge was a good fellow, and, after surrendering his own men, attended to some of the wounded Welsh. Two machine guns and sixteen prisoners were taken out of a place called Jolie Farm, and thirty prisoners out of Rudolf Farm – concrete kennels in a chaos of craters – and three officers and forty-seven men came out of the ruins of a house somewhere near the Iron Cross. All the Welsh troops behaved with great courage, and a special word is due to the runners, who carried messages back under fire, and to the stretcher-bearers, who rescued the wounded utterly regardless of their own risks. Afterwards the mule drivers and leaders were splendid, bringing up supplies under heavy barrage fire. Wales did well that day, and the Welsh miners, who had already proved themselves as great diggers and great tunnellers and very brave men, showed themselves cool and fearless in the assault.[5]

Of the subsequent attack on Langemark, Gibbs wrote:

The enemy put up a fierce resistance except at points where underfed boys had been thrust out in shell holes, as in the neighbourhood of Langemarck, to check the first onslaught of our men if possible, and if not to die. Behind them, as storm troops for counterattack, were some of the finest troops of the German Army. Behind the immediate supporting troops were massed reserves whom the German command held ready to hurry up in wagons and light railways to any part of the field where their lines were most threatened, or when instant counterattacks might inflict most damage on our men.

In gun-power the enemy was and is strong. He had prepared a large concentration of guns south-east of our right flank, and whatever may be his reserves of ammunition he has gathered up great stores for this present battle. The ground was hideous, worse than in the winter on the Somme. That seems strange, with a hot sun shining overhead and dust rising in clouds along traffic roads behind the battle-line as I saw it today. That is the irony of things. Where our men were fighting yesterday and to-day, there are hundreds and thousands of shell holes, some three feet deep and some ten feet deep, and each shell hole is at least half full of water, and many of them are joined so that they form lakes deep enough to drown men and horses if they fall in. So it was, and is,

Captured German pillbox

around the place where Langemarck village stood, and where the old lake of the château that no longer stands has flooded over into a swamp, and where a double row of black tree-stumps goes along the track of the broken road where the people of Langemarck used to walk to church before the devil did in so many old churches and established little hells of his own on their rubbish-heaps. So it was yesterday and remains to-day all about, the stumps of trees sticking up out of a mush of slimy, pitted ground which go by the romantic names of Glencorse Wood and Inverness Copse, and Shrewsbury Forest and Polygon Wood. The photographs of our airmen taken yesterday in low flights over these damned places reveal the full foulness of them. Seen from this high view, they are long stretches of white barren earth pock-marked by innumerable craters, where no man or human body is to be seen, though there are many dead and some living lying in these holes, and they are all bright and shining, because the sun is glinting on the water which fills them, except where dense clouds of smoke from great gun-fire drift across.

The courage of men who attacked over such ground was great courage. The grim, stubborn way in which our soldiers made their way through these bogs and would not be beaten, though they slipped and fell and stuck deep while the enemy played machine gun bullets on to their lines and flung high explosives over the whole stretch of bog-land through which they had to pass, is one of the splendid and tragic things in our poor human story.

I told yesterday how some of our English battalions took Langemarck like this, leaving many comrades bogged, wounded, and spent, but crawling round the concrete houses, over the old cellars of the village and routing out the Germans who held them with machine guns. At the blockhouse on the way up, called Au Bon Gîte, an oblong fort of concrete walls ten feet thick, the Germans bolted inside as soon as they saw our men, slammed down an iron door, and for a time stayed there while our bombers prowled round like hungry wolves waiting for their prey. Later they gave themselves up because our lines swept past them and they had no hope.[6]

Arthur Moore was the war correspondent for *The Times* and he reported the advance of the 38th (Welsh) Division thus:

HOW THE WELSHMEN FOUGHT AND DIED. THE 'COCKCHAFERS' WIPED OUT.

The story of how, on July 31st, the Welshmen shattered the Guards Fusilier Regiment, or the famous Berlin 'Cockchafers,' is (says the *Times* Special Correspondent) almost pathetic, for it was a proud regiment.

The 'May Beetles' – Maikafer is the German word – were the pets of their Emperor, who, every year on the First of May, has sent them a little packet containing a live cockchafer with his compliments. But it takes a lot of beetles to make a meal for a beast like the Welsh Dragon, and on July 31st he ate his fill. All three battalions of the Fusiliers were in the line – the first in the front system, the second in the next, and the third in support behind. They had only been in two days and were fresh, but the first two battalions simply crumpled up and disappeared before the Welsh attack, offering scarcely any resistance, and the third did little better. Of the 660 prisoners which the Welshmen took, over 500 were the 'Cockchafers,' the remainder coming from the 9th Grenadier and the 3rd Lehr Regiments, with a few from other units.

But it was the 'Cockchafers" battle. They were the pièce de résistance. Of the 3,000 men nominally constituting the three battalions, we may probably assume that some 1,800 have actually been in the trenches. Such a regiment, in fact, any regiment, can hardly have yielded over 500 prisoners, all in small detachments, until it had had at least as many killed and wounded. So what miserable remnant of them really got away, though the Regimental Commander and his Staff did succeed in bolting, it is impossible to say. We took the regimental battle headquarters out the other side of Pilkem and a very nicely appointed headquarters they had been, but, with the desertion which so often characterises German higher officers, the Commander and his Staff had moved back as soon as the trouble began. Among the unwounded officers we took was one battalion commander, but it was the regiment as a whole that suffered, and one of the younger prisoners, who had borne himself well up that point, when he saw the masses of his comrades in the prisoners' cage and heard how many of them we had taken, simply broke down and cried like a child. This blotting out of a regiment, with all its pride, was like that of the 18th at Thiepval last year, and is a truly pathetic thing.

UP AND OVER PILKEM RIDGE

I have said that prisoners surrendered in small detachments, and that fact summarizes the story of the attack, for here the advance was just like what it was on other parts of the field. We had pounded the German lines unmercifully beforehand, and when the attack began the Welshmen themselves say with enthusiasm that our barrage was almost perfect. In the dark of the early morning it was the men's best guide as they went forward behind it.

Just behind the actual front line the Welsh Regiment got a bunch of prisoners, and in the strongly fortified position called 'Makensen Farm,' nor far beyond, they got more prisoners and a noble store of ammunition, with great stocks of rockets, Very lights, trench mortars, and such odd trifles. On the left the Fusiliers, fighting along the south side of the railway line to Thourout, had some trouble, and picked up a handful of prisoners at a strong position known as 'Zouave House.' But here, as on the right, there was nothing like a serious check all the way to Pilkem village.

The whole line had, of course, to go up the slopes of the ridge, and not unreasonably, had apprehended that there might be trouble as they topped the slope and the enemy machine guns could sweep the ridge. But the trouble was never formidable. Everywhere were scattered concrete 'pill-boxes' and strong points, and in some the garrisons showed real fight. But the Welshmen were not to be denied. They stalked and bombed or rushed each fortress as they came to it, small units having little independent battles of their own, in which individuals behaved with the utmost gallantry.

'Jolie Farm,' halfway through the advance on the right, yielded two machine guns and 16 prisoners. 'Rudolphe Farm,' with the orchard surrounding it, produced another 30. Three officers and 47 other ranks came from a clump of buildings which was a telephone exchange and regimental intelligence headquarters, and 40 more were captured in a farm by the point known as the 'Iron Cross,' on the other side of Pilkem at the extreme easterly point of the spur of the ridge. So it was Boches, Boches all the way, in small detachments or nests of 'Cockchafers.' Perhaps the most interesting set of specimens taken was at the ruins of a large dressing station near a regimental headquarters, where 16 wounded prisoners, too seriously hurt to be moved, were taken, and with them 22 unwounded men, who certainly were not the legitimate dressing station staff. They merely got under the Red Cross for refuge when our men came along.

THE 'COCKCHAFERS" POEM

The village of Pilkem itself, which, of course, is quite non-existent as a village, offered no difficulty, but around it is one of the most magnificent trenches the Germans have ever constructed, some 10ft. across and 12ft. deep, and full of concrete structures and dugouts of the most elaborate nature. It is really a triumph of industry, but our guns had spoiled its looks badly, and though some parties of the enemy in it fought here and there, it offered no more formidable resistance than many other points.

In the later stages of the advance the South Wales Borderers did very fine work, and with some Fusiliers, they carried the advance on right to the Steenbeck. No troops, in fact, in all the battle did their job more thoroughly or with greater dash than the Welsh. They had had rather a trying time in the trenches before the attack, but it only hardened them and made them keener when the attack took place and the Germans never had a change. First

Cockchafers

came the torrents of our shells, and then the Welshmen with rifle and bomb and bayonet. Many of the 'Cockchafers' are men of fine physique, and must be good soldiers. But they met better, and were fairly smothered from the start.

Among the interesting minor booty which we found are copies of the regimental poem celebrating the valour of the 'Cockchafers,' telling how in 1870 they flew to France and desolated it, and how in this war, when called to fly over the Rhine, they took wing and Belgium ceased to exist. Then Hindenburg called to them and they flew east and broke the Russians. Then Austria called, and south they went, and flew over the Carpathians, and how the British gnashed their teeth when the 'Cockchafers' swarmed out against them. It is quite a nice poem, but it needs another verse.

The whole organisation of the attack seems to have been magnificent. Here, as elsewhere, our system of transport and behaviour of the transport troops was splendid, so that supplies were reaching the Welshmen on the ridge by 3 o'clock that afternoon. Over the dreadful shell-swept ground this is not to be achieved without real heroism, and in battle after battle our transport service has shown that it is manned by heroes. As always, too, I have heard the greatest praise of gallantry of the runners who take messages backwards and forwards in all stages of the battle while it is going on.[7]

A further report came the following day:

WELSH DASH – HOW THE COCKCHAFERS WERE ROUTED (From the Press Association's Special Correspondent). BRITISH FRONT, Wednesday.
This is the fourth day of fine weather, and the guns are very busy along most of the important points of the front. From what we have come to regard as very minor matters in this era of great events, there is virtually nothing to record at the moment, so the only thing to do is to hark back to the late great event and relate something further of the splendid tale which will not be told in anything approaching entirety for years to come. I have gathered some more details of the carrying of a large slice of the Pilkem Ridge by the gallant Welsh troops, in the course of which operation the Grenadier Fusiliers Regiment of the 3rd Guards Division,

known as 'The Kaiser's Own Cockchafers', were so severely cut up that they will do very little cockchafing again for a long while to come.

During the previous day the canal on the front of the Welshmen had been spanned by 19 bridges. Aerial reconnaissance on the eve of the attack revealed that the guns had been almost completely withdrawn from the front line (although a number of small parties were distributed among the shell holes close to the badly battered trenches), but that they held their second line in strength. This second line was studded with nests of concrete cupolas each of which held at least one machine gun. It was still dark when the men went over the top. They declare that our barrage was wonderful in its precision, and that it was a great experience to stride forward in the wake of such a perfectly-ruled curtain of creeping fire. The ascent of the ridge proved to be less difficult than had been apprehended. The intensity of our artillery fire drove the Huns to cover, and our men were upon them so quickly when the deadly rain of shells had passed over their heads that they were unable in many cases to put up a show of defence at all, and either surrendered or broke away in a dazed fashion to seek fresh concealment. Mackensen Farm was carried and found to be full of ammunition. The Welsh Regiment mopped up large bunches of prisoners in the German second line trench. Jolie Farm yielded two machine guns and 16 Huns. Rudolph Farm proved good for 30 prisoners, and a house nearby added three officers and 47 other ranks to the haul.

When the total count was completed it was found that the Welshmen had taken seven officers and 622 other ranks as the result of their attack. A striking feature of the fighting, I am told, is the sheer contempt our lads have for the Boche when he is out in the open. In many cases they did not even trouble to collect the kamerading creatures, but hustled them in football scrimmage fashion, shouting to them to get back to our lines, and it was a great spectacle to see them bolting away from their own barrage with their hands up. Of course, large batches were found. These were marshalled to the rear under guard. The famous troops who wear the flash took Pilkem village, or, rather, the brick-strewn spot where it once stood. They found a remarkable trench running around the place some 12ft. wide and 10ft. deep and this took some little while to get across.

Some extraordinary instances of heroism and resource were told to me. There was the case of a soldier who stealthily crept right up to a machine gun emplacement, and then lobbed it through the slit out of which the machine gun was firing, doing in its drum. Another man firing from his hip with a Lewis Gun knocked out three machine gun crews with their weapons as they emerged from a deep dugout. A private in a group which had lost its officer unobtrusively, but firmly, took charge over the head of a corporal who appeared to be suffering from shell-shock. He knew that he had to try and get into touch with a battalion commanded by a colonel, and as he led his men forward he was incessantly shouting out, 'Anybody seen the colonel?' At last he found the unit he was seeking.

But the proudest feat of the glorious day was undoubtedly the rolling up of the Cockchafers by the Welshmen. Like most troops opposing them, this crack corps had only come into the line a few hours before the battle, and they were, therefore, perfectly fresh. Indeed some of the battalions were caught by our artillery during the process of relief, and suffered considerably. The three battalions of the Cockchafers were deployed one behind the other, the third battalion being in reserve. Our waves swept upon the front battalion, which literally went to pieces. The next battalion fared no better. The reserve battalion stood for a while, but the last seen of what remained of it consisted of little parties of men wandering about as though out of command, occasionally loosing off their rifles, but more bent upon escaping to cover than anything else.

Our troops found copies of a most bombastic poem singing the praise of this regiment of Guards Fusiliers, relating how the Kaiser bade them go to Belgium, and how in consequence Belgium was no more; how they heard the call of the East, and rushed across to make Hindenburg the hero that he is; how they next responded to the appeal of their brethren in the Carpathians and polished off all enemies in that part of the world, and how they came face to face with the British. Although this part of the paean rather tails away in utterly meaningless heroics, the Welshmen have put the best possible finale to this modest effort, which completely eclipses the story of Bill Adams at the Battle of Waterloo.[8]

In addition to these reports, which were initially circulated in national newspapers, the Welsh newspapers naturally carried their own reports on the fighting.

WELSH FUSILIERS' RUSH AT PILKEM – STORMING
CONCRETE SHELTERS – THE LATE CAPTAIN EDWARDS.
Particulars of the death of Acting Captain A.S. Edwards, Royal Welsh Fusiliers, who was killed in action on the 31st of July, have been received. 'He was (says the writer) in charge of B Company, which met in its advance one of the many farmhouses, all of which were converted, by means of concrete gun emplacements, into miniature fortresses. They were momentarily in a tight corner, and Lieut. Edwards advanced himself as far as the door, when he was shot down from within. His death was instantaneous. He is buried just near the spot, about half-a-mile beyond Pilkem.'

Colonel the Hon. Henry Lloyd Mostyn, who was the first Colonel of the 17th Battalion, in a letter of sympathy, said; 'I shall always, I assure you, have the pleasantest recollection of your gallant boy, who served under me in the Welsh Division for six months. He was a most promising and capable young officer, and devoted to his duties. All ranks will much regret his loss.'[9]

It was not long, however, before the casualties began to arrive home to change the previous 'gung-ho' mood:

GRAPHIC STORIES OF THE NEWEST PUSH
Cardiff received its first convoy of casualties from the great push in Flanders shortly before nine o'clock on Friday morning, the Red Cross train conveying two officers and 134 rank and file being met at the Great Western Railway Station by Major E.J. Maclean and Lieutenant Hayward, from the 3rd Western General Hospital; Major Sir John Courtis (in command of the Motor Transport), and Mr. William Harry (in charge of the Voluntary Aid Detachments).

Members of Welsh units in the convoy included:
43571 Lce.-cpl. J.R. Reese, R.W.F. (sprained ankle).
54506 Pte. G.P. Jones, Welsh Regt. (sprained ankle).
56161 Pte. T. Pursehouse, R.W.F. (gunshot wound right leg).
285199 Pte. A. Evans, Welsh Regt. (gunshot wound left shoulder).

56436 Pte. G. Morris, R.W.F. (gassed).

39642 Pte. H. Bann, R.W.F. (gunshot wound head).

54281 Pte. W.A. Jones, Welsh Regt. (gunshot wound right arm).

48957 Pte. F. Reed, Welsh Regt. (gassed).

20181 Pte. T. Davies, R.W.F. (gassed).

In spite of their disabilities, the men seemed quite cheerful, and those who were well enough to enter into conversation assured a *Western Mail* representative that 'the greatest battle of the war had opened auspiciously, and that Fritz's number was at last up.'

'We have got them absolutely beat this time,' said one of the East Surreys, 'and it was rough luck on us that the torrential rains and thunderstorm came on to impede our progress. Though I am an Englishman, I am glad to be in a position to pay a warm tribute to the troops from Wales for the valour they showed in the great assault they made in the St. Julien region. The Welsh were positively without fear, and went to the assault like tigers springing upon their prey. They simply lost themselves with enthusiasm when they found that they were pitted against the Kaiser's favourite Fusilier Guards, and gave the enemy no chance to escape.

'They mowed down the 'Cockchafers," he continued, 'as they were grass, and it was really thrilling to watch their skill with the bayonet against the more daring of the enemy. I dare not give you the names of the Welsh battalions or units engaged, but you will, doubtless, hear all about their grand work soon from our field-marshal.'[10]

The praise for the work of the Welsh battalions continued in the reports which were carried the following week:

WHAT A CARDIFF CORPORAL SAID

The Welsh were embarrassed in their work of clearing the redoubts and consolidating the new position by fugitives who insisted on being taken prisoners (writes Mr. Percival Phillips in the *Daily Express*). A party of five 'Cockchafers' approached a Sergeant with plaintive gestures and formed a semi-circle around him. 'I haven't time to attend to you,' he said. 'Go down the hill and get out of this.' They were more inclined to follow him about until he swore at them fiercely and threatened to punch the head of the most importunate unless he let him alone. 'The "Cockchafers,"' in the language of a Cardiff corporal, 'had their tails down,' and all of them were very meek and amiable.

'All the Welsh troops behaved with great courage (says Mr. Philip Gibbs in the *Daily Telegraph*), and a special work is due to the runners, who carried messages back under fire, and to the stretcher-bearers, who rescued the wounded utterly regardless of their own risks. Afterwards, the mule drivers and leaders were splendid, bringing up supplies under heavy barrage fire. Wales did well that day, and the Welsh miners, who had already proved themselves as great diggers and great tunnellers and very brave men, showed themselves cool and fearless in the assault.'[11]

From Mr. Hilaire Belloc's war review in this week's *Land and Water* it transpires that the Welsh troops engaged in the battle of Flanders fought on the right flank of the French divisions and took Pilkem. Contrary to reports which have appeared in French newspapers it appears that the Welsh were not at St. Julien, the village which has twice changed hands since its capture on July 31. Mr. Belloc says: 'On the first 2,500 yards or so, from just north of what used to be the Steenstraate bridge over the canal to a point just north of the ruins of Boesinghe, were two French divisions under General Anthoine. Immediately on their right would seem to

German prisoners

have been the Welsh troops opposite Pilkem and upon the sector where the Allied line of what used to be the Ypres salient held English troops, thence afterwards, the Anzac troops. The Welsh carried the ruins of Pilkem and came down towards the brook on the further side, while the English troops in the centre reached to St Julien (which is another crossing of the brook), Frezenberg and Westhoek.

Among the incidents in this principal part of the actions we must note the Welsh troops destroying the 3rd Battalion of the Prussian Grenadier Guards during their capture of Pilkem. The division to which these German troops belonged, the 4th Guards Division was caught actually in process of relieving the 23rd Bavarian Division during the night between Monday and Tuesday, and to this must in part be ascribed their very heavy loss. The French troops to the north of the Welsh pushed on beyond the objectives assigned to them, and during the morning got leave to reach the Steenbeck itself. Their departure was a difficult one. They had the canal to cross (as had the British troops immediately to their right) and it is a country in which trenches are almost impossible and in which most works show above ground.'[12]

The achievement of the 38th (Welsh) Division in driving the Germans from Pilkem Ridge was soon portrayed in the press as an example of how Wales as a nation could contribute to the final victory:

THE WELSH AND THE COCK-CHAFERS

It is to be hoped that the stirring story of how the men of the Welsh Regiments overwhelmed the Kaiser's 'Cock-Chafers,' will be fully and faithfully told to the people of the Principality in their own vernacular tongue. No part of the country has done better than Wales in sending the best of her sons to fight in the world-war, and there is no people more responsive than the Welsh to tales of high courage. The accounts of the magnificent stand made by the Welsh at Mametz nearly twelve months ago is a matter of pride in all the land from Holyhead to Cardiff. The complete defeat of the 'Cock-Chafers' – the Guard Fusiliers Regiment of the Potsdam – on Pilkem Ridge will be still more popular when it becomes known throughout the country-side. Alas! The price of victory has to be paid in the blood of young boys scarcely out of their teens. But, however poignant the anguish for their parents, it is some consolation to think that they made the supreme sacrifice for their King and country. No better antidote to the virus of pacifism could possibly be supplied than particulars of the gallantry of our men in the struggle with the flower of the Kaiser's Army. It might even be excellent propaganda work to scatter broadcast a good Welsh translation of the German leaflets which the Welsh captured with their prisoners. The leaflet is described as containing a poem laudatory of the glorious history of the 'Chafers' – the Kaiser's pets before whom not only Belgium trembled, but all the armies of the East. These are the men who went down before the onslaught of the clerks, of the ironworkers, the colliers, and the quarrymen of 'the old country.' We have heard too much about the pro-Germans, the Pacifists, and the fomenters of strikes in various parts of Wales, so that the notion has gone abroad that the Welsh people are inclined to be out of touch with the Empire generally on the question of the war. It is untrue. The Welsh people are as steadfast to-day as they were two years ago, when Merthyr Tydfil sent Mr C.B. Stanton to Parliament with such an overwhelming majority. And they will be keener than ever when the tale of the prowess of the Welsh Regiments on Pilkem Ridge is fully unfolded to them.[13]

A vivid description of the conditions in which the fighting in August took place appeared in print in the middle of that month:

The night was clear and dry, and the British battalions, creeping silently across the bridges of the Steenbeck, lay in the ooze and waterlogged craters, and watched the ceaseless rain of shells dropping on their hidden foes. Some of the wounded men whom I saw limp into a dressing station this morning, encased in mud and weary almost beyond the power to talk, still remembered this lurid spectacle of the night, and the impression of its appalling force remained with them through the crowded hours that followed. I doubt if so many men ever before have lain down so quietly in a swamp, weighted down with heavy kit and the tools of battle, rising out of it at the first faint streak of dawn to flounder forward into an unknown land. The German batteries were sullenly active.

They ploughed the mud with shell, and spread an evil cloud of gas at random, but their fire appeared to die away as the night wore on, and when our own barrage was lowered across the fields, it seemed to brush aside the counter-strokes of the German gunners. Some of the wounded thought this was because their guns were knocked out a group at a time. Enough were left to dot the crater fields before Langemarck with stray missiles during the morning, but the men didn't seem to think it a strong or effective bombardment, and some of them referred to it quite contemptuously. The mud was their greatest grievance. It clung to their legs at every step. When a heavily laden infantryman pulled one boot free, he carried great cakes of clay with it, and even with the cowering Prussians plainly visible in their craters, he had to stop and shake free his feet.

The approaches to Langemarck were mere bogs at the best – actual ponds at the worst. Successive rainstorms had flooded the fields. In some places, wherever there were gullies, water lay at the bottom, and the roads of pre-war days had wholly disappeared in a desert of shell holes and debris of three years' trench life. The men could not drive direct at this goal – a group of grey and blackened

Waterlogged ground near Pilkem, 10 October 1917
© Imperial War Museum

377

ruins hemmed around with clusters of crumbled wire, invisible in the smoke that settled with the first outbreak of the massed artillery. The smoke and the morning mist not only hid the site of Langemarck; it gave comfort to innumerable machine gunners still surviving in the craters and in bits of farmhouse cellars.

The infantry had to pick their way slowly – ever so slowly – through the slime and the water, and carefully surround these isolated redoubts, as they loomed through the fog, flinging their bombs until the inmates came out or were killed, as pleased them best. Frequently they had to pause to pull their comrades from the treacherous mire – figures embedded to the waist, some of them still trying to fire their rifles at a spitting machine gun and yet, despite these almost incredible difficulties, they saved each other and fought the Germans and went through the floods to Langemarck.[14]

There was further praise for the courage of the Welsh soldiers in October:

GALLANTRY OF WELSH TROOPS. Flanders, Tuesday.
The fighting which developed out of the German counterattacks of yesterday morning continued at intervals during the day and into the night. As a result we seem to have largely, if not quite, restored our position beyond Cameron House, whilst elsewhere we have gained more than 100 yards of advance, owing to the gallantry of Welsh troops who pursued the wavering enemy. I am told that the ground is strewn with German corpses, and that the enemy has suffered frightfully in his unsuccessful attempt to regain some of the shell hole areas. Press Association.[15]

In addition, there was reporting of the daily life that took place behind the lines once the battalions were withdrawn temporarily for rest and refitting:

FOOTBALL BEHIND THE LINES. FRENCH TROOPS AMAZED AT OUR HILARIOUS TOMMIES
Lieut. Douglas James has written the following interesting letter to his father, Mr A.H. James, Albert Street, Haverfordwest, which reveals a more pleasant side of Army life at the front than that

generally portrayed: 'Not far away a famous French Regiment was stationed, and they hearing that a Welsh Regiment was in a neighbouring area challenged us to a football match (soccer). We were only too delighted to meet them, so after tea on Friday we selected a good team, and accompanied with a few hundred spectators, we fell in and marched to the arena. As we entered the field in martial array the French band in attendance broke out into a spirited military air which warmed our blood and awakened in us memories of our marches through Llandudno over two years ago. The field was bedecked with the flags of our Allies, and above them all and high above the grand stand floated the Tricolour and the Union Jack side by side. We halted there and stood to attention, and then the French officers, many of them of a very high rank, and wearing their picturesque uniforms adorned with many war decorations came down and 'saluted' us, and bade us welcome. It was a glorious sight, and I was delighted at the scene – the first real demonstration of mutual admiration that I have seen out here between the two nations.

The match was a good one, and though the French played a hard and fast game, we won by 3 goals to 2. After the match we were entertained right loyally and everyone was highly delighted. They knew we belonged to the Premier Welsh Regiment, the old 23rd, and were loud in their praise for the magnificent way in which the division in which we are, took that great Boche stronghold, the Pilkem Ridge. Our men are not only great fighters, but fine singers, and as a finale we formed up and, as only Welshmen can, we sang all the Welsh national airs and, before finishing up with the National Anthem, our boys sang the R.W.F. battle song – a stirring piece which gives 'Kaiser Bill' a very bad name. The French were greatly delighted, and wondered at the hilarious spirit of our men. You can't beat the British Tommy. So ended a grand day, and we marched back to camp in the very best of spirits.[16]

The impact of the call for strike action in the Welsh coalfield in the autumn of 1917 on the troops fighting at the Third Battle of Ypres was reported on:

ABERAMANITE DISOWNS ABERAMAN

Mr. R. Bell, 44 Lewis Street, Aberaman, has received a letter from his son, Sapper Robert Bell, R.E., France. The latter saw in the newspapers that Aberaman Colliery had a majority for Down Tools, and he writes: 'I do not at all wonder that your spirits are not up to concert pitch. What in the name of the Lord sort of conglomeration of humanity does Aberaman shelter now? I can assure you that the result of the ballot has been awaited with the keenest interest by the Welsh Division out here, and I feel almost ashamed to admit to my comrades that I possess the slightest connection with renegade Aberaman. Anyway, thank God it is not my birthplace. I notice also a letter from a correspondent in the paper in which he complains of being refused a ballot paper on account of being over age – in the military sense I take it. Anyway, did the refusal to be allowed to vote extend to yourself because you are over military age, or did the fact of your possessing a son on active service put you in a position to demand a vote? Well, to hell with the traitorous blighters who place Aberaman in favour of down tools. Ye gods! If it is notoriety they sought, good luck to them, they have got it; and if anyone asks me again where I worked last, I am going to tell them my last job was ringing the Lighthouse bell on the Inchcape Rock; employers' name, the Abbot of Aberbrothock; address, somewhere on the East coast of Scotland. What is it that all the eligible applicants at Tribunals are afraid of? Is it leaving home, or is it afraid to die, because they will all have a deuce of a reckoning to contend with when the lads of the Welsh Division get home again.

I am enclosing a token of gratitude from a relative of our late Colonel, who was killed at Langemarck, to each individual Sapper who took part in that glorious charge on the 31st of July last at Pilkem and Langemarck. I know there is a certain amount of soft soap about it, but I can assure you that it is with no small feeling of pride that I look back on that date, because if I don't do another day out here, I am satisfied that my individual bit has been done. Well, I have just exploded myself now and feel much better for putting my thoughts on paper. Forgive me for the abrupt style of my epistle: Bob.'[17]

Early the following year one reporter visited the former battlefield:

THE STORY OF PILKEM RIDGE. 'COCKCHAFERS' RAN LIKE RABBITS – THE CORPS THAT 'NEVER SURRENDER.'

On a recent mid-winter morning I made a pilgrimage to Pilkem Ridge, the tract of bleak country north of Ypres which as long as man goes forth to war, will be cherished by all Welshmen as the scene of one of his nation's most brilliant military achievements and the burial place of many of her honoured dead. I was one of the first civilians who have yet been permitted to cross this extended ridge, and here, as in other districts that I visited, the use of steel helmets and the carrying of respirators was a necessity.

Following a scramble through the unspeakable isolation of ruined Ypres, we drove our car northward, and leaving it in as safe a place as we could find, set forth on foot across the windswept two mile tract of land that develops in a north-easterly direction to Caesar's Nose, Stray Farm and Iron Cross. We were under shellfire a good part of the time, and in this district the German 9-inch guns send over heavy shells that make life very uncomfortable even at long distances. Now and then an incendiary bomb flamed to earth by way of variation in the proceedings.

We visited the old dugouts that were for so long the home of the Welsh battalions prior to the great advance of last July.

When intimation of the approaching push reached the Welsh Division, the Divisional Staff arranged for the construction of a system of trenches that would make possible a nearer approach to the enemy before beginning the advance over the open ground. This work was very expeditiously carried out by the Welsh troops, so much so that when, shortly before the push Lieutenant-General the Earl of Cavan, whose troops had formerly been quartered there, visited the place, he expressed to one of the leading Welsh Divisional Staff officers his gratification and amazement at the magnitude of the preparations that had been made.

ATTACK ON PILKEM RIDGE

It was early on the morning of July 31st that the attack upon Pilkem Ridge began. At 3.50, just before the dawn broke, the Welsh Division left their trenches and began the advance on the first objective which was a line about 500 yards beyond the German front line trenches. The 113th Brigade was on the left, the 114th on the right, and the 115th in reserve. The artillery preparation had been very good and the first objective was taken without much trouble. But even this early in the attack there were Welsh casualties, and it was here that Private Ellis H. Evans (Hedd Wynn), the winner of the bardic chair at last year's Welsh National Eisteddfod, was shot dead by a sniper.

After the first objective was won there was a brief breathing space. Then at 4.15 a second advance was made, the objective here being the top of the ridge of Pilkem, which contained the German second line trenches. The taking of this ridge by the Welsh troops was a brilliant episode, for at the word of command they leaped forward, and advancing at a tremendous pace, fairly rushed the ridge, hustling and bayonetting the Germans, many of whom were captured in their trenches. Among the heroes of this advance was Captain T.S. Richards, one of the soldier sons of Mr. Tom Richards, M.P., who for his bravery received the Military Cross. Just as the battalion was being hard pressed in the attack on the German trenches at Caesar's Nose, Captain Richards reorganised a portion of the line, and thus saved the situation at a critical moment and enabled the attack on that point to be successfully carried through.

German prisoners waiting to be interrogated. Note the Gibraltar cuff title on the standing prisoner's sleeve.
© Imperial War Museum

Among the troops captured were the Third Guard Fusiliers, otherwise known as the Berlin Cockchafers, the Third Lehr Regiment, another of the crack German corps, and the Ninth Grenadiers. It is interesting to recall the fact that the Lehr Regiment fought with the British in 1704, and when they were taken at Pilkem the word 'Gibraltar' was found upon their regimental arms.

'We took altogether,' said a Welsh Brigadier to me, 'about 600 of the Cockchafers. We swarmed on them at a moment when they were disorganised. They were about to be relieved from their position, there was gas about, and they had their gas masks on. Confusion resulted, and many of them surrendered with but little resistance in a way that belied their much-vaunted reputation.'

A Welsh Brigadier who was an eye-witness to the scene remarked to me that the dash of our men on the Cockchafers was so furious that the Berlin cracks 'ran away like hares and rabbits.'

One of the Welsh intelligence officers went up to a captured German officer in the cage and said, 'We are taking plenty of your fellows.' The haughty Cockchafer refused to believe the report and said proudly, 'Oh, no, we never surrender.' That day, however, proved the exception to the rule.

HOW THE 17th BATTALION R.W.F. ADVANCED

The third objective was along the railway through Iron Cross Ridge. This was also successfully captured, and then, in accordance with pre-arranged plans, the 113th and 114th Brigades held this position while the 115th, which had previously been in reserve, went through and sent out two battalions, the 17th Royal Welsh Fusiliers and the 10th South Wales Borderers, who attacked and reached the last objective, which was the Steenbeck River. On that day the Welsh Division, who in the advance had the Guards Brigade on their left and the Highlanders on their right, took more ground than anyone else. In the whole area taken there were found about 280 of the pill box strongholds. Of these about one-third had been destroyed by the artillery barrage preceding the advance; the others were captured by the advancing infantry by a series of flank attacks.

The total distance from where the attack started to the Steenbeck is rather over three miles, and between five and six hours elapsed between the start and the capture of the final objective which was reached by about 9.30.

To the average Welshman the term 'ridge' will convey a very wrong idea. The slope the whole way up was a very gradual one. The Pilkem Ridge itself, i.e. not more than 50 feet above sea level and only about 35 feet above the height of the Yser Canal.

The weather at the outset was fine, but it rapidly became very bad, and the country was little more than a mud swamp. Owing to the big shell craters, which soon filled up with water, it was well-nigh impassable, and one of the Welsh brigadiers told me that the next day he went up and on his way back he slipped into a shell hole, and the mud was so thick that it took two men all they could do to pull him out.

I am assured from another source that some of the poor fellows sank in these shell craters and were never seen again; and I heard of one who, in being hauled out, suffered dislocation of his lower limbs owing to the suction of the mud.[18]

In another article the bravery of the Welsh soldiers was juxtaposed with the human cost of the battle:

STIRRING ACCOUNT OF HEROIC DEEDS BY WELSH TROOPS
BY SPECIAL CORRESPONDENT OF *THE SOUTH WALES NEWS*, CARDIFF
MORE ABOUT PILKEM RIDGE NOTABLE INDIVIDUAL DEEDS;
VISIT TO A WELSH CEMETERY
Practically every portion of the Principality, both north and south, was represented in the Welsh triumph on Pilkem Ridge, for of the battalions who participated there were two from the Rhondda Valleys, one that is closely associated with Cardiff, two from Gwent, one from Swansea district and another from Carmarthenshire. The other battalions engaged were Royal Welsh Fusiliers drawn from all parts of North Wales.

Despite the big area of ground which was taken and the fact that so much of it was a singularly exposed character, the Welsh Division casualties at Pilkem Ridge must be regarded under the circumstances as very light.

Naturally enough on such a day there were many individual acts of bravery, but two there are that stand out for special mention, and the hero of each was a South Walian.

A GALLANT WELSH FUSILIER

Just as the top of Pilkem Ridge was being reached a great many gaps were being created in the Welsh lines by the German machine guns which had been cleverly placed. At a time when everyone was wondering how it could be silenced, Corporal James Llewellyn Davies of the Royal Welsh Fusiliers, who was a native of the Ogmore Valley, and whose home was at Nantymoel, took upon himself the responsibility of performing the task. With reckless bravery he pushed through the Welsh barrage, and rushing round the gun bayonetted one of the gunners and called on the other to surrender. Davies had the gratification of bringing the latter back a prisoner, together with the gun. Davies, however, was severely wounded, and subsequently died of his wounds, but his heroism was rewarded by the bestowal of the Victoria Cross upon his next-of-kin.

Later in the attack another V.C. was won by Sergeant Ivor Rees, a Llanelly steelworker. His act was performed at a point between Iron Cross and the Steenbeck River. Here there was a big concrete emplacement containing a machine gun. Sergeant Rees took the lead in the attack on this, and so successful was he that he not only secured the gun, but killed five Germans by bombing and captured 30 prisoners.

Many other Welsh honours were won that day, but these twain may be noted without in any way detracting from the merit of the others.

Pilkem Ridge still bears abundant evidence of the havoc wrought on that grim day. The whole of the ground surface is churned up into vast shell craters, many of which, when I visited it, were filled with ice. Much of the ground is honeycombed with dugouts and trenches – many of them of German construction. Large numbers of unexploded shells, fragments of shrapnel, portions of abandoned field guns, and other indications of what the late Sir Edward Reed once described as:

'The dire implements
Which sombre science with unpitying pains,
That love of neither man nor God restrains,
To warring hosts presents.'

were to be seen scattered to right and left or collected into heaps awaiting the attention of the Salvage Corps.

Ever and anon the firing of a big gun on the German front beyond St. Julien would be followed by the burst of a shell on the ridge near us, for the lie of the ground is such that it can be easily seen from the German observation posts. There had been a bitter frost the previous night, and as a result the fragments of debris from the bursting shells were widespread.

On the top of the ridge near the shell-scarred ruins of Stray Farm which was for a time the headquarters of one or other of the Welsh units, the views open spaciously in all directions. Northward we could see far beyond Houthulst Forest, and eastward beyond St. Julien to the front of Passchendaele, where the big German guns were belching forth fire and death-dealing shells. To the south lay the welter of debris that was once Ypres, and beyond this stretched the Ypres-Menin road, where, on that October day of 1914 a comparative handful of Welsh and South Wales Borderers and Worcesters barred the road to Calais against 26,000 Germans.

It was a scene to arouse the emotions and stir the blood.

A WELSH CEMETERY

Scrambling in a westerly direction across the shell holes and the now deserted trenches, we reached that point of the ridge known as Caesar's Nose. A couple of hundred yards north of this spot there stands a plain white cross which marks the site of one of the four Welsh cemeteries wherein are laid to rest the mortal remains of the Welsh Division who fell on July 31st of last year at Pilkem.

It is situated upon the bare slope, open in every direction to the winds of heaven, its only protection being a low fence of barbed wire supported at the corners and sides by corkscrew pickets. On the middle of the cross is the Red Dragon, and at the head of each of the graves is inscribed on a little metal tablet the name of him who sleeps beneath.

In a previous article I made reference to the death at Pilkem of Private Ellis H. Evans (Hedd Wyn), of Trawsfynydd, Merionethshire, to whom was awarded the Bardic Chair at last year's National Eisteddfod. He was the son of a Welsh farmer, and prior to the war he was the shepherd of his father's flock. One of the Welsh Brigadiers, who had taken much interest in young Ellis, told me that he had drunk deeply of the spirit of the Welsh mountains, and that he had mastered the alliterative measures of Welsh poetry in a very thorough matter.

One of our howitzer batteries was in action close to us as we made our way back across that bleak waste. It was joining in an effective chorus of reply to the Passchendaele Ridge. Not many yards away a marsh harrier, a bird of prey, that had evidently become accustomed to the artillery thunder, flew in characteristic fashion of the welter of desolation. The gathering twilight added mystery to this scene of war's sad aftermath. The ruined tower of the great Cloth Hall of Ypres stood grim and gaunt above the mists that were already wreathing the ruined city in a grey pall. Above we heard the whirr of motors and saw 'the pilots of the purple twilight' pass and repass in the darkening heavens. The heavy booming of the big artillery was ever and anon interrupted by the rattle of the anti-aircraft guns.

A forty-mile run back to our headquarters through the bitter frosty air concluded another day of absorbing interest.[19]

In his later work on the battle, Sir Arthur Conan Doyle outlined the difficulties the assaulting troops faced:

So notorious were the British preparations, culminating in the usual terrific bombardment, that the approaching conflict was discussed in the German papers weeks before it occurred. Their preparations had been gigantic, and took a new form which called for corresponding ingenuity upon the side of the stormers if it was to be successfully countered. The continuous trench had, save in the old system, been discarded as offering too evident a mark for the shattering guns. The ground was held by numerous disconnected trenches, and strong points arranged in depth rather than in breadth, so that the whole front should form one shock-absorber which would yield at first, but must at the last bring any pressure to a stand. Scattered thickly among these small posts there were concrete forts, not unlike the Martello towers of our ancestors, but sunk deeply into the ground, so as to present a small mark to gun-fire. These forts were made of cement and iron with walls so enormously thick that a direct hit from anything less than a six-inch gun could not possibly harm them. The garrisons of each were composed of twenty or thirty men, with two or three machine guns. There was usually no visible opening, the entrance being approached by a tunnel, and the windows mere slits which gave a broad traverse for a machine gun. They were contrivances which might well hold up an army, and it was a fine example of British adaptability as well as courage that they were able to make progress against them. The days of the gallant bull-headed rush were over, and the soldiers had learned in a cruel school that the fighting man must be wary as well as brave.[20]

Of the performance of the 38th Division he commented:

The advance of the Welsh Division, including as it did the two exploits of capturing the strongly fortified village of Pilkem, and of utterly scattering three battalions of one of the most famous regiments in the Prussian service, was worthy of the great reputation which they had won at Mametz Wood. The way in which the men followed up the barrage and tackled the concrete forts was especially worthy of mention.

The Cockchafers mentioned above were the dandy regiment of Berlin, and their utter defeat at the hands of a brigade of the New Army must indeed have been bitter to those who remembered the cheap jests which had been made at that Army's expense. Four hundred prisoners from this regiment found their way to the cages. Altogether 700 prisoners were taken, nearly all Guardsmen from the Third Division.

The Welsh had about 1,300 casualties, including Colonels Radice, Norman and Taylor. Among the dead was one Private Ellis H. Evans of the 15th Welsh Fusiliers, whose position and importance were peculiarly Cymric, since he was the winner of the Bardic chair, the highest honour of the Eisteddfod. An empty Bardic chair was afterwards erected over his grave. It is only in Wales that the traditions of Athens are preserved, and contests of the body and of the mind are conducted in public with equal honour to the victors.[21]

While the newspaper reports are unanimous in their praise for the actions of the Welsh troops at the Third Battle of Ypres, and in particular at Pilkem Ridge, it is interesting to note that there is no criticism of their conduct at Mametz Wood the previous year, only praise. It is apparent that the conduct of the Welsh in 1917 was only a further extension of the courage they had initially shown in July 1916.

CHAPTER 24

The German Perspective

IN HIS FAMOUS memoirs Ernst Jünger, who commanded an infantry company at the Battle of Langemark, described his time inside a strongpoint during the British artillery bombardment:

> … after a long search [I] found a few houses in the cratered landscape that had been discreetly toughened on the inside with reinforced concrete. One of these had been smashed the day before by a direct hit, and its inhabitants crushed as in a mousetrap by the collapsing roof plate.
> For the rest of the night, I squeezed into the overcrowded concrete box of the company commander, a decent grunt, who whiled away the time with his servant over a bottle of schnapps and a large tin of salt pork, stopping often to shake his head and listen to the steadily increasing roar of the artillery. Then he would sigh for the good old days on the Russian front, and curse the way his regiment had been pumped out. In the end, my eyes simply fell shut.
> My sleep was heavy and troubled; the high explosive shells falling all round the house in the impenetrable dark evoked

Ernst Jünger

389

extraordinary feelings of solitude and abandon in me. I pressed myself unconsciously against a man lying beside me on the pallet. Once, I was startled awake by a powerful impact. We lit the walls to check if the house had been breached. It turned out to have been a small shell that had exploded against the outer wall.[1]

Company Commander K. Lubinski of the 74th Infantry Regiment wrote:

Life in the cement block is hell. We are eleven men living here. Officers and other ranks share the lousy plank beds. Others are sitting on planks and chests, snoring by day and night. The plague of flies is terrible, the more so since the water-logged shell craters are still full of cadavers. Attracted by [this] the flies gather here by the thousand, invade the shelters, creep over our hands and faces, settle down on foodstuffs. One cannot risk being seen outside… and worst of all is the unbearable air.[2]

Another officer, L. Kalepky of the 86th Infantry Regiment, recorded the damage done to the German fortifications by the British artillery fire:

The bunkers were reasonably strong and could withstand even direct hits from shells of a calibre up to six inches, but owing to ground conditions in the area they could not be erected over a strong foundation. When a heavy shell opened a crater close to them, they would lean over, sometimes with the entrance down, with the soldiers trapped inside. There was no way of rescuing them, of course, and we suffered rather heavy casualties this way, not to speak of the painfully slow death of those trapped inside.[3]

Rudolf Binding, who commanded a squadron of dragoons, wrote of the artillery bombardment on 29 July:

I am scared. For the first time in this war I have doubts whether we shall be able to hold out against the odds. Thirty new four-gun batteries have appeared on the enemy's front in a single day, not counting those which may not have been spotted. Altogether there must be eight to ten thousand guns employed on this little bit of front. If one reckons that the main offensive is being made on a front of twenty-five miles, that means a gun to every four yards. Imagine all the ten thousand muzzles hurling out not only projectiles of iron and lead, but spreading poison gases as well; imagine only a fifth of this number of guns opposed to this concentration, all overworked pieces which fire, it is true, but not so accurately as on the first day; imagine an enemy airman cruising over each one of our batteries and directing on to it five times the fire which they can thunder, whereas they are perhaps unsupported by any air forces and simply have to sit tight: that is the picture which scares me. Verdun, the Somme, and Arras are mere purgatories compared with this concentrated hell, which one of these days will be stoked up to white-heat.[4]

He described the burial of the German soldiers killed by the artillery fire and the subsequent fighting:

One man after another goes west. Yesterday we were burying an officer of the 237th Reserve Infantry Regiment, who was under me when we first reconnoitered our way in Flanders, when another one came over and said to me: 'Now I am the last of the old crowd.'
    Incidentally this funeral was the most horrible performance in which I have ever taken part. There were sixty-nine to be buried, including four officers... There hadn't been time to dig out each man his full six feet of earth. Two long trenches, a man's length broad and almost touching one another, had been opened up three feet deep... and at the bottom of these the graves had been cut to another three feet, barely a pace being left one to the other. There they lay, one beside another, just like a bag of game after a day's shooting. Where the two trenches met stood the Protestant chaplain, on a plank laid across them, and uttered offensive platitudes which conveyed nothing to those present.[5]

At the end of the battle he commented:

It is appalling up at the Front. I have just come back from a visit to our best regiment, which is holding a position I know well to the north of Passchendaele and has had heavy losses in the very first days. It is right in the mud, without any protection, without a single decent dugout, for in this rapid withdrawal there is no time to dig. How many of those fellows who a fortnight ago were cheerfully celebrating the glorious record of their regiment will never laugh again; even the others who can laugh again do not laugh for long. 'My fellows are in tears,' reports one battalion-commander in despair, whose whole battalion lay covered by a regular blanket of British shells. Many of the men hardly speak. You see wild eyes gazing out of faces which are no longer human. They have a craving after brandy which can hardly be satisfied, and which shows how badly they yearn to lose the faculty for feeling. Men drink it who have never touched it before as though by instinct. Although nothing very much in the way of bombardment was being vouchsafed us, I found myself practically the only one going towards the Front; I saw nothing but men coming back. Only field-kitchens and stretcher-bearers – that is to say, people whose nerves are fed from the rear – were making their way forwards. Scores of men were streaming to the rear, one by one but without stopping, all in need of rest; not malingerers – no doubt merely men who need one day or two to come to themselves again. It is a perfectly honorable demand to make, but while the company-commanders are forced to send first one and then another, and then a third to the rear because they are no use in the line, the battalion-commander or the regimental-commander is

always calling out for more men to defend a position which is in danger, or to meet an expected attack.

One sees much magnificent conduct calmly and coolly shown in the middle of much which is less admirable and weaker. That type of man makes allowances for the others by increasing his own efforts. A battalion-commander, Freiherr

Rudolf Binding in later life

von G., stuck to his battalion for two days with a splinter of shell in his lung. He remained simply as an example; he knew it; and such examples have an effect. One cannot say that the morale is low or weak. The regiments simply show a sort of staggering and faltering, as people do who have made unheard-of efforts.[6]

Georg Bücher was an infantry officer who fought at the Third Battle of Ypres. In his memoirs he also wrote of the terrifying effects of the British artillery bombardment:

Sonderbeck burst into the dugout – he was the N.C.O. on duty. 'The big offensive has started!' he panted, his eyes rolling. I had never seen him in such a state of excitement. 'Already three men have been blown to bits,' he gasped, and hastily swallowed a mouthful of rum.

In a moment I was ready and hurried up the steps with him. There was an absolute downpour of earth and shell splinters – on every side the night was lit up by the explosions. Three of Sonderbeck's men were plastered on the walls of the trench or lying in fragments on the ground – the mess couldn't be cleared away while the bombardment lasted. I glanced at my wristwatch: it was time for Gaaten's spell of duty. I ran to his shelter. Armed figures were standing in the flickering candle-light which gave their faces a strangely wild and threatening expression.

'Time to go on duty!'

Five men followed Gaaten and me out of the dugout, which, as things were, was the only place of safety. I wondered whether their hearts were beating as wildly as mine. Shells were exploding all about us. The five silently took up their positions – they could only trust to luck.

There was a terrific explosion somewhere in the direction from which we had just come – a hissing column of flame and earth rose up from the trench. Gaaten's dugout and the four men in it had ceased to exist – a 15-inch shell had landed directly over it.

'Missed it by half a minute, Georg!' Gaaten shouted, his face ashen. I shook his hand and hurried away to the company-commander's dugout, where I arrived just in time to help carry Leutnant Kranz down the steps. He was already dead – a big splinter stuck out from the rent in the crown of his head.

By midday the communicators were impassable. The bombardment raged with undiminished intensity. We reported to Von Mall: twenty-seven dead so far, all mutilated horribly; there were very few wounded.

By the evening the parapets had disappeared. We reported to Von Mall: forty-one dead, all blown to shreds – we shuddered to look at them. All through the night the soil of Flanders was lacerated by most furious shellfire.

In the morning we reported to Von Mall: fifty-nine dead, all unrecognizable. More than twenty severely wounded men were lying in the dugouts...

At midday, when I was about to take my report to Von Mall, the ground heaved and rocked: somewhere close at hand hundredweights of explosive must have penetrated. I staggered out of my shelter and worked my way along the ruins of the trench while shell splinters hummed around me. Where the company-commander's dugout had once been, twelve steps deep and reinforced with balks of timber, was now a huge smoking crater not less than ten yards in diameter... Young Von Mall had been no coward, I said to myself as I stood before his open grave wherein no trace of him was to be seen or found.

We laid the remains of our eighty-four dead in the huge

German soldiers under artillery fire

crater – I had known every one of them. Not for a moment did the shells leave them alone – they were tossed up, flung about and blown to pieces.[7]

The shelling ceased at last and Bücher described the fighting that followed as the British attacked:

Suddenly the fire lifted from our trench – the enemy guns had lengthened their range. Zero Hour had come... I jumped up with a shout, helped to drag open boxes of hand-grenades up from the dugouts and ran around the trench bellowing orders.

There were only forty of us left. We stood waiting in the devastated trench, our strained eyes peering from beneath our steel helmets. We had nothing but our rifles and hand-grenades – the machine guns had all been smashed...

The enemy advanced carelessly towards us in groups followed by packed waves. Evidently they thought we were all dead. They were less than a hundred yards away. We fired about three clips of cartridges – within a minute we forty, firing at that beautifully compact target, had accounted for more of the enemy than the number of our casualties during the three-day bombardment, for the Tommies hadn't expected to meet with any resistance. No longer were they wandering carelessly towards us – their advance had become a wild rush.

Our retreat was no uncontrolled panic. Again and again a thin chain of us dropped into shell holes and lashed the khaki horde with our bullets, fired a few rounds and then retreated. Not every man rejoined the flight, for the enemy could shoot, too. Those who fell were left where they fell, although they shrieked for help. We couldn't help them – we had no choice, for behind us were murderous bayonets, hand-grenades, rifle-butts, spades.[8]

An officer of the 3rd Battalion of the German 34th Fusilier Regiment, which was in the front line of the Zonnebeke sector on 25 August, wrote:

The night passed fairly quietly. The food-carriers were able to get up from Zonnebeke and I was able to visit the sentries and front platoons several times, the last about 3.30 a.m. About 4 a.m., shortly after I had returned to the pill-box which sheltered thirty-six men of the supporting platoon, the enemy suddenly opened a terrific artillery bombardment on our position.

About 6 a.m. [the British infantry Zero Hour was 5.50 a.m.] a Sergeant near the entrance shouted out that he thought the English were coming. I hurried out. The air was filled with smoke and this together with a ground-mist made it difficult to see more than 20 yards or so. I could see no sign of the enemy. Then the shelling slackened only to move on and become stronger than ever behind us.

Suddenly I heard shouts of 'Englander' from in front. I called the men out and we took up a position in the mass of shell holes on either side. Almost at once figures appeared moving towards us through the fog. They were coming on at a steady pace bunched together in groups between the waterlogged shell holes.

We opened fire and threw hand-grenades into the midst of them and they at once took cover in the shell holes. I could see two of them fixing up a light machine gun which opened on us, hitting several of my men before we could silence it.

For a moment the attack here was held, but looking round I could see more English advancing past us to right and left, and realised that our only hope was to run for it. With the few men near me I started back towards Zonnebeke, but, after a few yards, saw it was hopeless as the enemy had already closed in ahead of us in their advance. The noise of the machine gun fire from the village made us hope that a counterattack would soon be made to regain the position and four of us ran back to the pill-box, a last and almost desperate refuge.

We had scarcely time to slam the door of thick oak planks behind us when it was ripped asunder by a hand-grenade, followed by others that burst inside among us. Two splinters from them hit me, one near the spine that made movement impossible for me. Seven or eight Englishmen came in and carried me out, laying me in a shell hole among three dead English and one of my Sergeants, also dead.[9]

The Germans soon began running back towards where their heavy machine guns were situated, shouting that the line had broken. The machine gun commander wrote later:

I tried to stop these men and make them face front again through the mist. Others retiring on my left were rallied by a subaltern and led forward again through the mist. Soon afterwards the enemy appeared twenty yards or so in front. They came on leisurely in groups as if they had the place to themselves, believing perhaps that the artillery barrage had killed us all. We opened a burst of fire into them and they quickly dropped to cover. Others now appeared behind and on both flanks. We raked the front with fire, but soon they concentrated their Lewis Guns on us. I got up to rush to better cover close by but a mass of bullets swept past at that moment and I was hit in three places, soon losing consciousness.[10]

The 10th Royal Welsh Fusiliers to the south of the railway were held up 600 yards short of the village. Survivors from the 3rd Battalion of the German 34th Fusilier Regiment had linked up with a rifle-grenade section around the machine gun post at the level crossing near the station. One of the 3rd Battalion described what happened next:

No sooner had they got into position than groups of the enemy appeared through the mist in front. The machine guns raked them with a hail of bullets and from then on fired almost continuously. To this day I still have a thrill of admiration whenever I think of

Garde Fusiliers earlier in the war

one of those gunners in particular who fired incessantly, his every movement utterly unruffled in spite of a stream of bullets sweeping past him.[11]

The 1st Battalion of the 34th Fusilier Regiment had been held in reserve and they were ordered to counterattack at 6.46 a.m. They crossed the Broodseinde Ridge and moved down the slope towards Zonnebeke. The company commander of Number 2 platoon wrote:

On approaching the village we came into the English artillery barrage, which was very violent. The ground was in a terrible state; the craters made by the high explosives were joining up with the older rain-filled shell holes, forming together small ponds with islands here and there formed by the crater edges which we had to use as stepping-stones. No one was allowed to halt or take cover, otherwise they lost touch and would never regain it.

By 7.30 a.m. we had reached the station road on the further side of the village and here near the level-crossing I came upon a machine gun post of the 3rd Battalion. Its two guns had been knocked out of action and the leader was lying dead. The rifle-grenade section was nearby with its commander severely wounded. A number of men, many dead or wounded, lined the road on both sides. This gallant band had held up the advance and paid the price, but we had arrived only just in time for the English were already beginning to move forward again up the slope from the Zonne brook to attack the position.

We lay down along the road, my line extending halfway to the church, and opened fire as fast as we could pull the triggers. Almost at once two of my other platoons, which had lost direction farther back, arrived together with a part of No.6 Company (2nd Battalion), and these reinforced my weakly held position, extending it to the village square.

The English artillery barrage had now gone on behind us and the infantry could not face our fire. After losing heavily, a number retired to the dead ground by the Zonne brook, leaving a firing line about 200 yards from us. The firefight continued throughout the morning, but the enemy made no attempt to advance. An English machine gun post located 200 yards west of the church caused much trouble and loss to us, but could not be silenced.[12]

The next British artillery bombardment of Zonnebeke began at 3 p.m. A subaltern of No.1 Company, 34th Regiment wrote:

I shouted to all to be ready. Machine guns were oiled, bayonets fixed and hand grenades got ready. Shortly after 6 p.m. the English artillery bombardment increased to drum-fire intensity; then suddenly a pause followed by shouts all along the line, 'They're coming.' The first waves of the English infantry came up to within 20 yards of us when our 4 machine guns and every rifle opened on them. They at once took cover in the shell holes and began to throw smoke bombs in our direction to cover the advance of the waves in rear of them.[13]

At this point the 5th and 9th Bavarian Regiments and other supporting troops came forward and charged the British. The same subaltern continued:

[It seemed] a spontaneous act of madness, but it was the last thing the enemy expected. His front lines got up and rushed back, taking the lines behind with them. We carried on as fast as we could over the broken ground and then as we got through the smoke an amazing sight greeted us. Great numbers of the enemy were fleeing panic-stricken down to and across the Zonne brook.

Our light machine guns were hurriedly placed in position and swept the retreating mass with bullets. As we watched this scene, I can only say we literally wept for joy at such a success. Klein Molen was now ours again, but it was clearly hopeless to pursue with our small disorganized force and with our flanks unsupported, added to which English machine gun fire was now enfilading our line from the direction of the church. So we took up a position east of the brook between Klein Molen and the railway, sent back a number of prisoners and supplied ourselves with captured rifles and ammunition, being short of the latter for our own.[14]

German dead near the Hannebeek stream

A German *Musketier*, Hanns Otto Schetter, left this account of his time at the Third Battle of Ypres:

In the night of 19/20 September we entrain to the front line. Ledeghem, the last station open to traffic, is our unloading stop. Many ammunition columns pass by us toward the front, and the cannonade grows in intensity – giving us a welcome! The enemy is firing fiercely and our own artillery is replying in kind. This morning the British infantry has broken through our first lines at Wilhelmstellung. Often we have to take cover on the side of the highway from the bursting shells. Anxiously I look ahead toward the front line where the shells are bursting with dark smoke clouds. Only stumps are left of the trees, and I try to figure out how I can best get through this hell. I am at watch at the roadside to look for vehicles of Regiment 231. We are moving forward with coffee containers and sacks of bread to our company which has occupied the shell holes and what is left of the trenches – the Flanders position. I am anxiously observing the battleground: concrete bunkers outline the position.

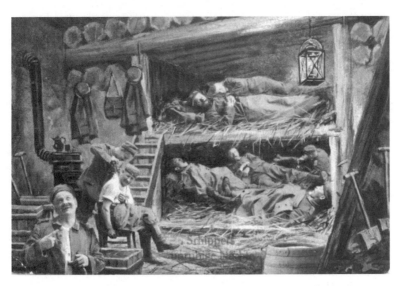

An idealistic image of German troops in their billet

There are no quarters for us, so at night we sleep in a barn on top of potatoes. At 3 a.m. we are awakened and we now move forward in single file on the Menin-Ypres road. On both sides of the highway our batteries are firing and their iron greetings receive prompt reply from the enemy. We have to move fast because it is almost 6 a.m. and we have to reach our front line before daybreak.

We reach the Front headquarters from where we are guided to our troops which occupy shell holes 150 metres ahead. The soldiers are reluctantly leaving their shell holes and are not eager for food. The whole earth is ploughed by the exploding shells and the holes are filled with water, and if you do not get killed by the shells you may drown in the craters. Broken wagons and dead horses are moved to the sides of the road; also, many dead soldiers are here. Seriously wounded who died in the ambulance wagons have been unloaded and their eyes stare at you. Sometimes an arm or a leg is missing. Everybody is rushing, running, trying to escape almost certain death in this hail of enemy shells on the highway, which is the only passage since the fields are flooded shell holes. I breathe easier when we reach our kitchen wagon. Today I have seen the real face of war.[15]

Kanonier Gerhardt Gurtler wrote of the reality of death on the battlefield:

In the newspapers you read: 'Peacefully they rest on the spot where they have bled and suffered, while the guns roar over their graves, taking vengeance for their heroic death.' And it doesn't occur to anybody that the enemy is also firing; that the shells plunge into the hero's grave; that his bones are mingled with the filth which they scatter to the four winds – and that, after a few weeks, the morass closes over the last resting-place of the soldier.[16]

This was the reality of the burials on the battlefield and the reason why so many men's bodies are missing. Their remains were scattered and lost before the fighting finished, their graves no longer marked and their incomplete bodies covered again by the earth.

The official history of the Guards Fusilier Regiment recorded their experience thus:

On 31 July at 4.15 a.m., the Artillery and mine fire increased to become a barrage along the entire front; the terrain beyond was gassed. From 5 a.m. onwards, the enemy shot at the frontline position with smoke and incendiary shells; all communication broke down, any dispatched patrols no longer returned, messengers did not reach their destination. After a short amount of time, the English launched an attack putting considerable pressure on the left wing of the regiment as well as the left neighbouring sector; the enemy penetrated the latter and, making use of the poor visibility and misty conditions of the funnel-like terrain, launched a surprise attack from behind against the regiment's companies of the Kampf und Betreitschaftsbattalion (Reserve Battalion). Everyone desperately defended themselves in all directions but finally succumbed to the enemy's crushing superiority after all ammunition and all means of close combat had been exhausted. Only a few remaining troops within both battalions succeeded in returning through the funnel terrain consisting of mud and tree debris and the thick veil of curtain fire; many remained there, lying severely wounded or completely exhausted. The Commander of 1st

Company, Lt. Eisenträger, was also wounded by shrapnel; it is safe to say that he would have been taken prisoner if it had not been for his brave orderly, B.F. Musolf, who, through the English barrage fire, carried him to safety on his back; that brave man was later awarded the Iron Cross 1st Class for his valiant action.

10th and 11th Company, who immediately took position south-west of the Steen stream, absorbed the remaining troops of I. and II. Battalions. Meanwhile, the regimental headquarters had moved its command post back to the Wilhelm Position, when the Commander of the Lehr-Infanterie-Regiment, which was positioned further to the left, casually announced that the English had already closed in on the command post.

At 9 a.m., the Commander of III. Battalion received the order to launch a counterattack against the English. Together with the other two Companies of the Reserve Battalion, they were to move from the Wilhelm Position onto the railway embankment; that attack was unsuccessful due to the enemy's onslaught of fire. Meanwhile, as the neighbouring regiment to the right retreated to a position behind the Steen stream and several enemy platoons were already moving toward the stream to the north and as our own artillery fire was so short that our troops were in danger, the regiment decided to join the retreat and occupy the eastern embankment of the Steen. That line withstood all further English attacks and any further advance was thwarted.

At approximately 3.30 p.m., the Reserve Regiment 229 of 50 Infantry Division, which had been given the order by the Division to counterattack at about 2 p.m., also reached the Steen.

In the evening, all remaining troops of the regiment were pulled away from the front of the Infantry Regiment 229 and were deployed as assault troops in the Wilhelm Position. The enemy's artillery fire slowly abated with nightfall; our artillery dispersed several advancing English platoons.

The morning of 1st August passed rather uneventfully. In the afternoon, however, heavy artillery fire started again, escalating into a heavy barrage. At about 10.30 p.m., an English attack was foiled by the Infantry Regiment 229. The constant rain by day and night had probably negatively influenced the English willingness to attack.

In the early hours of the following morning, 2nd August, in the pouring rain, the weary regiment assembled in the south-east of Schaap-Balie where it occupied the Flandern-Position as the Division's assault reserve. The regiment then replaced a battalion of the Reserve Infantry Regiment 261 on the 3rd August; utterly exhausted and soaked, they marched to Pitkem and Eeghem near Thielt where they set up camp on the 6th August.

Losses:

Fallen:

Captain V. Dettingen.

Lieutenants of the Reserve Schleicher, Horn, Betzga, Nauendorf.

Acting Officer Zacker.

83 NCOs and Guard Fusiliers.

Wounded:

Lieutenant Eisenträger.

Lieutenants of the Reserve Dressler, Klotz, Hammerstein, Lehm, Mener zur Hende, Bergmann, Küsters.

Acting Officer Sass.

292 NCOs and Guard Fusiliers.

Missing:

Lieutenants of the Reserve Steinhäuser, Vogt, v. Kaphengst, Dörschel.

Field Master Sergeants (Medical NCOs) Schulten, Mottek.

683 NCOs and Guard Fusiliers.[17]

The Germans bury their dead

Lance Corporal Adolf Hitler also served during the Third Battle of Ypres. He had joined the 1st Company of the 16th Bavarian Reserve Infantry Regiment, the List Regiment, at the start of the war and had fought at the First Battle of Ypres in 1914. Promoted to lance corporal, he was awarded the Iron Cross Second Class in December. Hitler was wounded in the thigh in October 1916 at the Battle of the Somme and hospitalised, only rejoining his regiment in March 1917. He wrote:

> With three weeks of continuous artillery, the English prepared for the great Flanders offensive. Now, the spirits of the dead seemed to come alive. The regiment braced itself in the filthy mud and dug into the shell holes and craters, unyielding, unwavering, and grew smaller and thinner, just as they had once before at this spot. Finally, the English attack came on July 31, 1917.
>
> Early in August we were relieved by fresh troops. What once had been the regiment was now a few companies. They staggered back, covered with mud, more like ghosts than men. Except for a few hundred yards of shell holes, the Englishman had won only death.[18]

Adolf Hitler (seated, extreme right)

Leutnant Adolf Meyer was an officer in the same regiment as Hitler; they moved into positions near Hooge on the main road from Ypres to Menin just a few days before the battle opened. He wrote:

> The English attack began. On a 25-kilometre front, the English threw division after division at our line. Heavy fog favoured the advance and the offensive. I reported immediately to the regimental battle station. Where the company strength in the last few days had sunk to an average of 50 men, on this morning the count was scarcely 30 and offered little defence against the attacking waves of the enemy and the extraordinarily strong tank offensive.
>
> At midday, two machine gun companies from the Reserve Infanterie Regiment 238 arrived as reinforcements. They had to be sent out in small groups from the regimental headquarters. Two officers (including myself) and the six dispatch runners led the way. From a hollow that protected us from observation, we had to cross some 200 metres, fully observed, of unprotected open ground. Because of the heavy machine guns and the ammunition boxes, we had to keep to the road where we were subjected to heavy artillery fire and machine gun fire. I can still see to this day two English tanks which had been brought to a halt by our artillery on the main road from Ypres to Menin, but which continued to give service in spite of it all by fearlessly spraying us with their machine guns.
>
> With their last ounce of strength, the few unwounded survivors dragged the machine guns and ammunition boxes into the foremost position. It was a miracle that all the guides from our regimental staff, both officers and the six dispatch runners, among them Hitler, had come through unscathed.[19]

During the ten-day British bombardment the List Regiment lost over 800 men. Overall, the Germans suffered catastrophic losses at the Third Battle of Ypres but were not broken.

General Ludendorff commented: 'The enemy charged like a wild bull against the iron wall which kept him from our submarine bases. He dented it in many places, and it seemed as if he must knock it down. But it held, although a faint tremor ran through its foundations.'[20]

Of the performance of the German soldier he wrote: 'What the German soldier experienced, achieved, and suffered in the Flanders Battle will be his everlasting monument of bronze, erected by himself in the enemy's land.'[21]

CHAPTER 25

Other Gallantry Medal Winners

IN ADDITION TO the awards listed in previous chapters, many other Welsh soldiers won gallantry medals for their conduct at the Third Battle of Ypres. It is important to recognise, however, that there must have been many acts of bravery and self-sacrifice during the course of the battle that went unreported or unseen.

The Distinguished Conduct Medal

Sergeant Alfred Speake of the 15th Welsh was awarded the Distinguished Conduct Medal. A native of Trealaw, Tonypandy, his citation ran: 'For conspicuous gallantry and devotion to duty. During the operations he shewed conspicuous gallantry and ability as a platoon Sergeant and as acting company Sergeant major. On one occasion, when all his officers had become casualties, he took command of the company, and was of invaluable assistance to the new company commander.'[1]

In January 1918 the announcement was made of two gallantry awards to another Welsh soldier:

A double honour has just been conferred upon Sergeant T.C.M. Phipper, of the Grenadier Guards, for singular bravery and devotion to duty on the battlefield. Sergeant Phipper is the son of Mr. and Mrs. Gilbert Phipper, of 34 Fleet Street, Swansea, and some years ago was a member of the Swansea Police Force, subsequently receiving an appointment at Portland Prison. The double honour consists of the Distinguished Conduct Medal and the Military Medal. The official report of the deed for which he won the D.C.M. states that at Pilkem Ridge, on 31st July, 1917, it was almost entirely due to Sergeant Phipper that battalion communication was kept up. During the attack he sent messages by flag and pigeon, whilst repairing the telephone wires, and it was owing to his courage and energy during the whole attack, which lasted three days with the exception of one hour, that communication was established the whole time. He received the Military Medal for gallantry on successive dates from October 1914 to October 1916. The fact was noted that Sergeant Phipper was repeatedly mentioned for general good service.[2]

This was in fact Thomas Charles Moore Phippen. His D.C.M. citation read:

For conspicuous gallantry and devotion to duty. In spite of constant shelling, by which the cable was frequently broken between Brigade and Battalion Headquarters, he personally organised a party and laid five lines himself, maintaining communications at a critical time by his gallant and prompt action. On the following day he displayed similar initiative and skill in connecting up the forward companies with their Battalion Headquarters.[3]

Phippen was born in Cwmbwrla, Swansea, and was working as a warehouseman when he enlisted in the Grenadier Guards in April 1904, aged 18. He was transferred to the Reserve in 1907 and married his wife Sarah the following year; they had three children. He was employed as a prison officer in Portland Prison, Dorset. When war broke out he was called up on 4 August and landed in France the following January. He was promoted to lance corporal in June 1915, made full corporal in July 1916 and Sergeant in October 1917. He was awarded the Military Medal on 30 October 1916 and was gassed in April 1918. He survived the war and was discharged in March 1920.

On 16 February 1918 a local newspaper carried the report of the presentation of the Distinguished Conduct Medal to a member of the Swansea City Battalion of the Welsh Regiment.

Another member of the Swansea Battalion was honoured on Saturday morning when the Mayor, Alderman Benjamin Jones, presented the Distinguished Conduct Medal to Sergeant F.W. White. On the 31st July, in the attack on Pilkem Ridge, Sergeant White, when his company had lost all its officers, took command during the critical time of holding the objective, once it had been gained, and the period of consolidation.

Sergeant White displayed such gallantry during these operations that he was recommended for the D.C.M., which was shortly afterwards awarded. The Mayor congratulated Sergeant White and Mrs. White, and called upon the Deputy-Mayor (Councillor Molynoux), Major Dyson Williams and Captain M. Williams, who also spoke. Cheers were given for Sergeant and Mrs. White, and also for Major Dyson Williams. Sergeant White joined up in November 1914, and resides at Clyne Valley.[4]

White's citation for his award read:

For conspicuous gallantry and devotion to duty. During the attack and capture of a position, he displayed exceptional initiative and fearlessness. He mopped up dugouts single-handed beyond his company's final objective, and, with his Company Commander and another man, rushed a fortified house and captured a machine gun, killing or capturing the garrison. When all his officers had become casualties, he commanded his company for two and a half days, showing a magnificent example throughout.[5]

Another local newspaper related more of the events that led to his award:

Sergeant F.W. White, Rhydydefaid, Killay, has been awarded the D.C.M. He is now serving with a Welsh regiment in France, and has been out about two years. In very heavy fighting Sergeant

White had every one of his officers and Sergeants knocked out, and no rations reached him and his party for three days. He and Captain Sandbrook captured two officers and sixty men, and Captain Sandbrook received fatal wounds. Sergeant White pays high tribute to the dead officer.[6]

Before enlisting, Frank Weldin White was a tailor's assistant. Born in Leominster in 1882, he had lived at 149 Arabella Street in Cardiff before moving to Swansea. He had landed in France on 3 December 1915, having risen to the rank of corporal. He survived the war, being discharged on 20 January 1920 to return to his home in Swansea and be reunited with his wife and three children.

The Distinguished Conduct Medal

The Military Cross

Captain Thomas Jacob Jones won the Military Cross at Pilkem Ridge. He survived the war and in 1919 was appointed as the headmaster of a new school in north Wales. A local newspaper carried an account of his career:

> The first headmaster of the new Central School at St Paul's, Captain T. Jacob Jones, B.A., M.C., is 32 years of age and began his teaching career under Dr P.B. Ballard, M.A., at Tonddu, Glamorganshire. He took the London Matriculation in 1904 and completed his degree in arts at Cardiff in 1908, specialising in Latin and History. During his varsity career Captain Jones was prominent as a Normal student, was a member of the Cardiff S.R.C. and a social worker under Prof. R.M. Burrows at the University Settlement.
>
> After 12 months as a certificated teacher in Nantyoel Elementary School, he was promoted to the position he now holds as form master at the Ogmore Vale Higher Elementary School, one of the first schools of that type opened in Glamorganshire.
>
> He is president of the Ogmore and Garw Association (N.U.T.), secretary of the Nantymoel Cymmrodorion Society, and at the outbreak of war was president-elect of the National League of Young Liberals for South Wales.
>
> While in the Army, close to Maubeuge, at the request of the authorities, he undertook the work of battalion education officer of the 17th R.W.F., over 200 students voluntarily attending his classes.
>
> His military record runs: October 1914, enlisted in the 13th Battalion R.W.F.; February 1915, transferred to the 17th Battalion R.W.F. March

The Military Cross

promoted corporal, and finally orderly room Sergeant. November, granted commission and appointed quartermaster and lieutenant 17th Battalion R.W.F. December 3rd, sailed overseas with 38th (Welsh) Division. December 1915 to February 1919, continuous service overseas. January 1919, awarded M.C. for services rendered, particularly for the period of the attack on Pilkem Ridge and Langemarck. November 1918, promoted to the rank of captain and quartermaster, 17th R.W.F. and February 1919, discharged.[7]

The Military Medal

Albert Ernest Hugall of the 13th Royal Welsh Fusiliers won the Military Medal at the Battle of Pilkem Ridge. Born in Barnsbury in north London in 1880, he was a clerk before enlisting in the 18th (2nd London Welsh) R.W.F. on 23 November 1915, aged 36. He lived at 19 King's Road, Stoke Newington, with his wife Florence Ada and son, Eric.

He returned home on 27 October 1917 and was presented with his Military Medal on 6 November. On 22 April 1918 he was killed in action and was buried in Bouzincourt Ridge Cemetery, north-west of the town of Albert. On 15 November 1918 Florence received his personal effects – his diary, letters, photos, tobacco pouch and pipe. The following June she was

sent Albert's identity disc. She died in 1974, having never remarried.

Born in Yeovil, Albert Evan Johnson joined the Glamorgan Constabulary and was stationed at Gorseinon in 1914 before joining the Welsh Guards. He was awarded

Albert Johnson

the Military Medal for 'capturing an enemy blockhouse and prisoners'[8] in October 1917. He rose to the rank of Sergeant and was wounded in 1918. After being discharged from the Welsh Guards he returned to his civilian occupation and retired as a police sergeant in 1945.

Thomas Norgate was also a member of the Glamorgan Constabulary. He was stationed in Gowerton but was born in Ropley in Hampshire. He enlisted in August 1915 and won the Military Medal for his conduct on 31 July when he displayed 'bravery and devotion to duty whilst acting as a stretcher bearer'.[9] He was later wounded and discharged from the Army in December 1918. By a coincidence, he was awarded his Military Medal in Barry on Armistice Day 1918 'amid hearty cheering'.[10]

John Harding won his Military Medal in September 1917 whilst serving as a sniper with the 14th Welsh Regiment. He had been in France for nearly two years and was the son of Mrs. Harding of 8 Spencer Street, Barry Dock. He wrote that on 29th July 1917: 'I volunteered to go out as a sniper with a pal. We were out for fifteen hours at a stretch, during which time there was a terrific bombardment. We accounted for three Huns.'[11] In May 1918 he was presented with the Military Medal by the Mayor of Leicester before a large assembly. He was in hospital in Leicester recovering from the effects of gas poisoning. Before the war Harding played football for St Mary's A.F.C., Barry. He was 27 years of age and all his brothers served during the war. He died on 16 April 1959.

Sergeant Evan Parry was awarded his Military Medal on 28 September 1917. From Silian, Lampeter, he was a coal miner and hewer at the Mardy Colliery in the Rhondda Valley. He served with the 15th Welsh Regiment and survived the war, being demobilised in January 1919 after serving on the Western Front since December 1915. His brother Thomas had been killed at Gallipoli in August 1915 while serving with the 6th Battalion of the Royal Irish Fusiliers. He has no known grave and is commemorated on the Helles Memorial.

J.W. Carter

Gunner J.W. Carter of the 113th Battery Royal Field Artillery won the Military Medal in September 1917. He received a note of congratulations from Sir Henry Rawlinson, commander of the Fourth Army. He was the second son of Mrs Carter of 17 Quarella Street, Cadoxton, Barry, and had been in France for 18 months. Before he enlisted he had been employed as a shunter on the Barry Railway and was formerly a pupil at Cadoxton School. He was recently married and had a brother, Private Bert Carter, with the Welsh Regiment in France.

Lance Corporal Robert Hartery of the 41st Machine Gun Corps was hospitalised after having been wounded on 26 August 1917. Hartery was awarded the Military Medal when, as a team commander of a machine gun company, he held his men together, continuing to fire on his target with remarkable coolness and ability, notwithstanding the fact that his team was under heavy fire and suffered casualties.

In a letter, the Captain commanding 41st Company wrote on 4 October 1917:

I am very pleased to enclose the ribbon of your Military Medal won at Ypres on 26th August 1917 for the following act of gallantry:
'At Ypres, as team commander during a particularly trying period, though his team was under very severe shellfire and suffering numerous casualties, he held his men together and continued firing on his target, with great coolness and ability.' I was very sorry indeed to lose you through being wounded and I can only hope you are now well on your way to recovery. Wishing you the best of luck.[12]

415

Mr. T. Ewbank, headmaster of Cadoxton Council Boys' School, received the following letter from Hartery, now stationed at the Command Depot, Alnwick, Northumberland. Hartery had been a member of the school's football team in the 1908–9 season when Cadoxton Boys secured the two Barry cups and medals for the championship:

> Dear Sir, – In this week's *Barry Dock News* I notice the report of Private Enoch Evans winning the Military Medal, also mentioning that Cadoxton School has two military medallists. I spent the latter part of my schooldays at the school, and won the Military Medal at Ypres on 26th August 1917. I was in France for two and a half years before being wounded, and during that time I was in every scrap. I enlisted in August, 1914 and am expecting to go to France again in a month's time.[13]

Bob Hartery had enlisted on 5 September 1914 with the 11th Battalion of the King's Royal Rifle Corps. His regimental number was R-2612. There are some Barry men on the town's Roll of Honour with numbers close to his, so they probably

enlisted on the same day. He later transferred to the Machine Gun Corps. After being in France for 30 months, Hartery, whose wife lived at 56 Lombard Street in Barry, was severely wounded in the thigh, wrist, arm and ankle and was brought to the 1st Eastern General Hospital, Cambridge. He spent six months on his stomach recovering from shrapnel wounds. In October 1918 Hartery was in Dundee

Bob Hartery

Hospital suffering from wounds to the chest and thigh. Later in life his son in law would assist him in removing shrapnel pieces from his neck. He broke his jaw in a fight when in his 70s and the doctor who saw the X-rays said he was worth more dead than alive, owing to the amount of metal still in his head.

One day, long after the war had ended, a man named Stan Lever walked into a shop in Barry where Bob Hartery's daughter Dorothy was working and said: 'I owe my life to your father.' Apparently, Stan had drunk his rum ration and that of others, then stood on the parapet of the trench shouting at the Germans. Bob Hartery had pulled him down and saved his life.

On 13 October 1917 it was announced that Sergeant Henry James Smith of the 19th Welsh (Pioneers) had been awarded the Military Medal. Born in Mitcheldean, Gloucestershire, in 1885, he played football for Cinderford before the family moved to Nantyglo in Monmouthshire, where he married and had six

children, also playing football for Ebbw Vale. He survived the war and died in 1956.

The announcement of his Military Medal stated that he 'showed great courage under very dangerous and trying conditions when in command of a working party after the officer in charge had been badly wounded.'[14]

In January 1918 Corporal Edwin Charles Ellwood, Royal Field Artillery, of 25 Travis Street, Barry Dock, was awarded a bar to his Military Medal.

Henry Smith

Corporal Ellwood, who had served 22 months in France, was home on leave when the opportunity was seized by the children and teachers of St Helen's School to make him a presentation of a valuable silver luminous wristwatch, suitably inscribed, in token of their appreciation of the bravery on the battlefield. The ceremony took place in St Helen's School before a crowded audience. The Rev P.J. Vaughan presided and in his address stated that this was the second presentation within a month made to an old boy of St Helen's School. He referred to the trying conditions at the battlefront and the bravery with which the troops suffered untold hardships and he congratulated Corporal Ellwood on winning the M.M. not only once but twice.

Mr. H. Wood, the headmaster, then related the incidents which led to Ellwood being awarded the Military Medal and bar. In July 1917 two officers and three men belonging to his battery were in a dugout when it was destroyed by a German shell, and they were buried in the debris. Ellwood volunteered to lead a party to try to rescue them. After working strenuously for nearly an hour, under fire all the time, they were successful in getting them all out – one of the officers, a captain, was dead, and the others were very badly crushed, but still alive. The next event was even more heroic.

On 12 October 1917, the infantry were to go over the top at 6 a.m. and Corporal Ellwood's gun, situated in Kitchener's Wood, was to take its part in the barrage to be fired. Just before the appointed time, a German shell burst not far from the gun. Nobody was injured, but a splinter had entered the gun and

jammed the shell inserted ready for firing. The gun was thus put out of action and there was nothing at hand to get the shell loose.

The infantry were depending on that gun to pave the way for them in the ten or twenty yard sector of the front allotted to it. Telling the others to get out of harm's way, Ellwood picked up a handspike and went to the mouth of the

Edwin Ellwood

gun and probed with it until he succeeded in loosening the shell. When it is remembered that these shells were meant for destroying wire entanglements, and they had a sensitive fuse, Ellwood was fortunate in extracting the shell without exploding it. The delay caused them to be ten rounds behind according to the timetable, but they made these up in the next fifteen minutes. Ellwood's officer told him that he was mad to attempt what he did, and said he would report him, but when the report was made, the Officer Commanding was so delighted with what Corporal Ellwood had done that instead of a censure he recommended him for further distinction and the bar was the result.

Councillor Dr O'Donnell J.P. then handed Ellwood the watch and in moving terms told him that his brave act was worthy of a Victoria Cross. He congratulated him on having escaped the dangers of the battlefield and made reference to the many brave men from the school who had fallen. He wished him well in the future and hoped that he would return safely and be able to wear his decorations with honour.[15]

John Williams of the Welsh Regiment won the Military Medal for his conduct on 31 July:

Mr. and Mrs. John Williams, of 66 Argyle Street, Swansea are justly proud of the record of their family, which has just been enhanced by the award of the Military Medal to their 19-year-old son Pte. John Clifford Williams of the Welsh Regiment. Mr. Williams himself is the schoolmaster in H.M. Prison, Swansea, and despite his many duties continues to attend the drills of the Y.T.C., where he held the rank of corporal. There are four sons of military age, all serving abroad – two in France, and the elder two (Bertram and Lawrence) in Salonika and Egypt. It was in an advance against the Cockchafers on July 31st that the young medallist displayed the conspicuous gallantry which earned for him the coveted distinction. At the time the younger brother was winning laurels, the elder was gassed just two miles away. The young soldier arrived home on leave on Thursday night, and was accorded a right royal reception. He enlisted when he was only 17 years of age. Mr. and Mrs. Williams have two younger sons, who are enthusiastic Boy Scouts.[16]

Corporal Augustus R. Taylor served with the 121st Brigade of the Royal Field Artillery and had taken part in the attack on Mametz Wood in 1916. He was awarded the Military Medal when, being the only N.C.O. on duty, he dressed and tended the wounded and also took ammunition up the line under heavy fire. From Penarth, he had joined the Army in 1915 and was a fine athlete, having played rugby for Cardiff in the season before the war, also playing for Penarth Water Polo Club.

Gus Taylor   The Military Medal

Mentioned in Dispatches

A regional newspaper report carried the praise given to a soldier for his actions in the trenches:

Private W. Richardson, Royal Welsh Fusiliers, who has been mentioned in dispatches, is the eldest son of Mr. and Mrs. G. Richardson, Llandegfan, and grandson of Mr. Samuel Richardson, formerly of Orme Road, Bangor. His Colonel writes: 'This man has done consistently good work during the 22 months that the battalion has been out at the front. All his duty has been performed in the trenches. He took part in the action at Mametz Wood, where his good work was commented upon, he was also in a successful raid, and finally throughout the whole operations on the Pilkem Ridge. He has always shown great cheerfulness and courage. In addition he has set an excellent example to men of new drafts by

the manner in which he has always carried out his duties.' Private Richardson joined the Army early in 1915, and went to the front in December, 1915. Previous to joining the forces he was in the employ of Mr. Boot, hairdresser, Llandudno.[17]

Mentioned in Dispatches
Oak Leaf

CHAPTER 26

Conclusion

THE THIRD BATTLE of Ypres ended on 10 November. On this last day of the battle the 1st South Wales Borderers were in action. A German barrage forced a gap in the lines between them and the 2nd Royal Munster Fusiliers and the German infantry counterattacked.

Tom Thompson was born in Eastburn in Yorkshire. Originally serving with the Lincolnshire Regiment, he had been transferred to the Monmouthshire Regiment and then to the 1st Battalion of the South Wales Borderers. Married in 1910 to Edith, he had joined the S.W.B. on 1 July 1917 and was killed on the last day of the battle.

The number of lives lost on both sides was enormous and the battle's popular name – 'Passchendaele' – has stood as a symbol of all that was wasteful about the Great War.

Yet it was not futile. To describe the months of fighting as such is disrespectful to the legions of men who fought and died in the countryside around Passchendaele. They were there because they generally believed in the cause for which they were fighting, and

Tom Thompson

fought for each other and their country. By late September it appeared that the German Army was on the brink of collapsing and Douglas Haig continued the assault because he believed that moment was in sight. He was wrong. The Germans held on stubbornly in the face of devastating artillery fire and infantry assaults.

In his memoirs General Ludendorff described the final days of the battle:

> Enormous masses of ammunition, such as the human mind had never imagined before the war, were hurled upon the bodies of men who passed a miserable existence scattered about in mud-filled shell holes. It was no longer life at all. It was mere unspeakable suffering. And through this world of mud the attackers dragged themselves, slowly, but steadily, and in dense masses. Caught in the advanced zone by our hail of fire they often collapsed, and the lonely man in the shell hole breathed again. Then the mass came on again. Rifle and machine gun jammed with the mud. Man fought against man, and only too often the mass was successful.[1]

Battlefield salvage photographed in 1938

The 38th (Welsh) Division had reinforced the reputation it had gained at home and in the press for its actions at Mametz Wood, and in the highest echelon of command in the British Army it had swept away any perceived stain on its character from its failure to capture Mametz Wood in a single day (unfair as that internal criticism was). The Welsh Guards achieved their objectives and picked up the highest of gallantry awards. Yet the bloody legacy of this ferocious fighting was felt right across the Principality and the war was to drag on for yet another year, with its most catastrophic losses yet to come in 1918.

A memorial plaque to the 38th (Welsh) Division was placed on a German bunker at Gournier Farm sometime after 1918. It reads 'IN MEMORY OF COMRADES OF 38th (WELSH) DIVISION 1914–18'. Although Gournier Farm was in the sector allotted to the 51st Division, a platoon of the 15th Welsh had assisted in clearing the enemy from this area on 31 July and this bunker changed hands many times during the day.

In August 2014 a magnificent Welsh dragon sculpture was unveiled alongside the road that runs from Pilkem to

Memorial plaque at Gournier Farm

Langemark. It now serves as a fitting memorial to those who participated in that dreadful conflict. As the accompanying plaque states: 'In remembrance of all those of Welsh descent who took part in the First World War.'

Hundreds of the Welsh soldiers and men of other nationalities who fought with the Welsh regiments at the Third Battle of Ypres have no known grave. They are the 'Missing'. On Sunday, 24 July 1927, the inauguration of the Menin Gate Memorial to the Missing took place. Field Marshal Lord Hubert Plumer unveiled the memorial and in his speech said:

> Our hearts are stirred by feelings of deep emotion as we stand here to pay a nation's tribute to the memory of the great army of men whose names are inscribed on this beautiful memorial, who have no known grave. One of the most tragic features of the Great War was the number of casualties reported as 'Missing, believed killed'. To their relatives there must have been added to their grief a tinge of bitterness and a feeling that everything possible had not been done to recover their loved ones' bodies and give them reverent burial. That feeling no longer exists; it ceased to exist when the conditions under which the fighting was being carried out were realised.
>
> But when peace came and the last ray of hope had been extinguished, the void seemed deeper and the outlook more forlorn for those who had no grave to visit, no place where they could lay tokens of loving remembrance. The hearts of the people throughout the Empire went out to them, and it was resolved that here at Ypres, where so many of the 'Missing' are known to have fallen, there should be erected a memorial worthy of them which should give expression to the nation's gratitude for their sacrifice and its sympathy with those who mourned them. A memorial has been erected which, in its simple grandeur, fulfils this object, and now it can be said of each one in whose honour we are assembled here today: 'He is not missing; he is here.'[2]

A year after the battle ended a poignant tribute appeared in a Welsh newspaper:

In loving memory of my dear son, Private A. Coslett, R.W.F., killed by a sniper on Pilkem Ridge, near Langemarck, 3rd Battle of Ypres, July 31st, 1917. From Mother, Brother Walter, and Sisters Florrie and Alice, and Brother Tom in France.

When alone in sorrow, and tears begin to flow,
There stands a dream of the sweet long ago,
And, unknown to the world, he stands by my side
And whispers, Dear Mother, death cannot divide.[3]

In fact, Albert Coslett of the 15th Royal Welsh Fusiliers had been killed on 4 August 1917. His brother Herbert of the Cardiff City Battalion had written home the previous summer to their mother at 36 Dinam Street, Barry Dock, stating that his brother had been shot in the heart during a bombing attack on the German positions. His brother had seen the grave and wrote that it was kept trim and tidy.[4]

Albert Coslett was only 19 years of age. He had been at the Front for four months and this was his first and final battle.

May Albert Coslett and his comrades never be forgotten.

Endnotes

Chapter 2: From Mametz Wood to Pilkem Ridge

[1]   Author's collection.
[2]   *London Gazette*, 26 July 1918.
[3]   *Cambria Daily Herald*, 25 May 1918.
[4]   Courtesy of Selena Hardie.
[5]   Courtesy of the People's Collection, Wales.
[6]   Courtesy of the People's Collection, Wales.
[7]   National Archives WO95/2559/3.
[8]   *Cambrian Daily Leader*, 12 January 1917.
[9]   Gundrey private papers. Reproduced by kind permission of Bernard Lewis, and Sue and Andy Thorndycraft.
[10] Ibid.
[11] Ibid.
[12] Ibid.
[13] *London Gazette*, 30 July 1919.
[14] Gundrey private papers, op. cit.
[15] Ibid.
[16] *Cambrian Daily Leader*, 12 January 1917.
[17] WO95/2559/4, National Archives.
[18] *Liverpool Evening Express*, 28 March 1917.
[19] *London Gazette*, 26 May 1917.
[20] *London Gazette*, 10 January 1919.
[21] *London Gazette*, 25 March 1917.
[22] *London Gazette*, 30 March 1920.
[23] *London Gazette*, 24 July 1917.
[24] *London Gazette*, 10 January 1919.
[25] *London Gazette*, 24 July 1917.
[26] Ibid.
[27] *London Gazette*, 11 January 1919.
[28] WO 95/2092/1, National Archives.

29 Ibid.
30 Ibid.
31 Ibid.
32 Ibid.
33 Ibid.
34 Ibid.
35 Ibid.
36 *Hemel Hempstead Gazette*, 31 October 1914.
37 Ludendorff, E., *My War Memories 1914–1918*, London, 1919, p. 429.
38 *London Gazette*, 16 November 1915.
39 *London Gazette*, 25 August 1917.
40 Ibid.
41 Ibid.
42 *London Gazette*, 25 August 1917.
43 *London Gazette*, 25 August 1917.
44 *London Gazette*, 3 October 1918.
45 *London Gazette*, 16 August 1917.
46 *Penarth Times*, 21 June 1917.
47 De Ruvigny, *The Roll of Honour 1914–1918*, p. 22.
48 WO 95/2553/3, National Archives.
49 Ibid.
50 Service Record, National Archives.

Chapter 3: The Battle of Pilkem Ridge: 31 July to 2 August

1 Dudley-Ward, C.H., *Regimental Records of the Royal Welch Fusiliers*, Uckfield, 2005, p. 328.
2 Von Kuhl, *Der Weltkrieg*, in Terraine, J., *The Road to Passchendaele*, London, 1997, p. 211.
3 WO 95/2553/3, National Archives.
4 Ibid.
5 Ibid.
6 Ibid.
7 Ibid.
8 Ibid.
9 Ibid.
10 Robinson, P., *The Letters of Major-General Price-Davies*, Stroud, 2013, pp. 174–5.

11   National Archives WO 95/2558/1.

12   Ibid.

13   Sheldon, J., *The German Army at Cambrai*, Barnsley, 2009, p. 314.

Chapter 4: The Welsh Guards

1   In Hicks, J., *Barry and the Great War*, Barry, 2007, p. 263.

2   Ibid.

3   Ibid.

4   Author's Collection.

5   *Citations of the Distinguished Conduct Medal in the Great War 1914–1920*, Uckfield, 2007, pp. 67–8.

6   Richard May, *Wokingham Remembers* website.

7   *Reading Mercury*, 18 August 1917.

8   *St Helen's Co-operative Book of Remembrance.*

9   *Merthyr Express*, 18 August 1917.

10   Hicks, J., *Barry and the Great War*, op. cit., p. 288.

11   www.bmj.com

12   *London Gazette*, 9 January 1918.

13   *South Wales Weekly Post*, 18 August 1917.

14   *Dundee Evening Telegraph*, 25 March 1940.

15   Dudley-Ward, *History of the Welsh Guards*, London, 1988, p. 159.

16   Courtesy of the Warden and Scholars of Winchester College.

17   Ibid.

18   Ibid.

19   *Roath Road Roamer*, courtesy of Glamorgan Archives.

20   *Taunton Courier and Western Advertiser*, 26 September 1917.

21   Unknown newspaper report 1917.

22   *Aberdare Leader*, 7 September 1918.

23   Ibid.

Chapter 5: The Royal Welsh Fusiliers

1   Dudley-War, op, cit., p. 328.

2   *Carmarthen Journal*, 10 August 1917.

3   De Ruvigny, *The Roll of Honour 1914–1918*, p. 44.

4   *Carmarthen Journal*, 10 August 1917.

5   *Chester Chronicle*, 18 August 1917.

6   Information courtesy of Ysgol Friars.

7   *North Wales Chronicle and Advertiser for the Principality*, 17 August 1917.

8   *North Wales Chronicle and Advertiser for the Principality*, 17 May 1918.

9   De Ruvigny, op. cit., p. 144.

10   *Wolverton Express*, 17 August 1917.

11   *Western Mail*, 1 October 1918.

12   Ibid.

13   *Llanelli Star*, 19 July 1919.

14   Service Record, National Archives.

15   WO 95/2555/1, National Archives.

16   *Cardigan-Cambrian and Merionethshire Standard*, 7 September 1917.

17   *The Breconian*, December 1917.

18   *Western Mail*, 4 August 1917.

19   De Ruvigny, op. cit., p. 237.

20   Service Record, National Archives.

21   De Ruvigny, op. cit., p. 96.

22   *Chester Chronicle*, 18 August 1917.

23   *Caerphilly Journal*, 20 August 1917.

24   Ibid.

Chapter 6: Hedd Wyn – The Soldier Poet

1   Llwyd, A., *The Story of Hedd Wyn*, Llandybïe, 2009, p. 77.

2   Simon Jones interviewed by Robin Gwyndaf of the Museum of Welsh Life, St Fagans, 26/09/1975. Recording AWC 4763-64.

3   *Y Cymro*, in Llwyd, A., op. cit., p. 129.

4   *Yr Herald Cymraeg*, 2 October 1917.

5   Peris Williams Collection, Bangor University, BMSS/4903.

6   Ibid.

7   *Y Brython*, 22 November 1917.

Chapter 7: The South Wales Borderers

1   De Ruvigny, op. cit., pp. 154–5.

2   Ibid.

3   Ibid.

4   Service Record, National Archives.

5   *Brecon County Times*, 14 March 1918.

6   De Ruvigny, op. cit., p. 41.

7   Atkinson, C.T., *The History of the South Wales Borderers*, Uckfield, undated, p. 330.

8   WO 95/2562/1, National Archives.
9   Ibid.
10   Ibid.
11   WO 95/2562/1, National Archives.
12   Courtesy of www.flintshirewarmemorials.com.
13   Courtesy of Selena Hardie.
14   *Biddulph Chronicle*, 1 September 1917.
15   Author's Collection.
16   *Hertford Mercury and Reformer*, 11 August 1917.
17   *London Gazette*, 26 January 1918.
18   De Ruvigny, op. cit., p. 286.
19   *Cardiff Times*, 8 September 1917.

Chapter 8: The Welsh Regiment

1   *London Gazette*, 29 November 1901.
2   Conan Doyle, op. cit., p. 142.
3   *Aberdare Leader*, 2 September 1916.
4   *Aberdare Leader*, 2 June 1917.
5   *Aberdare Leader*, 26 January 1918.
6   *London Gazette*, 26 January 1918.
7   http://www.newportsdead.shaunmcguire.co.uk.
8   Service Record, National Archives.
9   *Cardiff Times*, 1 September 1917.
10   *Amman Valley Chronicle*, 20 September 1917.
11   Military Cross Citations. Author's collection.
12   Ibid.
13   *Western Gazette*, 24 August 1917.
14   *Lincolnshire Echo*, 13 August 1917.
15   *The South Wales Weekly Post*, 14 August 1917.
16   Hicks, J., *Barry and the Great War*, op. cit., p. 148.
17   Author's Collection.
18   *Western Mail*, 27 August 1917.
19   *North Devon Journal*, 6 September 1917.
20   *Carmarthen Journal*, 10 August 1917.
21   De Ruvigny, op. cit., p. 106.
22   De Ruvigny, op. cit., p. 106.
23   *Western Mail*, 4 August 1917.
24   Marden, T.O., *The History of the Welch Regiment 1914–1918*, Uckfield, undated. p. 417.

[25] De Ruvigny, op. cit., p. 136.

[26] De Ruvigny, op. cit., p. 193.

Chapter 9: The Monmouthshire Regiment

[1] *Western Mail*, 14 August 1917.

[2] Service Record, National Archives.

Chapter 10: The Royal Artillery

[1] Gordon, H., *The Unreturning Army*, London, 2013, pp. 108–10.

[2] Hamilton, R. A., *The War Diary of the Master of Belhaven 1914–1918*, London, 1924, p. 358.

[3] Hamilton, op. cit., pp. 358–9.

[4] Hamilton, op. cit., p. 360.

[5] Hamilton, op. cit., pp. 360–1.

[6] *Cardiff Times*, 27 October 1917.

Chapter 11: The Royal Engineers

[1] *Reading Mercury*, 22 September 1917.

[2] IWM 85/51/1.

[3] Ibid.

[4] *Aberdare Leader*, 22 June 1918.

[5] *London Gazette*, 3 June 1918.

[6] *Cardiff Times*, 8 September 1917.

[7] De Ruvigny, op cit., p. 154.

[8] *Labour Voice*, 1 September 1917.

[9] *Glamorgan Gazette*, 10 August 1917.

[10] *Glamorgan Gazette*, 31 August 1917.

[11] *London Gazette*, 11 March 1916.

Chapter 12: The Tank Corps

[1] *Western Mail*, 4 August 1917.

[2] *Edinburgh Gazette*, October 1917.

[3] Anonymous, *The Tank Corps Honours and Awards 1916–1919*, Birmingham, 1982, p. 172.

[4] WO 95/1788, National Archives.

[5] Maurice, op. cit., p. 95.

[6] Maurice, op. cit., p. 94.

[7] Maurice, op. cit., p. 113.

[8] Maurice, op. cit., pp. 156–7.

Chapter 13: The Army Service Corps

1 Maurice, op. cit., pp. 156–7.

Chapter 14: The Field Ambulance Brigades

1 Anonymous, *Field Ambulance Sketches*, Leopold Classic Library, undated, pp. 120–1.
2 WO95/2549/1, National Archive.
3 http://www.northeastmedals.co.uk.
4 Courtesy of Stephen Lyons.
5 Ibid.
6 Courtesy of David Penman.
7 Ibid.
8 Ibid.
9 *London Gazette*, 26 January 1918.
10 Courtesy of David Penman.
11 WO 95/2550/1, National Archives.
12 Ibid.
13 Anonymous, op. cit., p. 139.

Chapter 15: The Welsh Victoria Cross Winners at Pilkem Ridge

1 Victoria Cross Citation. Author's Collection.
2 Snelling, S., *Passchendaele 1917*, Stroud, 1998, p. 43
3 Williams, W.A., *Heart of a Dragon*, Wrexham, 2008, p. 151.
4 *London Gazette*, 6 September 1917.
5 Snelling, op. cit., p. 46.
6 *London Gazette*, 14 September 1917.
7 *London Gazette*, 16 November 1916.
8 *London Gazette*, 8 November 1917.
9 *London Gazette*, 24 July 1915.
10 *London Gazette*, 26 November 1917.
11 *London Gazette*, 16 September 1918.
12 *London Gazette*, 11 December 1917.
13 *London Gazette*, 23 October 1919.

Chapter 16: The Royal Flying Corps

1 De Ruvigny, op. cit., p. 67.
2 *Liverpool Echo*, 20 August 1917.
3 Henshaw, T., *The Sky Their Battlefield 2*, London, 2014, p. 123.

[4] *London Gazette*, 16 August 1918.

[5] *London Gazette*, 16 September 1918.

[6] Ibid.

[7] *London Gazette*, 27 September 1917.

[8] *London Gazette*, 18 December 1917.

[9] *De Ruvigny*, op. cit., p. 122.

[10] Ibid.

[11] *London Gazette*, 18 July 1917.

[12] *London Gazette*, 17 September 1917.

[13] *London Gazette*, 5 July 1918.

[14] *London Gazette*, 18 July 1917.

[15] *London Gazette*, 17 September 1917.

[16] *London Gazette*, 18 March 1918.

Chapter 17: The Battle of Langemark: 16–18 August

[1] *Brecon and Radnor Express*, 17 January 1918.

[2] *Straits Times*, 21 May 1919.

[3] De Ruvigny, op. cit., p. 93.

[4] Ibid.

[5] *The Breconian*, December 1917.

[6] *Craven Herald*, 31 August 1917.

[7] De Ruvigny, op. cit., p. 43.

[8] *London Gazette*, 20 October 1916.

[9] De Ruvigny, op. cit., p. 119.

[10] *Herald of Wales*, 8 September 1917.

[11] De Ruvigny, op. cit., p. 143.

[12] De Ruvigny, op. cit., p. 146.

[13] *Roath Road Roamer*, op. cit.

[14] Hicks, J., *The Welsh at Mametz Wood*, Talybont, 2016, p. 55.

Chapter 18: The Battle of the Menin Road Ridge: 20–25 September

[1] De Ruvigny, op. cit., p. 237.

[2] Ibid.

[3] Author's Collection.

[4] *London Gazette*, 4 March 1918.

[5] *Roath Road Roamer*, op. cit.

[6] *London Gazette*, 22 March 1918.

[7]   *London Gazette*, 21 December 1917.

[8]   *London Gazette*, 22 March 1918.

[9]   In Chapman, P., *Tyne Cot Cemetery and Memorial: In Memory and In Mourning*, Barnsley, 2016, p. 143.

[10]   *London Gazette*, 6 February 1918.

[11]   *London Gazette*, 15 November 1918.

[12]   Courtesy of Amolia Williams.

[13]   Ibid.

[14]   *Wrexham Advertiser*, 6 October 1917.

Chapter 19: The Battle of Polygon Wood: 26 September to 3 October

[1]   Sherborne School Archives.

[2]   Richards, F., *Old Soldiers Never Die*, Uckfield, 2001, p. 245.

[3]   Richards, op. cit., pp. 245–6.

[4]   *London Gazette*, 6 April 1918.

[5]   Courtesy of Bruce Paul Wallace.

[6]   Service Record, National Archives.

[7]   *Aberdare Leader*, 15 November 1919.

[8]   Author's Collection.

[9]   *London Gazette*, 6 February 1918.

[10]   *London Gazette*, 3 September 1919.

[11]   *Wisden Cricketers' Almanack*.

[12]   *London Gazette*, 12 March 1917.

[13]   *North Wales Chronicle and Advertiser for the Principality*, 23 November 1917.

[14]   www.cairogang.com.

[15]   Ibid.

[16]   Ibid.

[17]   Service Record, National Archives.

[18]   *Barry Dock News*, 19 October 1917.

Chapter 20: The Battle of Poelcappelle, 9 October

[1]   http://www.inmemories.com.

[2]   *Melton Mowbray Times and Vale of Belvoir Gazette*, 26 October 1917.

[3]   *Letters Home 1914–1918*, Keeling. J. (ed.), privately published, 2010, p. 308.

[4]   *South Wales Weekly Post*, 3 November 1917.

5   *Melton Mowbray Times and Vale of Belvoir Gazette*, 14 September 1917.
6   Courtesy of Hugh Bierlijn.

Chapter 21: The Second Battle of Passchendaele: 26 October to 10 November

1   Roath Road Roamer, op. cit.
2   De Ruvigny, op. cit., p. 110.
3   De Ruvigny, op. cit., p. 286.
4   Courtesy of Alan Fennah, www.wartimememoriesproject.com.
5   *Burnley Express*, 21 November 1917.
6   *London Gazette*, 14 November 1916.
7   *London Gazette*, 28 March 1918.
8   *London Gazette*, 16 May 1916.
9   *London Gazette*, 28 March 1918.
10 www.stockport1914–1918.co.uk.
11 www.greatwar-frodsham.info.co.uk.

Chapter 22: Other Survivors' Accounts

1   Courtesy of Jeffrey Hughes and his Facebook site devoted to the 173rd Siege Battery.
2   Campbell, P. J., *In the Cannon's Mouth*, London, 1979, pp. 57–8.
3   National Library of Wales, FACS 665.
4   Courtesy of the Museum of the Royal Welsh Fusiliers.
5   Courtesy of the Museum of the Royal Welsh Fusiliers.
6   Macdonald, L., *They Called It Passchendaele*, London, 1978, pp. 200–1.
7   Davies, E., *Taffy Went to War*, Knutsford Secretarial Bureau, 1975, pp. 63–6.
8   Ibid., p. 86.
9   Courtesy of Colin Evans.
10 Macdonald, op. cit., pp. 247–8.
11 Grant, D. F., *The History of 'A' Battery 84th Army Brigade*, London, 1922, pp. 66–7.
12 In Hastings, M., *Forgotten Voices of the Great War*, London, 2002, p. 229.
13 Richards, op. cit., p. 247.
14 Richards, op. cit., pp. 254–5.

15   Davies, T., personal account, author's collection.
16   Courtesy of Trevor Tasker.
17   Dunn, J. C., *The War The Infantry Knew*, London, 1994, p. 399.
18   *London Gazette*, 17 April 1918.
19   Dunn, op. cit., p. 400.

Chapter 23: How the Press Reported the Battle

1   *Birmingham Mail*, 2 August 1917.
2   *Gloucester Echo*, 3 August 1917.
3   *Chester Chronicle*, 4 August 1917.
4   Translation courtesy of Anke Yee.
5   Gibbs, P., *From Bapaume to Passchendaele 1917*, Toronto, 1918, pp. 222–4.
6   Gibbs, op. cit., pp. 242–3.
7   *North Wales Chronicle and Advertiser for the Principality*, 10 August 1917.
8   *Herald of Wales*, 11 August 1917.
9   *North Wales Chronicle and Advertiser for the Principality*, 17 August 1917.
10   *Western Mail*, 4 August 1917.
11   *Western Mail*, 10 August 1917.
12   *Western Mail*, 11 August 1917.
13   *North Wales Chronicle and Advertiser for the Principality*, 10 August 1917.
14   *Yorkshire Post and Leeds Intelligencer*, 17 August 1917.
15   *Yorkshire Evening Post*, 2 October 1917.
16   *Haverfordwest and Milford Haven Telegraph*, 19 September 1917.
17   *Aberdare Leader*, 17 November 1917.
18   *North Wales Chronicle and Advertiser for the Principality*, 8 February 1918.
19   Ibid.
20   Conan Doyle, A., *The British Campaign in France and Flanders 1917*, Uckfield, undated, pp. 135–6.
21   Conan Doyle, op. cit., pp. 144–5.

Chapter 24: The German Perspective

1   Junger, E., *Storm of Steel*, London, 2004, p. 160.
2   K. Lubinski, Liddle Collection, University of Leeds.
3   L. Kalepky, Liddle Collection, op. cit.

4   Binding, R., *A Fatalist at War*, London, 1929, p. 178.

5   Ibid., pp. 179–80.

6   Ibid., pp. 193–4.

7   Hammerton J. (ed.), *The Great War – I Was There*, London, 1938, pp. 1,241–2.

8   Hammerton, op. cit., p. 1,244.

9   Wynne, G.C. Captain, *Landrecies to Cambrai*, Solihull, 2011, pp. 170–1.

10 Wynne, op. cit., p. 171.

11 Wynne, op. cit., p. 172.

12 Wynne, op. cit., p. 173.

13 Wynne, op. cit., pp. 174–5.

14 Wynne, op. cit., p. 175.

15 Macdonald, L., *1914–1918 Voices and Images of the Great War*, London, 1988, pp. 242–3.

16 Macdonald, op. cit., p. 255.

17 Schulenburg-Wolfsburg, Graf v.d., *Geschichte Des Garde Fusilier Regiments*, Berlin, 1926, pp. 181–3.

18 Hitler, A., *Mein Kampf*, Munich, 1925, p. 184.

19 Meyer, A., *Mit Adolf Hitler im Bayerischen Reserve Infanterie Regiment 16 List*, Neustadt-Aisch, 1934, pp. 73–4.

20 Ludendorff, op. cit., p. 492.

21 Ibid., p. 491.

Chapter 25: Other Gallantry Medal Winners

1   *London Gazette*, 17 April 1918.

2   *Herald of Wales*, 5 January 1918.

3   *London Gazette*, 26 January 1918.

4   *South Wales Weekly Post*, 16 February 1918.

5   Distinguished Conduct Medal Citation. Author's Collection.

6   *South Wales Weekly Post*, 8 September 1917.

7   *North Wales Chronicle and Advertiser for the Principality*, 13 June 1919.

8   Glamorgan Constabulary Records, courtesy of Gareth Madge O.B.E.

9   Ibid.

10 *Barry Dock News*, 15 November 1918.

11 Hicks, *Barry and the Great War*, op. cit., p. 293.

12 Hicks, *Barry and the Great War*, op. cit., p. 295.
13 Hicks, *Barry and the Great War*, op. cit., p. 296.
14 *Gloucester Journal*, 13 October 1917.
15 Hicks, *Barry and the Great War*, op. cit., p. 299.
16 *Cambrian Daily Leader*, 1 September 1917.
17 *North Wales Chronicle and Advertiser for the Principality*, 17 May 1918.

Chapter 26: Conclusion

1 Ludendorff, op. cit., p. 491.
2 Harington, C., *Plumer of Messines*, London, 1935, pp. 302–3.
3 *Barry Dock News*, 2 August 1918.
4 Hicks, *Barry and the Great War*, op. cit., p. 150.

Bibliography

Anonymous, *Citations of the Distinguished Conduct Medal in the Great War 1914–1920*.

Anonymous, *Field Ambulance Sketches*, Leopold Classic Library, undated.

Anonymous, *The Tank Corps Honours and Awards 1916–1919*, Birmingham, 1982.

Atkinson, C.T., *The History of the South Wales Borderers*, Uckfield, The Naval and Military Press Ltd., undated.

Binding, R., *A Fatalist at War*, London, 1929.

Brett, G.A., *A History of the 2nd Battalion The Monmouthshire Regiment*, Pontypool, 1933.

Campbell, P.J., *In the Cannon's Mouth*, London, 1979.

Chapman, P., *Tyne Cot Cemetery and Memorial: In Memory and In Mourning*, Barnsley, 2016.

Conan Doyle, A., *The British Campaign in France and Flanders 1917*, Uckfield, undated.

Davies, E., *Taffy Went to War*, Knutsford Secretarial Bureau, 1975.

De Ruvigny, *The Roll of Honour 1914–1918*, Uckfield, 2009.

Dudley-Ward, C.H., *History of the Welsh Guards*, London, 1988.

Dudley-Ward, C.H., *Regimental Records of the Royal Welch Fusiliers*, Uckfield, 2005.

Dunn, J.C., *The War The Infantry Knew*, London, 1994.

Farndale, M., *History of the Royal Regiment of Artillery, Western Front 1914–18*, London, 1986.

Franks, N.L.R., Bailey, F. W. and Guest, R., *Above the Lines*, London, 1996.

Franks, N.L.R., Guest, R. and Alegi, G., *Above the War Fronts*, London, 1997.

General Ludendorff, *My War Memories*, Uckfield, 2005.

Gordon, H., *The Unreturning Army*, London, 2013.

Grant, D.F., *The History of 'A' Battery 84th Army Brigade*, London, 1922.

Hamilton, R.A., *The War Diary of the Master of Belhaven 1914–1918*, London, 1924.

Hammerton J. (ed.), *The Great War – I Was There*, London, 1938.

Harington, C., *Plumer of Messines*, London, 1935.

Hastings, M., *Forgotten Voices of the Great War*, London, 2002.

Henshaw, T., *The Sky Their Battlefield 2*, London, 2014.

Hicks, J., *Barry and the Great War*, Barry, 2007.

Hicks, J., *The Welsh at Mametz Wood*, Talybont, 2016.

Hitler, A., *Mein Kampf*, Munich, 1925.

John, S., *Carmarthen in the Great War*, Barnsley, 2014.

John, S., *Carmarthen Pals*, Barnsley, 2009.

Junger, E, *Storm of Steel*, London, 2004.

Keeling, J. (ed.), *Letters Home 1914–1918*, privately published, 2010.

Langley, D., *Duty Done*, Baston, 2011.

Lewis, B., *Swansea Pals*, Barnsley, 2004.

Llwyd, A.,*The Story of Hedd Wyn*, Llandybïe, 2009.

Macdonald, L., *1914–1918 Voices and Images of the Great War*, London, 1988.

Macdonald, L., *They Called It Passchendaele*, London, 1978.

Marden, T.O., *The History of the Welch Regiment 1914–1918*, Uckfield, undated.

Maurice, Major R.F.G., *Tank Corps Book of Honour*, undated.

Meyer, A., *Mit Adolf Hitler im Bayerischen Reserve Infanterie Regiment 16 List*, Neustadt-Aisch, 1934.

Munby, J.E., *A History of the 38th (Welsh) Division*, London, 1920.

Parry, C.J., *The Story of the Order of St. John in the Principality of Wales*, Newport, 1996.

Richards, F., *Old Soldiers Never Die*, Uckfield, 2001.

Robinson, P. (ed.), *The Letters of Major-General Price-Davies*, Stroud, 2013.

Schulenburg-Wolfsburg, Graf v.d., *Geschichte Des Garde Fusilier Regiments*, Berlin, 1926.

Sheldon, J., *The German Army at Cambrai*, Barnsley, 2009.

Shores, C., Franks, N., and Guest, R., *Above the Trenches*, London, 1990.

Snelling, S. *Passchendaele 1917*, Stroud, 1998.

Terraine, J., *The Road to Passchendaele*, London, 1997.

Williams, W.A., *Heart of a Dragon*, Wrexham, 2008.

Wynne, G.C. Captain, *Landrecies to Cambrai*, Solihull, 2011.

Other sources

The archives of the Regimental Museum of the Royal Welsh, Brecon.
The archives of the Royal Welsh Fusiliers Regimental Museum, Caernarfon.
The Liddle Collection, University of Leeds.
War Diaries – held in the National Archives, Kew.
113th Brigade – WO 95/2552
13th Royal Welsh Fusiliers – WO 95/2555/1
14th Royal Welsh Fusiliers – WO 95/2555/2
15th Royal Welsh Fusiliers – WO 95/2556/1
16th Royal Welsh Fusiliers – WO 95/2556/2
114th Brigade – WO 95/2557/3
10th Welsh Regiment – WO 95/2559/1
13th Welsh Regiment – WO 95/2559/2
14th Welsh Regiment – WO 95/2559/3
15th Welsh Regiment – WO 95/2559/4
115th Brigade – WO 95/2560/1
17th Royal Welsh Fusiliers – WO 95/2561/2
10th South Wales Borderers – WO 95/2562/1
11th South Wales Borderers – WO 95/2562/2
16th Welsh Regiment – WO 95/2561/3
19th Welsh (Pioneers) – WO 95/2548/2
119th Brigade Royal Field Artillery – WO 95/2546/1
120th Brigade Royal Field Artillery – WO 95/2546/2
121st Brigade Royal Field Artillery – WO 95/2546/3
129th Brigade Royal Field Artillery – WO 95/2549/1
129th Field Ambulance – WO 95/
130th St John Field Ambulance – WO 95/2549/2
131st Field Ambulance – WO 95/2550/1
123rd Field Company Royal Engineers – WO 95/2547/1
124th Field Company Royal Engineers – WO 95/2547/2
151st Field Company Royal Engineers – WO 95/2547/3
38th Division Signal Company – WO 95/2548/1

Acknowledgements

To Wendy, whose endless hours of research, proof reading, support and love have made this work possible.

Damian Farrow for his Welsh translations.
Lieutenant-Colonel Ian Gumm of 'In the Footsteps' battlefield tours (www.inthefootsteps.com) for drawing the map of the plan of attack at Messines and for the maps of the Third Battle of Ypres.
Bernard Lewis for supplying original material.
G.P.G. Robinson of the Durand Group for the map of the British mines at Messines.
Jack Sheldon for his support in providing the German accounts.
Trevor Tasker for sharing his collection of original material.
Lee Odishow, sculptor of the Langemark dragon, for his assistance.
Daphné Vangheluwe for the cover photograph.
Anke Yee for her translation of the German poem and accounts.
The staff of the Regimental Museum of the Royal Welsh (Brecon) for their assistance.
Photograph of Lieutenant-Colonel G.F. Brooke courtesy of Bernard Lewis and Hugo Brooke.
Photograph of Gunner Ernest Buffin courtesy of Eric Nicholls.
Photograph of Randal Alexander Casson courtesy of the Warden and Scholars of Winchester College.
Photograph of John Charles Caveill courtesy of www.grangetownwar.co.uk.
Photograph of Rose Crowther courtesy of Glamorgan Archives.
Photograph of James Alfred Daniel courtesy of Steve John.
Photograph of Emlyn Davies and permission to use the extract from his memoirs, courtesy of his daughter Dilys Thomas.
Photograph of Kenneth Grenville Edwards courtesy of the Ysgol Friars website.
Photograph of Thomas Evans' family grave and home courtesy of David Healey.
Photograph of William Thomas Evans courtesy of Colin Evans.

Photograph of John Forster courtesy of
www.greatwar-frodsham.info.co.uk.
Photograph of Griffiths Ifor Gibson courtesy of Colston School.
Photograph of Fred Griffiths courtesy of Stewart Woodland.
Photograph and diary of S.G. Hughes courtesy of Jeffrey Hughes.
Photograph of Percy Lloyd Humphreys courtesy of Steve John.
Photograph of Beatrice James courtesy of Glamorgan Archives.
Photograph of David Lewis Jenkins courtesy of www.llanon.org.uk.
Photograph of Thomas Stephen Jones courtesy of Ian Williams and
Richard Evans www.newtredegar-ww1.org.uk.
Photograph of Wyndham Jones courtesy of the Tabernacle Baptist
Church, Newbridge, and Tim Bowers.
Photograph of Francis Henry Jordan courtesy of Steve John.
Photographs of Harold and Lionel Kent courtesy of Karen Derycke
of the Passchendaele Museum and Johnny Taylor of Merchant
Taylors' School.
Photograph of Frank J. King courtesy of Trevor Tasker.
Photograph of Harold Knapp courtesy of Glamorgan Archives.
Photograph of Charles Lancaster courtesy of the Biddulph and District
Genealogy and Historical Society.
Photograph of Ralph Lawrie courtesy of the University of Glasgow.
Photograph of William Charles Leinthall courtesy of the Shaun
McGuire's Newport's War Dead website and Paul Leinthall-
Cowman.
Photograph of John Charles Mann courtesy of the trustees of the
Royal Welsh Fusiliers Museum, Caernarfon and Wrexham
Museums.
Photograph of Derick Cecil Mason courtesy of David Ingham
www.burnleygallantry.co.uk.
Photograph of Alfred Morris courtesy of P. Kitcher.
Photograph of Arthur Mules courtesy of Bruce Paul Wallace.
Photographs and information relating to Frederick Noyes courtesy of
Robin Mellor.
Photograph of William George Owen courtesy of Mike Williams.
Photograph and letter relating to Private William W. Owen courtesy of
Amolia Williams.
Photograph of William Hugh Owens courtesy of Hugh Owens.
Photograph of Roger Alvin Poore courtesy of Sherborne School.
Photograph of John Shute Reid courtesy of Chris Foster.

Photograph of Allan Everett Renwick courtesy of Gwyn Evans.

Photograph of Aneurin Rhydderch courtesy of Steve John.

Photograph of Percy James Scannell courtesy of Christabel Hutchings of the Monmouthshire Antiquarian Association.

Photograph of Lovel Francis Smeathman unveiling the war memorial courtesy of www.herefordhsire-genealogy.co.uk.

Photograph of Geoffrey Lee Compton Smith courtesy of the trustees of the Royal Welsh Fusiliers Museum, Caernarfon and Wrexham Museums.

Photograph of Charles Taylor courtesy of Glamorgan Archives.

Photograph of the Tregaskis Brothers courtesy of Callan Chevin.

Photograph of Ernest C. Troman courtesy of David Langley.

Photograph of Victor Wallace Ward courtesy of David Langley.

Photograph of Thomas Glyn Williams courtesy of the Ysgol Friars website.

Photographs of the men of the 130th (St John) Field Ambulance courtesy of Helen Gleaves, Stephen Lyons, David Penman and the 130th (St John) Field Ambulance Research Group.

Photographs of the German bunkers and pillboxes courtesy of George Watson via Bob Grundy.

Also by the author:

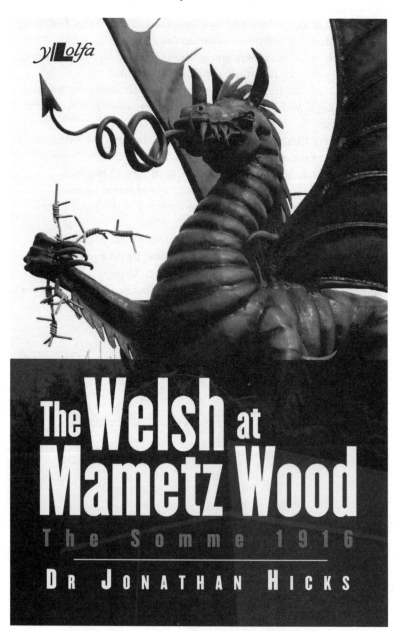

y Lolfa

The Welsh at Mametz Wood

The Somme 1916

Dr Jonathan Hicks

£12.99

£8.95

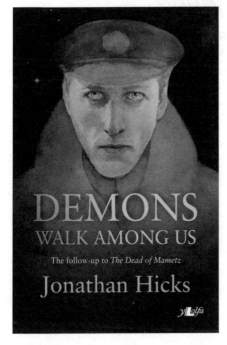

£8.95

The Welsh at Passchendale 1917 is just one of
a whole range of publications from Y Lolfa.
For a full list of books currently in print, send
now for your free copy of our new full-colour
catalogue. Or simply surf into our website

www.ylolfa.com

for secure on-line ordering.

Talybont Ceredigion Cymru SY24 5HE
e-mail ylolfa@ylolfa.com
website www.ylolfa.com
phone (01970) 832 304
fax 832 782